Immigrants to the Pure Land

Pure Land Buddhist Studies

a publication of the Institute of Buddhist Studies
at the Graduate Theological Union

Immigrants to the Pure Land

*The Modernization, Acculturation,
and Globalization of Shin Buddhism, 1898–1941*

Michihiro Ama

University of Hawai'i Press / Honolulu

Library of Congress Cataloging-in Publication Data
Ama, Michihiro.
Immigrants to the Pure Land : the modernization, acculturation, and
globalization of Shin Buddhism, 1898–1941 / Michihiro Ama.
    p. cm. — (Pure Land Buddhist studies)
    Includes bibliographical references and index.
    ISBN 978-0-8248-3438-8 (hardcover : alk. paper)
    1. Shin (Sect)—United States—History—20th century. 2. Shin (Sect)—
Hawaii—History—20th century. I. Title. II. Series: Pure Land Buddhist studies.
    BQ8712.9.U6A43 2011
    294.3'926—dc22

                         2010023445

The Pure Land Buddhist Studies series publishes scholarly works on all aspects of the Pure Land Buddhist tradition. Historically, this includes studies of the origins of the tradition in India, its transmission into a variety of religious cultures, and its continuity into the present. The series is committed to providing a venue for diverse methodological approaches, including but not limited to anthropological, sociological, historical, textual, biographical, philosophical, and interpretive, as well as translations of primary and secondary works. The series will also seek to reprint important works so that they may continue to be available to the scholarly and lay communities. The Pure Land Buddhist Studies series is made possible through the generosity of the Buddhist Churches of America's Fraternal Benefit Association. We wish to express our deep appreciation to the Institute of Buddhist Studies for its support.

University of Hawai'i Press books are printed on acid-free paper and meet the guidelines for permanence and durability of the Council on Library Resources.

Printer-ready copy prepared by Marianne Dresser.

Contents

Preface

The Pure Land Buddhist Studies Series was established to make available to scholars a wide variety of research on Pure Land Buddhism, an integral part of the Buddhist tradition. Originating in India as part of the diffuse developments leading to the formation of Mahayana, Pure Land Buddhism has spread throughout the Buddhist cosmopolis.

Topically, the series defines Pure Land very widely to include not only the cults of Amitābha and Amitāyus but also related topics. The scope of the series is the entirety of the Buddhist tradition in any location where Pure Land Buddhism has been found—South and Southeast Asia, Central Asia, East Asia, and today in the West. Methodologically, the series is also widely defined, including but not limited to textual, doctrinal, biographical, epigraphical, ritual, anthropological, interpretive, historical, and art historical approaches to the subject.

Michihiro Ama's *Immigrants to the Pure Land* provides an important window onto the early history of the Japanese form of Pure Land Buddhism as it has taken root in the West, specifically in Hawai'i and the continental United States. Much of the older literature on religion in the United States not only tends toward Eurocentrism but also understands changes and adaptations as being motivated by the dominant religious culture, which is seen as an active agent, while immigrant religions are largely understood to be passive recipients in the process. Without employing any of the jargon, Ama takes a different approach, consonant with subaltern and postcolonial theory. Instead of two abstracted monoliths—the dominant Protestant religious culture of the United States and the adaptive Buddhist religious culture from Japan—what we find in this study are the stories of living people struggling with an ongoing process of contestation in the engagement between Japan and the United States across the Pacific Ocean.

Speaking on behalf of the members of the Editorial Board of the Pure Land Buddhist Studies Series, we are pleased to present this volume to the scholarly world, confident that it will be of value not only to those within Buddhist studies but also to those working in studies of religion in the United States, and of the relations between religion and ethnicity, class, and race.

Richard K. Payne,
Series Editor

Acknowledgments

I am grateful to countless people for their support of this study. Without the Shinshū Ōtani-ha Fellowship for Pure Land Studies, concentrated effort on my research and writing would have been much more difficult; I am most grateful to the Higashi Honganji. I also thank the Humanities Center and the Department of East Asian Languages and Literatures, University of California, Irvine, for providing me with a grant and a graduate student researcher fellowship, and the Yokohama Zenkōji scholarship for International Buddhist Studies.

This book grew out of a dissertation submitted to the University of California, Irvine. Professor Duncan Williams, now at UC Berkeley, oversaw the entire process with great care. I also thank UCI faculty members Susan Klein, Edward Fowler, Jim Fujii, Anne Walthall, John Liu, and all the professors in the Department of East Asian Languages and Literatures, as well as its administrative staff, Mindy Han and Pat Eyster. A number of scholars helped my research in various ways. I thank Mark Unno, Shigeo Kanda, Alfred Bloom, and Richard Jaffe for reading the draft manuscript; the late Yūji Ichioka of UCLA for allowing me to explore his microfilm collections; Valerie Matsumoto for arranging some contacts in Stockton; Brian Hayashi for commenting on the paper I presented at the American Academy of Religions in 2003, which has become part of Chapter Six; Ronald Magden for providing local history related to Shin Buddhism in Seattle; and George Tanabe for initiating the review process at the University of Hawai'i Press. In Japan, I thank Shigeki Izumi for helping me transcribe the personal writings of Issei clergy, Akeshi Kiba for showing me unexplored materials related to modern Shin Buddhist overseas propagation, Tomoe Moriya for sharing with me her material concerning Imamura Emyō and reading the manuscript, Shiki Kodama for responding to my questions, and Mitsuhiro Sakaguchi for helping me investigate the study of Japanese immigration to Canada. Hiromichi Yamashiro provided useful comments on some of my terms, though I did not adequately incorporate his suggestions into the present work. I also thank Taku Yamamoto and Jessica L. Main for lending a hand in my research.

My gratitude is extended to Shin Buddhist ministers in North America. Akinori Imai, Bishop of the Higashi Honganji North America

District, supported me throughout the entire process. Chikai Yosemori, former Bishop of the Honpa Honganji Mission of Hawaii, provided me valuable information about early Shin Buddhist history in Hawaii. Chūhō Matsubayashi, former Rinban of the Nishi Honganji Los Angeles Betsuin, introduced me to some members of his congregation. Ōrai Fujikawa, Bishop of the Buddhist Churches of Canada, provided transportation during research in Vancouver. I also thank Bishop Kōshin Ogui, Bishop Thomas Okano, and Rev. Michael Endō and Rev. Koho Takata, through whom I gained permission to reproduce photos. Due to limitations of space, I am unable to list all the other ministers and Shin clergy, in the U.S. and in Japan, who provided assistance in my research; I am indebted to them all.

Leaders of various research institutions assisted me in accessing archival materials. I especially thank Cris Paschild, the former BCA archivist at the Japanese American National Museum, and the other research assistants for frequently pulling out boxes of historical documents; Gonnami Tsuneharu of the Centre for Japanese Research at the University of British Columbia for guiding me through the Japanese Canadian Research Collections; Kelly Haigh, Administrative Assistant at the UCLA Library Department of Special Collections, for finding me old monographs listed in *The Buried Past;* and staff members of the *Rafu Shimpo* for allowing me to examine original copies of the newspapers. Eiko Masuyama, an active member of the Nishi Honganji Los Angeles Betsuin in charge of its archives, brought me documents related to Itsuzō Kyōgoku and Julius Goldwater. In Japan, Nahoko Ishii of the Ritsumeikan University Library and Ms. Fukahori of the Ōtani University Library took care of my constant requests. Yasuyuki Fukumoto of the Bukkyō Ongaku Kenkyūsho was instrumental in getting me interested in the history of Buddhist *gathas*.

Many thanks to the wide range of Shin members and those related to local Buddhist organizations, both in the United States and Japan, who participated in my study in various ways: Ryō Munekata, Naomi Yamada, Shin'ichi Nishikawa, Ikuko Shimizu, Fumiko Groves, Ellen Hale, Sadie Yamasaki, Masayuki Ishihara, Brooke R. and Linda Whitted, Tadashi and Michiko Aoki, Marii Hasegawa, Nagatoshi Yoshinaga, Robert Akune, Mari Shimizu, Nobuyuki Izumida, Makoto Honda, and all those whose names I may have omitted here.

I wish to thank Buddhist sculptor Kokei Eri and photographer Naotatsu Kimura for allowing me to reproduce "Standing Image of Parte de Verre Amida Buddha" on the cover of the book.

My deepest appreciation is extended to my family. My father, Toshimaro Ama, made various comments on this study and sent me a variety of books and articles related to my research from Japan. My wife, Tomoko, helped to situate me in the best environment possible so that I could pursue my study singlemindedly (or egotistically), and Ayami often helped to divert my attention to non-academic matters. I only regret that I am not able to present this work to my mother, Noriko Ama, who passed away four years ago.

Finally, I thank the editorial staff. Since the beginning of my dissertation work, Peter Lait frequently proofread the manuscript, spotting my careless mistakes. Eiko Masuyama also proofread it. I thank the two reviewers who provided me with insightful comments; editor Marianne Dresser and Richard Payne, series editor of the Pure Land Buddhist Series, for their efforts to make the manuscript more presentable; and Patricia Crosby of the University of Hawai'i Press for overseeing the entire process.

This book was completed during my time at the University of Alaska, Anchorage. I was supported in this effort by the College of Arts and Sciences and my colleagues in the Department of Languages.

This work is dedicated to the Commemoration of Shinran Shōnin's 750th-year Passing.

Translation of Terms

In translating, I have used certain words interchangeably. First, following normal convention, the category "Shin Buddhism" denotes the Jōdo Shinshū tradition of Japanese Buddhism. Although the creation of such an English designation is unclear, "Shin Buddhism" seems to have appeared in the writings of D. T. Suzuki (1870–1966) and Gesshō Sasaki (1875–1926), the third president of Ōtani University.[1] The problem is what the "Shin" in Shin Buddhism represents. One probable reference is to Shinshū. In this context, *shin* would mean "truth" (*makoto*) in Japanese. If we accept this premise, then, Shin Buddhism refers to "True Buddhism." However, Shinran, who is posthumously regarded as the founder of Jōdo Shinshū, defined it as "the ultimate of the Mahayana" (*daijō no shigoku*). It also literally means "True School of the Pure Land." Therefore, the designation of "Shin Buddhism" as "True Buddhism" goes beyond a literal translation.

It is interesting to note, however, that there are many *kanji* characters that either read or sound like the word *shin*. One is "trust" or "entrusting," and another is "mind" or "heart" (*kokoro*). When these two characters are coupled, they form the word *shinjin*, the most important concept in Shinran's teaching: entrusting oneself to the Primal Vow of Amida Buddha (Skt. Amitābha, "Immeasurable Light," and/or Amitāyus, "Eternal Life"), who promised to liberate all sentient beings from their karmic shackles upon recitation of the phrase *Namu Amida Butsu* (literally, "I take refuge in Amida Buddha"); this phrase is known as the nenbutsu. *Shin* can also be read as "deep" (*fukai*), indicating "deep mind" (when combined with *kokoro*), another key concept in Jōdo Shinshū.[2] Lastly, *shin* can signify Shinran himself. Therefore, the choice of Shin Buddhism for Jōdo Shinshū may not be as problematic as it initially appears. With this in mind, I use both terms alternatively throughout this work.

I have differentiated "denomination" from "sect" (or school). "Denomination" denotes the suffix *-ha*, which appears in the names of branches of Jōdo Shinshū, such as Honganji-ha, Ōtani-ha, Takada-ha, and Bukkōji-ha. I use the term "sect" for the suffix *-shū*, which denotes different Buddhist schools or traditions, such as Jōdoshū, Nichirenshū, Tendaishū, and the like.

The designation of "Jōdo Shinshū" has its own history. The Japanese government did not acknowledge the name Shinshū, as in Jōdo Shinshū, until

1872. Although the Nishi (west) and Higashi (east) branches of the Honganji, as the largest denominations of Jōdo Shinshū, requested the Tokugawa *bakufu* (the feudal and dictatorial military government, also called the shogunate) to recognize the title, Jōdoshū, the school with which the Tokugawa family was affiliated, opposed it, because Jōdo"shin"shū made Jōdoshū sound "false," since a literal translation of the word *shinshū* means "true school." Prior to the Tokugawa period (1603–1867), Shinran's followers had been known as Ikkōshū, literally, "the school of singlemindedness (of reciting the nenbutsu)."[3]

The Meiji government (1868–1912) finally authorized the use of the name Shinshū in December 1872. In June 1881, the Nishi Honganji named itself Shinshū Honganji-ha (later modified to Jōdo Shinshū Honganji-ha), and the Higashi Hoganji called itself Shinshū Ōtani-ha.[4] I use these names interchangeably. At times, the "Honganji" is omitted and the terms "Higashi" and/or "Nishi" are used alone, to avoid undue repetition.

For the choice of words related to Shin Buddhist orders in the United States, I follow the nomenclature of the Buddhist Churches of America (BCA). For instance, "minister" designates an overseas Buddhist priest (*kaikyōshi*). "Mission" or "church" takes the place of "temple." "Nishi Honganji" has historically been romanized as "Nishi Hongwanji" for the sake of pronunciation, but I omit the "w" throughout this work except where it appears in citations. In the prewar period, "Honpa" was spelled "Hompa," and the first name of Bishop Emyō Imamura was rendered as "Yemyō." These usages do not appear in this work.

Lastly, a note about the treatment of Japanese names: traditionally, and in Japan, the family name precedes the first or given name. However, to avoid confusion, in this book all names, whether of Japanese nationals or second- and third-generation Japanese Americans, appear in the standard English-language format of first name followed by surname.

The word "Nikkei" is used as a collective term for people of Japanese ancestry living in North America, encompassing the Issei (Japanese nationals who immigrated to North America), the Nisei (the second-generation children of the original immigrants, born in North America), and the Sansei (third generation).

Immigrants to the Pure Land

Introduction

It is extremely pleasurable to view the full moon from the deck at the time of the lunar *Bon* [in August]. When I think of the verse, "With the distant view of a mountain and the moon, I bow my head thinking of my hometown," you, my wife and children, my sister and other family members cross my mind; hence, I have become a bit depressed. "The pain caused by viewing the moon alone in the three-thousand world" indeed describes my difficulty. However, I am here only to serve the Dharma. I made up my mind a long time ago. Moreover, why should I myself lament over who dwells in the world of light, which grasps and never abandons [sentient beings]?[1]

On his way to San Francisco in 1899, Shūe Sonoda, later to become the first superintendent of the Buddhist Mission of North America (BMNA), expressed to his father-in-law his anxiety about leaving his family behind and his determination to transmit Shin Buddhism in the New World. One year earlier, Hōni Satomi had moved to Honolulu as the first superintendent of the Honpa Honganji Mission of Hawaii (HHMH).

Prior to World War II, Jōdo Shinshū had become a dominant form of ethnic Buddhism in North America. By the mid-1920s, HHMH had built more than thirty Shin missions throughout the Hawaiian Islands. In the continental United States, BMNA had established Buddhist churches in the major California cities that had large Nikkei populations and had expanded its operations in Washington, Utah, Arizona, and New York. In Canada, by 1940, Shin missions had been founded in Vancouver, Maple Ridge, Steveston, New Westminster, and Royston (British Columbia); and Raymond (Alberta).

The rapid growth of Shin Buddhism in North America has been explained in two ways: through assimilation to the host society and reinforcement of ethnic solidarity. Scholars in the past defined Shin assimilation as a one-way process, in which the religion was transformed by modeling itself on Christianity. Partly due to the "otherness" of Buddhism as seen by Christians, together with the connection between Buddhist institutions and Japanese language schools, anti-Japanese activists considered Buddhists to be unassimilable. In order to overcome a sense of marginality, Shin Buddhists tried to conform to Protestant practices. They adopted the system of a board of trustees for organizational management, avoided the typical architecture of a traditional Japanese temple, and brought pews and lecterns into the worship hall. The liturgical changes included weekly Sunday services, in which the typical ritual format consisted of meditation, chanting of Buddhist scriptures, a sermon, the singing of *gathas* (hymns), the burning of incense, and announcements. The formation of the Young Buddhist Association (YBA) represented another form of Christian adaptation.[2]

Pioneering scholar Tetsuden Kashima questioned the equation of Buddhist assimilation with Christianity. In the 1970s, he examined how the Buddhist Churches of America (BCA) (the former BMNA, renamed during the war), adapted to help the Nikkei community survive and how it maintained itself while diverging from Japanese tradition.[3] He attributed the strength of the BCA to ethnic solidarity. Personal and social crises, including the deaths of resident immigrants, the hostility of Christian organizations, anti-Japanese campaigns, and the Pacific War fostered a sense of belonging to a Buddhist community. At the same time, Kashima argued that generational conflicts between the Issei and Nisei laity as well as between Issei and Nisei/Sansei ministers prevailed within the BCA because of these groups' differing familiarity with Japanese language and culture.[4] Despite these differences, Kashima showed that the organizational structure of the BCA was modeled on that of its mother temple, the Nishi Honganji in Japan.[5]

After the turn of the twenty-first century, the processes of transplanting and transforming Japanese Buddhist practice in the United States have continued to be debated by both American and Japanese scholars. For instance, George Tanabe has asserted that Shin Buddhist acculturation in Hawaii included the maintenance of "core" religious principles and traditional practices derived from Japan despite external modifications (Tanabe uses the metaphor of "grafting" in the horticultural sense).[6] Tomoe Moriya, a Japanese scholar, has investigated the activities of Bishop Emyō Imamura, who was the head of HHMH for more than thirty years and contributed to the birth of "American Buddhism."[7] Japanese scholar Masako Iino points out that the concept of *yamato damashii* (the spirit of Japan) persisted among Canadian Nisei Shin Buddhists.[8] Duncan Williams and Tomoe Moriya organized the Issei Buddhism Conference at the University of California, Irvine, September 3–5, 2004, to explore the early formation of Japanese-American Buddhism. A collection of papers presented at the conference edited by them, *Issei Buddhism in the Americas* (Urbana, IL: University of Illinois Press, 2010), describes Issei Buddhist activities.

Asian-American scholars have also argued that the assimilation of Buddhists of Japanese ancestry in the United States can never be considered linear when the relationship between ethnicity and religion is historicized. Lori Pierce has juxtaposed an analysis of race in Hawaii with the appropriation of Buddhism by Euro-Americans, arguing that it reflects the ideology of white supremacy during the prewar period.[9] Michael Masatsugu has conducted a comparative study of ethnic Japanese Buddhists and Euro-American converts from the beginning of World War II to 1966, when the Buddhist Studies Center, founded in 1949 by the BCA, was transformed into a seminary and renamed the Institute of Buddhist Studies (IBS).[10] Other scholars of Asian-American studies have included a discussion of Buddhism in their projects as well.[11]

This study adds a new perspective to these findings but simultaneously departs from them in significant ways. It contextualizes the acculturation of Shin Buddhism in the formation of the two nation-states, Japan and the United States, before World War II.[12] Acculturation generally suggests transformation of cultural practices, including religious values, from one place to another, but the domestic building and colonial interests of the two countries affected this activity significantly. Thus, American Shin Buddhists' efforts to define their religion between the two modern nation-states occurred within the acculturative process, which simultaneously constitutes an ethnic subculture and characterizes their crosscultural experience. Although similar concepts, such as inculturation (or enculturation) and emplantation, are available for the transnational examination of a particular religious practice, the choice of acculturation endorses Eileen Tamura's insistence of ethnicity and accentuates Shin Buddhists' ethno-religious identity in North America.[13]

In this work, I define acculturation as a blending process consisting of the "Japanization" and "Americanization" of Jōdo Shinshū. Japanization began after the Meiji Restoration (1868). The institutional spread of Western religion helped Shin Buddhism to reevaluate its Japanese character, and this operation continued in North America. Shin Buddhists brought worldviews formed and contested during the development of the Japanese nation-state along with their traditional cultural practices, and reappraised the spiritual values of their own tradition. At the same time, they responded to and became part of the state apparatus of Japan.

The Americanization of Shin Buddhism also had a political dimension. The concept of Americanization not only led immigrants to adapt to the customs of the host society, including Protestant practices, but also suggested the exclusivity and inclusivity of nationalism. American nativists promoted anti-Catholicism and anti-radicalism, whereas liberalists maintained that America's national distinctiveness derived from the activity of ethnic amalgamation.[14] For Shin Buddhists, Americanization suggested a process of assimilation into a host society dominated by Anglo-Americans, while at the same time it marked their discovery of the liberal and pluralistic aspects of "American democracy," which validated religious freedom and egalitarianism. Shin Buddhist acculturation thus encompasses various perspectives, often contradictory, that developed in the two nation-states.

Since the nation-states of Japan and the United States were mutually exclusive, the national identity of Shin Buddhists in North America remained equivocal. In Japan, modernity posed a question to Buddhists: how to become imperial subjects and simultaneously maintain their Buddhist faith. Buddhist leaders resolved this dilemma by conforming to the religious policies of the government, while keeping their faith to themselves. In this way, the Buddhist denominations were able to support Japan's colonial enterprises and establish a reputable position in the domestic sphere and on the Asian continent. In the United States, however, the situation of Shin Buddhists was complicated by another question: how to obtain American citizenship, or for that matter, how Japanese immigrants could become naturalized. Issei settlers in North America found themselves in a peripheral position: on the one hand, the Japanese government could not exercise the same kind of power in the United States as it did in China and Korea; on the other hand, the U.S. government did not welcome them. By delving into the unexplored religious "border" between Japan and the United States, this study proposes new ways of thinking about the relationship between the modern nation-state and Japanese Buddhism.

Acculturation occurred on a frontier. For Shin Buddhists, it came about as a result of the expansion of Buddhism in North America, otherwise known as "Buddhism moving eastward" (*bukkyō tōzen*). In this endeavor, a religious frontier was created in Hawaii, the United States, and Canada. David Chidester defines the frontier as a place where the concept of religion can be reexamined:

> [T]he frontier has been an arena in which definitions of religion have been produced and deployed, tested and contested, in local struggles over power and position in the world. In such power struggles, the term religion has been defined and redefined as a strategic instrument.[15]

Finding themselves in such a geographical position, Shin ministers reinterpreted doctrine, transformed rituals, and reconfigured institutional structures by incorporating some Protestant practices and the concept of democracy. Organizational leaders attempted to establish their locality in a society dominated by Anglo-Protestants without losing their faith and cultural heritage. At the same time, however, they found themselves in a quandary as to whether to promote Shin doctrine or the general teachings of Śākyamuni, because these two were not identical, and Euro-American converts demanded the latter.

Aims

This book has three aims. First, acculturation is examined at institutional, ritual, and doctrinal levels, since hierarchy, liturgy, and hermeneutics are the major components of organized religion. I divide these categories for two analytical purposes. In previous studies, scholars chose either organizational structure or ritual practice as the site of their primary investigation. By examining doctrine and incorporating its discussion into a social history of Shin Buddhism in the United States, this work will further the study of Asian-American Buddhism, which has previously lacked a consideration of hermeneutics, and place the intellectual activities of some Asian Americans in a broader framework of American intellectual history. Then by correlating the organizational, ritual, and doctrinal changes of Shin Buddhism, this study assesses whether or not doctrinal interpretation was the crucial factor for a denomination's structural assimilation. The evidence shows that organizational and ritual changes preceded doctrinal adjustment.

Second, *Immigrants to the Pure Land* compares the development of the Shin Buddhist diaspora in Hawaii and on the North American continent. Although official propagation of the Nishi Honganji began in Hawaii and the mainland United States at about the same time, the 1930s can be regarded as a watershed for the development of Shin Buddhism in North America. In Hawaii, the untimely death of Bishop Imamura resulted in the stagnation of the HHMH; meanwhile, on the mainland, under the aegis of Bishop Kenju Masuyama, the BMNA expanded to New York and created an independent Canadian bishopric. The demographic distribution, diplomatic relationships, and socioeconomic conditions of ethnic Japanese were also distinctively different in these regions. In this respect, the Hawaiian Shin clergy became more locally involved, while its mainland counterpart grew translocal.

Throughout the prewar period, Shin Buddhism in North America was never free from internal conflict. Collisions occurred between the Kyoto headquarters and the HHMH/BMNA, the central offices of HHMH/BMNA and local Shin missions/churches, and between clergy and laity. In other words, the Shin Buddhist diaspora was far from harmonious, contrary to the presumption of earlier scholarship. Further, this volume suggests that the causes of hostilities need to be studied together with the analysis of communal protocol in Japan, as these conflicts did not result from doctrinal differences. A great deal of animosity accompanied Shin Buddhism's establishment in North America, and this antagonism derived from the process of the Japanization and Americanization of organizational structures.

Third, this work narrates a history of Euro-American converts to Buddhism. Previously, scholars investigated the activities of Ernest Hunt and the Theosophists, including those who had converted to Theravada Buddhism. The effectiveness of those who had become priests at the BMNA is hardly known, although they were still the first group of Caucasians who became interested in Buddhism in the United States. Activities of such Euro-American Shin ministers as Robert Clifton (the leader of the BMNA English Department), Julius Goldwater (a relative of Senator Barry Goldwater), and Sunya Pratt ("America's First Female Priestess," so called by the *Los Angeles Times*), are introduced in connection with their relationships to the Issei clergy and the head temple in Japan.[16]

Resources

A highlight of the book is its intensive reliance on prewar Japanese documents kept at the BCA Archives, which have heretofore been largely overlooked. These documents make it possible to trace the activities of Issei ministers, the organizational leaders of Shin Buddhism in North America. In addition, they shed light on the relationships between clergy and laity; exchanges among Issei, Nisei, and Caucasian clergy; Shin Buddhist interactions with ministers of other Japanese Buddhist schools and the New Religions (*shin shūkyō*); and the development of the Nikkei pioneer community as a whole.

The discovery of new sources forces a critical review of the master narrative of Shin Buddhism in North America. The powerful presence of the HHMH and the BMNA, both of which were Nishi Honganji organizations, has largely overshadowed the overseas propagation of the Higashi Honganji. These two Shin orders were almost comparable in terms of the number of affiliated temples in Japan, and had exercised tremendous institutional authority over Japanese politics, the lives of the laity, and the Buddhist community as a whole. The history of the Higashi Honganji in North America has gone unnoticed, partly because of its limited presence and the lack of overseas records, its emphasis on propagation in Asia during the prewar period, and its loose organizational structure. By retrieving the history of the Higashi Honganji in Hawaii and on the West Coast, this study presents a more complex picture of Shin Buddhist history, but at the same time concludes that denominational differences appeared to be of little importance to congregations and that there was no distinct doctrinal development between the two Honganjis in North America.

Organization

This book has seven chapters. Chapter One provides a backdrop to the entire study by introducing a history of modern Shin Buddhism in Japan, of which there is little English-language literature available. Following a brief survey of Shinran's teaching and later developments by the Higashi Honganji and the Nishi Honganji, the reactions of Shin Buddhists to modernity in the early twentieth century are discussed, because the ensuing changes in North America reflect and parallel the modern development of Shin Buddhism in Japan.

Chapter Two analyzes the development of the HHMH and the BMNA. Shin Buddhism spread in Hawaii and North America as an "organized religion" with headquarters in Kyoto. So, the initial goals of the HHMH and the BMNA reflected the strategy of a Japanese headquarters for overseas operations. In Hawaii, ministers promoted their sectarian teaching to Japanese immigrants and aimed to introduce it to Caucasians, whereas on the mainland, their counterparts spread Śākyamuni's teachings to Euro-Americans while catering to the conventional demands of immigrants.[17] These differences are clearly shown in the documents of incorporation and the various by-laws of these different entities.

The organizational structures of the HHMH and the BMNA were simultaneously Americanized and Japanized. The Shin clergy modeled its organizations after Protestant congregationalism, including the system of boards of trustees and observance of by-laws. But the Nishi Honganji headquarters in Japan had already introduced the representative assembly of priests in 1881 as part of its modernization efforts. Further, the general structure of local Shin Buddhist gatherings had always been horizontal. Therefore, Shin priests did not freshly come to the democratization of their organizations after encountering Protestantism, even though the concept of "democracy" might have been novel to them.

Chapter Three traces the development of Shin ministries in Hawaii and on the mainland. In Nikkei communities, ministers' roles and responsibilities increased when immigrants saw Buddhism as one of their collective ties with Japan. With the expansion of a ministry, however, the acculturation of "faith" appeared on an individual level. As the background of Issei ministers differed from the spiritual interests of Nisei and Euro-American Buddhists, the HHMH and the BMNA diverged from conventional practices when bishops ordained members of the latter two groups. The establishment of an English department in these organizations was a new event. However, since the majority of Caucasian Buddhists were not necessarily interested in Shinran's teachings but found Śākyamuni's philosophy rational and logical, problems arose in the process of admitting non-Nikkei ministers. Caucasian commitment to the order was also weak, and most Euro-Americans did not stay long in the BMNA.

Chapter Four tackles the problem of ritual adaptation. As previously noted, it can be said that Shin Buddhist rites became Americanized following the Christian model. There is some truth to this observation, but ritual practices for some services also reflected liturgical changes in modern Japan. In their adaptations, too, the orientation of propagation—whether to promote Shin or Śākyamuni's teachings—became an issue. The moral teachings of Śākyamuni were the major themes of popular Buddhist hymnals, such as the *Vade Mecum* (1924) and the *Standard Gathas* (1939); and for the Caucasian "initiation" service, the BMNA leaders adopted a style conforming to the Theravada tradition.

The second half of Chapter Four discusses Buddhist architecture in North America. Shin Buddhists on the mainland continued using the facilities of a (usually) Protestant church building after purchasing it, unless they had enough money to remodel. At the same time however, the design of church buildings reflected Japanese cultural practices, the decisions of immigrants regarding permanent settlement, and the intentions of particular ministers, such as Bishop Imamura, who was aware of new trends in architecture at the Kyoto headquarters. To highlight this process of Japanization, studies of various scholars on the subject of Buddhist architecture are introduced.

Chapter Five investigates the ways in which some Issei ministers construed Shinran's teaching by borrowing concepts from Christianity, incorporating other Buddhist schools' practices, and studying modern democracy. Three cases under review are Takeichi Takahashi, who worked with Bishop Junjō Izumida of the Higashi Honganji in Los Angeles; Itsuzō Kyōgoku of the BMNA, who developed the Spiritual Activism of Manshi Kiyozawa (a Higashi Honganji scholar-priest and Japan's first religious philosopher); and Bishop Emyō Imamura of the HHMH, who had been educated under Yukichi Fukuzawa (founder of present-day Keiō University) and was associated with Kiyozawa. Each of the three interpreted Shin doctrine in a new light, through a pragmatic mode of thinking.

The hermeneutics developed by Takahashi and Kyōgoku differ, as the former represents the Americanization of doctrine, while the latter exposes its Japanization. Takahashi linked Shinran's teaching to John Dewey's instrumentalism and engaged in comparative studies of Buddhism and Christianity. Kyōgoku, on the other hand, expanded Kiyozawa's theory of self-exhaustion and attempted to bridge the gap between the concepts of self-power (*jiriki*) and other-power (*tariki*). Kyōgoku proposed a circular movement between the two, because the Shin tradition without a defined practice was unattractive to the Nisei and Caucasians in the presence of the strong structural system of Theravada Buddhism.

In addition to the hermeneutics of Takahashi and Kyōgoku, Imamura worked on the social dimension of Shinran's teaching. He wrote *Democracy According to the Buddhist Viewpoint* (1918) and critiqued the exclusionist discourse on Americanization. Two years later, Imamura participated in the 1920 territory-wide sugar plantation strike initiated by Nikkei workers and in Issei educators' protest over the Hawaiian territorial government ban on Japanese language schools. Through these incidents, he examined modern democracy from a Buddhist perspective.

The new doctrinal paradigm that Takahashi, Kyōgoku, and Imamura sought, however, had limitations. Although attempting to bring spirituality into the lives of the immigrants, they could not completely rid themselves of the doctrine of the two truths (the dual principles of secular and spiritual rules, *shinzoku nitai*), the core of the Shin Buddhist creed, which was related to the ideology of mundane authority. Ministers encouraged the Issei to be loyal to Japan and instructed the Nisei to be patriotic to the United States, while telling both generations to keep their faith to themselves. Regarding Buddhist scholars' connection with nationalism at that time, Michel Mohr notes that "[a] serious study of intellectuals active during the Meiji period often leads to the awareness that *it is much easier to condemn them than to make the effort required to understand them*."[18] I critically investigate the imperial connections maintained by the Issei clergy and identify the relevance of hermeneutical challenges made by these three individuals today associated with the doctrine of the two truths.

Chapter Six traces the history of the Higashi Honganji in North America and analyzes the interaction between the two largest Shin denominations. The Higashi headquarters in Kyoto, Japan, never tried to establish a base for propagation on the mainland. Instead, it seized opportunities and gained momentum whenever a local Nishi church divided into two groups and one of them sought an alternative affiliation. The first case concerns the split of Rafu Bukkyōkai (Los Angeles Buddhist Mission), where contention between the two parties was settled in the Los Angeles District Court. I argue that the differences between American legal practices and Japanese cultural applications were the loci of this lawsuit and that the Los Angeles Buddhist Mission's by-laws were the key to the settlement. In contrast to its accidental advancement on the mainland, the Higashi Honganji headquarters in Kyoto set out intentionally to propagate in Hawaii. Despite the presence of the two Honganji denominations, this research demonstrates that it is appropriate to treat the acculturation of Shin Buddhism as a relative whole.

Chapter Seven investigates the politics of acculturation by pursuing two objectives. First, the acculturation of Shin Buddhism is situated in a broader context by examining the Issei clergy's activities outside its own organizations. Second, acculturation is viewed as another example of ambivalence in the creation of Issei immigrant ethnicity. In the United States, BMNA leaders attended international religious conferences, where they endeavored to explain to the American public that Buddhism was a religion of world peace. In Hawaii, the Shin clergy supported the 1920 strike and the Issei educators' initial test case contesting the territorial government ban on Japanese language schools. The translocal and local activities of Issei Shin ministers, however, revealed their nationalistic concerns at the same time; hence I juxtapose their activities with those of their counterparts in Japan, who advanced onto the Asian continent and into other parts of the world.

Although the two branches of the Honganji were systematized under the rubric of Imperial Japan, there were several instances in which the critical ethos of Shin Buddhism survived in modern Japan. This independent attitude can be traced to Shinran. During the Meiji period, Kiyozawa personally criticized the Imperial Rescript. Kenmyō Takagi, another Higashi Honganji priest, opposed the Russo-Japanese War, the institutionalized practice of discrimination, and state-sponsored prostitution. Imamura's social engagement in Hawaii can be seen as reflecting the same spirit, especially when he questioned the laws of the United States. His assistance to the Nikkei workers in the 1920 strike and to the Issei educators in their initial test case can be read as another instance of Japanization, evoking Shin analytical attitudes, and as Americanization, involving the democratic principles developed in the United States, i.e., the human rights of workers and the freedom to learn a foreign language.

This book contributes to the crosscultural understanding of Shin Buddhism and demonstrates the complexity of a transnational Buddhist study. In 1997, Galen Amstutz published *Interpreting Amida,* in which he argued that Shin Buddhism had not received the thorough examination that it deserved from Euro-American scholars and Japanese nonsectarian academics. He traced the cause of these misunderstandings back to the reactions of intellectuals during the Victorian period of the nineteenth century, including antisectarianism.[19] It has been more than ten years since Amstutz's book appeared, but misunderstandings of Shin Buddhism still prevail, and only a few Euro-American scholars have shown interest in its study.[20] This present study aims to transcend a sectarian/antisectarian dichotomy. The comparative study of Shin Buddhism in Hawaii and on the mainland during the same time period, together with a close analysis of its sociopolitical conditions, will contribute to the history of American religions, the emerging study of American Buddhism, and the reexamination of modern Japanese Buddhism.

Chapter One

The Modern Development of Shin Buddhism

The Shin Buddhist response to modernity undertaken by the two Honganjis is worth examining for several reasons. In 1559, the head temple of Honganji achieved the rank of *monzeki,* which denotes a temple recognized by the emperor, imperial family, or an aristocrat.[1] By the sixteenth century, this temple complex had grown into "a formidable religious and political force" and "outstripped most other schools of Buddhism" in terms of its membership.[2] In the seventeenth century the Honganji was divided into Nishi (west) and Higashi (east) branches. The two Honganjis gave financial assistance to the Meiji government from the end of the Tokugawa period to the Meiji Restoration, with politicians such as Tomomi Iwakura and Kaoru Inoue often intervening in the modernization of these organizations.[3] Congregations regarded both abbots as living buddhas (*iki botoke*), whose status at the head temple corresponded to that of the divine figure of the emperor.

Modernity prompted the leaders of the two Honganjis to rethink their ideas of nation-statehood and restructure their organizations. Meiji politicians and nativists persecuted Buddhism and enforced the ideology of imperial Shintō. Despite initial resistance against the government, both the Nishi and Higashi Honganji branches sought an ideal relationship between Buddhism and the nation-state of Japan and ended up reinforcing national policies on religion. They also made an alliance with other Jōdo Shinshū denominations as part of the trans-sectarian Buddhist movement and competed with Christianity. In a denominational setting, Shin priests reexamined their organizational styles, rituals, and doctrine by studying the religious climate of Western Europe and its scholarship. Before further discussion of the modern development of Shin Buddhism, a brief review of Shinran's life and the doctrine propagated by Honganji is fundamental to the entire analysis.

Shinran's Life and Teaching

Shinran (1173–1263) is considered to be the posthumous founder of Jōdo Shinshū. Shin Buddhist scholars generally divide Shinran's life into four periods: his monastic training on Mt. Hiei, the center of Buddhist studies at that time; his departure from the monastery and encounter with his teacher, Hōnen (also known as Genkū, 1133–1212); his exile in Echigo province (present-day Niigata prefecture) and his efforts at propagation in the Kantō region after being pardoned; and his eventual return to Kyoto. According to Kakunyo's *Biography of Shinran* (*Honganji shōnin den'e,* commonly known as the *Godenshō*), Shinran was born to Arinori Hino, a Kyoto aristocrat. His parents died when he was young and his uncle, Noritsuna Hino, took him to a prominent Tendai monk, Jinen, who ordained the nine-year-old boy in 1181. Shinran then spent almost twenty years on Mt. Hiei as "a monk of the practice hall" (*dōsō*).[4]

What motivated Shinran to leave Mt. Hiei is unclear, but he apparently experienced a "turning of the mind" (*eshin*) after meeting Hōnen. Scholars have noted that Shinran was unable to pursue monastic practices or control his sexual desire. His frustration, inner conflict, deep sense of guilt, and fear of rebirth in hell led him to reassess his situation on the mountain. As a result, Shinran visited the Rokkakudō and sought a divine vision, which encouraged him to visit Hōnen, who was teaching the sole practice of nenbutsu (reciting the name of Amida Buddha, *Namu Amida Butsu*) in Yoshimizu in the eastern hills of Kyoto.[5] In the *Ken jōdo shinjitsu kyōgyōsho monrui,* better known as the *Kyōgyōshinshō* (*The True Teaching, Practice, and Realization of the Pure Land Way*),[6] Shinran writes: "Gutoku Shinran, disciple of Shakyamuni, discarded sundry practices and took refuge in the Primal Vow [of Amida Buddha] in 1201."[7]

Hōnen, inspired by the writings of the Chinese Pure Land Buddhist master Shandao (613–681), established Pure Land Buddhism as an independent school in Japan. Although Shandao had defined the nenbutsu (Ch. *nianfo*) as "the sufficient cause of birth" in the Pure Land, Hōnen redefined it as the "rightly established practice" (*shōjō no gō*) for birth in the Pure Land.[8] Hōnen carefully read the *Larger Sutra of Immeasurable Life* (Skt. *Sukhāvatīvyūha-sūtra;* Ch. *Wu liang shou jing;* Jpn. *Muryōju kyō*), in which Bodhisattva Dharmākara made forty-eight vows and became Amida Buddha (Skt. Amitābha, "Immeasurable Light," or Amitāyus, "Immeasurable Life") on the fulfillment of these vows. Hōnen saw the eighteenth vow of Dharmākara as the most crucial and named it the primal vow or original vow (*hongan*):

> May I not gain possession of perfect awakening if, once I have attained
> buddhahood, any among the throng of living beings in the ten regions of the
> universe should single-mindedly desire to be reborn in my land with joy, with
> confidence, and gladness, and if they should bring to mind this aspiration for
> even ten moments of thought [to call my name even ten times] and yet not
> gain rebirth there. This excludes only those who have committed the five
> heinous sins and those who have reviled the True Dharma.[9]

Hōnen recognized the act of reciting Amida's name as a spiritual contract between Amida and those seeking liberation from samsara (cycle of
life and death).

For Hōnen, the definition of the practice was more urgent than doctrinal classification. He saw himself living in the last Dharma age (*mappō*)[10]
and therefore unable to attain buddhahood despite his reputation of having great Buddhist wisdom. He considered himself an "ignorant and de-
luded person" (*guro*), and in his mind the recitation of Amida's name was
the "sole path of salvation." Whereas Shandao viewed the nenbutsu as
"the practice that accords with Amida's original vow," Hōnen saw it as
"exclusively selected by Amida Buddha." He discarded all other practices
and promoted the nenbutsu, since it was the easiest practice available to
anyone at any time and place. His simplification of Buddhist practices was
liberating, revolutionary, even radical. So novel were Hōnen's ideas that
he eventually faced criticism and suppression from the established
Buddhist schools of the time.[11]

The hostility against Hōnen and his followers reached a peak in 1206.
After secretly attending a nenbutsu service held by two of Hōnen's disciples, two of the former Emperor Gotoba's courtesans decided to become
nuns. Enraged by this event and at the urging of the monks of Kōfukuji,
who had previously requested that the emperor prohibit Hōnen's exclusive nenbutsu practice, Gotoba executed four of Hōnen's disciples and exiled him to Tosa (present-day Kōchi prefecture) and Shinran to Echigo
(present-day Niigata prefecture).[12] Considering this incident, Shinran
writes in the postscript to the *Kyōgyōshinshō*:

> The emperor and his ministers, acting against the dharma and violating
> human rectitude, became enraged and embittered. As a result, Master
> Genkū—the eminent founder who had enabled the true essence of the Pure
> Land way to spread vigorously [in Japan]—and a number of his followers,
> without receiving any deliberation of their [alleged] crimes, were summari-
> ly sentenced to death or were dispossessed of their monkhood, given [secu-
> lar] names, and consigned to distant banishment. I was among the latter.
> Hence, I am now neither a monk nor one in worldly life. For this reason, I

have taken the term Toku ["stubble-haired"] as my name. Master Genkū and his disciples, being banished to the provinces in different directions, passed a period of five years [in exile].[13]

Shinran expressed his anger at those who persecuted Hōnen's sangha and declared his independence from Buddhist authorities. In Echigo, Shinran married Eshinni, the daughter of a landed and military steward, and they had six children.[14]

Unable to see his teacher again, Shinran took his own path and spread Hōnen's teaching. He remained in Echigo until 1214 and later settled in Hitachi province (present-day Ibaraki prefecture).[15] His life must have been full of hardships and challenges. Alfred Bloom writes of the adversity faced by Shinran:

> The chief contribution of the period of exile to Shinran's spiritual development was the fact that it brought him face to face with the hard realities of the life of the common people which he had not known when he lived apart as a monk. His experience was perhaps even more radical than that of the ordinary peasant because of the painful transition of being thrust out of the pleasant confines of the capital into the rigorous life of the villager.[16]

Through conversations with people in the countryside, which he would never have had in Kyoto, Shinran's understanding of humanity and Amida's compassion deepened. He came to see himself as one of the "shackled foolish beings" whose karmic bondage was not so different from those of hunters and peddlers. Shinran considered "such peddlers, hunters, and others are none other than we, who are like stones and tiles and pebbles."[17] He was convinced, however, that

> when we entrust ourselves to the Tathāgata [Amida]'s Primal Vow, we, who are like bits of tile and pebbles, are turned into gold. Peddlers and hunters, who are like stones and tiles and pebbles, are grasped and never abandoned by the Tathāgata's light.[18]

Shinran spent the remaining thirty years of his life in Kyoto and kept in touch with his followers in Kantō. His return to the capital is another mystery, especially after Hōnen had already passed away. Scholars have indicated that Shinran might have become controversial in Kantō, as his teaching awakened the "peddlers, hunters, and others" to their fundamental equality of life, and the Kamakura *bakufu* (military government) reacted against this.[19]

During the last part of his life, Shinran continued to revise the *Kyōgyōshinshō* and produced other writings, including expositions of the

Pure Land teaching and hymns (*wasan*). Despite this productivity, in his later life he encountered family problems. First, Eshinni returned to Echigo without any apparent hostility toward Shinran. Then, in 1256, Shinran disowned his eldest son, Zenran, who had misguided Shinran's followers in Kantō and become a kind of guru. Seven years after this incident, in 1263, Shinran passed away at the age of ninety, while being looked after by his daughter Kakushinni.[20]

In the *Kyōgyōshinshō*, Shinran redefined Hōnen's teaching. He identified seven patriarchs of Pure Land Buddhism (*shichi kōsō*) and created the lineage by placing Hōnen's doctrine into the larger framework of Mahayana discourse. The seven masters identified by Shinran as Pure Land patriarchs are two Indian masters, Nāgārjuna (c. 150–250), founder of the Mādhyamika school, and Vasubandhu (c. 320–400), a master of the Yogācāra school; Tanluan (476–542), Daochuo (562–645), and Shandao in China; and Genshin (942–1017) and Genkū (Hōnen) in Japan. In Shinran's mind, these masters had classified Buddhism into two traditions, the path of sages and the Pure Land path. The first path is known as the gate of self-power (*jiriki/shōdōmon*) and the second as that of other-power (*tariki/jōdomon*). In addition, he regarded the Three Sutras of Pure Land Buddhism— the *Larger Sutra of Immeasurable Life,* the *Contemplation Sutra on Buddha Amitābha* (Ch. *Fo shuo guan wuliangshoufo jing;* Jpn. *Kan muryōju kyō*), and the *Smaller Sutra of Immeasurable Life* (Skt. *Sukhāvatīvyūha-sūtra;* Ch. *Amituo jing;* Jpn. *Amida kyō*), selected by Hōnen—along with Tanluan's *Commentary on Vasubandhu's Discourse on the Pure Land* (Ch. *Wangsheng lun zhu;* Jpn. *Ōjo ronchū*), as the sacred texts of Jōdo Shinshū.[21]

Shinran's teaching can be summarized as "one who entrusts oneself to the Primal Vow and says the nenbutsu attains Buddhahood."[22] Instead of re-iterating the nenbutsu, he paid more attention to the devotee's state of mind and emphasized the importance of faith in Amida's Vow. This mind of entrusting (*shinjin*) does not come easily, since ordinary people, full of egotistical concerns and suspicious of others, doubt Amida's salvific power.[23] For Shinran, Amida Buddha directs both the nenbutsu and *shinjin* toward the practitioner; hence, they represent Amida's activity to awaken sentient beings and inspire them to seek nirvana.[24] *Namu Amida Butsu* manifests itself in the logic of liberation: "the being of self-enclosure and deep egocentricity, symbolized by namu, [is] illuminated and transformed by boundless compassion, amida-butsu."[25] For Shin Buddhists, recitation after obtaining *shinjin* is a way to express their gratitude to Amida, not a self-disciplined act through which they would accumulate merit. "The individual who thus places his faith in the Other-Power is accepted as he is (*sono mama*), no matter how ignorant or sinful he may be."[26]

Shinran considered *shinjin* a matter of the present life, not of the after-life, and defined birth in the Pure Land as "skillful means" (*hōben*) to further develop Buddhist wisdom. By pointing out the unity of Amida's mind and of the mind of the practitioner, Shinran writes:

> [W]hen a person realizes *shinjin,* he or she is born [into the Pure Land] immediately. "To be born immediately" is to dwell in the stage of nonretrogression. To dwell in the stage of nonretrogression is to become established in the stage of the truly settled. This is also called the attainment of the equal of perfect enlightenment.[27]

The stage of nonretrogression (*futaiten*) suggests one's advance to ultimate reality without "backsliding." With the realization of *shinjin,* he or she begins to understand the oneness of life, though they still see things in a dualistic way and retain the "blind passions" (*bonnō*).[28] In other words, *shinjin* is the "unsurpassed wisdom" of the Buddha, which refers to the nonduality of the mind—"the experience of awakening."[29] Shinran, however, is modest enough to say that this stage is only "equal" to the bodhi-sattva's realization, not "identical" with it. He writes:

> Having immediately entered the stage of the truly settled
> On realizing true and real *shinjin,* a person will,
> Being the same as Maitreya of the rank of succession
> To Buddhahood, attain supreme enlightenment.[30]

Maitreya is a great bodhisattva who will become the next incarnated buddha. The individual who obtains *shinjin* gains the same spiritual quality as Maitreya and is assured of attaining buddhahood at the moment of death. By shifting the focus from practice to faith (*shinjin*), Shinran emphasized the importance of spiritual liberation attained in this life (as "having immediately entered the stage of the truly settled," or *shōjōju*) and avoided discussion of the afterlife.[31]

After Shinran's demise, however, his followers misunderstood his teaching. This confusion was partly due to the decreasing number of Shinran's immediate followers. One of his followers, Yuien, compiled a collection of Shinran's sayings, *A Record in Lament of Divergences* (*Tannishō*), in an attempt to correct the distortions of Shinran's teachings and to ensure thereby a rightful transmission. Together with the *Kyōgyōshinshō,* the *Tannishō* has been a core text for Shin Buddhists. For instance, Rennyo (1415–1499), the eighth abbot of the Honganji, noted in the colophon to the *Tannishō* that it is "an important scripture in our tradition."[32]

19

Rennyo and the Theory
of the Two Truths

Rennyo institutionalized Shinran's teaching two hundred years after his death. Both Japanese scholars and American Buddhologists have studied the religious and political leadership of Rennyo, who appeared to be the "restorer" of Shin Buddhism (*chūkō no so*) and transformed the Honganji into a powerful Buddhist order.[33] Mark Blum best summarizes his significance:

> By devoting considerable attention to the standardization of such things as retreats for study and practice, pilgrimage, funerary rituals, fund-raising, norms of behavior, support for women, and the assimilation of local dōjō into the greater church, Rennyo's integration of local, regional, and national forces reflects an institutional vision that formed a prototype for what later became normative in Japanese religion in the premodern and modern periods.[34]

During the fifteenth century, Rennyo attempted to unify Shin Buddhists throughout Japan, promoted confraternities—autonomous lay associations (*kō*)—as models of self-sufficient communities, and transformed the Honganji, which Shinran's followers had organized as his mausoleum, into the head temple of Shin Buddhists.

Rennyo explained Shinran's doctrine to the laity in a more comprehensive way, while at the same time diverging from Shinran. He communicated with his followers by sending colloquial letters (*Ofumi* or *Gobunshō*) written in *kana,* and therefore accessible to ordinary people unschooled in Chinese characters. Rennyo systematized the rituals connected with Shinran's teaching and formulated the daily Shin service for the laity. Like Shinran, Rennyo called his followers "Dharma friends" or "fellows on the same path" (*dōbō* or *dōgyō*) rather than "disciples." However, Shinran and Rennyo were quite different. Shinran had no intention of building temples or cultivating popular interest in organizations, whereas Rennyo stressed the lineage of Dharma transmission, built a series of large temples, and eventually institutionalized the Honganji.[35]

Their differences were also prominent in the application of the theory of the two truths, a metaphysical concept of Mahayana Buddhism that explains the doctrine of emptiness in absolute and relative terms.[36] Japanese Buddhists transformed this theory, denoting absolute truth as Buddha's laws and relative truth as mundane laws, or the rules of secular society. In other words, they saw "absolute truth" as part of the spiritual sphere and "relative truth" as that available to the secular realm.

In the volume on "Practice" in the *Kyōgyōshinshō,* Shinran cites a passage from Tanluan's *Commentary on Vasubandhu's Treatise on the Pure Land:* "True and real virtue is in conformity with the twofold truth based on dharma-nature,"[37] and further says that "faith [in the compassionate vow of Amida Buddha] must be the foundation [of our daily life and everyday activities]" (*shinjin ihon*).[38] He also emphasizes being in the community of those who are truly settled for birth in the Pure Land (*shōjōju*).[39]

Essentially, Shinran elevated the importance of spiritual principles over secular rules, but his descendants reversed the priority, Rennyo being no exception. Rennyo drew a parallel between "the law of the ruler" (*ōbō*) and "the law of the Buddha" (*buppō*), and in one of his letters urged the laity

> to follow publicly the law of the ruler and to resolutely hold on in one's heart to the faith in Amida's salvific power, while making secular moral obligations the foundation [for daily life].[40]

Observation of mundane rules was necessary for Rennyo, especially when his organization grew powerful enough to compete with regional warlords and the laity participated in civil conflict, such as the *ikkō ikki,* uprisings of single-minded Amidists. In applying the theory of the two truths, Rennyo also created the rhetoric of predestination in order to assure salvation in the afterlife. He blended the act of petitioning—to "beseech Amida for salvation in the next life"—into Shinran's teaching,[41] while for Shinran, Amida's salvation was assured for one who obtained the entrusting mind (*shinjin*).

The rhetoric of the afterlife became part of the Honganji's doctrine during the Tokugawa period (1603–1867). It is said that Ieyasu Tokugawa divided the Honganji into the Higashi and Nishi branches in order to weaken its power and popular influence.[42] (The Honganji had previously resisted two national unifiers, Nobunaga Oda and Hideyoshi Toyotomi.) As a result, the two branches of the Honganji implemented the shogunate's religious policies, such as requiring the registration of families at temples (*terauke danka seido*), developed loyalty to the political system, and maintained the special privileges achieved from their *monzeki* status. By preaching to their followers to practice perseverance in hardship (even though such suffering was caused by the social structure itself) and to long for a better afterlife, Honganji leaders reinforced the existing social order. The theory of the two truths thus served as an ideology of Shin Buddhism by which its authorities separated mundane rules (the laws of this world) and spiritual principles (salvation in the afterlife), and demanded that followers understand and accept their social positions.[43]

The Shin Buddhist Challenge
to Modernity

Tokugawa patronage of the two branches of the Honganji ended after the Meiji government abolished the rank of *monzeki* in 1871 and took away its privileges by separating Buddhism and Shintō. There were three urgent tasks that the leaders of the two Honganjis undertook at this time: to respond to the campaign to abolish the Dharma and destroy Śākyamuni (*haibutsu kishaku*) and establish relationships with the new government, to overcome the growing influence of Christianity, and to incorporate Western civilization into their denominations.[44]

The Shin Buddhist response to the developing nation-state was not unanimous. The government pronounced the "Promulgation of the Great Teaching" (*Senpu daikyō no mikotonori*), set up the Ministry of Doctrine (*kyōbushō*) in March 1872, and directed doctrinal instructors (*kyōdō shoku*), including Shintō and Buddhist priests, to educate the masses in the national teaching.[45] Mokurai Shimaji (1838–1911), one of the clerics who assumed the Nishi Honganji administration on the establishment of the Meiji government, wrote the "Critique of the Three Doctrinal Standards" (*Sanjō kyōsoku hihan kenpakusho*) in Paris during a religious study tour in 1872 and denounced Japanese politicians' efforts to establish Shintō as a state religion.[46]

Shimaji's efforts and Shin Buddhist leaders' inability to bridge the doctrinal differences between Shintō and Buddhism led the League of Four Shin Buddhist Denominations (Higashi, Nishi, Takada, and Kibe) to agree to withdraw from the Great Teaching Academy (Daikyōin). However, the Kōshōji, the Nishi Honganji's umbrella organization (which had been classified as *waki monzeki*, literally, "by the side of *monzeki*") opposed the decision made by the League of Four. In order to seek independence from the Nishi Honganji, which had to be recognized by the government, the abbot of Kōshōji supported the system of doctrinal instructors.

Within the Higashi Honganji itself, a group of priests, concerned that withdrawal from the Academy would bring about unfavorable conditions for their organization, initially disagreed with their own administration. However, the League of Four Shin Buddhist Denominations' opposition gained momentum when enlightened thinkers, such as Yukichi Fukuzawa, Amane Nishi, and Arinori Mori, and the print media, underpinned their efforts and discouraged the government so that it abandoned its plan.[47]

With the closure of the Great Teaching Academy, Shin leaders ironically acknowledged the quasi-state religion of Shintō. Shimaji initially advocated the separation of religion and state and even considered Shin

Buddhism as a source of resisting political authority. However, he seemed to agree with Kowashi Inoue, the intellectual power behind Hirobumi Itō and one who played a major role in drafting the Constitution of the Empire of Japan, on defining Shintō as not a religion. According to Inoue, Shintō was an "imperial tradition" and not under the rubric of "religion," in which politicians and intellectuals lumped Buddhism, Christianity, and later Sect Shintō together. In the case of Shimaji, Buddhism could furnish necessary spiritual guidance, while Shintō merely provided the rituals for honoring one's ancestors. Buddhism represented spiritual truth, while Shintō, related to imperial practice, fell into the category of mundane truth. Therefore, these two spiritual traditions were not in conflict for Shin Buddhists.[48]

With the theory of the two truths, the two Honganjis became embedded in the nation-state apparatus. Honganji leaders came to ignore the supremacy of Buddhist faith, as declared by Hōnen and Shinran, in the presence of so-called state Shintō. Although local congregations initially protested the state practice of enshrining Shintō talismans in their temples, Higashi officials announced its legitimacy.[49] In September 1871, the nineteenth abbot of the Nishi Honganji, Kōnyo (1798–1871), encouraged the congregations to observe the theory of the two truths and to be loyal subjects of the emperor. In February 1873, Higashi administrators ordered its priests not to read or otherwise rephrase passages in Shinran's works and other texts, such as the *Biography of Shinran* (*Godenshō*), in which Shinran had questioned imperial authority.[50] In 1892, the Higashi head temple began to celebrate *Shūtokue* (literally, "repaying one's indebtedness," a major ritual honoring Shinran, eminent monks, and those who contributed to the temple's development) and to honor secular rules by dedicating a Buddhist service to the emperor. This event paralleled the major annual service of *Hōonkō* in honor of Shinran's passing.[51] Further, the two orders sent their priests to the army for propagation among the military (*gunjin fukyō*) and into prisons to convert inmates (*kangoku kyōkai*). By initiating overseas propagation (*kaigai kaikyō*) in Korea, China, and Siberia, the two Honganjis supported the Sino-Japanese War (1894–1895) and the Russo-Japanese War (1904–1905).[52]

In the meantime, the government bestowed imperial honorary titles of Kenshin ("Seeing Truth") on Shinran in 1876 and Etō ("Illuminated Wisdom") on Rennyo in 1882, after recognizing the dedication of the two branches of the Honganji at the beginning of the Meiji period.[53] By 1911, the Higashi had constructed an imperial gate (*chokushi mon*) emblazoned with the imperial symbol of the chrysanthemum to honor members of the imperial family when they visited.[54]

The theory of the two truths also concealed the contradictions and injustices of modern society. Honganji leaders overlooked the growing poverty and discrimination experienced by their congregations and regarded these problems as not caused by sociopolitical factors but as a reflection of one's own perception.[55] There were a few Shin priests who recognized the perversion and attempted to reverse the priority of the two truths, but their efforts were short-lived, largely because Buddhism, as the organizational religion, was swallowed up in the rising tide of nationalism.

Shin Buddhist opposition to Christianity also involved state power. Five branches of Shin Buddhism (Higashi, Nishi, Takada, Kibe, and Kōshō) made an alliance and submitted a proposal to the government in July 1868 to convert hidden Christians (*kakure kirishitan*) in Uragami, in present-day Nagasaki prefecture. However, the government rejected the proposal, preferring Shintō priests to play that role.[56] In the same year, the Nishi Honganji set up the Department of Defeating Wrong Teachings (Haja gakka) in its academy, and the Higashi Honganji established the School to Protect the Dharma (Gōhō jō), through which scholar-priests linked the expulsion of Christians with defending the Dharma and Japan.

Although the government lifted the ban on Christianity in 1873, the Buddhist clergy as a whole continued to reject Christianity. In 1890 the government attempted to enact the Religions Bill, which aimed to promulgate ordinances dealing with Buddhism and Christianity on the same level, but Buddhist leaders opposed it, pointing out Buddhism's long history in comparison to Christianity's recent arrival in Japan. The bill was brought to the Lower House of the Japanese parliament in 1899, but a committee in the House of Peers rejected it, responding to the Buddhists' demands.[57]

Reforms of the Two Branches of the Honganji

As a response to Western civilization, Shin Buddhists went through changes in organizational style, ritual format, and doctrine. In the Nishi Honganji, clerics from the Suō and Nagato domains (or Chōshū domain, present-day Yamaguchi prefecture), such as Mokurai Shimaji, Tetsunen Ōzu (1837–1902), and Renjō Akamatsu (1841–1919), reformed its administration. These men worked with Takayoshi Kido (1833–1877), a Meiji-period statesman, who played a significant role in the Meiji Restoration along with Takamori Saigō (1827–1877) and Toshimichi Ōkubo (1830–1878), since Kido also came from the same region.[58]

The reformists restructured the Nishi Honganji by eliminating feudal characteristics from the denomination's bureaucracy. They dissolved the abbot's entourage and acolytes, consisting of about four hundred people, who had monopolized the administration, and abolished the hierarchical order of the head temple, branch temples, intermediary temples, and small temples (*honmatsu seido*) as a response to the new policy of "one Majesty with a million subjects." They also terminated the system in which certain temples had enjoyed a privileged relationship to the abbot's family, and placed all temples directly under the authority of the head temple. Three branches of Jōdo Shinshū, the Higashi Honganji, Takada, and Kibe, followed suit and terminated their *honmatsu seido* in April 1876.[59]

After the ban on the hierarchical temple-ranking system, the Nishi Honganji introduced its first representative assembly (*shūe*) in 1881. The reform administration led by the aforementioned priests from the western provinces lost power after the death of Takayoshi Kido, with whom they had strong connections. At the same time, the twentieth abbot, Myōnyo (1850–1903), attempted to regain power and sought relations with the next generation of politicians, such as Sanetomi Sanjō (1837–1891) and Tomomi Iwakura (1825–1883). Myōnyo even tried to bring down Shimaji by labeling him a heretic, and he planned to transfer his administrative office from Kyoto to Tokyo.[60] When the conflict between the clergy from the western provinces and Myōnyo escalated, previously neutral scholar-priests called for a representative assembly. They took the initiative and outlined an assembly plan adopting a system of constitutional monarchy, in which the abbot still held the ultimate authority of the teaching as the lord of the Dharma (*hossu* or *sōzu,* the authority of the school). Politicians, including Iwakura and Kaoru Inoue, also examined the outline and recognized the Nishi Honganji's constitution. The assembly was inaugurated on October 3, 1881, before the opening of the National Diet Assembly in 1890.[61]

The Higashi Honganji followed suit, but the introduction of a representative assembly was delayed, as the organization faced more difficulties in its restructuring. Contrary to the Nishi branch, in which reformists made good connections with the court and royalists at the time of the Meiji Restoration, the Higashi branch initially sided with the Tokugawa regime, which had resulted in Ieyasu Tokugawa's grant of an estate to Kyōnyo, the first abbot of the Higashi Honganji.

The modern reform of the Higashi involved a great deal of pain and hostility. Gonnyo (1817–1894), the twenty-first abbot, assisted in the cultivation of Hokkaidō under the name of "Hokkaidō propagation" (Hokkaidō *kaikyō*), as a demonstration of his loyalty to the new government (and as a way to expand the Higashi Honganji's diocese). The new Higashi administration eliminated the aristocratic retainers (*bōkan*), who had connections with the Tokugawa family. However, on October 3, 1871, some of these retainers assassinated Senshōin Kūkaku, one of the organizers of the School to Protect the Dharma, blaming him for the reform. Following this, two chief administrators, Shundai Ishikawa and Kaien Atsumi, requested the governor of Kyoto to oversee their administrative reforms. The two men later grew hostile to one another, and Kaoru Inoue mediated between them in June 1883. The Constitution of the Higashi Honganji was finally enacted in September of the same year.[62]

The Higashi's attempt to restructure the organization was, however, only half completed, and progressive priests with an intellectual background challenged the administration. Higashi officials set up a representative body (*shijunsho*) in 1883, but it served merely as an advisory committee to the abbot. The Shirakawa Party, organized by Manshi Kiyozawa (1863–1903), Bunyū Nanjō (1849–1927), and Senshō Murakami (1851–1929), criticized the administration in 1896 for neglecting doctrinal studies and rebuilding the two large temple halls without deliberate financial plans.[63] Their efforts led to the establishment of an assembly (*giseikyoku*) in 1897, which convened to discuss administrative regulations and oversaw the budget.[64]

Modernity also altered the ritual practice of the two Honganjis. Immediately after the Meiji Restoration, the Nishi branch abandoned the Buddhist rites associated with the Tokugawa family and began commemorative services for former emperors. After returning from their religious studies tour in Europe, Shimaji and Akamatsu, who had visited the birthplace of Jesus Christ in Bethlehem, commemorated the birth of the founder, Shinran. Nishi included this service in its annual religious calendar from then on.[65] In April 1911, the two branches of the Honganji held Shinran's 650th Memorial Service in Kyoto and for the first time mobilized a great number of regional followers to travel by train to the head temples.[66]

For the glorification of their rituals, Shin Buddhists incorporated Western music.[67] Zenjō Toki of the Nishi Honganji composed a song for the birth of the founder around 1887. Other Shin clergy wrote songs for transsectarian occasions.[68] The first full-scale ritual that included Western music, on December 16, 1917, attracted attention. A group of five hundred boys and girls affiliated with the Nishi Honganji Osaka Betsuin (a regional temple in Osaka) performed the Buddhist service accompanied by violin and organ (*ongaku hōyō*). This performance represented the fulfillment of Abbot Kōzui Ōtani's plan to modernize Shin rituals, since he had earlier proposed to have some of Shinran's hymns arranged with Western melodies.[69]

Modernity affected Shin Buddhist doctrine as well. Kōyō Sakaino (1871–1933) and others formed the Association of Pure Buddhists (Bukkyō Seito

Dō Shikai) in 1899 and initiated the movement of New Buddhism (*shin bukkyō*), whose objectives included the establishment of a strong faith, improvement of society, free debate on Buddhism and religion, denial of superstition, rejection of the hierarchy of Buddhist orders, and the separation of Buddhism from politics. Through the journal *Shin bukkyō*, Sakaino and others denounced war and insisted on a ban on prostitution.

Often contrasted with New Buddhism is the "Spiritual Activism" (*seishin-shugi*) of Manshi Kiyozawa. He attempted to reconstruct the Shin Buddhist teaching by incorporating Western philosophy and searched his own religious identity through his intellect without resorting to emotionality or mysticism. He thus emphasized the importance of having direct religious experience and achieved spiritual fulfillment by entrusting himself to Amida Buddha. He was able to obtain a settled mind (*anjin*), despite physical and mental suffering caused by his own efforts to make sense of Buddhism in modern times. Scholars have characterized Sakaino's activities as an outwardly oriented practice, and those of Kiyozawa as inwardly directed.[70] (Kiyozawa's scholarship and activities are discussed further in Chapter Five).

Other Shin Buddhist leaders included Shōshin Itō (1876–1963) of the Higashi Honganji, who initiated the movement of selfless love (*muga ai undō*) to deal with social problems; and Rōsen Furukawa (1871–1899) of the Nishi Honganji, who tried to create a modern form of Buddhism while tolerating various kinds of criticism directed toward it.[71]

In addition to these individual activities, the Nishi and Higashi branches of the Honganji systematized the doctrine and introduced Shin Buddhism to the West. Before the publication of the Taishō Tripiṭaka (*Taishō shinshū daizōkyō*) in 1924, scholar-priests compiled the *Outline of Shinshū* (*Shinshū taikei*), otherwise known as the Tripiṭaka of Shinshū. The first volume was published in November 1916, and this project took more than eight years to complete. It consisted of one hundred and thirty-four sections in three hundred and sixteen volumes, including the Three Pure Land Sutras; the seven Pure Land patriarchs; commentaries; Shinran's magnum opus, the *Kyōgyōshinshō*, and his hymns, letters, and biography; Rennyo's *Letters;* etc. The Tripiṭaka of Shinshū was designed for the Shin clergy to study orthodox scholarship, develop future doctrinal studies, and propagate Shin Buddhism more effectively.[72]

Some scholar-priests also foresaw the internationalization of Shin Buddhism. Renjō Akamatsu had his *A Brief Account of Shinshū* (*Shinshū ryakusetsu*) translated into English and submitted it to the World's Parliament of Religions in Chicago in 1893 along with other theses, including Kiyozawa's

The Skeleton of a Philosophy of Religion (Shūkyō tetsugaku gaikotsu).[73] Ryōon Fujishima published *Le Bouddhisme Japonais: doctrines et histoire des douze grandes sects bouddhiques du Japon* in 1889. The Higashi Honganji printed the *Principal Teachings of the True Sect of Pure Land* in 1910.[74] Gesshō Sasaki wrote *A Study of Shin Buddhism* and Zenken Usami translated and published *Buddhas Reden über Amitayus* in 1925.[75] In this way, modernity urged Shin scholars to reshape the course of the propagation of the religion.

The search for a modern Shin Buddhist studies was, however, not without its own problems. The Ministry of Education recognized Ryūkoku University (the Nishi Honganji's academic institution) and Ōtani University (the Higashi Honganji's academic institution) in 1922. In this new educational system, what had traditionally been called the "study of the school" (*shūgaku*) was replaced by Shin Buddhist studies (*Shinshū gaku*) as a sign of modern scholarship; however, those who advocated the reinterpretation of doctrine collided with conservative scholars.[76] Naotarō Nonomura of Ryūkoku University not only denied the existence of the Pure Land and one's karmic connections to the three worlds of the past, present, and future, but also separated the two kinds of entrusting (*nishu jinshin*) at the core of Shin doctrine: namely, believing deeply that one is "a foolish being of karmic evil caught in birth-and-death" and believing decidedly that "Amida Buddha's Forty-eight Vows grasp sentient beings." For Nonomura, these were two different matters to be unified in a Mahayana paradigm of oneness.[77] According to the doctrinal authority of the Nishi Honganji, however, Nonomura's interpretation was incorrect, because the two kinds of entrusting were like two sides of a coin, with both reflecting Amida Buddha's compassion. The Nishi administrators eventually defrocked and expelled Nonomura and set up the Institute of Shin Buddhist Studies to protect the orthodox doctrine and monitor new interpretations. The institute later outlined thirty themes on the concept of *anjin* and seventy themes on doctrine.[78]

In the Higashi Honganji too, debate between conventional and progressive scholars heated up. Daiei Kaneko (1881–1976) of Ōtani University eliminated the mythical and physical aspects of Jōdo Shinshū and defined the Pure Land as an "ideological realm" coupled with self-realization and an entrusting mind. However, traditional scholars misunderstood Kaneko's interpretation as an application of Kantian Idealism or a psychological analysis of the Pure Land. After much debate, the university expelled him in 1928, and he was defrocked the following year.[79] In 1930, Ryōjin Soga (1875–1971), also from Ōtani University, introduced a new concept: that Bodhisattva Dharmākara was a manifestation of the eighth consciousness (*ālaya-vijñāna*). This was an interpretation with which the Higashi doctrinal authority disagreed, and Soga was forced to resign from his position.[80] Senshō Murakami pronounced that the doctrines of Japanese Buddhism were not related to Śākyamuni's original teachings. Murakami was simply applying the modern studies of history and comparative religion to Buddhist studies, but the Higashi authorities could not agree with his scholarship and expelled him from the order.[81] The headquarters eventually reinstated these men after modern knowledge began to prevail in academia, but such heretical debates suggest that the organizational authority often squelched academic integrity.[82]

Modern scholarship finally encouraged the two branches of the Honganji to reevaluate Shōtoku Taishi (574–622), a statesman of the Asuka period (593–710), who according to modern Japanese scholars is said to have incorporated the Buddhist teachings into polity for the first time in Japanese history. On February 28, 1920, Higashi administrators informed its affiliated temples to hold a 1,300th-year commemorative service for Shōtoku Taishi in April. The following year, Nishi officials enshrined a scroll painting of him in the altar area of the Amida Hall.[83] Through these events, the two Honganjis created a Dharma lineage from Shōtoku to Shinran and celebrated Shōtoku as the founder of Japanese Buddhism.

The culmination of the Shin Buddhist rites was reached in 1923, when the two Honganjis celebrated the 700th-year anniversary of "Establishing the Teaching and Opening of the Sect" (*rikkyō kaishū*).[84] Shin leaders had formed the Federation of Shinshū Branches (Shinshū kakuha kyōwakai) in August of the previous year to commemorate this event.[85] The following year, it produced the *School Song for Shinshū* (*Shinshū shūka*) with the assistance of two scholars. This was sung by the clergy and laity of all Shinshū denominations, especially at Sunday schools.[86] Other events prior to 1923 suggest the simplification of services. In 1921, the Nishi Honganji's Representative Assembly approved the inclusion of the Japanese readings of Chinese characters in sutra-chanting service books and the accompaniment of Western music in the recitation of Shinran's hymns. Ideas for a service book for the laity were also exchanged.[87]

Summary

Modernity steered Shin Buddhists to take the doctrine of the two truths to a new level. The directive to observe mundane laws meant that they become imperial subjects and accept imperial Shintō into their daily lives. In order to differentiate spiritual principles from secular rules, Shin leaders did not recognize Shintō as a religion and encouraged their congregations to keep their Buddhist faith to themselves. While making external adjustments, Shin leaders restructured their organizational styles, examined rituals, and interpreted doctrines anew. These activities continued in North America, where the propagation of Shin Buddhism involved the introduction of a representative assembly of clergy and laity, the reinterpretation of the "Pure Land" and "other-power," and the observance of services relating to the imperial tradition and Western music.

Chapter Two

Changes in Organizational Style

The eastward transmission of Shin Buddhism commenced at the turn of the twentieth century. The Nishi Honganji initiated a full-scale campaign in North America after certain individuals laid the foundations of religious activities. These preliminary events, however, set a trajectory of propagation that resulted in different approaches in Hawaii and on the mainland. First, there were several Shin priests in Hawaii who had privately followed a large number of their fellow immigrants from Hiroshima and Yamaguchi prefectures. Second, the Nishi Honganji had sent its scholar-priests to the mainland for religious study prior to consigning *kaikyōshi* (ministers) to the communities of Japanese immigrants on the Pacific Coast. The presence of other Japanese Buddhist schools, which had arrived in Hawaii before the Nishi Honganji, was another factor that caused ministers in Hawaii and on the mainland to take separate paths.

When officially involved, the Nishi Honganji made a strategic decision in North America. The Kyoto headquarters directed its propagation efforts in Hawaii toward providing spiritual support to Issei plantation workers,[1] and encouraged sectarianism after witnessing the advancement of Jōdoshū (another Pure Land school) on Hawaii, the Big Island, in March 1894, and of the Higashi Honganji on Kauai in 1899. In addition, Gyōun Takagi built the first Nichiren temple in the Islands on the southeast coast of Hawaii in 1902, and Sen'ei Kawahara established the first Sōtō mission in 1905 on Waipahu plantation, near Pearl Harbor, on Oahu.[2]

In contrast to the situation in the Hawaiian Islands, a much greater need for interfaith dialogue and the lack of other Japanese Buddhist schools on the mainland set the stage for Shin clergy there to seek a transsectarian path.[3] There was a great demand for explaining Śākyamuni's philososphy to Euro-American participants, along with administering to the spiritual necessities of Issei pioneers in California and Vancouver.

This chapter compares the expansion of the Honpa Honganji Mission of Hawaii (Honpa Honganji Hawaii Kyōdan; HHMH) and of the Buddhist

Mission of North America (Hokubei Bukkyōdan; BMNA) through exploring the links between these two orders' organizational changes and goals of propagation, arrangement of by-laws, and establishment of Buddhist associations. As well, it presents a historical survey of the two orders. In North America, Buddhist organizations were incorporated under state law and regulated through by-laws, but success in the modification of the organizational structure to suit the legalization of a religious body did not mean that the development of the HHMH and the BMNA was trouble-free. First, the Kyoto headquarters often interfered with these orders, as it sent superintendents (*kantoku*) (this title was later changed to bishop, *sochō*) and *kaikyōshi* to North America. Second, conflicts within the order persisted. A case in point was the constant collision between the BMNA office and regional churches and among local churches themselves. In addition to these internal problems, the HHMH and the BMNA, two of the largest Buddhist organizations in North America, attempted to establish their dominance over other Japanese Buddhist schools and also competed with Protestant churches. By highlighting conflicts and various forms of competition, this study suggests that these Shin Buddhist communities were not as harmonious as past studies have presented.

Prior to Official Propagation

There were two phases in the early immigration to Hawaii: from 1885 to 1894 was a period of contract labor (*kanyaku imin*), while 1894 to 1908 were years of free migrants (*jiyū imin*).[4]

During the first period, the Japanese government recruited immigrants from the coastal regions of Hiroshima and Yamaguchi prefectures, as these were overpopulated and destitute areas.[5] The Japanese foreign minister, Kaoru Inoue, and Takashi Masuda, president of Mitsui Bussan (a trading company), who negotiated labor migration with the Hawaiian consul general, Robert Walker Irwin, were both from Yamaguchi prefecture. They considered people from Yamaguchi courageous enough to go to a foreign country, and those from Hiroshima realistic and law-abiding.[6] In the period of free migrants, approximately 125,000 Japanese sailed to Hawaii.[7]

By 1924, the total population of Japanese in Hawaii had reached 125,368 (58,721 immigrants and 66,647 Hawaii-born citizens). Breaking this number down by prefecture, 24.3 percent came from Hiroshima, 20.6 percent from Yamaguchi, 15.7 percent from Kumamoto, 13.1 percent from Okinawa, and 4 percent from Fukuoka. The remaining 12.4 percent came from seventeen other prefectures.[8] In other words, immigrants from the Chūgoku region (mainly Hiroshima and Yamaguchi), which was the stronghold of the Nishi Honganji, dominated the Japanese community in Hawaii. The followers in Hiroshima were especially known as Aki *monto* (Aki was the name of a premodern province, corresponding in the present day to the western part of Hiroshima prefecture).[9]

After the Japanese immigrated to Hawaii, several Buddhist priests, including Sōryū Kagahi of the Nishi Honganji, moved to Honolulu to provide spiritual support. Kagahi was born in 1855 into a temple family in Bungo province (present-day Ōita prefecture). As the resident minister of Kōtokuji (a temple affiliated with the Nishi Honganji), he was concerned about the welfare of his countrymen who had immigrated to Hawaii. In January 1889, he visited Abbot Myōnyo and the chief administrators, including Shimaji and Akamatsu, in Kyoto and explained the need for the propagation of the Nishi Honganji in Hawaii. Having no information about the conditions of the immigrants, the Kyoto headquarters considered Kagahi's request premature, though they encouraged him to carry out such efforts privately.[10]

Based on his efforts and findings in Hawaii, Kagahi sought once more to gain the official support of the Honganji. On March 2, 1889, he established a Honganji propagation office on Emma Street in Honolulu and delivered sermons on weekends. He also built the first Japanese Hawaiian Buddhist temple on the Big Island in April 1889, with the assistance of Saiji Kimura, a supervisor of plantation workers. Kagahi's sincerity led him to win support from the Japanese immigrants, who had realized the importance of maintaining their Buddhist faith. Kagahi returned to Japan on October 19, 1889, hoping that the abbot would now recognize and support his work. As a response to growing public interest in Hawaii, the Kyoto headquarters became sympathetic to Kagahi—until the administrators discovered that he had equated Amida Buddha with the Christian God in order to gain a propagation permit from plantation managers. The headquarters canceled its involvement in Kagahi's project and withdrew the promised funds immediately. For Kagahi, however, drawing such a parallel for non-Buddhists was simply "skillful means" (Skt. *upāya*), necessary for Buddhism to gain access to a society dominated by Christianity.[11] Not until 1897 did the Nishi Honganji positively evaluate propagation efforts in Hawaii.

After Kagahi had given up his plan, Buddhist propagation stagnated in Hawaii. Those who had trusted him and donated money were confused when he discontinued his efforts. The situation worsened when Honganji priests who were not qualified for overseas propagation took over Kagahi's enterprise and collected donations without proper authority.[12] Finally, in

March 1897, the Nishi Honganji headquarters sent Ejun Miyamoto to the Islands to examine the immigrant situation. After his investigation, Miyamoto urged the headquarters to become directly involved. In June, he assisted a group of sixteen Shin followers in Honolulu to petition for official propagation. In August, he helped another group of eight in Hilo, and recognized two priests who had been propagating privately as legitimate Honganji *kaikyōshi*.[13]

On the Mainland

At the beginning of the Meiji period, the Nishi Honganji headquarters sent a group of priests to study abroad. In January 1872, five priests, including Shimaji and Akamatsu, set off for Western Europe, with one of the group traveling to North America. In 1875 Tosui Imadate came to the United States to study at a university in Philadelphia. Two more priests made brief stops in North America on their religious tour to Europe.[14] Banryū Yatsubuchi participated in the 1893 World's Parliament of Religions in Chicago, though not as a representative of his order.

In 1898, the Nishi Honganji headquarters sent two more priests to San Francisco. In 1897, Nisaburō Hirano, a devout Shin Buddhist follower who was frustrated with the lack of Buddhist services in San Francisco, had visited the head temple in Kyoto. Responding to his request, the Nishi Honganji dispatched Eryū Honda and Ejun Miyamoto, who arrived on July 6, 1898, to investigate the situation. In the meantime, a group of young men met at the home of Dr. Katsugorō Haida to discuss the founding of a Young Men's Buddhist Association (Bukkyō Seinenkai; YMBA), and this organization was inaugurated on July 30 at 909 Market Street. On September 1, eighty-three members of the San Francisco YMBA petitioned the Kyoto headquarters for propagation.[15] On September 17, the YMBA established the first Buddhist church in the United States at 7 Mason Street.[16]

Although the group of immigrants petitioned for a minister right away, the Japanese consulate-general in Seattle delayed the Nishi Honganji headquarters' response to the immigrants and its advance in America. The consulate-general thought that sending Buddhist priests to a Christian country would provoke anti-Japanese sentiment and upset diplomatic relationships between the two countries. In response, Renjō Akamatsu proposed not to publicize propagation as an official project of the Nishi Honganji, but to simply send ministers to San Francisco.[17] As a result, Shūe Sonoda and Kakuryō Nishijima arrived in September 1899 (later the Kyoto headquarters marked their arrival as the beginning of the Nishi Honganji's certified propagation in the mainland United States). A reporter from the *San Francisco Chronicle* interviewed the two and published an article, "They Teach the Buddhist Faith," on September 12, 1899. The headline the following day, however, took a more aggressive tone: "Missionaries of the Buddhist Faith. Two Representatives of the Ancient Creed Are in San Francisco to Proselyte." The article appeared with a picture of the two priests wearing robes (Fig. 1).[18]

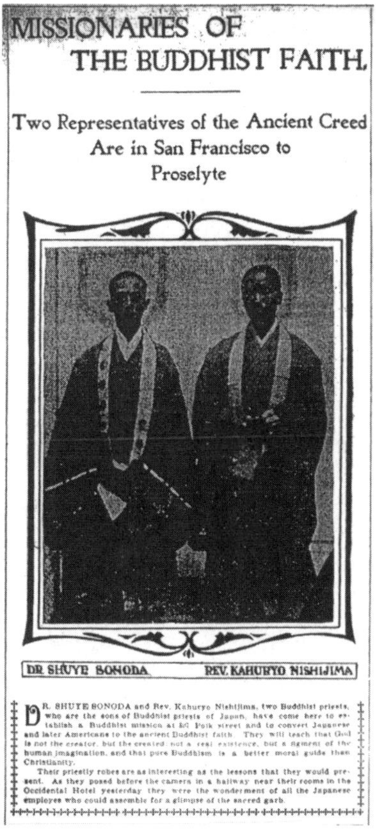

MISSIONARIES OF THE BUDDHIST FAITH.

Two Representatives of the Ancient Creed Are in San Francisco to Proselyte

DR. SHUYE SONODA — REV. KAHURYO NISHIJIMA

DR. SHUYE SONODA and Rev. Kahuryo Nishijima, two Buddhist priests, who are the sons of Buddhist priests of Japan, have come here to establish a Buddhist mission at [illegible] Polk street and to convert Japanese and later Americans to the ancient Buddhist faith. They will teach that God is not the creator, but the created: not a real existence, but a figment of the human imagination, and that pure Buddhism is a better moral guide than Christianity.

Their priestly robes are as interesting as the lessons that they would present. As they posed before the camera in a hallway near their rooms in the Occidental Hotel yesterday they were the wonderment of all the Japanese employes who could assemble for a glimpse of the sacred garb.

Fig. 1. Shūe Sonoda and Kakuryō Nishijima. (From the *San Francisco Chronicle*, September 13, 1899.)

In Canada, Japanese Buddhists held their first gathering in Vancouver in 1904. In the fall of that year, fourteen laypeople gathered at Yuichi Nagao's residence to discuss the possibility of constructing a Buddhist temple in Vancouver, and they requested the Kyoto headquarters to send a minister. In response to their petition, Senju Sasaki arrived in October 1905.[19] In contrast to the immigrants in Hawaii and California, dominated by people from Hiroshima and Yamaguchi prefectures, in British Columbia people from Shiga and Wakayama were more dominant than settlers from other regions in Japan. In 1891, the Imin Kōbe Kaisha (company) recruited the first group of immigrants from Hiroshima, and they arrived in Canada as contract laborers for the coal mining industry. Although immigration from Hiroshima and other prefectures such as Kumamoto and Fukuoka continued, Shiga and Wakayama eventually came to be known as "prefectures for having comrades come to [Canada]" (*yobi yose imin ken*). Especially those originating from Shiga tended to become contractors or foremen in the lumber business and kept strong connections with their birthplaces. More than half of the Shiga immigrants were *Kōshū monto,* referring to Shin Buddhists in Hikone (present-day Shiga prefecture); hence, Shin Buddhism was the dominant Japanese ethnic religion in Canada as well.[20]

Nishi Honganji headquarters' strategies varied in Hawaii and on the mainland. First, the careers of the superintendents (*kantoku*) sent to these two regions were distinguished. Hōni Satomi, the first superintendet of the HHMH, was a trailblazer. Nishi Honganji headquarters also assigned him to Hokkaidō, Vladivostock (Russia), Chishima (Kuril Islands), and Formosa (Taiwan).[21] On the other hand, Shūe Sonoda, a promising scholar who later received a further assignment in 1900 to study in Germany, became president of Bukkyō Daigaku (present-day Ryūkoku University) and received the Nishi Honganji's highest academic honor of *kankagu* in 1911.[22] Sonoda and three subsequent superintendents were all graduates of Tokyo Imperial University (present-day Tokyo University).[23]

Second, the geopolitical concerns of the Nishi Honganji headquarters were reflected in the naming of overseas propagation facilities. It specified the propagation units in Taiwan, Korea, the South Pacific, and Sakhalin as *fukyōsho* (布教所), and the ones in Hawaii and Siberia as *fukyōjo* (布教場). In North America, Kōyū Uchida, the fourth bishop of the BMNA, called the local facility a *bukkyōkai* (仏教会). These titles echoed Japan's diplomatic relationships with—and, to some degree, its imperial designs on—different foreign countries.[24] The suffix *sho* was given to the names of facilities in Japan's colonies, whereas the suffix *jo* was designated for facilities in Hawaii and Siberia, which the Nishi Honganji headquarters might have regarded as Japan's future territory, considering popular domestic sentiment at the time.[25] In the mainland United States, however, such territorial concerns were absent in the naming of Buddhist facilities.

Shin Buddhist Teaching or Śākyamuni's Doctrine

The HHMH grew faster than its counterpart on the mainland. As a response to two petitions from Honolulu and Hilo, the headquarters recognized Sanju Kanayasu, who had already been stationed in Hilo, and sent Shōi Yamada to Honolulu in October 1897 as the first *kaikyōshi*. Satomi soon followed, dispatched by the headquarters to Hawaii in January 1898.[26] After building the first temple hall in the area of Honolulu called Fort Lane in December 1899, Satomi returned to Japan. Emyō Imamura, whom Satomi accompanied to Hawaii in February 1899, succeeded him and became the second superintendent on January 20, 1900.[27] Under the Kyoto headquarters' new organizational system of 1918, Imamura became the first bishop (*sochō*) of the Hawaii District in the same year.[28] Until his death from a stroke on December 22, 1932, Imamura presided over the HHMH

師法猛恵院勝超故

Fig. 2. Emyō Imamura. Photo from the *Chōshōin ibunshū* (courtesy Honpa Hong-wanji Mission of Hawaii).

(Fig. 2). By 1924, the HHMH had established more than thirty-three missions throughout the Hawaiian Islands.[29]

Unlike the HHMH, the heads of the BMNA changed frequently, which left an absence of a long-term propagation strategy. Within six years, the superintendent was replaced four times: Shūe Sonoda (September 1899), Tetsuei Mizuki (December 1900), Kentoku Hori (March 1902), and Kōyū Uchida (August 1905). During Uchida's tenure, his title changed to bishop in 1918. Until his return to Japan in September 1923, due to illness, Uchida was in charge of the BMNA for eighteen years.[30] For the next three years, three acting bishops led the organization. Hōshō Sasaki took office in October 1926 as the fifth bishop, but served for less than two years. Between August 1928 and June 1930, there was no formal head at the BMNA until the Kyoto headquarters appointed Kenju Masuyama as the sixth bishop in July 1930. In the meantime, Itsuzō Kyōgoku served as interim bishop. By 1924 the BMNA had established a total of twenty-three Buddhist churches, and by 1932 nine more. In 1936, Hōzen Seki established a church in New York.[31] In Canada, the BMNA had founded three churches by 1920 and at least ten more by the 1930s.[32]

Although the HHMH and BMNA started out as Honganji branch offices (Honganji *shucchō sho*), their characteristics developed quite differently. The former doubled as the Honolulu *fukyōjo,* while the latter placed itself in the San Francisco YMBA. The HHMH was elevated to the status of *betsuin* (regional temple) in 1906, with Imamura serving both as bishop of the HHMH and *rinban* (custodian of a *betsuin*) of the Honpa Honganji Hawaii Betsuin.[33] On the mainland, however, a bishop never served as *rinban.* On his arrival in San Francisco, Uchida saw two signboards on a single building, "Honganji Branch Office" and "YMBA." He consolidated the two and renamed the organization the San Francisco Bukkyōkai, known as the Buddhist Church of San Francisco. His reasoning for the change was that the name "Honganji Branch Office" might turn away those who had been affiliated with other Buddhist sects in Japan, and the name "YMBA" could give an incorrect impression to middle-aged Japanese.[34] In this way Uchida avoided using the title "Honganji" on the mainland, whereas Imamura encouraged keeping this term in the names of facilities in Hawaii. Their decisions were based on whether or not other Japanese Buddhist schools were present in their respective regions.[35]

The Incorporation and By-laws of Missions and Churches

The differing relationships between Japanese immigrants and the host society in Hawaii and on the mainland made an impact on the orientation of Shin Buddhist propagation in North America. Uchida's decision to promote Śākyamuni's teachings on the mainland was nothing new. Sonoda and Nishijima had made initial contacts with Euro-Americans who were interested in Buddhism. In fact, Sonoda's efforts were supported by the San Francisco YMBA and the Dharma Sangha of Buddha, one of the earliest Buddhist associations in the United States, which was founded June 27, 1900, and where Sonoda and six Euro-Americans had served as directors.[36] The Caucasian members were J. R. Guelph Norman, Kathleen Melvena McIntire, Jenny Ward Hays, Charles Frank Jones, Eliza R. H. Stoddard, and Agnes White.[37] The Constitution of the Dharma Sangha of Buddha states:

> That the purposes for which it is formed are, to constitute a society to maintain churches and to propagate the doctrines of Gautama Siddartha [sic], the Buddha Sakyamuni, as set forth in the sacred scriptures of His disciples, and to that end:
>
> 1st To teach the doctrines embraced in the generic term, Buddhism.[38]

Neither "Shinran," "Honganji," "Jōdo Shinshū," nor any English equivalent is found in this document. The mission of the Dharma Sangha of Buddha was to reach out to the modern world. Sections I and II of Article I in the by-laws state:

> SECTION I. This Corporation is known as the DHARMA SANGHA OF BUDDHA, its members recognizing the universal nature of the Law of Life and Being, of Religion, and of the Divine nature in man as set forth in the TRI-PITAKA of the Buddha Sakyamuni, showing the Law of Life to be the object of Faith and Religion, of Science and Philosophy immutable and eternal Truth, harmonizing the spiritual and human nature in man, bringing all men into the bond of fellowship and uniting all humanity in the universal spirit of Truth.
>
> SEC[TION] II. The establishment of the Kingdom of Righteousness by the fusion into one of all forms of religion, in order to promote scientific and

[p]hilosophical research, the physical, intellectual, moral, and spiritual welfare of man, being the main object of this Corporation. These By-Laws are to be construed with the object of furthering that end.[39]

The Dharma Sangha of Buddha was not only committed to the study of Buddhism, but also sought connections among Buddhism, the humanities, and science. In San Francisco, Sonoda and Nishima taught Śākyamuni's doctrine to Euro-Americans on Sunday afternoons. The Dharma Sangha of Buddha celebrated Śākyamuni's birthday on April 8, and Dr. Norman lectured on Buddhism. It also began to publish a bimonthly English journal, *The Light of Dharma,* in April 1901.[40]

Their active engagement with Caucasians, however, did not mean that Sonoda and Nishijima ignored Japanese immigrants. They delivered Jōdo Shinshū sermons to Shin followers on Saturdays, lectured on Buddhism for a general Japanese audience on Sunday nights, and held a gathering of the Buddhist Women's Association (BWA) every other Thursday night. They also initiated a Japanese-language journal, *Beikoku bukkyō,* in January 1900.[41]

Imamura, on the other hand, attempted to introduce Shinran's teaching to a non-Japanese community. When Henry S. Olcott visited Hawaii in 1901, Imamura invited him to lecture on Buddhism. In the same year, when the HHMH celebrated Shinran's birthday, Imamura extended his invitation to the usurped Queen Lili'uokalani and Mary Foster, a prominent landowner in Hawaii. How much they understood of Shin doctrine is unclear. However, Foster later donated land to Imamura in 1907, when he discussed the future founding of a junior high school with her.[42] In 1914, Imamura celebrated the publication of *The Essence of Japanese Buddhism* by Ryūsaku Tsunoda, who had come to Hawaii in 1909 to serve as the principal of the Honganji's junior high school and girls' high school. Despite its broad title, this book was one of the earliest attempts to present Shinran's life and teaching in English.[43] Imamura's choice for propagating Shin Buddhism was clearly stated in the by-laws of the HHMH incorporated in 1907:

> The doctrinal basis of this Mission shall be in substantial accord with the doctrine of Shinshu Sect of Buddhism, and the object of this Mission shall be to promote the happiness and general welfare of the community by:
>
> Propagation and preaching of the doctrine of Shinshu Sect of Buddhism.
>
> Educational work, charitable work and other works which are necessary concerning the promotion of general welfare of the community. (Article 2)[44]

The objective of the HHMH was to promote Shin Buddhism. According to Article 3, "[T]his Mission may establish its branches, if necessary, throughout the Island of Oahu and other Islands of said Territory." According to Article 4, "Any person who believes in the doctrine of the Shinshu Sect and agrees to support the purposes and objects of this Mission may become a member thereof." Throughout the Hawaiian Islands, the word "Honganji" became a suffix to the title of a local *fukyōjo* and was placed after the name of the corresponding plantation site, such as Aiea Honganji and Waialua Honganji. When translated into English, the word "mission" was attached, such as Aiea Honganji Mission and Waialua Honganji Mission.[45]

Obtaining the governor's approval of the charter was, however, difficult for Imamura. Governor George R. Carter rejected it in July 1906, because "the language of this charter would be incompatible with the best future interests of the Territory."[46] He considered the HHMH a Japanese institution whose priests indoctrinated immigrants and their children to remain loyal to Imperial Japan, as it had supported Japan's war with Russia, made donations to its home country, and celebrated the emperor's birthday. Imamura and lay leaders submitted a second petition to the governor's office, with the help of a Buddhist sympathizer, Lillian Shrewsbury Mesick, who tried to correct the governor's misunderstandings of the HHMH's activities by publishing articles in a popular magazine, *Paradise of the Pacific.* The Caucasian law firm of Thompson and Clemons assisted Imamura and announced in public that based on their findings of the Japanese language school curriculum and an interview with Imamura, the HHMH represented "nothing prejudicial to the interests of American citizenship." The new governor of Hawaii, Walter F. Frear, who took office in 1907, responded favorably and signed the charter of incorporation recognizing HHMH as an "ecclesiastical, eleemosynary, and educational organization."[47]

In contrast to the Shin clergy in Hawaii, its mainland counterparts continued to promote Śākyamuni's doctrine. The Articles of Incorporation of the Buddhist Church of Sacramento, filed with the California Secretary of State on June 15, 1901, state:

> [T]he purpose for which the corporation is formed is to constitute a religious society to teach and propagate the doctrines of Guatama Seddartha [*sic*], the Buddha Sakyamuni, as set forth in the Sacred Books of Buddhism.[48]

The objectives in the Articles of Incorporation of the Buddhist Church of San Francisco, dated July 8, 1913, were "the spreading and propagating the fundamental principles of the Truth as inculcated and taught in the Buddha Dharma; and to expound and teach the same."[49] In 1918, Uchida defined the goal of BMNA as "to unify [all] Buddhists by propagating the teachings of Buddha."[50] He recommended his clergy to append the suffix *bukkyōkai* to the name of each facility, and translated the term as "Buddhist church," i.e., the Buddhist Church of San Francisco, the Fresno Buddhist Church, and the Buddhist Church of Sacramento.[51]

The Seattle Bukkyōkai was the first Buddhist church that Japanese immigrants established outside of California. Initially founded as the Seattle YMBA on November 15, 1901, its members sought incorporation and formed a business corporation known as the "Buddhist Mission Society." The State of Washington issued a corporate charter on January 27, 1906, to three trustees, Selma Anderson, Charles Rowland, and Gendō Nakai (the resident minister). At the time, two of the three stockholders were required to be American citizens; Article II, Section 33 of the Washington State Constitution (amended in 1889) prohibited land ownership by foreigners. Anderson was a Buddhist sympathizer and remained active in Seattle until the late 1930s.[52] The Articles of Association of the Buddhist Mission Society state:

> 1st The Name of the Proposed Corporation is "BUDDHIST MISSION SOCIETY."
>
> 2nd The Purpose for which it is proposed to be formed is,—"To purchase, hold, mortgage, sell and convey real estate and personal property of every kind and description whatsoever situated."[53]

It is interesting to note that the three trustees registered the Buddhist Mission Society as a real estate company. A similar incident of an organization not initially registered as an independent Buddhist association also occurred when Buddhists formed a group in Raymond, Alberta, Canada, "organized under the auspices of the Japanese society."[54] In other words, Japanese nationals in Raymond placed a religious department (*shūkyō bumon*) related to Buddhist services within the organization of a Japanese society (*nihonjin kyōkai*).[55]

There was a third type of by-law, indicating efforts to propagate the doctrines of both Śākyamuni and Shinran. The original charter of the Canada Buddhist Mission's Incorporation is unavailable, but the by-laws of the YMBA formed in 1906 as its predecessor state in Article 4:

> The purpose of this association is [for its members] to take refuge in Buddha [Shakyamuni]'s teaching and become followers of [the doctrine of] the Two Truths and Two Practices, while nurturing and training the mind and body.[56]

The theory of the two truths and two practices refer to the Honganji's set of beliefs: the dual principles of spiritual and secular rules. This by-law demonstrates the congregation's sectarian affiliation and its basis in Śākyamuni's teachings at the same time. An examination of these by-laws leads to the conclusion that the objectives of Shin propagation in North America were threefold: 1) Śākyamuni's doctrine, 2) Shin Buddhism, or 3) both.

The Japanization
of Organizational Style

Although the HHMH and BMNA modeled their religious bodies after the Protestant Church, their incorporation simultaneously demonstrated the process of "Japanization." The systematization of general meetings, by-laws, boards of trustees, and charters of incorporation were the phenomena of a joint-stock company in the United States. When applied to a religious body, they reflected the notion of congregationalism, the same organizing principle by which the early Puritans had identified their church as a voluntary association and integrated the values of grass-roots American democracy.[57] Most Buddhist ministers in the HHMH and BMNA, however, served as presidents of nonprofit organizations, following the Japanese pattern of temple management, where priests were in charge of administration.[58]

Imamura might have reflected the systematization of the HHMH on the Kyoto headquarters' modern administrative style. The Nishi Honganji had introduced a system of representative assembly in 1881, as mentioned in Chapter One; hence, the idea of setting up a general meeting or convention (giseikai) at the HHMH was not new to them. There was, however, a difference between the headquarters and the HHMH. In Japan, representatives of the organization's Diet (parliament) were restricted to the clergy.[59] This was also the case in Hawaii when Imamura gathered the first convention in February 1908 in the name of a ministers' meeting (kaikyōshi kaigi). After 1923, however, he included lay delegates from all the Islands to the annual convention of HHMH.[60]

The management of the overseas Buddhist groups was also related to the formation of religious confraternity (kō), a cultural practice of Japan. The confraternity was originally a group of monks who studied Buddhist texts together, but it later evolved into a socioreligious gathering, in which those sharing a common faith met and assisted with Buddhist services at local temples. The confraternity was also found in local religious gatherings and in Shintō. The feature of this type of religious body was to transcend hierarchy in daily functions, such as family status and the vertical relationships in households. By distributing religious duties equally among the members of the confraternity, they could exchange opinions and contribute to the maintenance of their entire community.[61]

In the case of the Honganji, Rennyo, the eighth abbot, particularly encouraged Shin followers to meet on a regular basis and discuss their understanding of the teaching. He helped to systematize these gatherings (*yoriai*) as a way for the congregation to respect equitable relationships. Shin confraternities later developed into autonomous assemblies instrumental for the expansion of the Honganji organization.[62] During the 1900s, Shin Buddhist immigrants continued to organize various confraternities in Honolulu, Palama, Moiliili, etc.[63]

Difficulties in Early Propagation and Stable Establishment in Hawaii

According to Imamura, there were four difficulties during the early propagation period. First, the Nishi Honganji had gotten a bad reputation because of the imposter priests who had deceived immigrants and collected donations under false pretenses. Second, the Kyoto headquarters could not financially assist Imamura's enterprise since it was more preoccupied with propagation in Korea and China. Third, Christian churches were attracting immigrants by offering assistance in learning English. Fourth, there was no propagation facility at a local level, so finding a place for Dharma gatherings was difficult.[64] Imamura's objective was to establish a self-sufficient organization capable of competing with the Protestant Church.

In the beginning of propagation efforts, it was extremely difficult and exhausting work for Buddhist ministers to gain the trust of the settlers. Issei plantation workers were young single men, most of whom entertained themselves by drinking, gambling, and womanizing. Imamura recalled:

> Even during daylight they (bachelor laborers) gambled openly and those who did not participate were being ostracized as sub-human. Into this smoke filled, imbibing, gambling scene I floated with my briefcase to speak of the Dharma. *"Bonze!"* "Bad luck!" Such abuses to my face were common. Some behind me were urging each other to scatter salt. "Beat him up!" was common. I had expected a certain amount of this but found myself unprepared for the reality. . . . I persevered and tried to talk to a few who seemed less unfriendly, but they too hesitated for fear of scorn from others. No one would listen.[65]

Imamura was often discouraged from his own propagation efforts. These experiences, however, increased his interest in the Shin Buddhist teaching and his appreciation of Amida Buddha's compassion even more. Other ministers encountered difficulties as well: ethnic hostitlity led a group of Puerto Ricans to threaten Hiseki Miyazaki, and young YMCA members incited by a Christian extremist attacked Jōshō Enpuku. One night, a gang of Japanese immigrants approached Hakuda Takeda at Makaweli camp, where after officiating an observance of a Buddhist service his congregation had lodged him in a room that prostitutes often used to carry out their business.[66]

Two events helped Imamura win the trust of the Japanese community. In December 1899 a Chinese clerk in Honolulu died from plague, and the city authorities burned down the contaminated house in China Town. The fire spread quickly and destroyed almost all the buildings in the community, and thousands of Chinese and Japanese were left homeless. Because the area was off-limits except to doctors, clergy, and journalists, Imamura literally worked as a servant for the Japanese residents. With the assistance of Shin Buddhist followers, he set up a charity called Kyōaikai to help the victims.[67]

The second event was Imamura's involvement in the Waipahu strike of July 1904, after which the construction of Buddhist missions at plantations became widespread. Imamura recalled:

> The reasons for their (Japanese laborers) strike were usual ones, such as the brutality of lunas, demand for higher wages, improvement of living quarters, and so on. Since it was during the Russo-Japanese War, the strikers were irritable and the strike was unusually violent. Although Consel [*sic*] General Saitō went there several times to calm them down and to stop their strike, they did not accept his advice. Because of my missionary work among the plantation laborers, I was asked by the plantation authorities to help them. So I went there and spoke before the excited audience. I spoke entirely from the religious standpoint to calm them. The result of my advice was helpful and the strikers returned to work (after eleven days of strike). I felt the great power of Buddha. The English papers reported this news.
>
> After this incident, the planters and the Caucasians in general recognized the fact that Buddhism had important meaning to the Japanese and was necessary to stabilize the labor population on the plantations. Since that time the plantations provided land for a preaching center (temple) and when the temple was newly built or rebuilt, they made monetary donations and also they helped us in various ways, thus enhancing our spirit as Buddhist missionaries.[68]

The Waipahu disturbance showed that by this time, Imamura had established a good relationship with the Japanese workers. The plantation owners also recognized his leadership, and in order to minimize conflict and commotion they also supported the Honganji's religious activities at plantations.

With the collaboration of his fellow ministers, the HHMH won recognition from Euro-Americans. Because of Tessan Funakura's successful mediation in a labor strike in Wailuku, Maui, in 1904, a planter donated a building to the HHMH.[69] And on January 9, 1909, Hiseki Miyazaki performed a wedding for a Caucasian couple on Kauai, the first time a Japanese clergyman officiated at a wedding of Euro-Americans.[70] Not every Japanese, however, understood Imamura's long-term vision. Most immigrants initially ignored his plan to build a Honganji high school with dormitories for students from rural Oahu and the neighboring islands. Improving education for plantation children, which at the time ended at the sixth grade, was Imamura's greatest concern, but their parents who were not planning to settle permanently devalued further education.[71]

The HHMH was not free from internal conflicts. Opposing Imamura's instructions, some ministers avoided studying English, returned to Japan on very short notice, confused their private affairs with public matters, did not report their propagation activities, privately discussed their transfers to other propagation facilities, or personally asked lay members to select their assignments.[72] Due to the lack of historical records at the HHMH, it is hard to estimate the frequency of problems between the clergy and laity; however, it is likely that various kinds of tensions did exist. Furthermore, two Nishi Honganji priests from Hiroshima came to Hawaii as nonauthorized *kaikyōshi* and built their own organization, the Shinshū Kyōkai Mission of Hawaii in 1914.[73] Discrimination against Okinawans, led by people of other prefectures, prompted Chirō Yosemori of the HHMH and the Okinawan laity to build their own temple, Jikōen, in 1938.[74]

Sometime during the 1930s, Imamura contacted Bishop Kenju Masuyama of the BMNA to request a transfer of one of his ministers to the mainland. A rivalry developed between Jōsen Deme, director of the girls' junior high school in Hilo, Hawaii, and Jōnen Nishiura, the minister of Hilo, after the congregation debated the separation of education and religion. Nishiura returned to Japan, but Deme wished to stay on. Considering Deme's potential, Imamura sought an alternative for him.[75]

Trouble Experienced by Buddhist Churches on the Mainland

While the *fukyōjo* were initially built at Hawaii's plantation sites, the origins of the *bukkyōkai* on the mainland varied. For example, by 1902 approximately three thousand immigrants had flocked to San Jose at harvest time and subsequently formed a small Japanese town. Within the community, a demand for a *bukkyōkai* grew.[76] In Vacaville, Christians were the first to found a church, but Japanese pioneers there wished for a

Buddhist association. In 1909 Bishop Uchida sent to their community Jitsuzen Kiyohara of the Yūzū Nembutsu sect, who happened to be studying in Northern California under his care.[77] In White River, Japanese settlers built a Buddhist church next to a Japanese language school in October 1912. Outside California, Japanese nationals founded Buddhist churches in Salt Lake City, Utah, in 1912, and Denver, Colorado, in 1915.[78]

There was obvious competition with Christianity at times in California. In Guadalupe, the Japanese community unanimously agreed to establish either a Christian or Buddhist church, but not both, in order to avoid religious conflict. Because the residents received a positive reply from the Los Angeles Buddhist Church one day earlier than they heard back from the Christian church, the Guadalupe Buddhist Church was established, and it was incorporated in August 1913.[79] In Cortez, twelve Buddhist families maintained their religion in the strong presence of a Presbyterian church. They requested the Stockton Buddhist Church for an affiliation during the 1930s; Shin ministers regularly visited them and continued services in Cortez until the outbreak of World War II.[80] In Pasadena, Shin Buddhists faced opposition from anti-Asian and pro-Christian Caucasians, who strongly believed that Pasadena should remain a Christian community.[81]

In Vancouver, confrontation between Japanese Christians and Buddhists was caused by an ideological contest over the assimilability of the Japanese into the host society. The religious quarrel became distasteful: the Japanese Christians preached "When in Rome, do as the Romans do," while YBA members fought back, saying, "Those who go to the Pure Land and Heaven cannot meet again." Japanese Christian priests severely denounced the drinking, smoking, and gambling habits of the Issei workers, and the workers protested violently, but this was not the case with the Shin clergy, who more or less tolerated such vices.[82] At one point, the Nikkei media was divided, with factions supporting one or the other of the religions: *Kanada Shinpō* sided with Christianity and *Tairiku Nippō* with Buddhism.[83] Further, the laity put the construction of the Steveston Buddhist Church on hold because of concerns about the misconceptions of Anglo-Canadians, who saw Buddhism as a sign of Japanese nationalism.[84] In Kelowna, two Christian priests opposed the Buddhist propagation initiated by Gijin Taga in 1927. But Buddhist ministers and a group of over a hundred people continued their efforts and established a *bukkyōkai* in January 1933.[85]

There was at least one exception to the hostility of a Western monotheistic religion toward Buddhism. When Buddhists in Raymond decided to found their church, James Walker, the Mormon bishop of the Raymond

Second Ward, helped them purchase one of its old buildings for $5,000. Discrimination against the Japanese in Alberta was not as harsh as it was in British Columbia, since Japanese-Canadian residents had the right to vote and served in provincial offices and the military. Because the Mormons and the Japanese established amicable relationships, this atmosphere of religious tolerance was later extended to the exchanging of spiritual fellowship between Japanese Christians and Buddhists in Raymond.[86]

Despite the differences in setting up a Buddhist church, there was a general pattern through which local *bukkyōkai* became independent. Tetsuden Kashima writes:

> [W]ith any sizable number of Japanese in any sector a Bukkyō Seinen Kai was formed, in the main by young male Issei. As the group became larger with the influx of Japanese, splinter groups were established, each with the capacity to support a resident *kaikyōshi*. Thus, there were established clusters of related organizations around the new temples in the San Francisco Bay area, Los Angeles, Fresno, lower central California, and Seattle.[87]

Some of the *bukkyōkai* started out as branches of a mother church, or a larger church supported a start-up group by supplying a minister. A group of Buddhists in Lodi, California, for instance, had been members of either the Sacramento or San Jose churches. When the Hiroshima Prefectural Association in Lodi became an independent organization, its majority members, who were also Shin Buddhists, made their church autonomous in April 1929. A Buddhist group in Florin won independence from the Sacramento church in March 1918, that of El Centro from Brawley in February 1925, and that of Walnut Grove from Sacramento in February 1931.[88] In Washington, too, the Buddhist associations in White River, Tacoma and Pierce County, Yakima, and Spokane became independent from the Seattle Buddhist Church.[89]

Some *bukkyōkai* were established in response to a particular crisis. The Buddhist association in Intermountain, Utah, emerged when Bishop Uchida held a memorial service in fall 1912 for the community of railroad construction workers in Ogden. In San Diego, California, the death of ten Japanese farmworkers caused by an overflow at the nearby Otay Dam in 1916 led the Japanese residents to seek a Buddhist minister who could officiate at their funeral services. In Steveston, British Columbia, Japanese fishermen often drowned, so the Japanese community needed a Buddhist cleric to perform funerary rites.[90]

Between 1920 and the beginning of the Pacific War, Japanese immigrants faced a number of crises caused by a series of anti-Asian laws, but the *bukkyōkai* continued to grow. Such adversity tested the faith of Nikkei Buddhists, as Kōsei Ogura writes:

> After the passage of the immigration law of 1924 discriminating against the Japanese, the number of Buddhists increased rapidly, and so did that of the Buddhist churches. Before that event, some of then had been hesitant in declaring themselves Buddhists, considering such an act impudent in a Christian country. But the immigration law made them more defiant and bold in asserting what they believed to be their rights; it made them realize the necessity of cooperation for the sake of their own security and welfare, and naturally they sought the centers of their communal activity in their Buddhist churches.[91]

Anti-Japanese sentiment ironically stimulated the Issei pioneers to hold on to their religious heritage, and they built twelve more Buddhist churches during the interwar period (according to the statistics mentioned above).

Although anti-Japanese activist pressure worked against Nikkei Buddhists, there were many rivalries within the BMNA. In 1932, Ogura saw the causes of the problems as political contention among the members and competition among ministers.[92] The outcome of such disturbances was "the independence of a separate church, or the split of the old one into two churches."[93] However, he avoids a full discussion about the nature of conflicts within the BMNA, perhaps because he had been an insider (he served as a *kaikyōshi* at various churches on the West Coast), and perhaps his reticence was a result of the lingering effects of agitation in his time. New findings at the BCA Archives show that there were three kinds of problems, albeit often intertwined: conflicts between the clergy and laity involving dissension and territorial disputes; tensions between the BMNA office and local churches; and confrontations between Buddhist churches and Japanese language schools.[94]

Conflicts between the Clergy and Laity in the BMNA

Discord between the clergy and laity initially appeared as interpersonal problems, but when certain individuals formed a group and opposed their priest, differences of opinion affected the operation of the entire church. In February 1934, a group of the Portland Bukkyōkai laity, including a former president, reported to the BMNA Ministers' Meeting that about sixty members had withdrawn from the church, after breaking off their relationship with Yoshihiro Tokunō. At the same time, eighteen others attempted to force Masao Washioka to resign. The church was split, with factions supporting one or the other of the clerics.[95]

In El Centro, too, the Buddhist church was divided. A group of laity and the board president expressed their concern over Tairyō Sawada to Bishop Sasaki in November 1927. Although the board president and two delegates from the BMNA office agreed to remove Sawada, some other board members opposed that decision, demanding that he stay, and criticized the board president. Itsuzō Kyōgoku, chairman of the BMNA Advisory Committee (Sanjikai) between 1926 and 1929, reconciled the two groups and the BMNA office eventually transferred Sawada to Santa Barbara in August 1929.[96]

Even prominent priests became the target of criticism. Anonymous members of the Seattle Buddhist Church spread a rumor concerning Yūhaku Shimizu. After investigating the matter, however, the board of trustees issued a statement in September 1925 to the effect that the rumor was untrue and the minister was innocent. The board also expressed its appreciation of Shimizu's dedication to the church and refused the Kyoto headquarters' request to issue a subpoena to him. Kyōgoku was himself wrongfully accused of mishandling the Fresno church's funds in 1930. The church's board of directors and the accuser came to an agreement: the complainant was to leave the *bukkyōkai*; the trustees would audit the church's accounts in the presence of the plaintiff and a minister representing the BMNA office; and the plaintiff was to drop the lawsuit.[97]

Problems in Vancouver

Trouble establishing a church in Vancouver continued for some time because two groups of laity supported one of the two clerics. Senju Sasaki, the first minister of the Vancouver church, returned to Japan after successfully constructing a new church hall in February 1911. Jun'ichi Shigeno inaugurated the Canada Bukkyōkai in September 1913, but relations with Gungai Katō, who had begun to work earlier, were strained. Although Katō left the church, Shigeno continued to be controversial because of gossip. A party of those who wanted to expel Shigeno collided with a group of laity who supported him in October 1920. The anti-Shigeno group left the church and formed another Buddhist association, called the Honganji Bukkyōkai, which the provincial government recognized on February 11, 1921. Nishi Honganji headquartes also supported this new organization by sending Takunen Nishimoto as its resident minister.[98]

Nishi Honganji administrators eventually tried to reconcile these two *bukkyōkai.* Senju Sasaki, the former minister in Vancouver, made the first attempt in February 1923, without much success. The conflict finally ended in September 1924 when the Japanese consul and two priests of the BMNA office intervened.[99] The delegates of the two churches agreed to consolidate and respect the decision of the Kyoto headquarters, which would appoint the ministers. They named the merger of the two organizations the Honpa Canada Buddhist Mission (Honpa Canada Bukkyōkai).[100]

Although Shigeno and Nishimoto resigned as the result of this consolidation, discontent still festered. A group of parishioners who opposed the merger contacted Junjō Izumida, the head priest of the Higashi Honganji in Los Angeles, in summer 1925. Upon its request, he initiated the Higashi's advance in Vancouver.[101] In November 1925, the Nishi Honganji sent Gijin Taga to the Honpa Canada Buddhist Mission (HCBM) to expand its operation, but due to his unpopularity, a further schism developed within the mission. Taga exercised the Japanese custom of benefice paid to the clergy—he took the contributions offered by the parishioners for whom he conducted services as his own benefice, and his personal income increased while the church's revenue decreased.[102] In July 1928, the president of the board petitioned the BMNA Advisory Committee for Taga's transfer. Giyū Tōfuku, one of the advisory members, came to Vancouver on August 15, 1928, and agreed to send him back to Japan. On January 8, 1929, however, another church member insisted for unknown reasons that the BMNA office allow Taga to remain in Vancouver.[103] Since the BMNA office did not carry out Tōfuku's plan immediately, the president of the Honpa Canada Buddhist Mission, Eikichi Kagetsu, sent a reminder to the interim bishop, Kyōgoku, on July 27, 1929.[104] Kyōgoku wrote to the Committee of Honpa Canada Bukkyōkai on January 1, 1930, and finally removed Taga.[105]

Despite these upheavals in Vancouver, the contributions of the two suspended priests to the development of the church are worth mentioning. Nishimoto founded the YMBA within the Honganji Bukkyōkai in 1920 and opened the first Sunday school in 1921. Shigeno "initiated" two Euro-Americans in 1913, Mr. and Mrs. Group, who were given the Dharma names Shaku Kakuryo (or Kakuryō) and Shaku-ni Myokaku (or Myōkaku), respectively. Although ordered back to Japan by the Kyoto headquarters, Shigeno did not return to Japan but continued his service at the church on Franklin Street. He then moved to Toronto where he lived out his life.[106]

Trouble in Vancouver continued after the establishment of Honpa Canada Buddhist Mission. The territorial disputes emerged when the local *bukkyōkai* sought independence. On August 19, 1930, those who were living in the area around Nanoose Bay and Comox on Vancouver Island urged the BMNA office to deny the jurisdiction of the Royston Bukkyōkai, which extended beyond Nanaimo. According to their petition, its territorial expansion demonstrated the egotism behind the enterprise initiated by Royston Lumber Company managers. Further, the resident minister of the Royston Bukkyōkai, Kōgyō Osuga, who was also serving as a Japanese language teacher on Vancouver Island, breached an agreement made with a group of educators in Comox and tried to expand his operation.[107] The Kyoto headquarters, however, ignored all these accusations and recognized the Royston Bukkyōkai located at the lumber company.[108]

The BMNA office recorded another territorial dispute between the Honpa Canada Buddhist Mission and one of its branch temples, the New Westminster Buddhist Mission. In 1931, the propagation zone of the HCBM was set between the northern bank of the Fraser River and the previously agreed upon boundary of the jurisdiction, while that of New Westminster was established between the southern bank of the river and the border.[109] But on April 30, 1932, the HCBM board president reported to Bishop Masuyama that Ryūzan Hayashi, the resident minister of the New Westminster Buddhist Mission, had rescinded the agreement and begun propagation in Steveston (near Vancouver) without the HCBM's consent. Although Hayashi made gestures of reconciliation to Seishō Ishiguro of the HCBM, he and the laity of New Westminster broke the agreement again and called for their organization's independence.[110] In addition, there was a third case of contention, after which the BMNA office witnessed the agreement for a propagation zone made between the Steveston Bukkyōkai and the HCBM on December 6, 1932.[111]

A series of disputes in Vancouver partly led to the opening of the Nishi Honganji's Canadian District. When local Buddhist associations voiced their demands for independence, the clergy and laity of the HCBM were concerned with losing their authority in the British Columbia diocese. Owing to the physical distance, the BMNA office could not act promptly, so in the early 1930s the dissatisfied HCBM leaders demanded that Bishop Masuyama establish a separate Canadian office within the Mission.[112] In June 1933, the Kyoto headquarters and Masuyama recognized the Canada Buddhist Church as being separate from the BMNA, with its own bishop's office (Canada Kaikyō Kantoku Jimusho) housed in the HCBM building.[113] Since the status of this mission was elevated (with a bishop's office), Masuyama asked the board president to recognize the independence of local Buddhist churches.[114] Masuyama initially also served as the head of the Canada Buddhist Church, but Zenyū Aoki took over this position on April 8, 1936, and became the sole designated bishop in Canada.[115]

Granting Special Privileges
to Churches

As to setting up the bishop's office in the Honpa Canada Buddhist Mission, granting special privileges to large regional churches was one way to minimize local conflicts. In the mainland United States, unlike the founding of the *betsuin* in Hawaii in 1906, the Honganji Buddhist Church of Los Angeles was the first to obtain such status on September 7, 1931, as the central temple in Southern California. [116] Witnessing the emergence of the Higashi Honganji Los Angeles Betsuin on November 10, 1922, Bishop Uchida tried to upgrade the status of the Honganji Buddhist Church of Los Angeles to a *betsuin,* but the Kyoto headquarters turned down his request for unknown reasons. The BMNA still urgently needed the establishment of a *betsuin* in order to unify branch temples in California. [117] Upon completion of paying off the debt from the construction of the church hall, Bishop Masuyama again requested *betsuin* status on August 24, 1931. This time, Kyoto headquarters accepted his proposal and bestowed the title. [118] For Masuyama, this promotion would also resolve contention between the Los Angeles Buddhist Church and the Gardena Bukkyōkai, which had sought independence from the latter. [119]

Recognizing the Honganji Buddhist Church of Los Angeles as a *betsuin* was, however, not without problems; it simultaneously promoted a sense of inequality with other *bukkyōkai*. Members of the Watsonville Honganji Buddhist Church, formerly a branch of the Salinas Buddhist Church that became independent in 1927, were critical of the headquarters' decision. They argued that temple ranking would encourage nonconformity among the congregations of other churches; that the designation of the *betsuin* title first had to be discussed in the BMNA General Meeting; that continuing such a practice reflected a Japanese sectarian style of temple management; and that Los Angeles was far from being the center of the Buddhist churches scattered all over the U.S. [120] Masuyama, however, granted *betsuin* status to the Fresno Buddhist Church on November 4, 1936, in order to unify the Central California district of the BMNA and contain the advance of the Parlier Higashi Honganji and other Japanese Buddhist sects. [121]

Tensions between the BMNA Office
and Local Churches

During the period of early propagation, two incidents reflected local churches' hostility against the central authority, and as a result, the ministers involved abandoned their affiliations with the Nishi Honganji. In

February 1908, two groups in the San Jose Buddhist Church came into a conflict involving Reverend Hōnen Takahashi's disagreement with the BMNA office. Takahashi's group became independent in the summer of that year.[122] Takahashi returned his robes to the Kyoto headquarters on August 20, 1908, and then became affiliated with the Yamamoto branch of Shin Buddhism, although superintendent Uchida denied Takahashi's claim.[123] Manjō (or Mansei) Ichimura reconciled the two Buddhist groups, and Takahashi returned to Japan in fall 1917 with his minister's registration reactivated.[124] In Los Angeles, the Buddhist clerics sought settlement of their dispute in court, after Uchida and the Kyoto headquarters attempted to consolidate three Nishi Honganji churches in September 1916. (This incident is discussed with a detailed analysis in Chapter Six.)

In order to minimize disobedience among the clergy, the bishop administered an oath to resident ministers. During Masuyama's tenure, many written contracts (*seiyakusho*), signed by ministers coming from Japan and witnessed by clergy at the Kyoto headquarters, were filed. According to these contracts, the minister was to obey the bishop's orders, act according to the instructions of the BMNA office, and agree to return to Japan if his conduct brought disgrace on the priesthood.[125]

Despite the hierarchical relationship between the bishop and ministers, the BMNA office often could not control the congregations. Members of the Buddhist Church of San Francisco disagreed with BMNA officials over the unification of their church and the office of the BMNA. Bishop Masuyama visited Siam (present-day Thailand) in 1935 and came back with relics of the Buddha given by the king. Upon his return in August, the BMNA decided to construct a new building and dedicated it together with a stupa for these relics on February 11, 1938.[126] To make the best use of the new facility, the ministers and delegates of the laity discussed restructuring the BMNA organization in 1939 and proposed the unification of the Buddhist Church of San Francisco and the BMNA office to create the North America Honganji (Hokubei Honganji).[127] The immediate response from the Buddhist Church of San Francisco, however, was negative, since a lay group that particularly valued the forty-year history of the church's independence sought to first resolve the practical problems that would be caused by the unification, including the financial burden and transfer of personnel.[128]

The overall confrontation, cited above, could be seen as trivial in the development of a more than forty-year history of the BMNA, but these incidents are enough to call into question the stereotype of Buddhists as peaceful individuals. Scholars have pointed out the hard-working, frugal, and law-abiding nature of Shin Buddhists overseas. The Japanese cultural ethos linked with Buddhism seemed to sustain the harmony of the Nikkei community, but these accounts portray only one aspect of Shin Buddhist life in North America. Although there has been no explanation of Shin Buddhist disputes, Terry Watada surmises that it was unlikely that a minister's personality and mobilization of supporters were the major factors leading to a schism in a *bukkyōkai;* such a generalization would overestimate the ministers' influence.[129]

The causes of personality clashes and churches' seeking independence in North America need to be considered in relation to the cultural practices of immigrants. In Japan, a religious confraternity (*kō*) was originally built on the basis of an agrarian community. The *kō,* whether Buddhist or Shintō, kept its own autonomy and rarely held any religious services with other, neighboring associations. This isolated practice suggests the importance of common ancestral worship within the community and in the maintenance of its internal order. In the case of Shin Buddhism, each confraternity held its own observance of *Hōonkō,* the most important annual ceremony commemorating Shinran's death, in which the laity of other Shin Buddhist communities did not participate.[130]

For Shin Buddhists, the *kō* was tied to ancestor worship in some areas. Through exploring the connection between Shin Buddhist practice and folk tradition during the late Tokugawa period, Shiki Kodama argues that there was a religious gestalt of a Shin Buddhist "trinity," in which Shin Buddhists equated Shinran with Amida Buddha and with one's ancestors, and Amida was often referred to as *oya-sama* (parent). For them, enshrining Shinran also meant honoring their own ancestors, so there was no need to deify the mortuary tablets of deceased family members, a practice observed by followers of other Buddhist denominations.[131] Since one of the confraternity's objectives was to honor the ancestors of its own members, it is hardly surprising that Shin Buddhists in North America sought to establish a sense of belonging connected to their native locales. Religious practice combining ancestral worship and faith in Amida Buddha was most likely the tradition found in Shin Buddhist communities in Hawaii and on the mainland.[132]

In addition to the widespread practice of ancestral worship, other cultural factors can be seen in territorial disputes among Buddhist churches. One such element was the connection between the establishment of *bukkyōkai* and regional identity promoted by prefectural associations (*kenjinkai*), and further localization within the same prefecture from which residents had moved to North America. For instance, a study conducted on

Mio-mura (in present-day Wakayama prefecture) suggested that there had been two competing groups within the village divided by geography.[133] About half of Mio-mura's residents had emigrated to Steveston; one may suspect that such local competition continued there. Another study indicates that immigrants from Hatsusaka-mura (on the eastern side of Lake Biwa in Shiga prefecture) created their own enclave in Vancouver, as the men who had migrated to Canada married women from the same village, temporarily returned home, sent their children back to Japan, and sent funds to their families in Hatsusaka-mura.[134] These studies point to internal rivalries within the Nikkei community, where Japanese nationals formed quite a few associations and clubs.[135] The territorial disputes among Buddhist churches, therefore, need to be examined on this premise.

Rivalries between the Buddhist Churches and Japanese Language Schools

During the interwar period, the rising Nisei population made the continuation of Japanese language education controversial. Although the Nisei group occupied less than one-third of the total Nikkei population in California in 1920, by 1930 it was more than half.[136] There were 138,800 people of Japanese ancestry in the entire United States in 1930, of which 68,300 (48.5 percent) were Nisei.[137] During the 1920s, the vast majority of the Nisei in Hawaii attended Japanese language schools, and Buddhist organizations directly sponsored ninety of the one hundred and ninety schools, though it was hard to estimate how many of these schools actually remained purely nonsectarian.[138] On the mainland too, almost every Buddhist church had a Japanese language school.[139]

The development of Buddhist churches' language schools in Hawaii and the mainland also differed. On the mainland, Buddhists opened the first Japanese language school, while in Hawaii it was the Christians who did so.[140] In Honolulu, Takie Okumura, an influential Congregational minister, denounced the Nishi Honganji's Japanese language school program for Japanizing the Nisei. But his protest seemed ineffectual, as Buddhists had sponsored about 39 percent of the one hundred and sixty-three language schools in Hawaii by 1920, and most of these Buddhists were affiliated with the Nishi Honganji.[141] On the mainland, the relationship between Buddhists and Christians concerning the management of Japanese language schools is unknown, although Buddhists stressed linguistic mastery while Christians emphasized moral education. When Hawaii's governor, Wallace Rider Farrington, endorsed the Department of Public Instruction's

January 1, 1923, decision to restrict foreign language schools under Act 30, Buddhist leaders in Hawaii united with other educators to question its constitutionality. In California, however, this was not the case, perhaps because of the intensity of the anti-Japanese movement and the lack of solidarity among Buddhist clerics, for whom the physical distances between churches and congregations were far greater than those of their counterparts in Hawaii.[142] (The significance of Shin Buddhist involvement in the Hawaiian lawsuits is discussed in Chapter Seven.)

When a Japanese language school was affiliated with a Buddhist church in North America, the minister served as its schoolteacher. He was called *sensei* (teacher), instead of *goin-san* or *jūshoku*, which are the common terms for a resident Buddhist priest in Japan.[143] There are several reasons for conjoining the language school with a church. First, though busy on the weekends holding religious services for various purposes, ministers were relatively free during the week. Second, teaching was a part-time job and immigrants needed full-time work. Third, a small number of parents could not afford the cost of operating language schools, so they asked the *bukkyōkai* for help. Fourth, the church could obtain extra income and subsidize the minister's salary by supporting a language school.[144] Combining the two organizatons was supposed to be mutually beneficial.

New findings, however, demonstrate that there were cases of conflict between the two organizations. In the Olaa community on the Big Island, a schism grew over the management of a Japanese language school after a three-year absence of a resident minister. When Hōsui Takeshima took over the ministerial duties at the Puna Honganji Mission in October 1909, he became a scapegoat. A local newspaper harassed him for six months and reported that someone was even planning to attack him physically.[145]

In the mainland, too, Buddhist churches and Japanese language institutions ran afoul of one another. At least two incidents resulted in the advance of the Higashi Honganji in Central and Northern California (Chapter Six recounts these stories). In addition, there was an incident involving the Buddhist Church of Oakland and the Wantō Japanese language school (Wantō Gakuen). According to the records, since construction of both a new church hall and a school facility would prove financially difficult, Japanese nationals in Oakland decided to first rebuild the church hall and use the old hall as the Japanese language school. But Wantō Gakuen later claimed that the Buddhist church broke the agreement and refused to rent out the building for this purpose.[146]

During the 1930s, two priests expressed their anxiety over the church's role in language schools to the BMNA office. On April 18, 1934, Inshu

Yonemura of Fresno requested Bishop Masuyama to transfer him, since the church and the language school were in conflict and he could not solve the problem.[147] Seishō Ishiguro reported to Masuyama on February 11, 1935, that an individual representing the language school at the Fairview Buddhist Church in Vancouver, Canada, had expressed his dislike of its resident minister, Kakusai Tada. To the complainant, it was disgraceful not to receive Masuyama's immediate attention on the matter.[148] Yonemura, who was then relocated and served as a language school instructor in Coachella Valley, California, reported to Masuyama on May 5, 1936, that one individual was agitating a group of parents at the school and spreading rumors that the Japanese association in Coachella Valley was falling apart.[149]

Contention between Buddhist churches and Japanese language schools show not only the lack of Buddhist faith of those involved, but also the issue of separation of religion and education. As mentioned earlier, some parents brought their children to schools affiliated with a mission or church not because they wanted their children to study Buddhism, but because the community could not afford to build its own school. Further, those who demanded separation of religion and education claimed that religious leaders had played the role of educators only in the early days of immigration. As Issei settlers secured their economic foundation, separationists urged them to seek independent education for their children so that the Nisei could gain upward social mobility.[150] Bishop Imamura, however, pointed out that the lives of the youth in Japan were becoming mechanical and individualistic because of the lack of religious education. For him, religion and education were inseparable. Louise Hunter writes:

> Buddhist educators . . . did not see how they could create the desired bond of sympathy and mutual understanding between the first- and second-generation Japanese without making the religion of the parents intelligible to the children.[151]

Despite local hostilities between Buddhist churches and Japanese language schools, the BMNA as a whole worked together with other Issei educators. Between 1912 and 1929, twenty-three Shin ministers attended the annual conference of the Northern California Japanese Language Association. Five of them, including Bishop Uchida, participated in the First Conference held in San Francisco on April 4, 1912, and agreed to interpret the Imperial Rescript, the basis of Japanese language schools, more liberally. The objective of the Issei educators was to combine Japanese and American curricula as well.[152] Tansai Terakawa, the resident minister of the Stockton Buddhist Church, who also served at a Japanese language school in Stockton between 1929 and the early 1930s, advocated that the education in those institutions should be free from any strict ideology, including religious doctrines. He believed that education should provide broader perspectives to the Nisei, along with understanding the Issei, Japan, and the Nisei themselves.[153]

During the 1930s, the BMNA attempted to systematize its Japanese language school curriculum. In 1936, it moved to unify communication among the schools, sought a better curriculum, and assigned five ministers, including Terakawa, to investigate the best teaching methods from a Buddhist perspective, compile textbooks, bring schoolteachers and managers together, find language instructors, and form alliances between the language schools and the Sunday schools.[154]

Summary

The transformation of Shin Buddhist organizational structure entailed the processes of Americanization and Japanization. The HHMH and BMNA operated according to state laws and the articles of incorporation. The objective of the HHMH was to promote Shin Buddhist doctrine, while that of the BMNA was to introduce Śākyamuni's teachings to the American public. Their choices were linked to the activities of an earlier unofficial propagation. In the process of Japanization, conflict and competition prevailed, as differences of opinion were found between the central authority in Kyoto and local missions and churches in North America, clergy and laity, Japanese language schools and Buddhist missions and churches, and Buddhists and Christians.

Chapter Three

The Development of
Shin Buddhist Ministries
in North America

The Americanization and Japanization of the Honpa Honganji Mission of Hawaii (HHMH) and the Buddhist Mission of North America (BMNA) are coupled with the expansion of their ministries. Their structural features reflected the spiritual concerns of the Issei, Nisei, and Caucasian ministers, who simultaneously maintained and transformed the teachings, practices, ordinations, and other rituals. By the 1930s, the HHMH and the BMNA had established ministerial duties for the three groups of priests, but a watershed event in the history of Shin Buddhism took place in Hawaii and on the mainland during that time period. With the death on December 22, 1932, of the charismatic leader of the HHMH, Bishop Emyō Imamura, whose tenure had lasted for thirty-two years, propagation in Hawaii began to stagnate. In contrast to the HHMH, the BMNA expanded in the 1930s under the supervision of Bishop Kenju Masuyama, who served in the office from July 1930 to February 1938 and who readily admitted Nisei and Euro-Americans to the ministry. Under his orders, six hundred Caucasians received Buddhist "initiation."[1] During that time, the bishop's office in Canada also became independent from the BMNA, and Masuyama helped Hōzen Seki establish the BMNA's first Buddhist church in New York.

The 1930s was also an era in which Shin Buddhist women became more active. Laywomen not only expanded their roles at local churches, but also created a transnational network to collaborate with their Japanese counterparts. From Hawaii, Imamura sent several Nisei women to Japan where they received ordination. On the mainland, clerical leaders considered admitting women into the ministry.

The Life of an Issei Minister

It is unreasonable to compare lives of early Issei ministers with their affluent counterparts in Japan.[2] In Hawaii, a minister's salary was based on donations made by the congregation, whose earnings were determined by the economy of a particular plantation. In 1918, Imamura described the hardships of being a minister:

> Throughout the Hawaiian Islands, the minister's residence is small enough to accommodate only one household. Some of them are experiencing much more inconvenience. At a site where a new temple hall was just constructed, the minister's family lives in one or two rooms behind the altar. It is unthinkable for these ministers in Hawaii to live leisurely as some wealthy priests do in Japan. The Hawaiian ministers must be determined to share grief and anxiety with the immigrants.[3]

Buddhist priests at large temples in Japan lived in affluence, receiving substantial donations from their parishioners, but ministers in Hawaii did not. Imamura's description also indicates that the relationship between the clergy and laity in Hawaii was unlike the inequality found in Japan, where priests still enjoyed certain privileges not shared by their congregations.[4]

A minister's salary on the mainland was modest as well. Junjō Izumida in Los Angeles received a monthly wage of $50 in 1908.[5] Yoshihiro Tokunō and Gijin Taga, who served at the Honpa Canada Buddhist Mission in 1926, received $80 and $100, respectively.[6] By this time, the BMNA office had established a guideline for benefices: for a single chief minister, over $120; for a married chief minister, $150; for a single assistant minister, $90; and for a married assistant minister, $125.[7] According to the BMNA budget in 1927, the bishop received an annual income of ¥5,000 (approximately $2,500), and his secretary earned ¥2,400 (approximately $1,200).[8] In the early 1930s, the average salary was $125, but the earnings of twenty ministers were under $100, while those of another fourteen were over $200.[9] The salary for Euro-American Buddhist ministers on the mainland is unknown, but in Honolulu, Imamura secured an annual stipend of $1,800 for Thomas M. Kirby and $1,500 for Ernest Hunt in 1926.[10]

Ministers on the mainland often faced financial difficulties, as many churches ran into debt due to the construction of church buildings and the overall economic depression in the United States.[11] In January 1927, the Buddhist churches in Seattle, Portland, Watsonville, Vacaville, Alameda, and Berkeley owed liabilities. In Alameda, El Centro, Brawley, Vancouver, San Francisco, and Salt Lake City, the boards of directors were unable to pay their ministers' salaries.

In Fresno, Itsuzō Kyōgoku lived without payment for one and a half years. According to Marii Hasegawa, his second daughter, the Kyōgoku family left Fresno and moved to Lompoc at the end of 1931, where her father taught Japanese in order to provide for his wife and three daughters.[12] In October 1931, the San Diego Buddhist Church discharged Shōdo Gotō because of financial difficulties.[13] At White River, the church had debts amounting to $3,200 between the end of 1928 and January 1931, and the board decided that Giryō Takemura should take care of future deficits on his own.[14] At El Centro, Tenrin Kawamoto personally borrowed money every month when his church could not pay his salary. But the owner of a Japanese store refused to lend him more money after discovering that Kawamoto's church was in the red.[15]

Yūtetsu Kawamura lived without a salary for the first six months of his assignment at the Raymond Buddhist Mission in Alberta, and received only $30 a month starting in 1935. He was shocked at the lack of public utilities in Alberta, where there was neither a telephone nor electricity, and his residence had neither toilet nor bath. The Buddhist mission still owed $3,000 from the purchase of the church building, and it was extremely difficult for Kawamura to pay off this debt, because the Japanese residents near the mission were not Nishi Honganji members.[16]

A minister's routine exceeded his religious vocation. In Hawaii, the *fukyōjo* often served as something like a town office in Japan. According to Imamura, when a child was born, the parents notified the territorial government. At the same time, they asked a minister to help them register it at the Japanese consulate and even to name the child. When a couple married, a minister was obliged to issue a marriage certificate. If the family had enough savings and wanted to transfer the money to their relatives in Japan, the minister helped them write a letter and negotiate the transfer at the bank. Ministers were also asked to mediate between two parties in a particular dispute. Sometimes the minister's attempt to bring the parties to reconciliation succeeded, but when it failed, both sides ended up blaming the minister. Further, ministers signed most of the administrative paperwork required by the Consulate on behalf of their countrymen. The Japanese consul also asked favors of ministers; for example, when the Japanese government needed funds for damages caused by a natural disaster, the consulate would request ministers to collect donations at their missions. However, in part because of these daily contacts, ministers were able to develop closer relationships with their parishioners, and provide ethical advice and spiritual guidance without giving offense.[17]

Some of the ministers assisted the Issei pioneers with their English. In Canada, Senju Sasaki initiated nonreligious philanthropic activities. As he was competent in English, he compiled a special English-Japanese dictionary for hospital patients who had difficulty communicating with doctors and nurses. He also made weekly visits to hospitals to help Japanese-speaking invalids.[18] Imamura organized night schools for immigrants to learn English, and Buddhist sympathizers like Mrs. Lillian S. Mesick and Mrs. Barber offered help.[19] On the mainland too, the Buddhist Church of San Francisco set up an English language school for Japanese immigrants in 1903. The Seattle Buddhist Church, including its Port Blakely branch, the Buddhist Church of Sacramento, and the Guadalupe Buddhist Church followed suit.[20]

Expectations Placed upon Ministers

At the Ministers' General Conference in 1916, Imamura described what kind of person he thought would make an ideal minister, and voiced his concerns over the future propagation of Buddhism in Hawaii. His instructions included the reexamination of one's own faith, an understanding of the situations faced by immigrants and the importance of Nisei education, and the need to learn about the United States:

> The mission of a Buddhist minister is to realize in his life the all-embracing love of Buddha [Amida]. So we must always stand firm in our belief, and try to do our best with a thanksgiving spirit.
>
> Think always more of the teaching than of yourself.
>
> Make the reverence of Buddha and the love of your fellow-men your abiding motives.
>
> Be always contented with a simple and frugal life.
>
> Do not forget to teach that luxury and extravagance lead to the inevitable destruction of home and the community at large.
>
> a. A Buddhist minister must show his virtue of obedience by living up to the instructions given out by his superior.
>
> b. Punctually and promptly you must discharge duties of your own.
>
> A minister should think of himself as a leader of the world, terrestrial as well as celestial. To give the proper guidance to the people, you must keep your mind always alert even to the daily occurrences of the community and of the world at large.
>
> Japanese people here seem to be making their own homes in the plantation. What one calls "Aggregation life of the Camp," will be a story of the past in the near future. So the minister must help them to realize the Anglo-Saxon idea of "Sweet Home" with Buddha [Amida] as the universal parent. The necessary and adequate conditions of realizing this idea may be many, but four requisites are to be specially noticed[:] (a) A clean and beautiful dwelling; (b) The good faith of the wife; (c) The balance of income and expenditure; [and] (d) The education of children.

How to beautify one's own dwelling is a matter of great interest in every respect. The traditional artistic instinct of the Japanese people should be brought to a test in this connection. But more than anything else, every minister must be an example to his countrymen in cleaning and beautifying his church and its premises.

To foster the virtue of wives, the importance of pious obedience to her elders, single-minded devotion to her husband and love and self-sacrifice for her children's sake, must be dwelt upon in your sermons. These are the three cardinal virtues of a good wife in every good home. In connection with material prosperity, habits of thrift and industriousness ought to be emphasized. Thrift reduces expenses; industriousness brings larger income. Drive every kind of idle luxury out of your plantation.

As to the matter of education, you have your Educational Homes in your charges. Do your best to make them more efficient, in perfect accordance with the American principle of good citizenship taught in the public instruction.

As you well know, Japanese children born here are entitled to be American citizens by the Constitution of this Country; but their parents are not by any means to be nationalized into Americans. From this discrimination of parents and children, it is logically to be expected that there may arise a pathetic division of the Sweet Home in the matter of Nationality. Parents may feel lonesome in some way or other, and will need your consolation. Give them solace; tell them that good parents must think more of the future of their children than their own. To give in this life is to receive in the next.

For their child to be a good American Citizen, parents must secure a birth certificate from the proper authority in the first place; must send their children to the public school regularly; must have them take an interest in various movements in Americanism. Every Buddhist minister knows this and sees to it that the parents may not amiss in their conduct in this regard.

Whenever you preach, you must not forget that you are preaching to Americans as well as Japanese. So you must always try hard to study America and Americans. Right understanding of true Americanism is essential to your missionary work.

As to the attitude toward the other sects and denominations, we must be always tolerant and must work together with ministers of different faiths whenever the general welfare and enlightenment of the plantation or community call for harmony.

You ministers are at the same time the heads of the Educational Homes. So you must always see how public instruction is carried on, and do everything in your power to co-operate with it as the parent of every enlightened home will do with the school.[21]

Ministers not only provided spiritual support to the Issei plantation workers but also offered spiritual guidance to their children. Buddhist education required a triadic interaction of home, school, and mission, although women were largely subjugated in a patriarchal system. In order to guide the Nisei, it was incumbent on ministers to learn English and develop sufficient knowledge of the current circumstances of the United States. The HHMH modified and reprinted Imamura's address in 1931, so his vision of an ideal minister persisted, though it is unknown whether or not the laity in Hawaii had the same kind of expectations of its ministers as did Imamura.

New findings suggest that the laity was not necessarily concerned with a minister's deftness in spiritual guidance. The board president of the Steveston Buddhist Mission in British Columbia petitioned Bishop Kenju Masuyama for a resident minister on April 22, 1932. In the petition, he attached a nine-page description of the *bukkyōkai*'s history and the specific requirements for such a person, together with an explanation of his remuneration.

> Ministers need to be:
> Younger than forty years old, healthy and married.
> Determined for permanent settlement and dedicated and active.
> Eloquent and capable of dealing with new hot-blooded young immigrants.
> Interested in sports. He is more welcomed if competent in Japan's martial arts, such as judō and kendō.
> His wife was to be:
> Educated enough to be a leader in the Buddhist Women's Association or Young Buddhist Women's Association.
> More welcomed if she is acquainted with the Japanese arts, including flower arrangement or tea ceremony.
> More welcomed if she has the basic knowledge in music as she can teach Buddhist hymns.
> Compensation:
> The minister's monthly salary shall be 100 dollars. Due to the bad economy, the bukkyōkai's budget has to be tight; however, when things get better, his salary shall be increased.
> Housing will be provided, free of charge.
> The bukkyōkai shall pay the utilities, including the water and electricity bills.
> For his travel expenses to Steveston, the bukkyōkai shall give him 250 dollars.[22]

For the Steveston Bukkyōkai followers, the performance of cultural activities was a necessity, and spiritual guidance appeared to be a formality.[23]

This petition, however, did not suggest a lack of Buddhist faith within the church. The Japanese fishermen who had settled near the mouth of the Fraser River were quite devout. A poet of Japanese ancestry described their lives in Steveston at that time:

> While reciting nenbutsu in the ocean covered with a dense fog,
> I suddenly notice a voice of my grandfather catching salmon.[24]

Fishermen often died while at sea. In October 1907, just after the Vancouver Riot, Sensuke Musashi and Kosaburō Ono purchased a small Buddhist altar and formed a Buddhist Club (*bukkyō kurabu*). A group of laypeople gathered on the second floor of a pharmacy and learned how to recite sutras from Fukumatsu Nakamura, known as "Amida-san." They went to the families of their kinsmen and conducted funerals. Eventually, when a Buddhist minister arrived in Vancouver, a relationship developed between him and the followers of the Buddhist Club. In 1924, the members decided to build a Buddhist church. In spring 1928, they began construction of the Steveston Bukkyōkai after raising $8,000, despite a financial crisis in the Japanese community when the association of Japanese fishermen sued the Canadian government on account of reducing the number of licenses issued to them.[25]

On July 20, 1933, another petition for a resident minister was made by the Raymond Buddhist Mission in Canada, after Shinjō Nagatomi was forced to leave because his visa had expired. The board president strongly desired the continuation of the spiritual guidance offered by Nagatomi, who "had shown a white path of illumination in the darkness of ignorance."[26] He expressed his regret that the *bukkyōkai* was unable to compensate Nagatomi enough for his dedication, including sharing his own food and shelter with the laity. The minister who would take up Nagatomi's post would have to "leave behind all his personal greed in order to complete the mission of guiding sentient beings." Interestingly enough, the board president preferred priests sent directly from Japan, not those already working in the United States.[27]

The Issei laity was unconcerned about the clergy's fluency in English, but this was not the case with organizational leaders. Like Bishop Imamura in Hawaii, the leaders of the BMNA office were concerned with a new minister's ability to communicate with the Nisei. For instance, the fifth bishop, Hōshō Sasaki, outlined the requirements of a minister in 1927:

> Ministers must be at least thirty years old, and have enough experience in rituals and propagation. After arriving in San Francisco, they are required to

take part in at least a three-month English language program and observe religious practices at a church.

I hope to designate all the ministers to teaching positions at a church's Japanese language school. For the purpose of Nisei education, it is necessary for them to live permanently in the United States.

The Kyoto headquarters should send a group of priests to academic institutions located in New York, Boston, Los Angeles, San Francisco, and Seattle, in order for them to study various subjects in the United States. Afterwards, they can either serve as leaders of the clergy here or find employment at the headquarters in Japan.

The secretary of the BMNA office [though he, himself, is a minister] must have a good command of English.[28]

The first two requirements were necessary for the Issei clergy to interact with the Nisei laity, but it was extremely rare for ministers from Japan to be fluent in English. The clerical leaders, therefore, felt compelled to develop a Nisei ministry for the sake of English-language propagation. Bishop Imamura and Bishop Masuyama eventually sent a group of Nisei minister candidates to Kyoto. After receiving ministerial training in Japan, they returned to the United States as Nisei *kaikyōshi.*

Birth of a Nisei Ministry

The emergence of the Nisei ministry also reflected Nisei Buddhists' search for religious identity. They were caught between anti-Japanese activists, who considered Buddhism a "foreign religion," and their Issei parents, who nurtured Shin Buddhism as a cultural and spiritual heritage of Japan. The progressive Issei clergy and Nisei laity resisted exclusive Americanization by insisting on freedom of religion as guaranteed under the Constitution; they simultaneously negotiated with Issei elders by adapting Buddhism to a new environment. Being an "American Buddhist" for a Nisei required a lot of effort, especially when Nikkei Buddhists participated in Hawaii's territory-wide sugar plantation strike in 1920, and the exclusionists saw Buddhism as an "enemy religion."[29]

Issei ministers helped Nisei Buddhists develop their religious identity in a Nikkei subculture. Bishop Imamura transformed the YMBA and YWBA, which originally started out as the organizations of Issei Buddhists, into Nisei lay organizations. They later merged and became the YBA, known as Bussei. In order for the Nisei to understand Buddhism, Imamura instructed Issei ministers to "emphasize the teachings of the historical Buddha and the ethical elements of Buddhism rather than its more philosophical and metaphysical aspects."[30] He helped a group of Nisei organize the First Pan-Pacific YMBA Conference in Honolulu in 1930.

On the mainland, too, the YMBA and YWBA developed on a national level: Nisei Buddhists established the North American Federations in 1926 and the YBA League of Canada in 1928.[31] Under the supervision of Kyōgoku and Terakawa, Nisei Buddhists participated in various activities. The YMBA and YWBA joined together as the YBA, published the journal *Bhratri,* and organized the First Canada-Hawaii-American Conference in San Francisco in 1932.[32] In Canada, the national league of Nisei Buddhists held annual conferences promoting the exchange of ideas among local churches, published the journal *Kōgen,* sponsored various sport events, and organized the Sunday School Association, which included one hundred and ten teachers and twelve thousand students by 1939. Although the Canadian Buddhists were no longer a part of the BMNA at that time, the YBA groups on the Pacific Coast from Vancouver to California often held intercontinental conventions.[33] The spiritual interests of those who became Nisei ministers and their enthusiasm for propagation evolved through these Bussei activities.

During the early interwar period, the offices of the HHMH and the BMNA initiated the Nisei Ministers' Program, though their campaign first commenced in Hawaii. Son'yū Ōtani, the fourth son of the twenty-first abbot of Nishi Honganji and Emperor Taishō's brother-in-law, served as Executive Director of the Kyoto headquarters and toured North America between 1925 and 1926. He encouraged Imamura to educate Hawaiian-born youths in Japan; hence, Shigeo Takeda and Takeo Miura left Honolulu to study at Ryūkoku University in Kyoto at the end of 1926. Son'yū Ōtani also founded five-year scholarships for local high school graduates to become ministerial candidates in Hawaii.[34] In 1927, Imamura sent two more candidates to Kyoto, Iwasaburō Yoshikami and Ralph Honda. Takeda, Miura, and Yoshikami registered themselves at Sentokuji, Imamura's home temple in Fukui prefecture, in order to receive ordination (*tokudo*).[35] As registration at a local temple in Japan was the only way to become ministers, Imamura negotiated with the headquarters to authorize registration of non-Japanese ministers at the overseas *betsuin* in their region.[36] After being ordained, Takeda immediately returned to the Hawaii Betsuin and served as its minister, while enrolling in the social work program at the University of Hawaii. Miura and Yoshikami also returned to Hawaii. Imamura later sent one more candidate, Fusato Marutani, to Japan.

Kanmo Imamura, the eldest son of Bishop Emyō Imamura, was probably the first native-born Hawaiian to receive ordination in Kyoto. Kanmo was born in August 1904 in Honolulu, and ordained at the age of nine, as Emyō expected him to be his substitute at Sentokuji. According to the regulations of both branches of the Honganji, nine years of age is the minimum for someone to be eligible for ordination, since Shinran took tonsure at that age. There were three steps in becoming a full-fledged overseas minister; receiving ordination (*tokudo*); obtaining a Dharma teacher's (*kyōshi*) certificate, and receiving official appointment to propagate outside Japan (*kaikyōshi*).

Kanmo Imamura became a *kyōshi* on June 16, 1931, and returned to Hawaii in 1934. He served as director of Hawaii's YBA the following year, but moved to Berkeley in August 1941.[37] Kanmo Imamura became one of the key Buddhist leaders in the Bay Area in the 1950s and led the Berkeley Bussei. He promoted Buddhist dialogue with Caucasians, including members of the so-called Beat Generation, such as Allen Ginsberg, Jack Kerouac, Gary Snyder, and Philip Whalen.[38]

The BMNA Educational Program for Nisei ministers developed under the aegis of Bishop Masuyama. Prior to his arrival in 1930, the BMNA had established its Endowment Foundation (Hokubei Kaikyō Zaidan), and one of its objectives was to train Nisei ministers. It states:

> The training of able men is the best of farsighted policy. In this world of human beings, Man is the central figure of all enterprises. In order to teach Buddhism to the Americans and the second generation of Japanese parentage, it is of primary importance to have a devoted minded person with a thorough knowledge of Buddhist principles and at the same mastering both Japanese and English languages. However, there is no other way of obtaining such a person except by training. For instance by choosing a suitable person among second generation or other Americans and sending him to Japan to be trained in Buddhist institutions.[39]

Because of the lack of educational facilities, training had to take place in Japan, and Issei ministers insisted that the Nisei candidates learn Japanese. Upon advice from a resident minister in Santa Barbara, Masuyama sent Noboru Tsunoda to Kyoto in 1931 as the BMNA's first student to study abroad (*ryūgakusei*). Tsunoda had helped the church's Sunday school for many years, served as a role model for other Nisei, and, with his parents' consent, sought to pursue Buddhist studies.[40] Masuyama asked the Kyoto headquarters to pay for his lodgings and food. Ryōtai Matsukage, who later became the seventh bishop of the BMNA after taking over from Masuyama, took care of Tsunoda's daily affairs. Kōyū Uchida, who had been the BMNA's fourth bishop, was now Director of Propagation at the Kyoto headquarters and supervised Tsunoda's academic progress.[41] Tsunoda married in Japan and returned to California, serving in the BMNA Education Department from October 1939.[42]

In 1931, Masuyama outlined further qualifications for Nisei ministerial candidates. At minimum, the candidate needed to have graduated from a junior college with a letter of recommendation from a resident minister. He ought to have a high academic standing and speak both Japanese and English. Since he was obliged to work for the BMNA after coming back, the BMNA office would give him a monthly stipend of $15 during his training in Japan. To achieve this goal, Masuyama requested all other ministers on the mainland to put $5 a year into a common fund.[43]

Until the beginning of the Pacific War in 1940, the BMNA sent at least three more Nisei candidates, who on their return, served as ministers in the United States. Masaru Kumata (Dharma name Shaku Kenryō), a native of Seattle, sailed to Japan in December 1932 as the second *ryūgakusei*. He married in Japan, and on his return to the U.S. he was appointed YBA Director in April 1941. During the war, he was Bishop Matsukage's assistant and advised him on legal matters.[44] Kiyoto Nagatani, a native of Walnut Grove, California, graduated from the Chūō Bukkyō Gakuin, an academic institution of the Nishi Honganji, in March 1937. Newton Ishiura, a native of Kauai, Hawaii, attended Ryūkoku University between 1938 and 1941. Nagatani later worked at Stockton while Ishiura served at Bakersfield.[45]

Canada's first Nisei candidate to become a minister set off for Japan in 1938. Takashi Tsuji, an active member of the YBA League of Canada, announced his intent to become a Buddhist minister after participating in the Bussei. His father, a devout Buddhist who was disappointed by the lack of Shin ministers, had encouraged one of his sons become one. Although Tsuji's Japanese was limited, he survived at Ryūkoku University with a subsidy from the Buddhist Mission of Canada, and headquarters ordained him with the Dharma name Shaku Kenryū. In November 1941, when diplomatic relations between Japan and the United States deteriorated, he returned to Canada and assisted in Sunday services for the first time in Vancouver.[46] From 1968 to 1981, he served as the tenth bishop of the BCA.[47]

It is hard to assess whether a Nisei minister sought to study Buddhism in a general sense or found Shinran's teaching most important. Noboru Tsunoda, the first Nisei minister, initially had planned to enter medical school and become a doctor. But his experience in the Pan Pacific YMBA Conference in 1930 inspired him to change career directions. He realized the need to propagate Buddhism among Euro-Americans, but he wrote:

"[U]nless the religion is strongly believed in by the Second Generation Buddhists, themselves, that Buddhism, now in its flower, will suffer a lingering death." Tsunoda decided to enter the Buddhist ministry "for the welfare of his fellow men."[48] In the case of Masaru Kumata, though he wrote in a Dharma essay that Buddhism is a "faith founded on knowledge," he avoided discussing "entrusting mind" (*shinjin*), one of the key concepts in Shin Buddhism.[49] Their writings therefore give the impression that the Nisei ministers might not have been interested in Shinran's teaching at first, or that they might have felt compelled to study Śākyamuni's doctrine before Shinran's, because the majority of Nisei and Euro-American Buddhists would not understand the latter without sufficient knowledge of the former.[50]

Euro-Americans' Admittance to the Nishi Honganji Order

If the creation of the Nisei ministerial program was the point of departure from the Japanese tradition, then the establishment of English Departments at the HHMH and the BMNA marked a significant organizational shift. In the past, Euro-Americans had never been affiliated with the Nishi Honganji in Japan, and those admitted by the HHMH and the BMNA were not primarily interested in Shinran's teaching. Because of their interest in and focus on Śākyamuni's philosophy, Caucasians' entry into the ministry also required a modification of Jōdo Shinshū rituals (Chapter Four includes a discussion of this topic).

Kirby, Hunt, and Imamura

The BMNA was the first to admit Euro-Americans into the ministry. In the 1920s, Bishop Uchida ordained Thomas M. Kirby and Robert and Alice Clarke.[51] Kirby, an Englishman, moved to New Westminster, British Columbia, Canada, in 1904 and traveled to Japan in 1913 to study Buddhism. He taught at Heian Junior High School and Bukkyō University in Kyoto, both run by the Nishi Honganji. In 1915, he visited Zen master Shaku Sōen in Kamakura (near Tokyo) and received the Dharma name Sōkaku. Kirby then returned to Canada in March 1916 and began to propagate Buddhism to Caucasians at the Canada Buddhist Mission, with the help of Jun'ichi Shigeno.[52]

After Kirby moved to San Francisco, Bishop Uchida ordained and appointed him as chief minister of the BMNA English program.[53] At Imamura's request, Kirby advanced to Hawaii in 1921 where he served as head of the HHMH English propagation program. In 1922, the Clarkes assumed the position he had vacated, leading the English-speaking group in the

Bay Area.[54] In the same year, Uchida ordained J. M. Hayes and Dr. Adolph Brodbeck.[55] In Hawaii, Kirby and Ernest Hunt led English propagation efforts in the early 1920s. For the next five years, Kirby taught fundamental Buddhism to Euro-Americans in Honolulu. His vitriolic lectures, however, included attacks on Christian beliefs, and his interpretation of Buddhism eventually diverged from Imamura's. Kirby left for further study in Japan in 1927 but later abandoned his Buddhist beliefs.[56]

In the meantime, Imamura developed a close relationship with Ernest Hunt, born August 16, 1876, in Hertfordshire, England. In 1915, he and his wife, Dorothy, moved to Hawaii and opened Buddhist Sunday schools in the plantation camps on the Big Island of Hawaii. On August 11, 1924, when Imamura conducted Hawaii's first Buddhist ordination, Hunt received the Dharma name Shaku Shinkaku, and his wife was given the name Shinkō.[57] After Kirby's departure, Hunt took over his position and looked after a biweekly forum, a gathering of Euro-American Buddhist sympathizers, in Honolulu.[58]

The HHMH English department developed further. On July 8, 1928, Imamura and Hunt "initiated" nine members of the forum. Those recognizing the Buddhist faith were Mr. and Mrs. Adolph Constable, Mr. and Mrs. George Wright, Mrs. Carl Scheid, Mrs. Merlyn McGrew, Mr. Julius Goldwater, Mrs. Flora Maddock, and Miss Gloria Will. They found the buddhadharma to be compatible with European civilization and traced their racial backgrounds to Indo-European origin. In 1929, the HHMH admitted eight more Caucasians.[59] Imamura also sent a young student, W. E. McGuffin, to Kyoto along with a group of Nisei minister candidates.[60]

The publications of the English department included the *Vade Mecum* (1927), a revised edition of the one published in Hilo in 1924; *The Symbolism of Buddhism* (1927); and *Buddhism in Hawaii* and *An Outline of Buddhism* (1929).[61] Imamura and Hunt worked together, and the former allowed the latter to propagate to both Nisei and Caucasians. By 1928 Hunt had converted sixty Euro-Americans. He won recognition from the government and began Buddhist services at hospitals and prisons in Honolulu. He also established a direct branch of the Mahabodhi Society (based in New York) in Hawaii. When Tai Xu, a prominent abbot of the Lin Yin Temple in Hangzhou, China, visited Hawaii on April 12, 1929, Imamura and Hunt agreed with him to remove sectarian barriers and work for a cosmopolitan form of Buddhism. They established a branch office of the International Buddhist Institute (IBI) in Honolulu and published an English journal, the *Hawaiian Buddhist Annual,* from 1930 to 1934.[62] The mission statement of the IBI includes:

1. To disseminate the Teaching of the Buddha in the English speaking community of the Hawaiian Islands.

2. To allay all prejudice and misunderstanding regarding Buddhism.

3. To give all who desire it a chance to hear in the English language what Buddhism really is.

4. To help the Hawaiian-born of Japanese ancestry by pointing out to them in the English language the outstanding features of their religion, showing them that it is the Highest Wisdom.

5. To co-operate with all other Buddhist societies irrespective of sect or school in any undertaking that will directly or indirectly reform the thought and therefore the attitude of mankind towards the problems of life.

6. To strive earnestly to decrease sadness and suffering (evil) by fighting against every cause that tends to bring it about.

7. To encourage everything that helps to increase wholesome pleasure (good).

8. To banish the war thought and establish the thought of peace.

9. To foster international mindedness.

10. To demonstrate in a practical manner universal sympathy and belief in the Oneness of all life by practicing mutual aid, and extending kindness to animals and all forms of life.[63]

The objectives of the IBI in Hawaii were not only to disseminate Buddhism but also to initiate an ecumenical Buddhist movement. The first issue of the *Hawaiian Buddhist Annual* testified to the orientation of the IBI, as it included articles written by residents in India, England, France, Germany, Japan, China, Hawaii, Denmark, the United States, Ireland, South Africa, and Hungary.[64]

The cosmopolitan Buddhism that Imamura and Hunt were seeking in Hawaii, however, was enigmatic, especially when their goals of propagation are closely examined. Imamura still wished to universalize his sectarian teaching, Shinran's Pure Land Buddhism, but Hunt went beyond Imamura's trans-sectarian cooperation and planned to replace Japanese forms of Buddhism in Honolulu with the ethical teachings of Śākyamuni.[65] Despite differences in the orientation of propagation, Imamura held Hunt in high esteem and even offered to reduce his own earnings to increase Hunt's income.[66]

After Imamura's sudden death on December 22, 1932, Hunt became isolated from other Issei ministers, and the HHMH English program fell apart. The impact of Imamura's thirty-two–year tenure was so overwhelming that searching for his successor was extremely difficult. A columnist in the *Chūgai Nippō* suggested that the next bishop be chosen from the Issei ministers in Hawaii, despite the politics involved with the selection process.

The same columnist also wondered if the Kyoto headquarters could send one of its executive leaders.[67] The headquarters eventually sent Zuigi Ashikaga to Hawaii as the third bishop, but he returned to Japan shortly after completing the work left behind by Imamura.

The HHMH revealed a nationalistic streak when it elected Gikyō Kuchiba, a Hawaiian Issei minister who was unable to speak English, as the fourth bishop in September 1935.[68] Priests sent by the Kyoto headquarters had become jingoistic by that time and saw Hunt's faith in Theravada Buddhism unfit for Shin propagation. Together with senior Issei ministers, they made various rationales for pressing Kuchiba to dismiss Hunt, such as complaining about his high salary and promoting Nisei ministers who could speak both English and Japanese.[69] Kuchiba fired Hunt in 1937. A Nisei minister, Shigeo Takeda, who opposed Kuchiba's decision but was obliged to deliver the notice of dismissal to Hunt, took over the English program.[70]

Hunt had his own problems. Ashikaga proposed that a group of Issei ministers teach him the Shin Buddhist doctrine. In Hunt's eyes however, it was unnecessary to study Jōdo Shinshū, because he was only concerned with the ethical teachings of Theravada Buddhism. Further, Hunt confused the concept of *shinjin,* entrusting oneself to Amida Buddha, with the Christian concept of "faith," which Japanese ministers could not accept.[71] He finally left the HHMH and became affiliated with Sōtō Zen in Honolulu. He died on February 7, 1967, at the age of ninety-one.[72]

The Growth of the BMNA
English Propagation Program

Contrary to the expansion of Hawaii's English Department in the 1920s, it was not until the 1930s that the BMNA English Department became strong. Bishop Masuyama, who assumed the BMNA office in July 1930, started "initiating" Caucasians into the Nishi Honganji order again. Records show that he admitted three people in 1933: Francis G. Geske, Richard K. Prosser, and Robert S. Clifton.[73] Masuyama conducted a "ceremony of initiation" (*nyūmon shiki*) when the number of Euro-Americans who desired to propagate Buddhism in the United States was increasing. In Masuyama's mind, "initiation" was not the same as "confirmation" (*kikyō shiki*), the first ceremony in which a Japanese professes oneself as a Shin Buddhist, somewhat similar to Christian baptism, which "prohibited one from converting to other religious faiths." He would consider ordaining them if he found their practice and study satisfactory after one year; hence, Masuyama requested the

Kyoto headquarters to make special arrangements for them. By 1934 he had initiated more than forty-five Caucasians.[74]

With these Euro-Americans, Masuyama established twelve gatherings of the Buddhist Society of America. Among them he ordained (*tokudo*) Geske, Prosser, Clifton, and Julius Goldwater, and recognized them as Buddhist "missionaries" (*senkyōshi*).[75] As of 1934, society members included:

Chief Director: Right Rev. Kenju Masuyama, Bishop of the Buddhist Mission
    of North America
Director: Rev. Tansai K. Terakawa
Director: Rev. Robert S. Clifton

Local Units:
    San Francisco Buddhist Society: Rev. Robert S. Clifton, Leader,
       and Rev. Richard Prosser, Assistant
    San Mateo Buddhist Society: Rev. Richard Prosser, Leader
    North Oakland Buddhist Society: Rev. Francis Geske, Leader
    Central Oakland Buddhist Society: Mr. William Reuter, Leader,
       Mr. James K. Stewart, Associate
    Los Angeles Buddhist Society: Rev. Julius A. Goldwater, Leader
    Tacoma Buddhist Society: Mrs. G. M. Pratt, Leader
    Berkeley Buddhist Society: Mr. James K. Stewart, Leader
    Rapelje (Montana) Buddhist Society: Mrs. Fern Tolley Bush, Leader
    Houston Buddhist Society: Mr. Thomas Ascardi, Leader
    Portland Buddhist Society: Mr. Ralph R. Phillips, Leader
    San Diego Buddhist Society: Mr. Gerard Arts, Leader
    Seattle Buddhist Society: Mr. N. Earl Brown, Leader[76]

Most of these societies were located on the Pacific Coast and were related to local *bukkyōkai.* But even in Montana and Texas, where the BMNA did not establish propagation centers, a group of Caucasians admitted by Masuyama set up a society.

Masuyama continued to accept "white missionaries" in the mid-1930s. He ordained Frank B. Udale on March 1, 1935, with the Dharma name Kyosen (or Kyōsen); S. Alex White on April 8, 1936, as Hogen (or Hōgen); Sunya G. Pratt on April 23, 1936, as Teiun; and Violet I. White (the wife of Alex White) on May 30, 1937, as Hosui (or Hōsui).[77] But it was unclear how the Nishi Honganji headquarters classified their status. For a minister working outside Japan, there were three levels of ranking: ordination (*tokudo*), Dharma teacher (*kyōshi*), and overseas propagation (*kaikyōshi*). Some of the Caucasian ministers cited above took ordination twice, traveling later to Japan to re-ordain there. Clifton received his second ordination on

Fig. 3. Robert Clifton re-ordained in 1934 at the Nishi Honganji in Kyoto (photo licensed by Corbis).

October 17, 1934, and became a Dharma teacher on December 18, 1934, and *kaikyōshi* the next day[78] (Fig. 3). Prosser likewise took a second ordination in Kyoto on August 15, 1936, and Alex White on December 15, 1939. White became Dharma teacher on October 1, 1940, and *kaikyōshi* on March 14, 1941.[79] Goldwater had previously taken initiation in Honolulu under Bishop Imamura in July 1928, but repeated it with Masuyama on June 7, 1934. He further took ordination on April 15, 1937.[80]

How well the Euro-Americans ministers understood the Shin Buddhist teaching was also unclear. Brodbeck, who took ordination under Bishop Uchida, made a vow of entrusting himself to Amida Buddha, yet emphasized the importance of keeping the precepts (a more Theravadin approach to praxis).

Brodbeck's Confession

Rejecting all religious austerities, I rely upon [Amida] Buddha, the Eternal Life, with the whole heart, for our salvation in the future life, as well as in the present: believing that at the moment of my faith in [Amida] Buddha my salvation is completed. From that moment invocation of his name is observed to express gratitude and thankfulness for Buddha's love. Being thankful for the reception of this doctrine from the founder, I keep the precepts which are fixed for my duty during my life. Namu-Amida-Butsu.[81]

Reciting Amida's name in gratitude for Buddha's compassion was one of the orthodox Shin doctrines; however, keeping precepts was not. Prosser, Goldwater, Pratt, Udale, and White all agreed that Śākyamuni's philosophy was much more rational than Christianity, as blind faith was not involved. They considered the notions of enlightenment, nirvana, compassion, and wisdom most appealing, but never mentioned Shinran. Interestingly enough however, their pictures, except for Prosser's, show that they did not shave their heads, like the Japanese Shin clergy, who also did not shave their heads (Fig. 4).[82] Their practice suggests that they either

REV. JULIUS A. GOLDWATER   REV. KENNETH PROSSER

REV. SUNYA N. PRATT

REV. S. ALEX WHITE   REV. FRANK BODEN UDALE

Fig. 4. Five Caucasian priests. From *Why I Became a Buddhist* (courtesy Buddhist Churches of America).

adapted themselves only outwardly, or understood Shinran's attitude of "neither monk nor layman," since he had not shaved his head and called himself Gutoku ("stubble-haired").[83]

Julius Goldwater played a significant role in the propagation of Buddhism in Los Angeles. He was Jewish and a relative of Senator Barry Goldwater, and he was the first Caucasian to become a Buddhist priest in L.A.[84] He had become interested in Buddhism in Honolulu in 1924 when he met Carl Scheid, a resident of Yakima, Washington, a German who had moved to Hawaii after his wife's death and studied Buddhism.[85] With his ordination, Goldwater actively organized the Buddhist Brotherhood of Americans at the Nishi Honganji Los Angeles Buddhist Temple and helped the Issei clergy. He delivered Dharma sermons in English at major services and held study classes for English-speaking people.[86] With an emphasis on the basic doctrine of Buddhism, he introduced Caucasians to the *Tannishō,* the most well-known text in Shin Buddhism.[87]

Sunya Pratt, born in England on February 6, 1898, moved to Tacoma, Washington, and became America's first female Buddhist priest.[88] The ordination ceremony took place in front of the altar at the Tacoma Buddhist Church, officiated by Masuyama and assisted by Goldwater, on April 23, 1936, in the presence of her two children (Fig. 5). Pratt also knew something of Shinran's teaching. She discussed the limitation of self-power and the importance of faith:

Fig. 5. Sunya Pratt ordained in 1936 in Tacoma. Officiating is Bishop Kenju Masuyama; on the right is Julius Goldwater (licensed by AP Images).

> [T]rusting to the instructions left by Buddha, to repress doubting until results show themselves, and to have faith that within us is that power which can and will attain—the power of Amida Buddha.[89]

Pratt seemed capable of connecting the faith aspect of Shin Buddhism with the teachings of Śākyamuni Buddha, as she studied Shin texts in English. These texts were obtained from Gendō Nakai in Japan, who had been the resident minister of the Seattle Buddhist Church between 1902 and 1907.[90] In one of her letters to the BMNA English Department, dated November 24, 2505 (Buddhist calendar year), she writes:

> Dear Brother,
>   I have just been looking up the list of books I mentioned when I visited you, especially referring to Shin Shu, and have found the following sent me by Rev. Gendo Nakai, many of which you may already have.
>   The Praise of Amida [by] K. Tada
>   Selected Essays [of] Kiyozawa Manshi
>   Shinran and His Work [by] Arthur Lloyd
>   The Tannisho translated [by] Ryokyo (Ryūgyō) Fujimoto
>   Buddhabhasita Amitatyuh Sutra [translated by] Utsuki

The Discourse on Buddhist Paradise [by] Utsuki

The Essence of Japanese Buddhism [by] R. Tsunoda

The Ideals of the Shinran Followers [by] G. Matsutani

Principal Teachings of the True Sect of Pure Land [by] Y. Okusa

A Catechism of The Shin Sect [by] A. K. Reischauer

A Study of Shin Buddhism [by] Gessho Sasaki

Shinranism in Mahayana Buddhism and the Modern World [by] T. Takahashi and J. Izumida

Buddhism and Faith [by] Masatoshi Mori

Synopsis of the Jodo Shinshu Creed

Life of the Shonin Shinran [by] Gessho Sasaki and [D.] T. Suzuki

Hymns of the Pure Land [by] Oshima

And of course Shinran and His Religion of Pure Faith by Rev. Nakai.

The other publications are mostly already on the list that you already have. Dr. Goddard's books can be obtained from the Dwight Doddard Estate Thetford Vermont.

[I] Am feeling quite sleepy after my trip—and am endeavoring to get everything caught up before the weekend.

My best regards to yourself and your wife, and all the good wishes in the world. Please give my respects to O Socho San.

Yours in [the] Buddha

(signed) Sunya Pratt.[91]

In most of her letters, Pratt uses the year-count based on the Buddha's entry into nirvana (or the year that Buddha was born). The year 2505 suggests 1939, and "O Socho San" means bishop. The person Pratt addressed as "Dear Brother" is unknown, but it was probably Tansai Terakawa, who was in charge of the English program at the time. Although living in Tacoma, Pratt kept in close contact with the BMNA office, continued to be a member of the BCA after World War II, and served at the Tacoma Buddhist Church until her death on February 11, 1986.[92]

Goldwater and Pratt admitted other Caucasians. Goldwater initiated eight people on June 17, 1934; another eight on January 13, 1935; five on August 17, 1935; and three in September 1936. As of 1939, he had been planning to admit another four in September.[93] Together with Tatsuya Ichikawa, Pratt held initiation services for six Caucasians in February 2503 (probably 1937).[94] She reported to the BMNA English Department whenever she admitted new members to the Seattle Buddhist Church.[95] Other Euro-American ministers might have done the same at their locations, but there are no records available to confirm this.

Despite the growing presence of Caucasians in the BMNA, their commitment to the organization varied. During the 1920s, Robert Clarke thought that he would be able to help lessen discrimination against Japanese immigrants by demonstrating similarities between Buddhism and Christianity to the American public. In a heroic tone, he addressed the Japanese pioneers: "Are you willing to back me up with the necessary funds, and are you willing to work to bring a better understanding between yourselves and your brothers, the American people?" Clarke planned to visit churches on the Pacific Coast, introduce the Buddhist teachings to Caucasians, and publish a Buddhist journal, but this enterprise was expensive. He requested a group of Japanese to pay him $300 per month on top of his travel, lodging, and advertising expenses.[96] It is unknown whether Bishop Sasaki supported his plan or not. At any rate, Clarke's name does not appear in the BMNA English Department after 1930, which may suggest that he left the organization. His motivation might have been in question or perhaps he was unable to work with the Issei clergy.

Robert Clifton once sought to expand his power within the BMNA. When he went to Japan to receive second ordination, he spoke at the Tsukiji (Nishi) Honganji in Tokyo on December 8, 1934. He also petitioned the Kyoto headquarters to recognize his authority as head of the BMNA English program. At that time, Clifton was planning to establish more Buddhist societies in Chicago, New York, and Washington D.C.[97] Despite his initial enthusiasm, however, he left the BMNA in 1935 for unknown reasons. Upon receiving a Federal Bureau of Investigation (FBI) inquiry concerning Clifton during the Pacific War, Kumata, who was helping Bishop Matsukage at the time, sent a letter to Terakawa on April 1, 1942, to inquire about Clifton's whereabouts. Terakawa replied:

I do not know where he is at present. Rev. Seki in New York City might know because he told me at [the] minister's conference last year that Clifton had visited his temple several times. . . .

He visited Japan about September of 1934. I do not know who they were but some Japanese Buddhists financed his trip. He toured Japan lecturing on Buddhism. He received formal ordination from Hongwanji and returned to America about January of 1935.

Upon his return, he organized the International Buddhist Institute, opening [an] office on Pine Street near [the] Headquarters, but it lasted only a month or so and then closed for reasons unknown.

In [the] early summer of that year, he left San Francisco leaving word that he was entering a sanitarium because of his health. Never since we have received any communication or information concerning him whatsoever until April 1937, when he wrote to Bishop Masuyama from New Jersey saying that he was married. . . .[98]

Be that as it may, Clifton left the order and discontinued his communication with the BMNA. But records show that he founded the Western Buddhist Order in London on October 24, 1952, together with Hunt and others. He was ordained again in Laos in 1955 (supposedly in the Theravada tradition). After assisting the Penang Buddhist Association in Malaysia, he died there on February 6, 1963.[99]

Alex White, similarly to Clifton, also requested the BMNA office to expand its operation. White asked both the Nishi Honganji Kyoto headquarters and BMNA office to propagate Buddhism in the United States. During his stay in Japan from October 1939 to April 1940, the Nishi administrators asked him to report on the current situation of Buddhism in America. White later wrote in a letter to Bishop Matsukage:

> I have proved my sincerity and my competence to the highest authorities of Hongwanji and as a token of their appreciation of my work they conferred upon me such honors as have never before been granted to any man of my race. They realized where my sympathies are, and still, owing to the age old game of church politics, no action has yet been taken on the innumerable things they themselves perforce admitted as well worth of urgent consideration.[100]

White was concerned with the aging Issei congregation and the growing number of Buddhist sympathizers. In his mind, however, the BMNA had been using the Japanese style of propagation for the past fifty years. He called for its leaders to study American psychology, establish military chaplains and a Buddhist university empowered by the laws of the state of California, and restructure its English Department so as to develop Nisei education programs and reorganize the YBA.[101]

Because Caucasian ministers' commitment to the BMNA and the HHMH differed, there were several instances of suspicion among the Caucasian clergy and laity. Pratt reported to the BMNA that on May 24, 2505 (probably 1939), *The Tacoma Times* published an interview with Fred McIntosh, whom Masuyama had initiated on April 22, 1936. In the article she found major discrepancies in McIntosh's understanding of Buddhism.[102] Another instance shows that Clifton warned the BMNA office about Frances Geske somewhere between 1933 and 1934.

> Dear Mr. Sasaki,—
>
> Frances Geske's address is number 605 Alcatraz Ave., Oakland. I made this inquiry at the request of Bishop Masuyama and Mr. Terakawa.
>
> Also I discovered that he is planning to do many things that would be very harmful to Buddhism. It is very necessary to have him come over here and have a talk and surrender his certificate before it is too late.

He is trying to get engagements in vaudeville theatres as an ex-Buddhist priest and has also offered his services to a Christian Church in Oakland to "expose" Buddhism. You see how serious this is.

Sincerely,

R. Clifton.

Will you please call this to Bishop Masuyama's attention?[103]

The Buddhist faith of the Caucasians who took "initiation" and even ordination was uncertain. At the same time, it was difficult for the Issei clergy to discern their real motivations to become ministers and their levels of understanding Buddhism. Despite these problems, the BMNA office had created an annual budget of $200 by 1936 to assist in the propagation of Buddhism to Euro-Americans (*hakujin dendō*). The bishop was further obliged to obtain additional money from the Kyoto headquarters for this project.[104]

Though the relationship between Issei ministers and Caucasian clerics was not always amicable, there was one instance of trans-sectarian alliance between a Euro-American monk of the Tibetan Buddhist tradition and Shin ministers. In 1936, at the San Diego Buddhist Temple, B. A. Baird often officiated at services with Hōzen Seki and Yoshinao Ōuchi. Baird had studied in the Tibetan lamasery of Chorten Nyima for four years. After being ordained, he returned to the United States and began propagation in San Francisco. He eventually came back to San Diego, where he had spent his childhood, and joined the two Shin Buddhist priests. Despite his religious background, Baird appeared to have dressed in robes identical to those worn by the Shin clergy (instead of typical Tibetan Buddhist robes), which suggests that he also incorporated Shin practice into his liturgy.[105]

Further Expansion of the BMNA in the 1930s

The BMNA advanced to New York during the late 1930s. Based on the assessment of Hōzen Seki, who had founded the Arizona Bukkyōkai in 1933, Masuyama negotiated with the Kyoto headquarters to subsidize Seki's project with an annual budget of ¥1,200 for two years, beginning in 1936. Masuyama states:

It is rare to find a minister in the BMNA who would dare to go to places where Buddhism had not taken root and dedicate his entire life to propagation. Reverend Seki's success in Arizona would be an unusual enterprise nowadays. I ask the headquarters to consider providing extra care to such outstanding ministers. The advancement to New York has been one of our concerns, but we neither collected money nor found a candidate who could carry out such a mission in the past. I believe that Seki is the most adequate for this project.[106]

By the mid-1930s, the growth of the Buddhist churches on the Pacific Coast had been stabilized, so Masuyama sought a further eastward transmission of Buddhism with the headquarters' support. Seki was a man of adventure and previously had helped the BMNA advance in Mexico.[107]

In September 1936, the BMNA officials initiated a campaign, "Flying Propagation to the East Coast," and publicized the dedication of a statue of Amida Buddha at the New York Bukkyōkai. Two Nisei pilots, Katsumasa (Benny) Chōjin and Katsumasa (John) Takemoto, YBA members of Oakland and Alameda, respectively, planned to make a nonstop flight from Alaska to Tokyo. In preparation for this unique event, the BMNA's campaign to New York fulfilled their test flight. They flew from Alameda to New York, making brief stops to collect donations from various Buddhist churches. Seki carried the statue and three different kinds of gifts with him: Buddhist sutras for the President of the United States, Franklin D. Roosevelt, fresh fruit and vegetables from Guadalupe and Salinas for the Japanese ambassador, and a souvenir for the Japanese consul and the Japanese residents of New York. Many Japanese corporations, including banks and trading companies in New York, also supported Masuyama's project.[108] Seki felt that such a public display was necessary in order to impress the Japanese residents of New York, who had earlier rejected Buddhism because of the presence of three Japanese Christian churches.[109]

With the establishment of Buddhist churches in the 1930s, the activities of the *fujinkai* (the Buddhist Women's Association, BWA) also expanded. As one of the early organizations, the BWA, often led by the resident minister's wife, had operated in the background in nearly all churches.[110] In a recent study, Aya Honda analyzes the social network of the Seattle Buddhist Church's BWA in the prewar era. There were two aspects of its activities, religious and social. Religious activities included serving refreshments after services (*reikai*) and making arrangements for home services (*katei shūkai*) for those unable to attend the temple on a regular basis. Social activities included visiting church members at home to celebrate marriages and births and paying calls on those who were hospitalized. The BWA also set up cultural classes to teach culinary and sewing skills.[111]

According to Honda, the Seattle BWA grew to become one of the church's decision-making groups during the 1930s. When new church buildings were being constructed, members of the BWA designed the kitchen facilities. At major services, their representatives delivered congratulatory messages to the congregation. Their proficiency in raising funds was reflected in their ability to collect and donate $6,000 for new construction. The BWA skillfully coordinated gatherings of the congregation and hosted various cultural festivals. For instance, Honda writes, "[T]he bon Odori could not have functioned without the Fujinkai's involvement."[112] In 1938, the Seattle church's BWA even initiated the Northwest Buddhist Women's Federation (Seihokubu Bukkyō Fujin Renmei), which brought together the activities of local Buddhist women in Portland, Oregon; and Yakima, White River, and Tacoma, Washington.[113]

Buddhist women in North America were closely linked with their counterparts in Japan. In 1908, the Nishi Honganji headquarters in Kyoto had founded the Federation of Buddhist Women's Associations, encompassing one hundred and twenty-one local groups throughout the country.[114] Buddhist women in the United States purchased the monthly journal *Buddhist Women* (*Bukkyō fujin*), published by the Federation, and donated money to their counterparts in Japan. During the 1930s, they even sent "comfort bags," which contained small items necessary for overseas travel, to Japanese soldiers stationed in Manchuria.[115]

Due to the strong presence of the BWA, the role of women in the ministry gained more attention during the 1930s. In 1933, BMNA officials discussed the possibility of setting up a ministerial training program for women, but because of budget limitations and other priorities, adoption of the proposal was postponed.[116] Prior to this, the BMNA office had promoted assistant female clerics (*kyōshi* 教士, different from *kyōshi* 教師, "Dharma teacher") and recognized a handful of such women on January 14, 1925.[117] In 1909, Nishi Honganji officials in Kyoto developed a system of clerical assistants who were both men and women. Assistant priests were those who had only taken confirmation rites; they were not in a position to officiate at Buddhist services, though the headquarters allowed them to deliver daily sermons.[118] On the mainland, assistant female clerics served as Sunday school teachers.

There was another female minister at the BMNA besides Pratt. Aiko Hotta, an active member in Seattle, studied Buddhism in Japan between the late 1920s and early 1930s. During her stay, she met Hōjun Sugimoto and married him. She was ordained as Aijun Sugimoto and assisted her husband, who also became a minister of the BMNA.[119] Unfortunately she died in a car accident in 1932.[120]

In Hawaii, Imamura's investment in Nisei Buddhist women bore fruit during the 1930s. He awarded scholarships to Hatsuko Yamauchi, Kinu Hirasa, Misao Ichikawa, Mitsue Hamada, and Tsugiko Noda, who then traveled to Japan to study at the Wariko Kai's Higher Girls' School (present-day

Kyoto Women's University) and the Buddhist Central Institute in Kyoto.[121] Almost all of them received ordination (*tokudo*) and the status of Dharma teacher (*kyōshi*) between 1932 and 1934. In addition, the head temple ordained Tomiko Ōhara and Yoshiko Shimabukuro in 1938. Although further research is needed on their involvement in the HHMH after their return to Hawaii, some of the women members kept the mission open when the War Relocation Authority transferred the ministers to internment camps on the mainland.[122]

The Relationships between the Headquarters, the BMNA, and the HHMH

Differences in the number of female Nisei ministers and of Euro-American clerics in Hawaii and on the mainland show that the BMNA and the HHMH had separate programs and different relationships to the Kyoto headquarters. The head temple in Japan (*honzan*) supervised propagation on the mainland and continued to pay the BMNA bishop's stipend and its Endowment Foundation (Hokubei Kaikyō Zaidan).[123] When the BMNA created the bishop's office in Canada in 1933, Masuyama requested from the Kyoto headquarters an annual budget of ¥1,200 for propagation in Canada.[124] How much the Kyoto headquarters financed the operation of the HHMH is unclear, but if Imamura's description is correct, the HHMH was a self-sufficient organization.

The Kyoto headquarters strived to maintain its bonds with the districts of Hawaii and continental North America. It fostered a sense of belonging to the head temple in the Issei and Nisei congregations in two ways. First, based on Masuyama's request in 1931 and 1932, the headquarters rewarded those who had dedicated themselves to the development of the BMNA, including the establishment of local Buddhist churches and the Endowment Foundation.[125] Masuyama also succeeded in negotiating with the leaders of the Fresno Buddhist Church when they asked the BMNA office and Kyoto headquarters to subsidize a debt of $13,000. By giving letters of appreciation and gifts sent by the headquarters to those who made extra efforts to rebuild the church, Masuyama encouraged others to do the same.[126] It is most likely that Hawaiian Shin Buddhists also received rewards from Japan in like manner.

Second, the Kyoto headquarters sent members of the abbot's family (*renshi*) to the BMNA and the HHMH to encourage the clergy and laity. The impact of Son'yū Ōtani's tour to the mainland and Hawaii in 1925 and 1926 was tremendous. He conducted confirmation ceremonies (*kikyō shiki*), lectured on Buddhism, read out the abbot's statement (somewhat like a papal encyclical), and officiated at commemorative services. Through the appearance of an Ōtani family member, the laity donated a considerable amount of money to the HHMH and the BMNA.[127]

In the English-speaking districts of the Nishi Honganji, the bishops of these two organizations should have shared similar goals in spreading the Dharma, but there hardly seemed any collaboration between the two. Uchida and Imamura did not establish a strategic alliance (they were distant relatives). Knowing that Uchida would eventually return to Japan, ministers in Hawaii suggested that Imamura should serve as General Bishop, uniting the HHMH and the BMNA.[128] Imamura himself realized, after his study tour of the continental United States in fall 1918, the necessity of transferring the center of Buddhist propagation to the mainland.[129] It was not until 1938, however, that the BMNA office recognized the need for an exchange program for ministers in Hawaii and on the mainland.[130]

The dialogue between Imamura and the leaders of the BMNA also appeared to be quite formal, business-like discussions that avoided bigger themes such as the future of Jōdo Shinshū in America (but also in a sense too informal, as the discussion was wide-ranging; however, since it was not done in an official setting, no notes were taken). Records show that Imamura from time to time exchanged correspondence with Uchida, Sasaki, Masuyama, and Kusuhara; however, their exchanges appeared to be perfunctory, such as discussing extending the trips of Japanese visitors from Honolulu to the mainland and notifying one another of Son'yū Ōtani's itinerary.[131] Since the BMNA bishops almost always stopped over in Hawaii on their way back and forth from San Francisco to Japan, Imamura would have had opportunity and reason to communicate with them, but there are no available records of such communications.[132] Judging from the orientation of religious programs, it was less likely that the leaders of these two organizations reciprocated their visions of future propagation, and, as it appeared, the BMNA and the HHMH kept their distance from each other.

Summary

The acculturation of an organizational structure took place in the development of the ministry. Issei clergy faced financial hardship due to the necessity of constructing new church buildings and the economic depression in the United States, which affected the immigrants' livelihood. The creation of a Nisei ministerial program showed an aspect of Japanization and the Issei clergy's ambivalence concerning its attachment to and departure from Japanese practices. The establishment of an English department was a sign of Americanization, leading to a major deviation from tradition. But this process stagnated when the Kyoto headquarters and the BMNA office required Euro-Americans to maintain Japanese cultural practices. Several Caucasians were at the same time unsure about their Buddhist identity. The primary mission of the English department was to promote Śākyamuni's teachings in America, particularly true in the case of the BMNA, where Uchida and Masuyama ordained several Caucasians, in contrast to the HHMH, where Imamura ordained only the Hunts.

The 1930s was a critical period for the development of these two organizations. In Hawaii, Imamura and Hunt sought a cosmopolitan Buddhism through nonsectarian and international ties. After Imamura's death in 1932, however, the HHMH discontinued its search. In this respect, Ruth Tabrah writes:

> In the eight years since Yemyo [Emyō] Imamura's death his idea of a cosmopolitan, American Buddhism as the focus of the Hawaii Mission had not been carried forward. The ideal, like his vision of worldwide propagation, was to become a temporary casualty of the war years ahead, and to remain dormant for at least a decade following the deep emotional wounds of World War II.[133]

Imamura's successors did not carry out the further organizational development he had envisioned. The HHMH English Department nearly dissolved when Bishop Kuchiba dismissed Ernest Hunt. On the mainland, Masuyama and his successor, Matsukage, succeeded in expanding the BMNA in the 1930s. Masuyama reformed the BMNA and created seven departments: the English Department, YBA, Sunday School, Education, Propagation, Publication, and Social Affairs. He celebrated the construction of a new building together with the dedication of a stupa for the Buddha's relics and permitted the independence from the BMNA of Canadian propagation efforts. While Imamura made basic Buddhism available to the Caucasians with the intention of universalizing Shinran's teaching, Uchida and Masuyama promoted Śākyamuni's teachings as the key objective of the BMNA. It was not until the late 1930s that the BMNA office began to promote Shin Buddhism in English in cooperation with the Kyoto headquarters' Translation Department.

The expectations of the Nisei and, in particular, the Caucasians of the BMNA and the HHMH compelled the Issei Shin clergy to loosen the configuration of its ministry. The heads of the two orders admitted Caucasians by performing rituals for them, but since liturgy required the attendee's active participation, confirmation and ordination ceremonies also deviated from tradition. The transformation of worship is the subject of Chapter Four.

Chapter Four

The Transformation of
Shin Buddhist Rituals
and Architecture

Victor Turner defines the performance of ritual as "distinctive phases in the social process, whereby groups and individuals adjust to internal changes and adapt to their external environment."[1] Issei Shin ministers at first practiced the ritual protocol prescribed by their head temple in Kyoto. Previous studies have said that Buddhist rituals became Protestantized when Issei ministers attempted to keep the interest of and cater to the demands of young Nisei followers. Referring to Isao Horinouchi, Carl Becker, for instance, writes:

> Since few white Americans ever set foot inside a Buddhist church in America, much less stay for a whole service, there was little pressure from the Americans themselves. Rather, the [I]ssei, or first-generation Japanese, desired to show their loyalty to their new country and culture by adopting more aspects of Western derivation; and the [N]isei, or second generation, were leaving the Buddhist fold at rates that made the [I]ssei in charge feel that only further Americanization could stem the tide of their dissatisfaction.[2]

In the early propagation of Buddhism in the United States, the Japanese immigrants themselves sought alterations to the rituals. Becker's assessment is correct: The sequencing of the Buddhist service, the music, pews, and even church architecture were signs of adapting to Christian forms.[3] But this represents only one aspect of the acculturation. When Americanization and Japanization of Shin ritual are woven together, the acculturation of the Buddhist service appears to be more complex. First, ritual practice appeared to be discursive in the early period of Shin propagation. Only during the 1930s did the BMNA standardize the procedure of major annual services and work out a dress code for ministers. Second, the composition of Buddhist songs or hymns, known as *gathas,* demonstrates not only a two-way process of acculturation but also the re-importation of the hymnal to the Buddhist community in Japan and the BMNA's borrowing of the hymnal from the HHMH. Third, clerical leaders emulated Theravada rituals for the initiation and ordination of Caucasians, diverging from traditional Shin practice in Japan. Finally, since the facilities of missions and churches were the center of Buddhist ritual activities, the second half of this chapter investigates the relationship between variations of architectural design and cultural practices of Shin Buddhists.

Ritual Transformed

Early Services

There were two types of services in the early period of propagation: regular and special. Regular services usually consisted of reading a scriptural passage, reciting Amida's name, and singing a hymn.[4] Regular services initially appeared as "sermons" (*sekkyō*). On the mainland in the late 1900s, sermons were given on Sunday evenings between 7:00 and 8:00. The Buddhist Church of Oakland, however, offered sermons at 3:00 P.M. on Sundays, and the Watsonville Buddhist Church at 2:00 P.M. on Saturdays and Sundays.[5] The scheduling of Sunday services was meant to accommodate the laity's work schedule, such as working on Sundays, demanded of workers in seasonal jobs.[6] During the 1900s the Hawaii Betsuin held regular services at 2:00 P.M. each Sunday and at 7:00 P.M. on the 16th and 18th of every month. These services were accompanied by a weekly Sunday school session beginning at 9:00 A.M., and a gathering of the Buddhist Women's Association, which met at 2:00 P.M. or 7:00 P.M. on the first Sunday of each month.[7] To cater to the demands of Euro-American Buddhist sympathizers, the clergy of the Buddhist Church of San Francisco and the Los Angeles Rafu Bukkyōkai separated Shin sermons and lectures on Śākyamuni's doctrines.[8]

Special services were annual commemorative events, such as the celebration of the births of Śākyamuni and Shinran, *Hōonkō* (the service honoring Shinran's passing), and *Ohigan* (services performed during the spring and fall equinoxes). Although attendance at regular services was modest, usually no more than fifty people, attendees at special services easily exceeded one hundred.[9] Donations given at special services were important financial sources for the church. The Issei pioneers in North America also celebrated *Kigen-setsu* (marking the advent of Emperor Jinmu's rule in Japan) and *Tenchō-setsu* (Emperor Meiji's birthday). At the inauguration and graduation ceremonies of Japanese language schools affiliated with Buddhist missions in Hawaii, Shin ministers often read the Imperial Rescript on Education.[10]

For the commemoration of Śākyamuni's birthday, Shin ministers invited Buddhist sympathizers to their services. The clergy of the Buddhist Church of San Francisco and the Rafu Bukkyōkai in Los Angeles held services in both English and Japanese. In San Francisco, the congregation gathered twice on

April 12, 1908. The English-language service began at 11:00 A.M. with ring-ing the temple bell, followed by singing a *gatha,* recitation of a sutra and sutra passages, singing another *gatha,* the pronouncement of a congratu-latory message, two sermons, and singing one more *gatha.* The *gatha* singing was accompanied by an organ or piano. Shin minister Kaizō Kii delivered a Buddhist sermon on the theme "A Vivid Manifestation of Truth," and Dr. Mazzininanda spoke on "Buddha, His Life and Bachin [*sic*]." After the service, the Buddhist Women's Association offered refreshments. The Japanese service, which began at 7:30 P.M., was twice as long as the English one and included an expression of homage, congratulatory mes-sages delivered by representatives of the church's various organizations, and a sermon.[11]

In Los Angeles, the congregation celebrated Śākyamuni's birthday along with Shinran's. On May 20 and 21, 1916, there were three Japanese services, starting at 2:00 P.M. and 7:00 P.M. on Saturday, and 6:00 P.M. on Sunday. All services were accompanied by violin, piano, choir, and classical Japanese in-struments. The English service, which started at 3:00 P.M. on Sunday, con-sisted of five sermons: "Birth of Buddha" by Shin minister Tetsugai Jisōji, "Buddha from the Theosophical Viewpoint" by A. P. Warrington, "A Greater Humanity" by F. B. Austin, "Every Man and Woman My Brethren" by John Milton Scott, and "Friendship" by C. C. Pierce.[12]

In addition to these regular and special services, ministers had other re-ligious obligations. On the mainland, they visited groups of families who lived in communities far from the church and held sermons for gather-ings of regional followers (*chihō sekkyō* or *shucchō dendō*). In Hawaii, min-isters made propagation trips to nearby plantations (*kōchi dendō*). Issei clergy also officiated at funerals, memorial services, and weddings.

Shin Marriage Ceremonies

Scholars have previously concluded that officiating at weddings was a new Buddhist phenomenon in North America and that it represents a form of Protestantization. The procedure of Buddhist weddings was patterned after the style in the Episcopal Church, including such features as the bride's wearing a white wedding gown, bridesmaids, flower girls, veil bear-ers, and the performance of traditional popular music such as the *Wedding March.*[13] Referring to the practice of exchanging *juzu* (a string of beads sim-ilar to a Catholic rosary), Horinouchi writes:

> I believe that the placing of the "juzu" or rosary . . . over the hands of the
> bride and bridegroom is a substitute form of the wedding ring. Today, this
> juzu ceremony is one phase of the wedding that is uniquely Buddhistic in

form. Both bride and bridegroom receive a special juzu or rosary that symbolizes their marriage to each other.

In a brief explanation of the metamorphosis of a Buddhist wedding, we can conclude that Buddhism as an indigenous religion from Japan had had no formal experience with performing weddings in Japan. Buddhists were forced to accept a modified version of a wedding format established by Christianity in America. . . .[14]

Horinouchi simply traced the origin of the Buddhist wedding to the Christian tradition. Shin Buddhism in Japan, however, has had a long history of matrimony and a system of a son's inheritance of the temple from his parents. Shin priests emulated Shinran, who had renounced his monastic vows and married Eshinni. Records show that the Higashi Honganji Diet systematized the Buddhist marriage service in 1917. In 1923, the Federation of Shinshū Branches outlined procedures for the wedding service as a response both to local priests, who had been performing them at their own discretion, and to Crown Prince Hirohito's marriage in 1924.[15] These events suggest that the standardization of Shin nuptial rites in Japan occurred between the late 1910s and early 1920s.

Horinouchi also overlooked the fact that there had been a diversity of Buddhist wedding services in North America in the 1900s. As early as 1908, Bishop Imamura received permission from the territorial government to perform marriage ceremonies. Horinouchi speculated that Buddhist weddings on the mainland did not begin until 1914 or 1915.[16] However, Ronald Magden has recently shown that Gendō Nakai in Seattle officiated at one hundred and ninety Buddhist weddings from 1902 to 1907, because of the sudden influx of so-called "picture brides" after the Gentlemen's Agreement in 1908,[17] and Hōshin Fujii, Nakai's successor, carried out one hundred and ninety-five in 1910 alone. Fujii even conducted group weddings at the U.S. Immigration Office and in the dining rooms of Japanese ships on their arrival in Seattle.[18] During this period, Hiseki Miyazaki also held a nuptial service for the first time for a Caucasian couple on Kauai on January 9, 1909. In Honolulu, Kirby performed his first Buddhist wedding for a German bridegroom and his English bride in October 1925.[19]

What was unique to Issei Shin clergy was officiating at weddings in English.[20] In this transition, exchanging juzu and marriage rings became part of the wedding rites in Hawaii.[21] It is unclear whether the former practice first began in Hawaii and was later introduced to Japan, or vice versa; but the practice of exchanging rings had not been common for a Buddhist couple in Japan. (Exchanging juzu was recognized by the aforementioned Federation of Shinshū Branches.) Kissing in public was taboo for Buddhists both in Japan and in the Nikkei community, since such public displays of affection were rarely done in these cultures.[22]

The Standardization of Rituals and Robes

BMNA officials standardized the format of services in the mid-1930s. They defined a total of eight special annual services as of 1931: the New Year's Day celebration (*Shūshō-e*) on January 1st; the commemoration of Shinran's passing (*Goshōki*) held either on January 15th or in November, depending on the use of the lunar calendar; Nirvana Day (*Nehan-e*) on February 15th; spring and fall equinox services (*Higan-e*); the celebration of Śākyamuni's birthday during the week of April 8th; the celebration of Shinran's birth during the week of May 21st; and *Obon* in either July or August. Buddhist churches also honored Shōtoku Taishi in March, but no longer listed services connected with the celebration of imperial holidays. In 1933, the BMNA office set up the procedures for these services and the singing of *gathas* became routine. A sample of standard services became available, including a general sermon, wedding, funerary and memorial rites, and group services for the Buddhist Women's Association (*fujinkai*), the YMBA/YWBA, and the Sunday school.[23] The Hawaii Betsuin had also well systematized its regular services by the 1930s. According to an observation recorded in 1937:

> Regular services of the Honpa Hongwanji are held every Sunday at the temple for different age groups, and here also the innovations from the [W]est are apparent. The most obvious innovations are found in the four sections of pews which fill a large portion of the spacious hall, and in the [W]estern pipe organ, choir, and pulpit located to the right of the highly ornate Buddhist altar. Beginning at 6:30 am on Sundays, there is a sunrise service at the temple for adults. The children's ceremony for grade [school] children begins at 8:40 am for half an hour and serves as a brief gathering in the temple hall of all the Sunday School children prior to an instructional period which is conducted at the Fort Street Japanese Grammar School. The High School group's service which is conducted immediately after the children's service is mainly for young people between the ages of twelve and eighteen years. Student boarders at the high school dormitories are required to attend this service, which consists of several chants, responses, and hymns. The noisy conversations of the boys in the left section and the girls in the right section of the temple quickly subside as the organ begins to play and all bow their heads and press the palms of their hands together in silent meditation. The next hour is devoted to the young people's service. The addition of a sermon makes this service slightly different from the preceding high school service. Occasionally the sermon is delivered in English, but more often it is given in Japanese.

Congregational singing, accompanied by the organ, gives these services a distinctly [W]estern atmosphere.

The older people, mainly those between the ages of forty and sixty, gather at 1:30 in the afternoon to worship. This service is conducted entirely in Japanese and retains more of the Oriental flavor. Most of the women are dressed in the traditional ceremonial kimonos and many have their ceremonial "haoris" or coats. The entire congregation averages about seventy-five elderly men and women. Many arrive at the temple before the hour to enjoy a bit of visiting. The service is begun by the striking of the gong—at first slow and loud with the tempo gradually increased and the volume decreased. This is repeated several times. The congregation sits in silence until the sound from the gong has died away. Then the priests, seated before and to the side of the image of Buddha, begin to chant, followed by the people, some aided by books and some from memory, while still others remain silent. After twenty minutes of chanting, the priests lift to their faces the books from which they have been reading, and then replace them on the small desks in front of them. Then rising, they all leave. Later the head priest or a visiting priest reappears alone, and delivers his sermon from the pulpit.[24]

Sunday services became stratified according to age, and Issei and Nisei ministers delivered sermons in Japanese and English, respectively.

The BMNA office announced a ministers' dress code in 1933 and differentiated three kinds of robes: colored (*shikie*), black (*kokue*), and one for administrative use (*fuhō*). Ministers classified their dress according to three occasions: special, general, and regular services. The special services were further divided: those including *Hōonkō,* the celebrations of Śākyamuni's and Shinran's births, weddings, and commemorative ceremonies; and those including Nirvana Day, *Obon,* and funerary and memorial rites. General services referred to those held on spring and fall equinox days and the celebration in honor of Shōtoku Taishi. Regular services included weekly sermons and public lectures. For all these occasions however, a robe was worn over a Western-style shirt and tie, not traditional Japanese clothing.[25]

The practice of wearing Western clothes underneath the robe was another sign of the Americanization and Japanization of the rituals. It may have been modeled on the dress code of the Christian clergy, but Nishi Honganji officials in Kyoto had recognized the new cultural trend of Japanese people wearing Western clothes. For informal occasions, the headquarters allowed priests to wear a robe over Western clothes (according to the "Regulation of Minister's Dress Code," 1917). Further, delegates in the representative assembly (*shūe*) debated in 1927 whether or not a minister attending a meeting could wear Western clothes.[26] One such episode describes the ambivalent feelings of the North American congregation toward clergy wearing Western clothes. When Son'yū Ōtani visited from the Kyoto headquarters and conducted a confirmation ceremony in California, he wore a robe over his Western clothes in the American style, but the laity requested that he put on a traditional kimono.[27]

The Production of *Gathas*

The systematization of rituals culminated in the publication in 1939 of *Standard Buddhist Gathas and Services: Japanese and English* (hereafter *Standard Gathas*), a prewar service book used in North America. This project involved complex exchanges among the Nishi Honganji Translation Committee in Kyoto, the BMNA, and the HHMH. There were three stages in the development of Buddhist *gathas* in the United States before World War II: the importation of Japanese songs to the United States, the use of English hymns created by the Hunts and A. R. Zorn in Hawaii, and a combination of bilingual songs.[28]

The production of Buddhist songs in Japan began at the turn of the twentieth century. A Buddhist priest in Hiroshima first published the *Buddhist Song Book for People Vol. 1* (*Tsūzoku bukkyō shōka shū dai ippen*) in 1903, which included thirty songs with each stanza accompanied by a single melody. In 1912, the Kyoto headquarters introduced its first service book, the *Sacred Text* (*Seiten*) for the clergy and laity alike, which included twenty-six songs with Western-style melodies. The fourth edition of the *Seiten,* published in 1923, was designated for the use of the BMNA. Between these years, in 1917, the HHMH compiled its own Buddhist hymnal entitled the *Praises* (*Raisan*).[29]

The *Raisan* was the forerunner of the Japanese Buddhist hymnal; the songs were sung by a choir with instrumental accompaniment. The *Raisan* debuted in 1918, when the HHMH celebrated the completion of its new mission hall. Kōsaku Yamada, a rising musician in Japan, who happened to be convalescing in Honolulu at the time, arranged the music to twelve lyrics, including "Praising the Virtue of Amida Buddha" (*Ondokusan*), the most popular Shin Buddhist hymn today. Yamada was asked to do the arrangements by Tokusui Kotani of the HHMH and his student, Yasuo Sawa, who was teaching at the HHMH Sunday school. In 1926, the *Raisan,* composed in polychordal melodies with piano/organ accompaniment, was introduced to Japan with the addition of several other pieces and became popular among young Japanese Buddhists, who had been familiar only with a single Western melody arranged to a lyric. Kōsaku Yamada's musical arrangements added to the appeal of the edited hymnal of the *Raisan.*[30]

The HHMH continued to be the leader in the composition of modern Buddhist songs. In 1924, Ernest Hunt compiled the *Vade Mecum,* the first service book in English, an anthology of one hundred and thirty-eight songs, including forty-seven written by Dorothy Hunt and fifty-one by A. R. Zorn. No musical notations were given for the one hundred and fourteen *gathas.* Although almost all of their themes were trans-sectarian, the Hunts did dedicate four hymns to Amida Buddha and Shinran.[31]

The *Vade Mecum* shows aspects of the Americanization and Japanization of Buddhist hymns. First of all, it reflected popular Christian sentiment. For example, the Hunts and Zorn portrayed Buddha as a deity, referred to him as "Lord," and even used war imagery in the description of Buddhist religion, based in similar descriptions of Christianity that were the product of Protestant triumphalism.[32] Despite these shortcomings, the *Vade Mecum* made a great impact on the systematization of the Honganji hymnal initiated by Nishū Utsuki, head of the Translation Committee in Kyoto. When the Nishi Honganji in Japan published the *Standard Gathas* in 1939, Utsuki reproduced most of the original English songs from the *Vade Mecum* since "it is [was] rather difficult to change the already prevalent forms among the younger American Buddhists."[33]

Further along in the process of making the *Standard Gathas,* there was a reversal in the course of the development of Buddhism in Hawaii. George Tanabe writes:

> The line of development of Buddhism in Hawaii did not always go from Japanese to English, as one might expect from a more simple model of cultural adaptation, and here we see that the Americanization of Buddhist worship services required Japanese hymns to follow in the pioneering footsteps of the English-only *Vade Mecum.*[34]

The success of the *Vade Mecum* in Hawaii encouraged Utsuki to compile a new hymnal, the *Standard Gathas,* integrating a collection of Japanese hymns with English ones reprinted from the *Vade Mecum.* Therefore, the *Standard Gathas,* with "no adaptation of a Japanese service book,"[35] was the most suitable for the "parallel use of both English and Japanese music and services" in "Hawaii and the American Continent."[36]

The *Standard Gathas* fit in well with the propagation of Śākyamuni's doctrines. There were fifty-seven hymns in English, of which fifty-one were reprinted from the *Vade Mecum.* Their themes included karma, morality, discipleship, and the Three Treasures (Buddha, Dharma, and Sangha). The *Standard Gathas* also contained excerpts from the *Dhammapada* and other Theravada texts.[37] There was scant mention of "rebirth in the Pure Land or faith in Amida's vow, and the lyrics use a diction that is more familiar to general Buddhism rather than the religion of Shinran." Thus, "the Theravadin flavor congenial to the Hunts" survived with "added Shinshū colors."[38]

Prior to the publication of the *Standard Gathas,* there had been several attempts to include English songs in a Japanese service book. In 1936, the Buddhist Sunday School in Canada compiled the *Buddhist Sutras and Songs* (*Kanada Nichiyō Gakko Seiten Sanbutsuka*). Also in 1936, the Kyoto headquarters published the *Sacred Shin Buddhist Text* (*Shinshū Seiten*), a revision of the *Sacred Text* published in 1912. In 1938, the *Sacred Shin Buddhist Text* was reprinted as the *Buddhist Service Book* (*Raihai Seiten*) "for the use of the temples in the United States" and replicated thirty English songs from the *Vade Mecum*.[39]

In the mainland United States, BMNA officials also endeavored to compile their own service book. In 1932, the ministers agreed to create a Buddhist hymnal in English as a way to express the American Buddhist spirit. The BMNA office encouraged the laity to write new Buddhist lyrics in either English or Japanese, and asked a group of professional musicians to select from these. Although unable to award prizes for the winners, the BMNA acknowledged applicants' efforts by printing their names in the hymnal.[40] The following year however, there was a setback in the discussion of compiling the hymnal, and the BMNA decided to use the one that the HHMH had already produced. Organizing the Japanese hymnal was also postponed because of financial limitations.[41] The BMNA service book eventually became available in 1938 together with the *Standard Gathas,* though this was probably the *Buddhist Service Book* mentioned above.[42]

While the Kyoto Translation Committee and the BMNA attempted to standardize the hymnal, local immigrants on the Big Island composed their own songs. Keiko Wells researched cases in which female Shin Buddhists in Kona wrote folksong lyrics between 1930 and 1950. They expressed their spiritual concerns openly, due to the absence of overt Christian hostility and encouraged by Shuun Matsuura, the resident minister of the Kona Honganji.[43]

Songs written by Ume Hirano were particularly self-reflective and showed the essence of Shin Buddhism. She used a traditional connotation of *oya-sama* (parent) for Amida Buddha and praised "her" virtue, creating an image of Amida as a loving mother (though it was common at that time to assign the male pronoun to Amida in English translations).[44] Hirano also conceptualized her own experience of the "turning of the mind," or conversion (*eshin*), and stressed the importance of first being in a state of despondency. Wells summarizes Hirano's ideas:

> One must fall [to give up one's ego completely] before being embraced by Amida, but one cannot be saved if one falls with any expectation of being saved. One must, Hirano taught, just fall.[45]

Hirano's interpretation was underpinned by the Shin doctrine of the twofold entrusting mind (*nishu jinshin*): understanding one's ignorance and at the same time realizing Amida's compassion. Hirano's composition testifies that the practice of singing Jōdo Shinshū themes continued among the Kona immigrants, although the *Vade Mecum* and the *Standard Gathas*, with their basic Buddhist themes, attracted the most attention among Shin congregations.

Publication of the *Standard Gathas* was part of several translation projects initiated by the Nishi Honganji in Japan in the early 1930s. Although a few people in the United States and Japan had previously rendered Japanese Buddhist texts into English, the Kyoto headquarters commenced translation work officially in 1933. Kōyū Uchida, former bishop of the BMNA, Ryūgyō Fujimoto, a former BMNA minister who had received a Master of Arts degree from the University of Southern California, and Nishū Utsuki, along with others, came up with a list of fifteen Shin Buddhist texts to be translated into English. These were *An Outline of Shinshū; The Life of Shinran Shōnin; History of Hongwanji; The Doctrinal Development of Shinshū; The Sacred Books; The Organization of Hongwanji; The Handbook of Shinshū; The Service Book; Buddhism and Shinshū; Hongwanji, Its Forces and Activities; Hongwanji, a Guide Book; National Life and Faith; Shōtoku Taishi; On the Western Views of Amida Faith;* and *Ethics of Shinshū.*[46] In 1938, the Kyoto headquarters shipped six texts, possibly the integration and editions of the fifteen mentioned above, to the BMNA office: *The Shin Sect: A School of Mahayana Buddhism; Buddhist Children's Stories; Three Lives of Buddhist Faith; The Seven Spiritual Fathers; A Living Faith;* and *Shinran and His Religion.*[47]

There is a discrepancy between the systematization of the *Standard Gathas* and the translations of these Shin Buddhist texts. Examining these lists, it is clear that the Kyoto headquarters intended to propagate Shin Buddhism at this time. The distribution of the *Standard Gathas*, however, suggested encouraging Shin members to study Theravada teachings, even though the orientations of these two forms of Buddhism were quite different. Theravadins strongly emphasize the moral teachings of Śākyamuni, whereas for Shin Amidists faith alone was the most important matter, so discussion of moral values would come only after the realization of *shinjin.*

The Nishi Honganji's difficulties in simultaneously propagating Theravada and Shin Buddhism increased when the quality of the Shin English translations was called into question. The English-language versions, translated by Japanese scholars, were still far more reflective of Japanese than English in terms of their construction and failed to reflect the

American way of thinking.[48] Limitations in transliteration suggests that neither Euro-Americans nor Nisei parishioners fully understood Shin Buddhist doctrine and its relationship to the teachings of Śākyamuni Buddha during the prewar period.

Rituals for Admitting Euro-Americans into the Order

The acculturation of Shin rituals became contorted when the BMNA modeled its ordination and initiation ceremonies for Euro-Americans on Theravadin forms. In 1933, BMNA leaders outlined the "Refuges and Precepts for Initiation of Lay Members":

> I TAKE MY REFUGE IN THE BUDDHA.
> I TAKE MY REFUGE IN THE DHARMA.
> I TAKE MY REFUGE IN THE SANGHA. (Repeat only once.)

> Kill not but have regard for life.
> Steal not but help each man to be master of the fruit of his labor.
> Keep from impurity . . . lead a life of chastity.
> Lie not, but be truthful.
> Invent not evil reports, neither repeat them.

> [The] bishop reads precepts and candidates all say together: We undertake to observe them all.

> Candidates for Initiation.
> Mr. Julian McFarland, Mr. S. Alex White, Mrs. S. Alex White, Mr. George White, Mr. Stanley White, Mr. Sanford White, Miss Lillian Lamm, Mr. B. P. O'Toole, Mr. Arnold Voland, Mr. James K. Stewart, Miss Emily Ingle, Mr. George Rosas, Miss Ella M. Pierce, Mrs. B. E. Grace, Mr. William Magistretti, Mr. Gerard Arts.[49]

In the ceremony, the candidates recited the Three Treasures and the Five Precepts, reciting after the bishop, who would not otherwise be personally bound to observe these precepts, according to Shin Buddhist tradition. The ordination ceremony was much longer than the initiation rites and was also derived from the Theravada tradition. The BMNA office drafted its procedure in the same year:

> The Ordination Ceremonial [Ceremony]. Based on the Authentic Service used today in Ceylon (present-day Sri Lanka).

> Opening Ceremony as usual.

> Adoration: Namo tassa Bhagavato Arhahato Sammsambuddhasa!

(The candidate in the dress of a layman, but having the robes of a Bhikkashu [*bhikṣu,* monk] in his arms, makes the usual obeisance to the Abbot, and standing says:)

"Grant me leave to speak. Lord, graciously grant me admission to the Sangha. (Kneels down). In compassion for me, Lord, take these robes, and let me be ordained, in order to destroy all sorrow, to attain Nirvana, and to enlighten my fellow creatures. (The Abbot takes the robes). In compassion for me, Lord, give me those robes and let me be ordained in the Brotherhood of our Lord Buddha."

(And the Abbot then bestows upon the candidate the bundle of robes, placing the band thereof around the candidate's neck, saying:)

"Brother, I do hereby ordain you a member of the Sangha."

(The candidate then rises up, and retires to throw off the dress of a layman, and to put on his robes. While he is changing his dress, he recites the following:)

"In wisdom I put on the robes. I wear them in all humility, for use only, not for ornament or show."

(Having put on the robes, he returns to his former position in front of the shrine, and says:)

"Grant me leave to speak, Lord. Graciously give me, Lord, the Three Treasures and Precepts."

(He kneels down. The Abbot gives the Three Refuges and the Precepts as follows, the candidate still kneeling and repeating them after him, sentence by sentence:)

"I take my refuge in the Buddha.
I take my refuge in the Dharma.
I take my refuge in the Sangha."

"Again I take my refuge in the Buddha.
Again I take my refuge in the Dharma.
Again I take my refuge in the Sangha."

"Once more I take my refuge in the Buddha.
Once more I take my refuge in the Dharma.
Once more I take my refuge in the Sangha."

"Kill not, but have regard for life.
Steal not, but help each man to be master of the fruit of his labor.
Keep from impurity, lead a life of chastity.
Lie not, but be truthful.
Invent not evil reports, neither repeat them.
Swear not, but speak decently and with dignity.
Waste not time in idle gossip.
Covet not, nor envy, but rejoice at another's good.

Cherish no hatred, but embrace all beings with love.
Free your mind from ignorance, be anxious to learn the Truth."

(The Candidate says:)

"I have received the Treasures and the Precepts. Thank you, Master. Namuamidabutsu!"

(The Abbot pronounces the invocation and the benediction:)

Invocation:

"O Thou Eternal One, Omniscient, Omnipresent, and Omnipotent, in loyalty and reverence, we offer Thee, gratitude and devotion, for that Thou hast enabled us, through our Lord Buddha, to learn of Thee, and to know the way to salvation. May these, Thy people, ever walk in the Holy Path, striving to free their minds from all selfish desires, until they shall have perfected themselves in purity and wisdom, for only by so doing can they enter the joy and peace of Nirvana."

(Turning to the new members of the Sangha:)

"May the Light of Amit[ā]bha, which guided the footsteps of our Lord Buddha, ever shine upon ye and illuminate thy path, so that ye may come at least to that blessed state of everlasting Peace."

After the ceremony, an oath between the bishop and candidate was exchanged. For instance:

A Promise

Shaku Rigon:

You are hereby ordained into the brotherhood with the firm promise that you will conduct yourself in accordance with the teachings and precepts of the Buddha, and that you will always endeavor and strive to be an uplifting leader of men.

In the event that your promise is unkept [sic], your dismissal will take effect.

October 19th, 1933

Signed: Bishop
Buddhist Mission of North America.

I hereby accept with the firm promise to conduct myself in accordance as outlined above.

October 19th, 1933

Signed:[50]

The initiation and ordination ceremonies for Caucasians suggest a complete divergence from the Honganji's ritual practice, as the candidates' pledge to observe the Five Precepts and/or Ten Precepts was essential in these services. Furthermore, when Julius Goldwater entered the priesthood along with the initiation of eight other Caucasians on June 17, 1934, he faced a statue of

Buddha "sitting cross-legged" on the altar of the Nishi Honganji Los Angeles Buddhist Church. The candidate, wearing robes, declared, "I have received the Three Treasures and the Ten Precepts, Namu Amida Butsu!"[51] The object of worship (*honzon*) in Jōdo Shinshū is not a statue of a sitting (Śākyamuni) Buddha, but a statue or image of a standing Amida Buddha.[52] In other words, Goldwater took the Ten Precepts and recited *Namu Amida Butsu* in front of an "unorthodox" *honzon*. Despite these differences between Theravada and Shin Buddhism, two examples of the initiation ceremony similar to the one cited above for lay members appeared in the *Standard Gathas* in 1939.[53] This suggests that the Nishi Honganij headquarters may have approved the BMNA's incorporation of the Theravadin ritual into its practice.

Architectural Co-option and Adaptation

Ritual adjustment was sought not only by modification of service styles but also by co-option and adaptation of the worship hall and exterior designs. As researchers have indicated, congregations that modeled themselves on Protestant practices used folding chairs and bench-type pews, set up a podium for sermons, had organ or piano accompaniment for services, and congregants entered the hall without removing their shoes. The adornments of the Buddhist altar, however, remained traditional, including the gong; hence, the interior of a church/temple was generally an eclectic mix of Japanese and American styles.[54]

At the same time, temple architecture was heterogeneous, reflecting the economic situation of the laity, cultural trends of the time, architects' preferences, and ministers' choices. Horinouchi argues that more than half of the Buddhist churches on the mainland before World War II were of Western-style architecture. Choosing such normative designs was one way for Shin Buddhists to avoid "arousing a negative reaction from the general society." At the same time, congregations often continued to use the Christian church building they had originally purchased if they did not have enough money to remodel it.[55] Horinouchi's analysis, however, does not apply to the study of Shin Buddhist material culture in Hawaii.[56]

Lorraine R. M. Palumbo identifies four types of Buddhist temples constructed in Hawaii between the 1890s and the outbreak of the Pacific War: in the style of a plantation house; in the style of a Japanese temple; buildings reflecting Hawaiian eclecticism; and buildings reflecting Indian/Western influence. The first three types coexisted in the period between 1896 and 1920. The last style, with elements of Asian Indian and/or Western architecture,

Fig. 6. A reminiscence of the plantation style. Photo from *A Grateful Past, A Promising Future*, p. 233 (courtesy of Honpa Hongwanji Mission of Hawaii).

predominated in temple designs from 1921 to 1941, when immigrants decided to settle permanently. During this period, many Japanese Buddhist schools founded head temples in Honolulu, following Indian/Western architectural styles, but the Honpa Honganji Betsuin was the first to complete its headquarters in 1918 with such an innovative design.[57]

Transitions between these four styles demonstrate the processes of Japanization and Americanization. The plantation house style was the most common form of temple design, since it was inexpensive, quick, and flexible to build (Fig. 6). It also produced an atmosphere of openness, without gateways, fences, or walls. The single building doubled as a temple hall and a school classroom. If there was enough space, two facilities were constructed on a single site. Unlike temples in Japan, the arrangement of the plantation house style did not allow a mission to be cut off from the surrounding neighborhood.[58]

The Japanese style became popular as early as 1898 (i.e., in the Honokaa Honganji and the Honomu Honganji), reflecting immigrants' longing for the mother country. (Fig. 7-1, 7-2) Palumbo suggests characteristics of Japanese style: a quality of homogeneity, conservation of materials and relatively straightforward construction, the use of the same precut materials (processed by a Caucasian middleman in California), and the expansion of outer sitting space. Immigrant communities could not, however, model their missions exactly on temples in Japan because of constraints in obtaining Japanese building materials.[59]

Fig. 7-1. A photo of the Honomu Honganji taken in 1900—the Japanese style. Photo from *A Grateful Past, A Promising Future*, p. 238 (courtesy of Honpa Hongwanji Mission of Hawaii).

Fig. 7-2. A photo of the Olaa Honganji Mission taken in 1907—the Japanese style. Photo from *A Grateful Past, A Promising Future*, p. 265 (courtesy of Honpa Hongwanji Mission of Hawaii).

When immigrants gave up their dreams of returning to Japan and sought permanent settlement and acceptance in Anglo-American society, they stopped holding on to traditional motifs.[60] The Hawaiian eclectic style was a combination of the plantation house style and Japanese design. The Honolulu headquarters of the two Buddhist organizations were constructed according to this model: the Honpa Honganji Mission built in 1899

Fig. 8. The Honpa Honganji Mission built in 1899 and used until 1918—the Hawaiian eclectic style. Photo from *A Grateful Past, A Promising Future,* p. 19 (courtesy of Honpa Hongwanji Mission of Hawaii).

(Fig. 8) and the Jōdoshū Mission in 1905.[61] (The Honpa Honganji Mission became the Honpa Honganji Hawaii Betsuin, which was later moved and rebuilt in 1918 in the Indian/Western style.) The Hawaiian eclectic style reveals the natural transitions of immigrants' lifestyles. Palumbo writes:

> Temples had to conform to the fact that the immigrants were no longer accustomed to their old way of life in Japan and that the congregation wanted a space that was more comfortable to be within. The functional needs of accommodating seats or pews caused the temple plan to change in the most natural way.[62]

When immigrants determined to settle permanently, their lifestyles spontaneously shifted toward the Western manner. They did not consciously set out to make their temple structures similar to Christian churches, at least not in the beginning, because the transition was "still more of a functional process of adaptation which [led] to the changes in plan."[63]

The choice of the Indian/Western style won recognition from the host society and marked a focal point in the development of the Nikkei community. The edifice of the Honpa Honganji Hawaii Betsuin has been popularly cited as Gandharan (Northern India) architecture (Fig. 9-1, 9-2). The building was constructed in 1918, designed by the architectural firm of Walter Emory and Marshal Webb (there were no Japanese architectural engineers in Hawaii at that time). Imamura describes the characteristics of his *betsuin:*

We believe that the Buddhist teachings and the designs should be one and the same. . . . It is a mixture of the old and the new. It is the modern architecture of the time combined with the old: a modern and ancient East-West architecture. The temple may look like Byzantine or Arabian architecture but this is something that is not comparable to any one type of architecture.[64]

Fig. 9-1. The Honpa Honganji Hawaii Betsuin built in 1918—the Indian/Western style. From *Chōshōin ibunshū* (courtesy of Honpa Hongwanji Mission of Hawaii).

Fig. 9-2. A photo of the Honpa Honganji Hawaii Betsuin taken during the 1950s. From *A Grateful Past, a Promising Future*, p. 92 (courtesy of Honpa Hongwanji Mission of Hawaii).

The Indian/Western style was the symbol of cosmopolitan Buddhism and embraced various religious traditions. Palumbo writes:

> The Buddhists chose the Roman Tuscan column and dome, Indian style stupa forms, and classical arched windows for their first temple instead of following the traditional Congregationalist Church design. It is reasonable that [Imamura] was not looking to copy the church form. In order to achieve distinction from his opposition, he chose an architectural type that suggested new thought or a new presence while still having a form based on tradition. Imamura wanted to create a new image for Buddhism without forsaking the identity of Buddhism in exchange for acceptance. These architectural elements signify stability, historical significance, and cultural identity.[65]

In the design of this building, Imamura created a new Buddhist image, one that Euro-Americans found impressive. At the same time, the Indian/Western building style served the Nikkei community well, since it accommodated schools, and had separate halls, kitchens, and space for parking, all of which various groups could use for different purposes. For the justification of compartmentalization, walls and gateways were constructed with electric lighting.

It is interesting to note that the design of the Honpa Honganji Hawaii Betsuin also indicates the Japanization of Buddhism in two ways. First, according to Richard Jaffe, the Indian/Western structure was already "popular within the Nishi Honganji during the Taishō and early Shōwa periods."[66] The architect, Chūta Itō, and Kōzui Ōtani, the Nishi Honganji abbot, had studied Indian/Southeast Asian Buddhist motifs and envisioned such a style for establishing a modern Buddhist identity and for universalizing Japanese Buddhism. Second, according to Tomoe Moriya, when discussing the construction of the Honpa Honganji Hawaii Betsuin, the majority of the congregation preferred a Japanese-style building, as opposed to Imamura's Indian/Western design.[67]

In other words, the Japanization of Buddhist architecture brought about an internal conflict. On one hand, the Honolulu laity sought to create a rustic image of Japan projected by a traditional-looking Buddhist temple. On the other hand, Imamura searched for a modern (or cosmopolitan) Buddhist identity in collaboration with his counterparts in Japan. Later, the building of the Tsukiji Honganji (a Nishi Honganji *betsuin* in Tokyo), constructed in 1934, was modeled after the architecture of the Honpa Honganji Hawaii Betsuin[68] (Fig. 10). The Buddhist Church of San Francisco also employed the Indian/Western style when the main worship hall was rebuilt in 1938 (Fig. 11).

Fig. 10. The Tsukiji Honganji constructed in 1934.

Although scholars have not yet investigated Buddhist architecture on the mainland, the process of acculturation can be observed in three sites. In Fresno, Kuninosuke Masumizu, a professional temple and shrine architect, designed the first temple hall. He was one of the earliest immigrants who attempted to found a Japanese community in Coloma, California. He and other residents of Aizu (present-day Fukushima prefecture) had escaped

Fig. 11. The Buddhist Church of San Francisco constructed in 1938. From *Buddhist Churches of America: A Legacy of the First 100 Years*, p. 306 (courtesy of Buddhist Churches of America).

the persecution led by the Meiji government and fled to the West Coast in 1869. With his skilled background as a carpenter specializing in temples and shrines (*miya daiku*), the Fresno Buddhist Church appeared to be a mixture of motifs from Japanese Buddhist temples and Shintō shrines. The three-story building was destroyed by fire in 1919, though a similar design survived in a reconstruction project (Fig. 12-1, 12-2).[69]

Two other Buddhist churches in California have been recently featured in a series entitled "Japanese Architecture and Gardens in America" in *The East*. Yukiko Y. McCarty examines the exterior designs of the San Jose Buddhist Betsuin, built in 1937, and the Nishi Honganji Los Angeles Buddhist Temple, constructed in 1925. George Gentoku Shimamoto sketched the design for the San Jose Buddhist Betsuin with the help of two legendary brothers, Shinzaburō and Gentarō Nishiura. It resembles the Founder's Hall (Goei-dō) of the Nishi Honganji head temple in Kyoto (Figs. 13, 14).[70] In Los Angeles, since no licensed Japanese architect was available, Edgar Cline, influenced by the "Egyptian Revival" style popular in Hollywood in the 1920s, designed the Buddhist church with a combination of Japanese, Chinese, and Islamic elements.[71]

Summary

In the past, the adaptation of Shin rituals drew the attention of scholars, who argued that this was an obvious sign of Protestantization, but this chapter demonstrates that the acculturation of Shin rituals included a process of Japanization. There were a variety of services, depending on the native languages of the speakers and attendees. The schedules of religious gatherings also differed depending on the work schedules of the laity. The acculturation of rituals included the development of Buddhist hymns in two languages, the practice of exchanging rings and *juzu* in weddings, and the regulations of clerical dress codes suited to the host society. The promotion of Theravada Buddhism through ritual performances was inevitable for the BMNA to accommodate Euro-Americans.

The architectural design of missions and churches also indicates the Americanization and Japanization of Shin Buddhism. A local *bukkyōkai* in North America often purchased a Christian church and continued to use it without remodeling it. When Japanese carpenters and funds were available, Issei laity constructed Japanese-looking structures. In Hawaii, four exterior patterns developed in response to immigrants' needs and wishes: the plantation house style, Japanese temple design, Hawaiian eclectic model, and Indian/Western influence. The last style particularly reflected the emergence of modern Buddhist architecture in Japan.

Fig. 12-1. The Fresno Buddhist Church Betsuin was built in 1902 but burned down in 1919. This photograph was taken in 1906. From the *Fresno Betsuin Buddhist Temple Centennial 1901–2001*, p. 13 (courtesy of Fresno Buddhist Church Betsuin).

Fig. 12-2. Photo of the Fresno Buddhist Church Betsuin taken in 1937. From *Fresno Betsuin Buddhist Temple Centennial 1901-2001*, p. 19 (courtesy of Fresno Buddhist Church Betsuin).

Fig. 13. The San Jose Buddhist Church, built in 1937. From *Buddhist Churches of America: A Legacy of the First 100 Years,* p. 310 (courtesy of Buddhist Churches of America).

Fig. 14. The *honzan* of the Nishi Honganji Head Temple in Kyoto.

Chapter Five

Shin Buddhist Doctrine
Reconstructed

C hanges in organizational style and rituals correspond to the rethinking of Shinran's teaching in North America. The reinterpretation of Shin doctrine was triggered by theological challenges from Christianity, interaction with Buddhists from other traditions, and democratic principles in the United States. In the prewar period, the two branches of the Honganji sent scholar-priests (*gakusō*) to various academic institutions in the United States and Western Europe. Several Nishi Honganji *kaikyōshi* also attended American universities and received Master of Arts degrees.[1]

These priests, however, were unconcerned with the adaptation of Shin doctrine to a new environment. Therefore, the primary focus of this study is the intellectual activities conducted outside research institutions, namely, the work of Dr. Takeichi Takahashi, Reverend Itsuzō Kyōgoku, and Bishop Emyō Imamura. Their pursuits appear unrelated, as they were geographically separate and there is no evidence of correspondence among them. It is also dubious whether these men consciously reinterpreted Shin doctrine by responding to or initiating changes in organizational structure and rituals. But an examination of their modes of thinking, taken all together, suggests that there was a shift in doctrinal interpretation, since in their teaching and ministries they responded to Christianity, the basic teachings of the Buddha, and democratic principles.

The sequence of this inquiry into the works of Takahashi, Kyōgoku, and Imamura is thematic. Takahashi studied Shin doctrine epistemologically, using John Dewey's instrumentalism, while Kyōgoku took a more practical approach, considering the daily activities of the Issei and Nisei. Kyōgoku extended the notion of "experiment" proposed by Japan's first religious philosopher, Manshi Kiyozawa (1863–1903), who was also a Higashi Honganji priest. Imamura, for his part, drew attention to the social dimension of Jōdō Shinshū and discussed democracy from a Buddhist perspective. Throughout the intellectual activities of these three individuals, pragmatism takes on a considerable role.[2]

Along with the thematic arrangement, a caution is in order. In *Shinranism in Mahayana Buddhism and the Modern World* (1932; hereafter *Shinranism*), Junjō Izumida and Takahashi are listed as coauthors. Izumida writes, "[Takahashi] advised me one day that he would like to write an English booklet on the True Sect in collaboration with me before his departure for the East, as a tribute to my past thirty years service for the American mission."[3]

Noting the pragmatism that underpins this monograph, however, it is obvious that Takahashi was the primary author. The book is difficult to comprehend because of his use of abstract words and an unorganized style of writing, but he attempted to compare Shinran's teaching with Western philosophy and Christian theology, and placed Shin doctrine within the Mahayana discourse by expounding on the significance of the *Kyōgyōshinshō*, Shinran's magnum opus, and the *Tannishō*, the well-known Shin Buddhist text. Takahashi called Shinran's teaching "Shinranism" and regarded it as a future-oriented, democratic religious outlook, though he does not thoroughly discuss what is meant by this.

A problem plagues the case study of Kyōgoku. His materials, collected and explored for this study, were not written in the prewar period. He came to the United States in 1919 and stayed until his death in 1953. He began the tradition of *bunsho dendō* (literally, "propagation through sending letters") after he had fallen ill and resigned as resident minister in September 1941. His new venture was interrupted by the war and internment, but after leaving the internment camp he resumed publishing the Buddhist journals *Jikishin* (Japanese) and *Tri-Ratna* (English). It is thought that more than five thousand copies of these journals circulated every month in more than ten countries, including Canada, South Korea, the Philippines, and countries in South America and Europe. The journals often included Kyōgoku's sermons from the prewar period. So the present study considers the line of his thinking that appeared during the immediate postwar period as the consummation of Kyōgoku's intellectual activity before World War II.

Although this chapter makes a first attempt to introduce Takahashi's and Kyōgoku's scholarship and beliefs, other scholars have studied Imamura.[4] Eileen Tamura discusses his achievements in relation to the ethnic identity of the Nisei in Hawaii, and Lori Pierce explores race and religion. The Japanese scholar Tomoe Moriya exclusively explores Imamura's intellectual activities and the management of the HHMH as a case study for the transformation of a Japanese religion in Hawaii.

Takeichi Takahashi

An examination of Takahashi's scholarship is worthwhile on two counts. First, he applied Dewey's instrumentalism to the modern interpretation of Shinran's teaching. Second, he made the first attempt to introduce the *Kyōgyōshinshō* in English by comparing Shinran with St. Paul and Western philosophers. By studying Takahashi's work produced seventy years ago, we can discover a level of transliteration of Shinran's doctrine in the prewar period.

Little is known about the life of Takeichi Takahashi except for his attendance at the University of Chicago. According to the registrar's records, he was born to Fusakichi and Kei Takahashi on March 31, 1889. After receiving a bachelor's degree from Lake Forest College in Illinois, he enrolled in the Department of Philosophy at the University of Chicago in fall 1921. Takahashi received a Master of Arts degree in December 1922 with his thesis, "The Primary Value of Conduct in Ethics," and became a Doctor of Philosophy in December 1927; his dissertation was "The Symptomatic Function and Value of Systematic Moral Judgment."[5] In 1930, Takahashi served as principal of the Japanese language school affiliated with the Higashi Honganji Los Angeles Betsuin. He later became Research Professor at the India Academy of America in New York, where he lectured on Mahayana Buddhism.[6]

At the University of Chicago, Takahashi learned a great deal about Dewey's line of thinking. Based on the pragmatism of Charles S. Peirce and William James, Dewey had developed what is known as "instrumentalism":

> "[I]nstrumentalism" might suggest to a mind not too precommitted that natural science and technology are conceived as instruments, and that the logical intellect of mind which finds its congenial materials in these subjects is also instrumental—that is to say, not final, not complete, not the truth or reality of the world and life. Instruments imply, I should suppose, ends to which they are put, purposes that are not instruments which control them, values for which tools and agencies are to be used.[7]

Dewey "reconstructed" Western philosophy by defining intelligence, including moral judgment, as a tool of inquiry into human activities. He realized the importance of actual experience and considered a theory simply a hypothesis from which one could conduct experimental tests for further observation.[8] In his doctoral dissertation, Takahashi elaborated on instrumentalism:

> In opposition to the traditional Aristotelian concept of the good, Dewey presents an instrumental concept. The actualities of any moral judgment are merely tools to an end; they are working-hypotheses. The world is neither an

eternally complete being nor an eternal consciousness. The problem of the world is essentially a problem of organization. The world is in the making; it is not ready-made for eternity. It is a process of making or of reorganization. The same is true of human nature itself; it is always a process of making along with its life conditions. Dewey regards the problem of human nature as being a problem of social conduct. The problem of social conduct is essentially a problem of social organization, a problem of communication in terms of social intelligence.

Any problem and its solution must always involve the future. Therefore, in Dewey's view, any actual solution is merely a means to an end: it is a living-hypothesis. Any value theory expressed in terms other than of human choice is an abstraction. It is only significant and real when it refers to a process of choosing. There is no absolute solution or absolute problem for Dewey.[9]

When human conditions change and society is in a state of flux, one needs to rectify theory and mobilize further intelligence by taking into account the present circumstances. In this way, future analyses can become more dynamic. Pragmatists aver that one should not generalize a phenomenon with antecedent bias.

Dewey redefined a "religious" quality of "religion" from a pragmatic perspective. The noun "religion" suggests a fixed doctrine and an institutional apparatus, while "religious" indicates a "religious quality in experience" that brings about "the better adjustment in life and its conditions." For Dewey, doctrine denotes a method by which a human being could grasp the truth, in a way similar to how science promotes inquiry. Therefore, he designates God as the unity of all kinds of purposes for the individual to desire and to act. God or the divine means "human choice and aspiration," not a supernatural being outside of human activity and nature.[10]

Takahashi could not yet have read Dewey's *A Common Faith* (published in 1934) at the time of his writing *Shinranism,* published two years before. Nonetheless, it was this concept of instrumentalism through which Takahashi interpreted Shinran's teaching.

Takahashi introduced Shinran's *Kyōgyōshinshō* to the United States for the first time. The goal of both Izumida and Takahashi was to introduce Shinran's teaching to Nisei Buddhists and to the American public in general. In the Preface to *Shinranism,* Izumida writes:

> My primary purpose and hope for the American mission has not been, from beginning to end, for old Japanese here, but for their children and Americans. Therefore, it has been my long cherished hope that I would be able to do something for them, which might remain long after my death, although I knew I could not possess such a mind as to fully realize my hope.[11]

Most of Izumida's life in the United States was taken up with meeting the religious demands of the Issei. He could not achieve his objective of presenting Shinran's teaching in English in his daily activities, but he often neglected his family and other duties to help those who sought to understand the Buddha's teachings. Takahashi understood Izumida's aim and saw him as being faithful to the Dharma. For Takahashi, Izumida was one of the very few ministers who sought spiritual purity in American society or "lotus-flowers in American ponds," because he had no real interest in mundane things, though many other ministers seemed to get involved in them.[12] Takahashi also attempted to communicate with Christians through the publication of *Shinranism.*

> We must find the universal in the individuals, as far as each individual can be true for itself on the basis of today's theory of relativity. We can find an international spirit of humanity in all different individualities of both the East and the West, though the ways of expression may differ. If this truth be doubted, even the basis of each national organization will be broken up. From the point of view of social psychology, we find a theoretical ground of international spirit and organization on the basis of the contemporary theory of relativity. Not only so, but also we can find enough reason for it in our sciences and metaphysics. Here is indicated thus the author's spirit in introducing Shinran's work, Kyo-gyo-shin-shyo to western minds which are expected to be mostly Christians.[13]

Takahashi believed that international harmony would be achieved through understanding individual and social difference, not by a single authority claiming universal truth. For him, the study of comparative religions served such a purpose.

Shinranism highlights two themes. First, Takahashi interprets Shinran's doctrine metaphysically, using a pragmatic theory, though he acknowledged that Shinran taught Buddhism "only religiously, according to his primary purpose which lies in the easy way of salvation for all human beings on earth."[14] Second, Takahashi explains how the dualistic relationship of Amida and sentient beings turns into the oneness of reality. To facilitate these discussions, he distinguishes Shinran from European philosophers, albeit making references to Aristotle. Takahashi then compares Shinran with Paul of the New Testament, drawing upon similarities and differences between Shinran's relationship to Amida and Paul's to God.

Like Dewey, Takahashi defines religion as something to be experienced in one's social life. He disagrees with the notion that religion consists of a set of static dogmas to which religious authority forces one to conform.

Religion is essentially the process of social conduct in the highest terms of value at any state. It is the most fundamental process of life which lie(s) above the individual; that is to say, it is the process of life in contact with the eternal harmonious whole by which all human superficial illusions are broken up in the depth of the human heart which shares most graciously in the eternal harmonious whole.[15]

Reality needs to be found within the individual, and religious values serve as tools for one to discover oneself in unity with all things. Such values are "things 'as there' to be tested out in future experience."[16] Takahashi applies this formula to the concept of Shinranism.

For Shinran the present life is not made to see a sun-set [sic] but a permanent rising-sun [sic] going up, up and up with a sublime grace of Amida. Man cannot, in his view, see the possible universe by either the head or the heart. Man cannot live through the possible universe by reasoning. Man cannot grasp through things yet to be by intuition. Man can live through the possible universe hoped for only by means of faith in Amida who has ever brought its full evidence to light with the Forty-Eight Vows. For Shinran the best is not "here," not "now," but is only "there" to be "had" in the future.[17]

For Takahashi, Shinranism requires an incessant reconstructive effort to seek a "harmonious whole." His understanding of religion is "scientific," as he considers science a method rather than knowledge. Shinranism is a religion of "natural empiricism," where one obtains faith through neither the supernatural working of the divine nor one's own merit, but a "natural process" of inquiring into "natural mysteries," such as the irrational aspects of life and the fundamental question of birth and death. Faith can never be grasped by the human intellect but only through experience, because "nature (reality) is thus presumed as an immeasurable series of realization[s] in terms of all kinds of human experience."[18]

In Takahashi's view, Buddhism is empirical, as it is said, "What is phenomenal, that is reality." This worldview, which recognizes the ubiquitous nature of reality, derives from Śākyamuni's own experiences. His road to attaining nirvana was long and arduous. The Buddha failed at ascetic practices and depended on a young girl, who fed and revived him, after which he sat under a *bodhi* (literally, "awakening") tree with great determination to pinpoint the cause of suffering.

Takahashi also considers Shinran empirical. Three of the forty-eight vows of Amida Buddha, the nineteenth, twentieth, and eighteenth vows, correspond to various kinds of Buddhist followers: to those believing in making merit, to those who depend on both their own goodness and on

Amida's virtue, and to those who entrust themselves completely to Amida's Primal Vow. Shinran defines the eighteenth vow as the decisive cause for birth in the Pure Land. Although the nineteenth and nwentieth vows were skillful means for Shinran, Takahashi interprets them as examples of the adaptability of the Buddha's teachings to various individuals, in response to different personalities and particular social conditions. Takahashi argues that Shinranism indicates a doctrine of individuation, because "reality must always be found in a very specific thing with reference to its particular social conditions."[19] As Shinran says, " [The Vow] was entirely for the sake of myself alone"[20]—one needs to discover the foundation of one's own life in the cosmic harmonious whole by giving up one's individualistic concerns.[21]

To illustrate Shinran's teaching in a Christian society, Takahashi juxtaposes Shinran's notion of entrusting mind (*shinjin*) with Paul's concept of faith. These two "saints" appear to be similar because Paul emphasized faith in Jesus, the Son of God who had died on the cross in order to bring about salvation for the entire human race, as much as Shinran emphasized entrusting oneself to the Primal Vow. However, the two men's understanding also differs. For Takahashi, Paul did not resolve how faith arises within the individual but claimed the importance of faith as "the most primary means to an end for salvation" and as "a mere individual reaction within the self." In contrast, according to Shinran, "faith itself is an end [in] itself," for it is "grace" directed to human beings by Amida Buddha.[22] The act of calling Amida's name signifies bridging a gap between "personality and impersonality into the depth of reality which is neither perfect nor imperfect . . . but the Bodhi (awakening) above cognitive value."[23]

To further clarify the relationship between sentient beings and Amida, Takahashi turns to a metaphysical discussion of emptiness, though the discussion is abruptly abandoned at a certain point. The real nature of emptiness does not require any presumed category, because "emptiness as an idea does not present emptiness as such at all according to the Buddha Sakyamuni. Emptiness or nirvana is neither being nor non-being."[24] By referring to the theory of the two buddha-bodies, Takahashi distinguishes two aspects of the Buddha: "the eternal Law-Master" as emptiness itself, and "the temporal Law-Master" as a manifestation of reality through Śākyamuni's activity. Takahashi then discusses that the state of emptiness is not something to be attained cognitively but experienced, in the case of Shin Buddhists through the act of the nenbutsu.[25] However, he does not clarify the relationship between Amida and Śākyamuni.[26]

There are other limitations in Takahashi's discourse on Shinranism. Though he applied modern philosophies to his reinterpretation of Shinran's teaching, Takahashi remained conservative in his belief: he recognizes and accepts the teaching of a physical rebirth in the Pure Land. For instance, he writes, "for the Nembutsu followers pure faith is the primary method for the attainment for rebirth" and "with this faith in the future rebirth, we can overcome all sufferings and pains on earth. . . . We can now fully enjoy life at ease on this basis of rebirth in the future life."[27] Instead of experimenting with Shinran's teaching for the growth of one's personality, what is "hoped for" or "believed in" appears to be merely a desire for a better afterlife in these contexts. Such a longing for life after death contradicts Shinran's earlier definition of "faith," which is "salvation" itself.

Another shortcoming of *Shinranism* is its absence of discussion concerning the implications of Shinran's exile. Takahashi completely omits any examination of passages in the *Kyōgyōshinshō* and the *Tannishō* in which Shinran strongly expressed his resentment at the imperial authority that denigrated the Dharma, executed four of Hōnen's disciples, and exiled others, including Hōnen and Shinran himself. By ignoring Shinran's social criticisms, Takahashi's discussion of a religious person and his social conditions, as well as of democracy, remains abstract.

> Women should not be treated lower than men because of their inborn weakness, but ought to have equal opportunities for their growth and realization. Children should be respected fully as children; they should be treated as ends in themselves. Common people ought to have an equal opportunity with others for their growth and realization; for they are equally children of the Law. Democracy in Shinranism is not merely a democracy of religious and ethical humanity in terms of divine love or human love, but also in terms of metaphysical claim of equality in the Law of Nature as such. . . . Although he [Shinran] had no interest in social and political philosophy, his doctrine had been worked out in the way of religious democracy from which ground we may properly deduce today's doctrines of democracy, humanity, international organization new individualism, etc. Shinranism is in this phase a democratic futurism.[28]

Takahashi's comparison of Shinranism and democratic religion appears inadequate. On a theoretical level, a Shin Buddhist has the capacity to relativize individual values and societal values, because Shinranism, based on the doctrine of emptiness, negates absolute values attached to all things. But Takahashi neither discusses racial discrimination in the United States nor expresses his doubts about Japanese imperialism. In his writings, he appears sectarian, even ethnocentric; in this, Takahashi was no different from the vast majority of Shin clergy and Japanese scholars of the time.

Although limited in his analysis of faith and suggestions concerning its relevance to modern society, Takahashi is a precursor to the comparative study of Shin Buddhism and Christianity. His discussion was theoretical but not practical, and there are no signs of its application to the Shin Buddhist community. In contrast to Takahashi's scholarship, Itsuzō Kyōgoku's proposal was more useful, as he was concerned with the daily activities of the laity. He attempted to bridge the gap between the faith aspect of Shin Buddhism and the practice related to Śākyamuni's doctrine by reexamining the Shin concept of other-power (*tariki*).

Itsuzō Kyōgoku

As a member of a temple family, Itsuzō Kyōgoku was naturally drawn to Buddhism in his youth (Fig. 15). He was born in 1887, the eldest son of Kenryū and Sada Kyōgoku, in Shimane prefecture in the western part of Japan, bordering the Sea of Japan. At the age of three, his family moved to Chōkokuji, the temple belonging to his grandfather, Jiun Tatsukawa, which was affiliated with the Nishi Honganji in Hiroshima. Though at first skeptical about entering the priesthood, which was expected of Itsuzō, at the age of eighteen his views changed, after the death of his father. In 1906, he entered Kanazawa Junior College (Kanazawa Daishi Kōtō Gakkō) and was ordained the following year.[29]

While living in Kanazawa (Ishikawa prefecture), Kyōgoku had many spiritual experiences. One episode from his youth reveals that a conversation with a German soldier led him to change his attitude toward Buddhism. A Major von Schultz was in Japan to study the Japanese Army, after Japan had prevailed in the Russo-Japanese War. Kyōgoku often visited Schultz to learn English and German. One day, still dressed in ceremonial robes, he encountered the major, who asked him about the surplice he was wearing over his shoulder, made of pieces of material sewn together. Kyōgoku explained that it was a Buddhist tradition, since the Buddha and his disciples had worn robes made from rags they had gathered from graveyards and garbage dumps. The major then asked him if pieces of beautiful gold brocade like the ones Kyōgoku was wearing could be found in such places in Japan. This conversation led Kyōgoku to reevaluate his understanding of Buddhism.[30]

At about the same time in Kanazawa, he met the philosopher Kitarō Nishida (1870–1945) and Haya Akegarasu (1877–1954) of the Higashi Honganji, who were later to shape the course of his career.

After graduating from college, Kyōgoku moved to Tokyo. He attended Tokyo Imperial University, majoring in English literature, and graduated with a bachelor's degree in July 1915.[31] (It is interesting to note that Manshi Kiyozawa had graduated from that same university and Kyōgoku later joined Kiyozawa's group, Kōkōdō.) While in Tokyo, Kyōgoku married Kiyo Akiyama in August 1912, and they had three daughters, Yurii, Marii, and Maya. Prior to his overseas assignment, Kyōgoku taught at a school run by the Nishi Honganji.

Kyōgoku and his family arrived in Los Angeles in August 1919. Kyōgoku's ministerial career can be divided into four periods: 1922–1931, serving at Fresno Buddhist Church; 1932–1941, retiring from the BMNA and living in

Fig. 15. Itsuzō Kyōgoku. From *Buddhist Churches of America: A Legacy of the First 100 Years*, p. 71 (courtesy Buddhist Churches of America).

Lompoc; 1942–1944, internment in Topaz, Utah; and 1944–1953, publishing the two Buddhist journals *Jikishin* and *Tri-Ratna*.[32]

Before moving to Fresno in 1922, Kyōgoku served at the Los Angeles Buddhist Church for two years. The Los Angeles members expressed their unhappiness when the BMNA transferred him, and requested the bishop to find someone as competent as Kyōgoku.[33] From the point of view of the BMNA office, Fresno was a strategic place in Central California, where a minister who could speak English, such as Kyōgoku, would be urgently needed.[34]

While serving at the Fresno Buddhist Church, Kyōgoku helped the BMNA administration and became one of its advisers (*sanji*) in January 1926, assisting the acting bishop, Ryūsei Kusuhara.[35] Kyōgoku carried out the duties of chairperson of the BMNA Advisory Committee between July 1929, after the fifth bishop, Hōshō Sasaki, resigned, and July 1930, when the sixth bishop, Kenju Masuyama, assumed the BMNA office.[36] In other words, Kyōgoku took on the responsibility for the BMNA administration during the yearlong absence of a bishop. His work consisted of managing the Fresno church and supervising the affairs of the entire BMNA, including ministerial transfers, settlement of church problems, and communication with the Kyoto headquarters. He also became adviser to the national Young Buddhist Women's Association (YBWA) in 1928.

Kyōgoku's major contribution during his time as BMNA adviser was the establishment of the BMNA Endowment Foundation (Hokubei Kaikyō

Zaidan). Bishop Masuyama recognized his dedication when requesting the Kyoto headquarters in 1932 to award those who had contributed to the development of the BMNA:

> Kyōgoku Itsuzō: previously served at Fresno.
> In spite of his hardships, his contribution toward the establishment of the Beikoku [Hokubei] [K]aikyō [Z]aidan and the leadership of the Young Buddhist Association are outstanding.[37]

Kyōgoku was the chairperson of the Foundation Committee that drafted its by-laws.[38] After the BMNA celebrated its twenty-fifth anniversary in 1926, ministers and lay representatives recognized the necessity of securing a strong financial foundation. During the 1930s, the committee aimed to raise $500,000. The urgent tasks to be undertaken by the BMNA were translating and publishing Buddhist texts and commentaries, sending Euro-American ministerial candidates to Japan for religious education, propagating the Buddhist teachings to Caucasians, organizing Sunday school texts, and developing Nisei organizations such as the YMBA and the YWBA.[39] Kyōgoku, together with other advisers, established the basis of the Foundation Committee and promoted the teachings to the youth through Sunday school programs.

After Bishop Masuyama's inauguration, however, Kyōgoku submitted his resignation from the post of resident minister of the Fresno church on December 26, 1931, and temporarily left the BMNA. The direct causes of his resignation are unknown, but the church was experiencing financial problems at the time. The laity's pledges could not be met during the Great Depression, which began in 1929 and lasted for about ten years. The church needed an annual budget of $2,000, but due to the lack of financial support, ministers had to make many sacrifices. The Kyōgoku family was often unable to pay the bill, and public utilities were cut off at their rented house.[40] Kyōgoku also felt responsible for educating his three children.[41]

Despite these difficulties, Kyōgoku and his wife were well respected in the Fresno Buddhist community.[42] He organized many YMBA and YWBA events in rural areas, started Buddhist education for both Issei and Nisei, and conducted Sunday school teachers' training classes. At one time, there were thirty-two Japanese language schools in Central California (from Madera to Bakersfield), often forming connections with the Fresno Buddhist Church. Throughout his career, Kyōgoku encouraged Nisei followers to express their understanding of Buddhist teachings.[43] Kyōgoku's wife, Kiyo, took care of the Buddhist Women's Association and served food and refreshments at various church functions.[44]

After leaving Fresno, the Kyōgoku family lived in Lompoc for the next nine years. Kyōgoku taught at a Japanese language school to make ends meet and support his children, though unfortunately his youngest daughter, Maya, died on August 9, 1934, from an illness.[45] Even though he had resigned from the BMNA, Kyōgoku still kept in touch with the organization in various ways. For example, he continued paying an offertory to the Kyoto headquarters and delivered sermons at nearby churches.[46] During his time in Lompoc, he studied Sanskrit and Pāli texts and read various books in English, all of which became resources for later propagation.[47]

Kyōgoku rejoined the BMNA on July 31, 1941, initially receiving an appointment to serve at the Stockton Buddhist Church. Two months later, however, he had a heart attack and relocated to Berkeley for treatment. Soon after, the Pacific War broke out, and he and his family were interned at the Topaz, Utah, camp. After their release, they moved back to Fresno, and Kyōgoku died there in 1953. Because of his strong conviction that Buddhism was not just for the dead (as opposed to what the majority of Japan's populace had practiced, so-called funerary Buddhism), Kyōgoku avoided preparing his own grave. He wished for his ashes to be scattered over the ocean at Lompoc.[48]

In his last nine years, Kyōgoku dedicated his life to propagation through publishing Buddhist journals. He founded two publications, one in Japanese, *Jikishin* (literally, "direct mind") and the other in English, *Tri-Ratna* (a Sanskrit term for the Three Treasures: Buddha, Dharma, and Sangha). He started *Jikishin* after receiving a moving letter from one of his Dharma school students. Kyōgoku states:

> One day, I received a letter from a young Buddhist soldier sent to the battlefields of the South Pacific as a translator. In the letter, he described how hellish his life was down there, as he often drifted between the worlds of life and death. Yet, he thanked me for having taught him Buddhism at Sunday school. Because of the nenbutsu and the Buddhist songs that he learned in America, he appreciated his own life. He even enclosed five dollars for me along with his letter.[49]

The letter encouraged Kyōgoku to provide further Buddhist education to the Nisei. Initially, he sent letters to the YBA leaders interned at Topaz and to Nisei Buddhist soldiers. Deeply disturbed by the deaths of these men on the European front, he published their stories in a leaflet titled "The Silver Moon" on May 30, 1949.

Kyōgoku eventually separated the Japanese- and English-speaking readership. He designed *Tri-Ratna* for Nisei Buddhists, including those stationed at overseas American military bases, and for Euro-Americans interested in Buddhism.[50] He circulated *Jikishin* among Issei Buddhists as a spiritual guide and source of information on Japan's rehabilitation after the war. He kept up personal correspondence with people in Japan, including those who had lived in the United States before the war and Nisei Buddhist soldiers who worked under the supervision of the U.S. Occupation authority.

As indicated in *Tri-Ratna*, Kyōgoku had made a tremendous impact on the Nisei laity through the Sunday school program. His objectives for Nisei Buddhist education included making Buddhism more accessible to the laity and reducing clerical specialization, transforming Buddhism from the mere "funerary religion" practiced in Japan to a "religion of daily life," and changing negative images of Japanese Buddhism (e.g., that it was a religion only for the retired or dead) to positive associations, such as creating the Land of Buddha.[51] George Teraoka considered Kyōgoku's activity a "hotbed of Buddhism" because Kyōgoku disseminated the seeds of the Buddhist teachings into the hearts of many young Japanese Americans. Teraoka was one of the so-called "three crows" in Fresno (*Fresno sanba karasu*), along with Dr. Kikuo Taira and Manabu Fukuda. Both of these men later became leaders of the BMNA national YBA movement.[52]

The Relationship between Kyōgoku and Kiyozawa

Kyōgoku's "hotbed of Buddhism" was underpinned by the modern Shin Buddhist discourse developed by Manshi Kiyozawa, a priest, scholar, and educator who sought a modern religious identity with a sense of crisis. The impact Kiyozawa made on the modern development of Japanese Buddhism was significant. Joseph Kitagawa considers him "one of the most influential thinkers during the 1890s" and Saburō Ienaga sees Kiyozawa as "a fleeting but splendid experiment for the modernization of Buddhism."[53] Kitarō Nishida places him as "one of the most important figures in modern Japanese religious philosophy."[54] Through his own religious experiences, Kiyozawa resolved differences between the modern concept of the self, which was "at least partly emancipated from the group structures and values of traditional society and at least somewhat aware of its individual capacities and options," and Buddhist identity, which denies the permanent, inherent existence of a self.[55]

Kiyozawa died quite young but he dedicated his short life to self-discovery. He was born into a low-ranking samurai family in Nagoya (west of Tokyo). Although his family was poor, the Higashi Honganji priests recommended that Kiyozawa study at Tokyo Imperial University because of his extraordinary intellect. With a scholarship from the Higashi Honganji, he studied religious philosophy under Ernest F. Fenollosa and became the first Japanese scholar in that field. After graduating, Kiyozawa served as principal of a junior high school in Kyoto run by the Higashi Honganji. Though he could have easily pursued an academic career and had a more prosperous life, Kiyozawa resigned in 1890 and began his own internal exploration to discover the basis of his religious identity. He gave up smoking and eating meat, separated himself from his family, and pursued ascetic practices. This period of his life is known as the "Minimum Possible." However, in 1894 he contracted tuberculosis and gave up his abstemious lifestyle. As his health deteriorated and with death imminent, he reached a much deeper level of understanding and appreciation of Shinran's teaching.[56]

Kiyozawa committed himself to the Higashi Honganji with a strong sense of gratitude. In 1895, he and a colleague attempted to reform its administration, believing that the headquarters had busied itself raising funds to rebuild the two temple halls and neglected the promotion of Shinran's teaching. Fearing Kiyozawa's campaign, the Higashi administration excommunicated him, but he was later exonerated and invited to serve as the principal of Shinshū University (present-day Ōtani University in Kyoto). Though his attempts at reform were not very successful, his efforts encouraged many young Higashi priests and quite a few from the Nishi Honganji and other Buddhist schools. Kiyozawa formed a study group called Kōkōdō, which published a Buddhist journal, *Spiritual World* (*Seishinkai*) from 1901 until 1918, well after his death. Kiyozawa died in 1903 at the age of forty-one, having never recovered from tuberculosis.[57]

Kiyozawa discusses the relationship between the finite and the infinite in his book *Skeleton of a Philosophy of Religion*.[58] It is said that if one sees the relative and imperfect nature of self as opposed to the infinite, the relationship between the finite and infinite is dualistic. But for Kiyozawa, the infinite does not mean a creator of the universe but the universe as an organic whole. He defines the correlation between the finite and the infinite as "whenever any particular finite thing or being is taken as the principal point of reference, all the other finites in the universe come to be seen as supports for its existence," and he considers such a relationship "the oneness of all things" (*banbutsu ittai*) or the "inter-dependent nature of all existence."[59] In this way, Kiyozawa avoided the use of Buddhist nomenclature as part of his effort to modernize Buddhism, and explained the concept of "dependent co-arising" or the notion of "the trichiliocosm in a moment of consciousness" (*ichinen sanzen*) in his own words.[60] He also used the terms "Tathāgata" or "the Infinite" to designate Amida Buddha, and defined it as a "religious symbol" through which he tried to reconcile differences between Shin Buddhism and other religions.[61]

Kiyozawa argues that a finite being comes to understand the infinite through "a final cause" or "an efficient cause." The former suggests the realization of oneness, in which *shinjin* is directed toward the practitioner as Buddha's wisdom; the latter indicates one's exertion to achieve spiritual attainment as similar to Śākyamuni's awakening. The efficient cause is the gate of self-power (*jiriki/shōdōmon*) whereas the final cause is that of other-power (*tariki/jōdomon*). Gilbert Johnston explains these differences by using the concepts of time and space. The ascetic practitioner sees his or her relationship with the infinite in terms of time, such as the length of practice required to come to self-realization. The Shin Buddhist recognizes his or her relationship with the infinite in terms of space, because Amida Buddha initially appears as external to oneself, though Amida's virtue is later internalized as *shinjin*.[62] For Kiyozawa, *shinjin* is the "subjective Spirit," constantly working to make him understand his co-relation with all other things.[63]

Kiyozawa coined the term "Spiritual Activism" (*seishin-shugi*) to describe subjective engagement with the "self." He defined *seishin* as "maintaining" peace of mind (*anjin*), suggesting the state of entrusting oneself to the great compassion (*daihi*) of the infinite (other-power). His three sources of Spiritual Activism were the Āgama sutras for "the establishment of self," the *Discourses* of Epictetus for "subjectivism," and the *Tannishō* for "faith in Other Power." Spiritual Activism is a form of "pragmatism," which "develops at the place where the relative enters into the Absolute and the finite meets the Infinite."[64] He rephrased it as activism (*jikkō-shugi*), subjectivism (*shukan-shugi*), or the way of introspection (*naikan-shugi*).[65]

Kiyozawa explored his intellect as part of his own experience. He often used the scientific term "experiment" (*jikken*), and emulated Śākyamuni and Shinran. For Kiyozawa, the Buddhist teaching is useless unless one can verify it through one's own experiences.[66] While he cognitively understood the definitions of self-power and other-power, he dared to pursue an ascetic life in order to examine his own fortitude. As a result, Kiyozawa contracted tuberculosis and collapsed. His wife and two sons died, and his attempts to reform the Higashi Honganji failed. These tragic events, however, only led him to a greater appreciation of Amida's compassion. In his last essay, "The Nature of My Faith" (*Waga shinnen*), Kiyozawa writes:

> My belief in the tathagata occurs at the limit of everything that I know. . . . And when I reached the conclusion that the meaning of life is incomprehensible, it

was at that point that my faith in the tathagata arose. Gaining faith (*shinjin*) probably does not require that one go through such a lengthy process of inquiry, so the course of events that led me to this conclusion may indeed seem accidental. But in fact in my case, it could not have been any other way. Within my faith there is an element which believes in the ineffectiveness of my own efforts. And to believe in my own ineffectiveness, it was necessary first to exhaust my entire range of intellectual faculties to the point where I could no longer even raise my head. This effort involved an incredible ordeal.[67]

Kiyozawa exercised his intellect in order to understand Shinran's teaching. But that same intellect at first hindered him from establishing faith in Amida Buddha; thus, it was unavoidable for him to exhaust all of his mental power. As a result, he set the path of "self-assertion, followed by collapse, self-negation, and acquiescence."[68]

As a modernist, Kiyozawa was analytical and experimental in his approach to the oneness of life. His method was different from mainstream Shin tradition of the time, in which the Honganji authorities had often characterized devotees as illiterate and ignorant, because Amida's compassion did not discriminate against such people. But when Shin Buddhism was challenged by modernity, people like Kiyozawa could not ignore rationality. Alfred Bloom describes his cognitive method:

> In the process of religious awakening one moves from attachment to ordinary views of objectivity to awareness of the subjective, inner realm, and finally transcends both objectivity and the subjective (small self) to awareness of the Absolute (large Self) which embraces and transcends the subject-object dichotomy. This process provides a rational basis for the principle of Other Power.[69]

Kiyozawa demonstrated that faith (*shinjin*) could be explained logically. For him, birth in the Pure Land was not a matter of the afterlife but rather of manifesting a settled mind in one's present life. By objectifying and transcending the self, Kiyozawa rejected egoistic individualism and the insistence on the "I." He expressed the attainment of *shinjin* as "one begins to feel freely contented in the face of any circumstance."[70] With this confidence, he was no longer obliged to conform to worldly ethics or concerned with the maintenance of morality. In other words, he advocated the superiority of spiritual principles over mundane rules.

From a spiritual standpoint, Kiyozawa's views were an implicit critique of the state. To his mind, the significance of secular truth is to recognize one's incapability of fulfilling one's duty in society and understand that the law of the state is imperfect.[71] Kiyozawa writes:

[T]he Shinshū worldly truth teaching is not something which sets out to impose prescriptions on human behavior. If it were offering regulations for our actions, we would expect its principle to be definite and precise. In fact, whether it be simple "rules," a general notion of duty to the laws of the state, or the five [Confucian] cardinal virtues of benevolence, justice, politeness, wisdom and fidelity, the forms [Shinshū statements take regarding such obligations] are decidedly vague. . . .

The worldly truth teaching is thus nothing less than the means to perceive absolute truth from its back side by means of *shinjin.* That is to say, as opposed to the positivity of absolute truth, worldly truth is appealing for its negativity. For that reason it is a great misconception to think the worldly truth teaching exists in order to compel people to uphold standards of human behavior, or by extension to benefit society and the nation. If the worldly truth teaching were expounded as a basic duty to the laws of the state or the precepts of benevolence and humanity, as a matter of course it would be conducive to the performance of [these duties] to some degree.

In fact [such concerns] are an appendant phenomenon. Since there is a degree of efficacy in these secondary aspects, however, their esteem in society has resulted in the main point [of the teaching] being overlooked entirely. Despite the fact that the essential thrust of the doctrine is religious, it is this appended moral elements that seem to be valued most highly; a strange set of circumstances indeed![72]

Kiyozawa wrote this essay in 1903, one year before the advent of the Russo-Japanese War. The "moral elements" to which he referred were those of the Imperial Rescript of 1890, which ruled the lives of the Japanese people at that time. For him, taking refuge in Amida Buddha was the most urgent matter in life; submitting oneself to the emperor and observing moral standards were circumstantial.

Kiyozawa's Spiritual Activism attracted many young Shin Buddhists, among them Kyōgoku. It was unlikely that the two men ever met, as Kyōgoku was just sixteen when Kiyozawa died in 1903. But Kyōgoku later joined the Kōkōdō group, and along with his colleagues he occasionally organized memorial services for Kiyozawa in Kanazawa and contributed articles to the *Seishinkai.*[73] In was in this context that Haya Akegarasu introduced him to Kiyozawa's thought.

Kyōgoku's relationship with Akegarasu was ambivalent. Akegarasu, who had been one of Kiyozawa's immediate students, passionately propagated his teacher's philosophy and attracted many followers. Akegarasu and his wife, Fusako, adopted Mitsuo, Kyōgoku's younger brother. But when Akegarasu married a second time after Fusako's death, Mitsuo became independent.[74] Kyōgoku also seemed to have moved away from

Akegarasu. Nevertheless, when Akegarasu visited North America in 1929, Kyōgoku offered him a place to stay, and they went to Yosemite with others (Akegarasu's trip to North America and its significance is discussed in the Chapter Six). For his part, Akegarasu, along with D. T. Suzuki, wrote a Preface to Kyōgoku's posthumous book, *Akarui bukkyō* (literally, "Bright Buddhism"), in which Kyōgoku acknowledged Akegarasu as the teacher who had led him to understand Shinran's teaching (*shin no manako*) and Kitarō Nishida as the one who had guided him in practice (*gyō no manako*).[75]

Kyōgoku's interaction with Higashi priests continued in the United States. He was often invited to the Higashi Honganji Los Angeles Betsuin and the Berkeley Higashi Honganji as a guest speaker.[76] At Kyōgoku's funeral, Rinban Kankai Izuhara of the Higashi Betsuin offered words of appreciation, representing his family, as they were related in Japan. Also, a son of the abbot of the Higashi Honganji, Kōshō Ōtani, who was studying in the United States at the time, offered incense as a special guest.

Efforts to Bring Together Shin Buddhism and Other Buddhist Traditions

As Kiyozawa stressed the importance of questioning the self, Kyōgoku followed suit and radically transformed his own life perspective. Before coming to the United States, he wrote:

> A life of skillful faith best summarizes my past.... Guilty, appreciation and impermanence were the most effective formulae that I often used. The *Tannishō, Goichidai kikigaki,* and *Waga shinnen* were my tables of logarithms and compass I always had.... My so-called Dharma sermons were based on explaining and verifying them, or showing their application.... Therefore, I must be independent from my masters, teachers, and friends. I must proceed as I listen to my own voice. I realized that I needed to return to whom I am as a living self, instead of pretending who I was, made up of principles and formulae.[77]

Kyōgoku stripped himself mentally naked and faced his true "self." This rigorous method of introspection continued to be his central theme in the United States. Kyōgoku attempted to bridge the gap between the basic teachings of Śākyamuni and Shinran. The two seem quite opposite, as Śākyamuni teaches the practitioner to control one's blind passions by pursuing certain acts, which Shin Buddhists would consider to be self-power, *jiriki,* whereas Shinran teaches the follower to entrust oneself completely to the Primal Vow of Amida Buddha, relying on other-power, *tariki.* For Shin Buddhists, practicing the six *pāramitā*s (giving, morality, patience, diligence, meditation, and wisdom)[78] and observing the five precepts (abstention from killing, stealing, lying, fornication or adultery, and consuming intoxicants) are unnecessary for attaining birth in the Pure Land. However, the lack of a clear "practice" in Shin Buddhism was puzzling for the BMNA's lay Nisei and Buddhist sympathizers in the United States. Considering this situation, Kyōgoku proposed a circular movement between self-power and other-power.

> After we have tried to follow the Five Precepts given to us by the Buddha as the basis for our life, we see as in a mirror our true self, the self which every day ignores the Five Precepts, the self which is weak, ignorant, and ugly. We see our self directly, not merely theoretically. This is the beginning of Wisdom, the Wisdom which comes from truly experiencing the first Five Paramitas—Dana, Right Behaviour (Five Precepts), Patience, Right Effort, Meditation. The Six Paramitas comprise the way of life to be followed by all those who desire Enlightenment, meaning in a broad sense all Buddhist[s]. To those fortunate beings who are able to carry out the Six Paramitas, the marvelous world of Wisdom is opened to them as step by step they climb toward the goal of Enlightenment. But for us, we can merely hear about that spiritual world for the more we try to walk the way of the Six Paramitas, the more our weak and incapable self is clearly revealed. Instead of climbing forward step by step we fall rung by rung and know that we are the most lowly, the most foolish, the most evil of men. Only through the painful process of trying to walk the Way of the Six Paramitas and in failing, do we see our true self directly, the self which is full of evil thought and actions. . . . We are always making use of extenuating circumstances to excuse our own faults but we never consider extenuating circumstances when passing judgment on others. We see only the facts of the crime and condemn others. Even when we think that we have judged ourselves harshly, we still find that we have been too easy on our wrong-doing.
>
> Let us try to analyse ourselves objectively without making excuses for ourselves. Then when we realize that we have not followed the Way of the Six Paramitas and see directly all the weakness and ugliness in ourselves, Namu Amida Butsu flows from our lips as an expression of gratitude to Amida's great compassion which enfolds this weak and ugly self of ours.
>
> The Six Paramitas which is the Way for those who desire Enlightenment becomes for those of us who try and fail, the way to perceive direct understanding through experience. And through direct understanding comes true faith, [shinjin, entrusting oneself into Amida's Primal Vow].[79]

Kyōgoku valued the process of trial and error on the practitioner's part, even though the official view of Shin Buddhism held that the mastery of the six *pāramitās* and the five precepts were the virtues (or merits) of Amida and had nothing to do with a Shin follower's own efforts. But in

Kyōgoku's mind, if a person cannot realize his or her own self-attachment, he or she cannot come to appreciate a life of interdependence or a state of oneness. So by referring to the first practice of the six *pāramitās*, *dāna* (offering, or giving), Kyōgoku explains that people often fail in this act because making offerings without expecting anything in return is a difficult task. But through introspection on one's tendency to anticipate something in return, one comes to understand one's own ego. This transformation of self is centered within the heart of Amida Buddha.[80]

Kyōgoku's conviction that absolute failure (*jiriki mukō*) leads to an appreciation of Amida's compassion resonates with Kiyozawa's understanding of morality. In his "Discourse on Religious Morality and Common Morality" (*Shūkyō teki dōtoku to futsū dōtoku no kōshō*), Kiyozawa concluded that the significance of morality is to understand one's inability to be perfectly moral, after which one comes to praise Amida's virtue.

> One may wonder, then, what the purpose of Shinshū worldly truth actually is. The answer is simply that it aims to lead the individual to the [above-stated] perception that one cannot, in fact, perform these moral tasks. Although there may be differences between those who have attained *shinjin* as it relates to absolute truth and those who have not, it should be noted that it awakens the individual to the perception that the impossibility of moral praxis is identical in both cases. By way of explaining the profound implications [of this truth], let us first turn to those who have not yet attained *shinjin*. Having perceived the difficulties in [common] moral practice, such people may become religious and thereby proceed down the road to the attainment of *shinjin*. At first glance, this may not seem like much, but in fact it is not a simple matter. For the single basic impediment blocking the entrance to *tariki* faith is the conviction that one is capable of practicing *jiriki* discipline. Although there are many kinds of *jiriki* disciplined praxis, the most common and universal is behavior considered ethical or moral. As long as one thinks proper moral action is indeed possible, the entrance to *tariki* religion is ultimately blocked. It is an indispensable condition for becoming religious that one experiences [the disappointment incurred] when honestly seeking to mold one's behavior to conform to ethics or morality, one realizes that ultimately things will not turn out as expected. . . .
>
> Although we attain "the great pacified mind" as a result of *tariki shinjin*, the habitual deluded mind of *jiriki* continues to arise nonetheless. Thereafter, when we hear teachings on worldly truth, they seem directed precisely at this deluded mind. Our reaction is to immediately attempt to put these ideals into practice. When we then engage in such practice, however, we eventually perceive how truly difficult this is. It is then we turn around and rejoice [once again] in our *tariki* faith. . . .

In other words, in the situation [of one who has attained *shinjin*], because their praxis is so difficult, the worldly truth teaching exists to deepen further with each thought a sense of gratitude toward the infinite compassion [of the Buddha].[81]

For Shin Buddhists, religious morality suggests the observance of societal customs and laws, but for Kiyozawa, it also indicates the five precepts and other Buddhist practices.[82] As mentioned above, he considered a human being part of "an organic whole" that is related to all phenomena, and argued that this sense of interconnectedness would evoke in him or her a sense of ethical responsibility for all other beings and things. But the individual is merely incapable of fulfilling his or her own duty. This is the "paradox of the self."[83]

By emphasizing the ethical dilemma, Kiyozawa establishes a circular movement of introspection and self-cultivation. He investigates the causes of self-limitation and the development of morality. Failure in moral experience leads one to search for an alternate spiritual basis, namely entrusting oneself in Amida Buddha. After attaining faith, the practitioner is encouraged to work on one's morality once again.[84] Kyōgoku follows suit. When one exhausts oneself in meritorious acts and understands the impossibility of fulfilling the six *pāramitās*, the gate to other-power opens naturally. By further practicing the six *pāramitās* and again experiencing failure, one understands one's weaknesses and how one's life is embraced through interdependent relationships. For Kyōgoku, the end of self-power is the beginning of other-power.[85]

Kyōgoku did not merely construct this circular movement on the intellectual level; he also put it into practice. Through communication with a Shingon priest, Shūnin Kagao, after World War II, he discovered that many Japanese soldiers, including Buddhists, were being detained in the Philippines as war criminals.[86] From Fresno, Kyōgoku assisted Kagao by sending them the *Jikishin*. The Buddhist journals and Kagao's efforts helped to ease the fear of those who were sentenced to be executed. Kyōgoku, concerned for the detainees' families in Japan, also helped them financially. Through the practice of *dāna*, the friendship between Kyōgoku and Kagao became a trans-sectarian movement. Kagao learned Shinran's teaching from Kyōgoku, while the latter was inspired by the former's tireless efforts to help the detainees.[87]

The importance of the six *pāramitās* led Kyōgoku to endorse trans-sectarian Buddhism. He urged the Nisei Buddhists to return to the teachings of Śākyamuni Buddha. But this did not mean to merely remove sectarian barriers. He writes:

All sects if traced to their origin, go back to the teaching of the Buddha, Shaka-muni. The Buddhists must not always stay under their sectarian founders; they should see the Buddha through them. If we go back to the teaching of the Buddha, all sectarian prejudices melt away and yet the special point of each sect becomes known more clearly.[88]

Kyōgoku encouraged the Nisei laity to see the importance of Śākya-muni's teachings through Shinran's eyes, and not to let the error of sectarian conflicts in Japan prevail in the United States.[89]

Based on his emphasis on Śākyamuni's teachings, Kyōgoku created a two-course curriculum for the BCA Sunday School Department, which was organized in 1947, and he was appointed chairperson of the Committee for Researching Sunday Schools. The curriculum seems to be the culmination of his activities in the prewar period. Earlier in Fresno, he had already initiated the recitation of the Three Treasures in English, developed the "class instruction" system with the use of special cards, and introduced English Buddhist texts to the senior class. Although these activities became standard practice in the BCA after the war, other ministers had regarded his efforts as "radical" in those days.[90] With a great deal of help from Arthur Yamabe and others, Kyōgoku created a set of one hundred and twenty-three lesson cards as supplementary teaching material. The BCA and HHMH used more than seven thousand sets, and even sent them to Japan to educate Japanese Buddhist children.[91] Because of his contributions, Kyōgoku is considered "the father of the BCA Sunday [S]chool Department as it has emerged today."[92]

Kyōgoku's promotion of Śākyamuni's teachings, however, was problematic for some of his colleagues who were only concerned with the propagation of Shin doctrine. For instance, the fifth BMNA bishop, Hōshō Sasaki, opposed Kyōgoku's idea of first introducing basic Buddhism to the Nisei and Euro-Americans and later teaching them Jōdo Shinshū doctrine.[93] Issei ministers' lack of enthusiasm for promoting Śākyamuni's teachings might have derived from their educational backgrounds. Most had studied Shin Buddhist doctrine at Bukkyō University (later Ryūkoku University) under the auspices of the Nishi Honganji. The first four bishops of the BMNA, however, including Shūe Sonoda and Kōyū Uchida, graduated from Tokyo Imperial University and were aware of a broader range of Buddhist studies. From the time of Acting Bishop Senju Sasaki (who served in this capacity from September 1923 to July 1925), the heads of the BMNA had always been graduates of Ryūkoku University. So there seemed to be two factions developing: one emphasizing Shin and the other promoting Śākyamuni's teachings.[94] Kyōgoku, however, did not ignore the propagation of Shin

Buddhism in the Sunday schools. At the end of the two-course curriculum ("The Life of Buddha" and "The Teaching of Buddha"), he planned to introduce the "Sermon on the Pure Land" and "Namu Amida Butsu." So, as can be seen, he was about to create a further program for Shin Buddhism, but died before that became a reality.

Kyōgoku's efforts to reinterpret Shinran's teaching in the United States suggest the Japanization of Shin doctrine. He developed Kiyozawa's Spiritual Activism in California, where he interacted with Buddhists from other traditions. Kiyozawa did not merely appropriate the findings of European Buddhologists in the search for his spiritual identity. Studying Western philosophy helped him to understand Shinran's teaching.[95] He distanced himself from the united Buddhist front in Japan and did not propagate the superiority of his particular order (see note 61). In like manner, Kyōgoku made sense of Shinran's teaching by studying and practicing the six *pāramitā*s. He neither universalized Jōdo Shinshū nor appropriated Theravadin Buddhist concepts into the Shin tradition. Kiyozawa and Kyōgoku not only comprehended Buddhism on an intellectual level but also put their theories into practice. By doing so, they found themselves incapable of attaining awakening through their own efforts. This dilemma led them to entrust themselves to a greater "Self," namely the Primal Vow of Amida Buddha, through which they were able to obtain spiritual liberation. Kyōgoku described the features of Buddhism as the "4 Ls" (Light, Love, Life, and Liberty).[96]

Kiyozawa and Kyōgoku, however, had their limitations. While Kiyozawa engaged intellectually with educated people, Kyōgoku interacted with the Issei and Nisei laity. In each case, their contributions were limited to their own communities. Kiyozawa attempted to reform the Higashi Honganji and Kyōgoku participated in the organization of the BMNA. Their lack of broader social interest is due to the nature of Kiyozawa's Spiritual Activism. While Kiyozawa prioritized spiritual truth over secular truth, he was indifferent to reforming society. In his social critique, discussed above, Kiyozawa did not necessarily regard state power as evil. By distancing himself from political authority, Kiyozawa emphasized the significance of finding spiritual freedom. The problem of the modern nation-state appeared to him only as the result of prioritizing his spiritual concerns. He simply hoped for the nation of Japan to become "purified through the illumination of the natural working of Amida."[97] Kiyozawa died before the advent of the Russo-Japanese War in 1904. The members of Kōkōdō stopped developing a blueprint of his model for redefining the theory of the two truths.[98] For Kyōgoku, too, Buddhism was something to be kept to oneself, and he was not concerned with the reinterpretation of the dual principles in the United States.

A further effort to reconstruct the theory of the two truths was made in Hawaii by Emyō Imamura, who investigated the possibility of creating a new doctrinal paradigm and discussed the concept of democracy from a Buddhist perspective. Like Kyōgoku, he was a progressive man and promoted the ideas of the "3 Ls" (Light, Love, and Life) to characterize Buddhism to Nisei Buddhists and Euro-American sympathizers. In contrast to Kyōgoku, who included "Liberty," spiritual liberation, as a fourth "L," Imamura added "Labor" as his fourth "L."[99]

Emyō Imamura

Imamura rediscovered a critical aspect of Buddhism that could be applied to society. He responded to the discourse of Anglo-Protestant exclusionists by demonstrating the liberal and pluralistic climate of American intellectuals; thus, he tried to redefine the United States as a more tolerant society. In this process, however, he also universalized Shin Buddhism and remained connected with the Kyoto headquarters. In other words, Imamura was ambivalent toward the two nation-states. As suggested by his words "America and Americanism [are] in the [process of] making,"[100] Imamura himself was in the midst of creating a new paradigm of the Shin Buddhist doctrine.

Emyō Imamura was born to Ejitsu Imamura, head priest of Sentokuji (affiliated with the Nishi Honganji) and his wife, Kōe, in 1867. Emyō's mother died when he was three, and his father later married Masao Satomi, the elder sister of Hōni Satomi, who later became the first superintendent of the HHMH. In 1884, Emyō and his father Ejitsu studied at the Kahōkan in Kyoto, a private school headed by Tokumon Ama, a Nishi scholar who held the highest academic position (*kangaku*) within the order. Priests from other Shin Buddhist denominations, Zen priests, and even administrators of the Magistrate's Office in Fushimi district (Kyoto) attended this school.[101]

Emyō Imamura later studied with progressive Shin priests and under Yukichi Fukuzawa. At the Futsū-kyōkō (later called Bungaku-ryō; present-day Ryūkoku University), run by the Nishi Honganji, he joined an association called Hanseikai, which in 1899 began to publish a monthly journal, *Hanseikai zasshi* (later known as *Chūō kōron*). Hanseikai initiated a temperance movement and promoted a new level of discussion on Shin Buddhist spirituality. Through this campaign, the clergy and laity worked together to search for a new Shin Buddhist identity. The members of Hanseikai once invited Manshi Kiyozawa and asked him to be a special associate of their overseas propagation group. Under these circumstances, Imamura became interested in the reform of his order and its overseas propagation.[102]

After graduating from the Bungaku-ryō in July 1890, Imamura entered Keiō Gijuku University (present-day Keiō University), founded by Yukichi Fukuzawa. His study in Tokyo was part of a project of the Nishi Honganji headquarters to send bright young priests to foreign and domestic universities (*naichi ryūgaku*). Fukuzawa was then calling for Buddhist reform and promoting Euro-American civilization to the youth, and his pedagogy attracted the attention of ambitious priests. Imamura graduated in 1893 and spent several years teaching at junior high schools before moving to Hawaii in 1899.[103]

Fukuzawa regarded religion as a means of moral education and taught Buddhist priests to become men of noble character. Although he was never a Buddhist, his parents had been affiliated with the Nishi Honganji, and his religious theses often included discussions of Shin Buddhism. Fukuzawa read Rennyo's *Ofumi* thoroughly and evaluated positively the propagation style and simple language Rennyo used to communicate with rural people, avoiding imposing Shinran's teaching upon them.[104] But Fukuzawa disagreed with Honganji officials who urged their parishioners to be grateful to the emperor. He questioned the ways in which Shin clerics linked the teaching with the ideology of the state. Masao Maruyama determined that Fukuzawa was wary of Japanese politicians who regulated all kinds of cultural activities related to religion, scholarship, art, and the economy.[105] In essence, Fukuzawa recognized the importance of religious autonomy.

He supported Kiyozawa's Higashi Honganji reform movement, but the two men differed in terms of their understanding of religion. Fukuzawa considered his own efforts a grassroots campaign designed for young clergy, and criticized the moral decadence of senior priests. He disliked the practice of worshiping the abbot as a living buddha, because the abbot had failed to demonstrate the authority of the Dharma. For Fukuzawa, Shinran was not merely a saint of the past or a figure to be revered, but an individual who demonstrated the significance of having religious morality. Fukuzawa insisted that Shin Buddhists needed to learn how their founder had actually lived.[106]

Though he was careful to separate religion and politics, Fukuzawa became contradictory when connecting religion and morality. He once wrote an article about the ideal role of Honganji abbots: they ought to give moral courage to Shin Buddhist soldiers and direct the two branches of the Honganji to serve the nation-state of Japan. In contrast to Fukuzawa, who regarded religion as a source of moral teaching, Kiyozawa stressed the significance of spirituality over morality and spiritual principles over mundane rules. Kiyozawa did not necessarily oppose the system of the Honganji having an abbot, but he was critical of the military propagation carried out by the two Honganjis.[107]

As Tomoe Moriya suggests, the ideas of Fukuzawa and Kiyozawa are helpful in analyzing Imamura's activities in Hawaii. Like Fukuzawa, Imamura was concerned about the critical assessment of a society that could be offered by religion, but he did not specify Shinran's teaching as a moral ideology. Like Kiyozawa, he struggled to define the significance of spiritual principles over mundane rules, but his efforts expanded beyond his own circle. Imamura approached the entire society of Hawaii from a Buddhist perspective and opposed conformity with the Anglo-American norm. He insisted that the Buddhist faith could someday fit together with the legal system of the United States.[108]

For Imamura, the importance of spiritual rules is to understand the nature of suffering. He defines spiritual principles as "the matter to overcome suffering by having a settled mind (*anjin*)" and secular rules as "man's moral life in the present." He further writes, "[O]nce the settled mind is established, action to the secular rules naturally arises," which suggests one's understanding of indebtedness and observance of laws and regulations.[109] But at the same time, he identifies the Buddhist way of life as "leaving the world by living there and living in the world by keeping distance from it."[110] From a standpoint that simultaneously connects and disconnects spiritual principles and secular rules and an understanding that suffering is a matter of course, a Buddhist is said to participate in worldly affairs spontaneously.[111] Being optimistic, yet determined in his religion, Imamura activated an interaction between spiritual and mundane rules in Hawaii, where anti-Japanese activists were condemning the HHMH.

Democracy and Shin Buddhism

Imamura made tireless efforts to address exclusionist misunderstandings of Shin Buddhism and insisted on the liberal and pluralistic sides of American democracy. In May 1918, he wrote *Democracy According to the Buddhist Viewpoint* (*Bukkyō yori mitaru minpon shugi*), and in March 1920 he published *The Spirit of the United States and Freedom of Religion* (*Beikoku no seishin to shūkyō no jiyū*) in Japanese.[112] In the former, he defines the sangha as a democratic association, given that Śākyamuni himself observed the precepts with his disciples and ignored caste distinctions.[113] Shinran is also said to have treated his followers as "honorable friends" (*dōbō*) or "honorable co-workers" (*dōgyō*), and refused to call them disciples.[114] By "surrender[ing] of the self through the agency of His Not-Self Power [Other Power],"[115] those who receive the entrusting mind, including Shinran himself, were supposed to be equal. For Imamura, Shin Buddhism was an egalitarian religion.

From the Buddhist point of view, Imamura considered both autocracy and modern democracy as a relative polity. By connecting a religious ideal of egalitarianism and the democratic principles of a modern nation-state, he pointed to the problems of "falsified democracy," which appeared to him as "an arbitrary government [led] by the mobs, unenlightened, and egotistic [politicians]."[116] He also questioned the ways in which American exclusionists linked autocracy to Japanese nationalism and modern democracy to American patriotism:

> Our solemn conviction gained in the light of the Buddha is this: If autocracy has no absolute value, neither has democracy. . . .
>
> Various practical problems concerning the relationship between America and Japan must also be settled in the light of the above discourse, that is, in the spirit of unity in variety. America has her own way of dealing with things, and so has Japan. Japan must not force America to accept what the latter has not in her natural constitution. Nor can America expect of Japan to adopt what is not agreeable to her native temperament. Each ought to respect the other's natural peculiarities. If Japan favors autocracy in whatever sense this may be understood, there is reason for it, social, historical, or otherwise: if America claims to be democratic, it is perhaps inevitable. There is no necessity to quarrel over these things. Let us open our eyes to a far greater aspect of life, where all our trifling discussions and misunderstandings are leveled. Let us never lose sight of this unifying principle, which is known in Buddhism as Dharma or the law. . . . We do not advocate democracy, nor do we rejoice over autocracy. They are both fragmentary views of life; for whatever our individual and national differences, are we not living in the unity of the Dharma, in the great Ocean of Love and Mercy of Amit[ā]bha Buddha?[117]

Imamura's opinions on international relations between the United States and Japan sound simplistic from today's standpoint, and his critique is directed more toward the condition of democracy in the United States. But he indicates that any kind of ideology, including thoughts and systems, has only relative value because human beings are imperfect. Yet Buddhism embraces heterogeneous differences just as they are. Imamura sought an alternative to the existing social organization in the United States, which was a far cry from its egalitarian principles and in which

Japanese immigrants were discriminated against by legislation. By doing so, he challenged anti-Japanese activists who connected autocracy with Buddhism and modern democracy with Christianity.[118]

Imamura's critique resonates with Alexis de Tocqueville's assessment of the political arrangement in the United States. Pointing out the inconsistency between the power of the majority and the sovereignty of the people, where the minority is often ignored, de Tocqueville is skeptical of any form of government.

> Omnipotence in itself seems a bad and dangerous thing. I think that its exercise is beyond man's strength, whoever he be, and that only God can be omnipotent without danger because His wisdom and justice are always equal to His power. So there is no power on earth in itself so worthy of respect or vested with such a sacred right that I would wish to let it act without control and dominate without obstacles. So when I see the right and capacity to do all given to any authority whatsoever, whether it be called people or king, democracy or aristocracy, and whether the scene of action is a monarchy or a republic, I say: the germ of tyranny is there, and I will go look for other laws under which to live.[119]

For de Tocqueville, only God is just, and any worldly form of human organization is imperfect. He rejects both autocracy and democracy because he values the sovereignty of the people. He further writes:

> The organization and establishment of democracy among Christians is the great political problem of our time. The Americans have doubtless not resolved this problem, but they furnish useful lessons to those who wish to resolve it.[120]

Certainly, de Tocqueville's warning of the dangers of linking modern democracy with Christianity was quite pertinent to Imamura. In *The Spirit of the United States and Freedom of Religion,* Imamura explores the connection between the egalitarian aspect of Buddhism and the liberal climate of the United States. He wrote this booklet after his tour of the mainland in 1918. When it was published in 1920, Imamura was involved in Hawaii's territory-wide sugar plantation strike (the significance of this event is discussed in Chapter Seven).[121] This booklet can be seen as a manifesto, expressing Imamura's longing for authentic democracy. In it, he lists monographs written by European scholars on studies of the United States, including de Tocqueville's *De la democratie en Amerique* (*Democracy in America*) and James Bryce's *The American Commonwealth.*[122] Would it be an exaggeration to say that Imamura was conducting his own (Japanese) version of American studies by exploring the tradition of religious freedom in the United States?[123]

According to Imamura, "Americanism" has two aspects, inclusivity and the exclusivity of nationalism. The former indicates pluralistic religious traditions such as those he observed on the East Coast: Puritanism, the Dutch Reformed Church, Quakers, Catholicism, and Judaism. Inclusivity also refers to liberal thinkers, suggesting the Founders Benjamin Franklin and Thomas Jefferson, the writer Ralph Waldo Emerson, and pragmatists such as William James and John Dewey. Imamura particularly sees the importance of empirical inquiry, though his detailed discussion of pragmatism is no longer extant. The exclusivity of American nationalism, which Imamura criticized, is patriotic ideology linked with the superiority of Puritanism and Anglo-American conformity.[124] He writes:

> To denounce religions other than Christianity in the name of Americanism is to betray the ideal of Americanism and to abuse it.
>
> Americanism has never been fulfilled, but it is in the process of its completion. It is still growing and flexible to change freely.
>
> Americanism is never exclusive but embraces all differences, as if hundreds of rivers flow into a great ocean, and a great sky displays millions of stars.[125]

Because of his belief in the liberal discourse on Americanism, Imamura was optimistic about the future of Buddhism in the United States. To his mind, Americans still had an opportunity to accommodate a different type of religion, unlike Europe, where the alliance of Christianity and the state had long prevailed.

While believing in the ideal of freedom of religion in the United States, Imamura encouraged HHMH members to change their attitudes toward Jōdo Shinshū. He made five proposals. First, Shin Buddhists should not be afraid of those who impose Christianity on them and who say that Christianity is the spirit of America. Instead, Shin Buddhists should examine their own faith from deep within. Second, Shin Buddhists should not hold on to Japanese traditions in the United States, i.e., being Buddhist only because of one's hereditary identification is pointless. Being a Buddhist without understanding the teaching is in contradiction to the American spirit, which denies mere subordination to traditional authority. Third, Shin Buddhists need to conduct a "pragmatic test" to demonstrate how Buddhism contributes to "real material good" in the United States. Fourth, Shin Buddhists should not feel offended about the foreignness of their religion, but seek its real benefits for themselves and others. Finally, Christianity is only an incentive for Shin Buddhists to promote Buddhism; thus, they should never get discouraged. However, their efforts will be insignificant if limited to the Nikkei community. They need to make a contribution to the lives of the American people as a whole.[126]

Imamura encouraged his people to remain confident. Forced to live with anti-Japanese laws, Shin Buddhists would wait for their day to come. They should propagate the teaching without hesitation, because there was a need to respect the minority in a true democracy. Further, Imamura inspired his congregation to make great efforts to actualize a U.S. legal system in which Shin Buddhists could voice their demands, such as nullifying discriminatory laws, and through which their wishes would eventually be fulfilled.[127] Imamura's vision of improving the existing legal system involves progressive thinking on the concept of the Pure Land. He avoids an ontological discussion of the Pure Land but demonstrates active engagement with it.

> Religiously considered, the ideal of the Shinshū is the realisation of the Pure Land in one's own life. The world as we find it is full of contradictions and struggles between different factors such as wealth and poverty, intelligence and ignorance, good and evil, beauty and ugliness. But in the countries of the Buddhas, especially in the Pure Land of [Amitābha], which is the ultimate ideal of Buddhism, all differences are annihilated, all disturbances are quieted, all forms of relativity are reduced to oneness, and all contradictions blend harmoniously in a higher form. . . . [T]here prevails in the Pure Land the oneness of nature and man, of the savior and saved, and the oneness of all beings ever born in it, and the perfect unity of the flesh and the spirit, as well as the identification of ideality and actuality.[128]

For Imamura, the significance of the Pure Land is to discover the oneness of life, where differences between the ideal and the actual no longer exist. He further writes:

> When a man comes to realise what all this means (i.e., every suffering existence is sure to find ultimate refuge in the love and mercy of [Amitābha]) in the deepest recess of his heart, his individuality breaks away from its bondage, and he recognises himself in others formerly regarded as not belonging to himself. When he is thus expanding, he cannot stop until the whole world is transformed into a Pure Land of [Amida]. For he is now an ideal being existing in the mind of [Amitābha] Buddha.[129]

According to the *Larger Sutra* (*Sukhāvatīvyūha-sūtra*), the vows undertaken by Bodhisattva Dharmākara drove him toward their fulfillment. Therefore, by modeling oneself on Dharmākara and making one's own pledge, a Shin Buddhist could strive to express his or her religious vision in the United States. For Imamura, the transformation of the *sahā* world (this world) into the Pure Land involved removing discrimination against the Nikkei community and renouncing war.[130]

Being a pragmatist, Imamura moved away from the conventional idea that many Shin Buddhists held at the time, seeing birth in the Pure Land solely as a matter of the afterlife. He writes, "[B]e born into the Pure Land every day" and "[M]editate and practice, as one desires for birth in the Pure Land."[131] In other words, Imamura rediscovered agency among those who had obtained an entrusting mind, since Shinran had characterized them as "having immediately entered the stage of the truly settled" (*shōjōju*) and recognized their spontaneity.

Imamura's Limitations

As one of "the truly settled ones," Imamura relativized Anglo-American conformity and valued the liberal aspects of Americanism; however, he could not dispense of the theory of the two truths per se. What he would say on one occasion might seem different from what he would say on another. The HHMH published *Five Appeals to American Patriotism* in 1917 as a text for Nisei Buddhists to study the political ideologies of the United States. It included the Declaration of Independence, Washington's Farewell Address, Monroe's Seventh Annual Message, Lincoln's Gettysburg Address, and Wilson's War Message. In the Preface, Imamura wrote:

> Those of Shinshu faith are earnest in the belief that in Shinranism is the foundation of their spiritual life, and that the laws of the land are the foundation of civil life. Since we live in this country, we must be faithful and obedient to the laws of the country. Moreover, it is generally considered that those who firmly believe in religion and faithfully obey the national laws are the most desirable citizens. To be faithful and obedient to the Land of the Stars and Stripes, one must thoroughly understand the spirit of the country. In order to do this it will be most desirable to truly comprehend the aforesaid five appeals to American patriotism.[132]

Five Appeals to American Patriotism came out before Imamura published *Democracy According to the Buddhist Viewpoint* and *The Spirit of the United States and Freedom of Religion,* and the spirit of questioning American nationalism is absent from it.

In contrast to his instructions to the Nisei, Imamura intermittently observed the imperial rules of Japan along with the Issei workers. At various occasions ministers read the Imperial Rescript in the Japanese language schools affiliated with the HHMH. The HHMH supported Japan's war with Russia by giving financial help and celebrated Japan's national holidays, including the emperor's birthday. Indeed, Imamura received the honor of "the Sixth Order of the Sacred Treasure" from Emperor Hirohito in 1928.[133] In the private sphere, however, Imamura did not enshrine a picture of the Emperor and Empress, although the practice was common among Japanese immigrants.[134] Further, he extended his critique to the national polity of Japan, writing, "[I]t is absurd to think that changeless tradition is good with a brain imbued with national polity, which was established when the emperor issued the Imperial Rescript."[135] Imamura's ambivalence reveals the dilemma he faced, being an independent thinker on one hand and, on the other, a leader of the HHMH connected to the Kyoto headquarters and the Japanese government.

The Climate among Liberal American Intellectuals

In order to better understand Imamura's effort to connect Buddhism and democracy in an intellectual history of the United States, it may be helpful to review how some American liberal thinkers thought about democracy at that time. According to John Higham, the movement of Americanization was ambivalent at least until the outbreak of the World War I.

> From its tiny beginnings at the end of the nineteenth century to its height in the First World War, the movement for Americanization was another indication of the growing urgency of the nationalistic impulse. Americanization brought new methods for dealing with the immigrants; it significantly altered the traditions of both nativism and confidence. At the same time, the movement embraced the underlying spirit of both traditions. Within the crusade for Americanization the struggle between nativistic and democratic instincts persisted.[136]

On one side, Americanization allowed immigrants to nurture their own cultures; on the other, it became a powerful ideology of the nation-state as created by Anglo-Americans, who imposed their political and social values on immigrants. Higham rephrases the inherent conflict of Americanization: "the impulse of fear and the impulse of love ran throughout its whole course, clashing in principle though in practice sometimes strangely blended."[137]

For an illustration of liberal Americanism, we can consider two intellectual thinkers. In 1916, Randolph Bourne published "Trans-National America," which called for the recognition of ethnic differences among immigrants from southern Europe. He critiqued Anglo-American conformity as a discourse on national uniformity.

America is coming to be, not a nationality but a trans-nationality, a weaving back and forth, with the other lands, of many threads of all sizes and colors. Any movement which attempts to thwart this weaving, or to dye the fabric any one color, or disentangle the threads of the strands, is false of this cosmopolitan vision.[138]

Americanization meant "Anglo-Saxonizing" immigrants. Bourne disagreed with this; he believed that the profound American spirit was one of genuine integration of various ethnicities. According to Christopher Lasch, Bourne did not envision a hodgepodge of different cultures within one nation but sought for "a culture beyond ethnicity."[139] Due to his untimely death in 1918, however, Bourne's challenge never came to fruition.

Bourne had once been a student of John Dewey and praised his notion of instrumentalism as a means of social criticism. Dewey published *Democracy and Education* in 1916 and defined democracy as something more than a political assembly:

A democracy is more than a form of government; it is primarily a mode of associated living, of conjoint communicated experience. The extension in space of the number of individuals who participate in an interest so that each has to refer his own action to that of others, and to consider the action of others to give point and direction to his own, is equivalent to the breaking down of those barriers of class, race, and national territory which kept men from perceiving the full import of their activity.[140]

For Dewey, democracy was a way of life in which people would be able to respect individual differences. Despite his liberal stance, however, he supported President Woodrow Wilson's decision for the United States to enter World War I in 1917. Dewey's support of the war disappointed Bourne, and he went on to attack Dewey's personal opinion and his philosophy as a whole.[141] Dewey, however, continued to develop his vision of democracy. In *Reconstruction in Philosophy* (1920) he writes:

Government, business, art, religion, all social institutions have a meaning, a purpose. That purpose is to set free and to develop the capacities of human individuals without respect to race, sex, class or economic status. And this is all one with saying that the test of their value is the extent to which they educate every individual into the full stature of his possibility. Democracy has many meanings, but if it has a moral meaning, it is found in resolving that the supreme test of all political institutions and industrial arrangements shall be the contribution they make to the all-around growth of every member of society.[142]

In an authentic democracy, individuals can evaluate their own government and the political structure of their nation-state. For the growth of individuality, Dewey meditated on a new style of learning that connected democracy and education.[143]

Although the liberal discourse on Americanization recognized ethnic diversity, it is questionable whether or not "Asian-ness" was part of that discussion. First, when demanding exclusionists to tolerate ethnic differences, altruistic intellectuals, including Bourne, were only concerned with immigrants from Eastern and Southern Europe.[144] Second, even those who were sympathetic to the Japanese focused their argument on the Nikkei's assimilability, not the preservation of a "different" ethnicity and culture.[145] Imamura's effort, therefore, can be seen as expanding the ethnic diversity of the United States by including the Japanese minority and developing the multiplicity of the American religious heritage by incorporating Shin Buddhism. Later, some YBA members in Hawaii became civil servants and struggled to carry out justice as laid down in the American Constitution, though how they undertook to implement Imamura's ideas needs further study.[146]

The interpretation of modern democracy was also one of the common concerns of the mainland Shin clergy. When Senator James D. Phelan (D-California) and Valentine S. McClatchy, publisher of the *Sacramento Bee,* criticized Shin Buddhism (after confusing it with Shintō) in the early 1920s, Uchida responded that "Buddhism is Democratic, an ideal long held by the citizens of the United States of America."[147] Uchida, however, did not fully discuss the notion of Buddhist democracy, as did Imamura in Hawaii.

Summary

The reinterpretation of Shinran's teaching required a pragmatic mode of thinking. Takahashi Americanized the doctrine, drawing strength from Dewey's instrumentalism. Kyōgoku, on the other hand, reflected on the correlation between Shinran's and Śākyamuni's teachings and Kiyozawa's Spiritual Activism. Imamura initiated an interaction between this world and the Pure Land and sought a new Buddhist identity in Hawaii.

These three individuals were, however, quite different and areas of further research related to their activities are still needed. Takahashi was a scholar and not necessarily affiliated with the Shin Buddhist order. His pursuits were personal and philosophical. Few among the laity seemed to understand the ideas in his book, *Shinranism.* On the contrary, Kyōgoku and Imamura served as leaders of Nishi Honganji organizations. Kyōgoku, however, was not involved in the entire operation of the BMNA for a long period of time. His activity was limited to Central California until the BCA adopted his Sunday school curriculum after World War II. Kyōgoku was mostly concerned with Nisei Buddhist education, and his relationship with the Euro-Americans admitted to the BMNA is unknown. It is also hard to identify how much the laity actually understood his concept of spiritual growth, from the exhaustion of self-power to entrusting oneself to other-power, and how much they put this theory into practice.

In Hawaii, Imamura supervised the development of his organization, rituals, and doctrine. On one hand, he attempted to universalize Shin Buddhism as the objective of the HHMH. On the other hand, he searched for a cosmopolitan Buddhism and hired Hunt, who, however, propagated the ethical teachings of Theravada Buddhism. It is unclear how Imamura reconciled these two forms of Buddhism. In addition, the relationship between Shin and Chinese Buddhism in Hawaii remains unexplored. (In fact, it is unknown whether or not there were Chinese immigrant Buddhist organizations in Hawaii at the time.) There is also no information concerning Shin Buddhist interaction with native Hawaiians.[148]

As concluding remarks on the correlation among organization, rituals, and doctrine, it is fair to say that changes in organizational style and rituals occurred before the reinterpretation of Shin doctrine. On the mainland, the BMNA promoted Śākyamuni's teachings, initiated Caucasians who had been members of the Theosophical Society, and responded to the trans-sectarian Buddhist needs of Japanese immigrants. The relationship between the doctrinal orientation of the BMNA and the notion of a united Buddhism (*tsū bukkyō*) as developed in Japan remains unexplored, except for Kyōgoku's attempts to bridge the teachings of Śākyamuni and Shinran. In Hawaii, efforts similar to Kyōgoku's have not yet been identified. However, Imamura opened up a new dimension for the discussion of Shin doctrine by taking democracy into account, though this experiment was not as fruitful as his "democratization" of HHMH organizational style and the construction of a new building in an Indian/Western architectural style (as discussed in Chapter Four).

This chapter has demonstrated that the relationship between Kiyozawa and Kyōgoku was explicit, while that between Kiyozawa and Imamura was implicit. Scholars have not yet examined the history of the eastward propagation of the Higashi Honganji, the denomination with which Kiyozawa was affiliated. Chapter Six presents a history of the Higashi Honganji and examines whether or not there was further development of Kiyozawa's Spiritual Activism in North America within his order. It also investigates whether or not there were clear differences in doctrinal interpretation between the two branches of the Honganji.

Chapter Six

A History of the Higashi Honganji
in North America

The Higashi Honganji propagation is historically important, as it illustrates simultaneous competition and cooperation between the two branches of the Honganji in North America. The Nishi Honganji and the Higashi Honganji are comparable in terms of size and membership in Japan, but the scale of the Higashi propagation in North America has always been smaller than that of the Nishi. In 1933 and 1934, the Higashi had seven ministers and 2,900 members in Hawaii, whereas the Nishi boasted sixty-one ministers and 14,464 members.[1] In Los Angeles alone, the Higashi had five ministers and one thousand members in 1937, while the Nishi had six clerics with five thousand members.[2] During the prewar period, the Higashi headquarters sent only twenty-four ministers to Hawaii and thirteen to the mainland;[3] the Nishi headquarters dispatched more than two hundred ministers to the HHMH and the BMNA, respectively.

The Higashi Honganji initially did not have a plan to propagate in the mainland United States. Bishop Uchida of the BMNA and the Kyoto headquarters attempted to consolidate three Nishi Honganji churches in Los Angeles in September 1916. One group in the Rafu Bukkyōkai, headed by Junjō Izumida, its resident minister, however, opposed this, and subsequently the other group sought a court settlement. This incident not only led to the beginnings of Higashi Honganji propagation on the mainland, but also demonstrated the differences between the jurisdiction as defined by American legal institutions and the authority exercised by the Japanese Buddhist headquarters.

With the affiliation of the Rafu Bukkyōkai, the Higashi Honganji began to expand on the mainland. The number of propagation centers on the Pacific Coast increased when a Nishi *bukkyōkai* split and one of the competing parties sought affiliation with the Higashi as an alternative to leaving the BMNA. In other words, the Higashi Honganji advanced to the mainland by chance and without much effort. In contrast, the Higashi headquarters in Kyoto was determined from the start to propagate in

Hawaii. Owing to the lack of records, the history of its propagation in Hawaii is difficult to trace; however, there seems to have been both cooperation and competition between the Higashi and the Nishi, albeit of a different degree of intensity from that observed on the mainland.

A case study of Haya Akegarasu's visit to North America in 1929 further helps to investigate the relationship between the two Honganjis. Akegarasu was a prominent but controversial disciple of Manshi Kiyozawa, and he had several friends in Hawaii and on the mainland. Kankai Izuhara, who later became the second *rinban* of the Higashi Honganji Los Angeles Betsuin, and Hōun Tamayose, resident minister of the McCully Higashi Honganji and one of the "most learned and influential leaders in the Okinawan community,"[4] were Dharma friends of Akegarasu. In addition, Itsuzō Kyōgoku and Taigan Hata of the Nishi Honganji had received spiritual guidance from Akegarasu before moving to the United States. Nishi Honganji congregations received Akegarasu positively, which demonstrates that denominational differences between the two Honganjis were less important to the laity than to the organizational leaders.

Three Higashi Honganji ministers responded to the laity's transdenominational attitudes in the United States. Shōsetsu Tsufura helped the Nishi Honganji advance to the East Coast by organizing a Buddhist association in 1945 (which later became the present-day Seabrook Buddhist Temple), and he served at the Cleveland Buddhist Temple from 1951 to 1955. Gyōmei Kubose, a disciple of Akegarasu, founded an independent organization, the Buddhist Temple of Chicago, in October 1944. Enshō Ashikaga started a Japanese language program and later taught Buddhist studies when the University of California, Los Angeles (UCLA), opened its Department of Oriental Languages in 1947. Tsufura demonstrated the cooperation between the two Shin denominations; Kubose initiated a trans-sectarian Buddhist movement in the Midwest; and Ashikaga contributed to the growth of Buddhist studies in the United States.

Buddhist Disputes over the Applicability of Japanese Practices to the American Legal System

Junjō Izumida (1866–1951) played a major role in establishing a Buddhist group in Los Angeles.[5] He was born in 1866, the second son of Hōjō Izumida, the resident minister of Anyūji, a Nishi Honganji temple in Nagasaki prefecture. The Izumida family later moved to Shōrenji in Saga prefecture. Junjō Izumida was ordained in 1893 and became a full-fledged minister in 1897. A year later, he taught at the Bungaku-ryō (present-day Ryūkoku University) in Kyoto, which was operated by the Nishi Honganji. In 1902, he traveled to San Francisco on the recommendation of an administrative minister, Renjō Akamatsu, who later held the highest academic position at the headquarters (*kangaku*). Inspired by the propagation centers in San Jose and Sacramento, Izumida decided to stay longer on the Pacific Coast. He returned home in 1903 and convinced his family and the members of Shōrenji of the necessity of his leaving Japan again. The following year, he returned to the United States, this time arriving in Los Angeles.[6]

The population of Japanese pioneers in Los Angeles was rapidly increasing, and a Buddhist temple was necessary to serve its need for funerals, memorial services, and spiritual guidance. In September 1904, Izumida formed a nonsectarian Buddhist group called Rafu Bukkyōkai at 229 East Fourth Street; the first building construction took place at South Savannah Street in Boyle Heights.[7] Two more Buddhist organizations related to the Nishi Honganji were created soon after: the Nanka Bukkyōkai in October 1905 (on Jackson Street) and the Chūō Bukkyōkai in October 1912 (1508 Turner Street). Kōyū Uchida was appointed as acting head minister of the Nanka Bukkyōkai, while also serving as the fourth superintendent in San Francisco beginning in August 1905. Teishin Kawakami established the Chūō Bukkyōkai, which Shinjō Haraguchi later joined.[8]

The Kyoto headquarters made a major attempt to unify these three churches in September 1916 when the Rafu Bukkyōkai split, with factions both for and against Izumida. There was an incident called *"Butsuzen chin-uri sōdō"* (literally, "a bloody fight in front of the Buddha") at the Rafu Bukkyōkai on September 17. The fight broke out among the board members when they were discussing the resignation of Izumida, who was president of the organization at that time. Tetsugai Jisōji, the associate minister, presided over the meeting, during which it was said that Izumida had mismanaged and embezzled church funds and had presented different financial records to the board and the superintendent of the BMNA. He was also accused of having made financial reports without proper signatures. At the meeting, some pro-Izumida members, upset by these accusations, physically attacked the accusers, Matsuba and Nakamura. Both sides eventually came to some kind of reconciliation, though these two individuals initially threatened to take Izumida and other members to court. It was also said that other ministers formed the Nanka Bukkōkai because of arguments over who would receive the donations.[9] Bishop Uchida, in charge of the BMNA office, seized the opportunity of the schism in the Rafu Bukkyōkai to push for consolidation of the three churches.

The Nishi Honganji headquarters in Kyoto supported Uchida's decision. On May 1, 1917, Uchida visited Los Angeles and urged the leaders of these churches to merge, though without success. The headquarters then sent Shūe Sonoda, former superintendent of the BMNA, to Los Angeles on June 26, 1917. In an interview published in the *Rafu Shimpo,* Sonoda said that the Nishi Honganji had too many missions (three) in Los Angeles and suggested that it would be better to consolidate them to minimize financial and ministerial difficulties. He further pointed out the decline in the quality of the ministers.[10]

The *Rafu Shimpo* subsequently reported that under the guidance of the Executive Council, headed by Sonoda, the three churches approved the consolidation. On September 4, representatives of each organization made proposals, including to unify the three churches into one large organization, which would increase membership and help the teaching be more efficiently propagated; to choose the best location for a new building in the Japanese community in Los Angeles and promote the teaching, charities, and various other social activities on behalf of the members; to combine the current assets and debts of each church and reorganize management; to appoint Uchida as the head minister of the consolidated church and reassign all other ministers working at the three churches; and to select ten members from each church to form a consolidation committee.[11]

Prior to this agreement, on August 13, 1917, the ministers of the BMNA had decided on the following points: to consolidate the churches simultaneously; to send Izumida back to Japan and remove Haraguchi from Los Angeles; to appoint Uchida as acting head minister of the consolidated church; to appoint Kudara as minister of the San Francisco Bukkyōkai to replace Uchida; to eliminate the board system and appoint ministers as presidents of the churches; to give Sonoda exclusive authority over the ministers; to ask Japan's Ministry of Foreign Affairs to stop giving out visas to ministers not authorized by the Nishi Honganji headquarters; and to send regular reports of propagation activity directly to Sonoda in Japan.[12]

The documents filed at the Los Angeles Superior Court, however, reveal that the Rafu Bukkyōkai's decision for consolidation was not unanimous.[13] The proposal for consolidation was presented at the Rafu Bukkyōkai's first general meeting on September 9, 1917, but the majority of the members rejected the motion, and Izumida respected their decision. After this meeting, those who were in favor of the consolidation banded together and tried to discredit Izumida as president of the church. The Executive Council accused him of taking temple property and funds and proposed an investigation into his alleged misconduct. The pro-consolidation members called a second general meeting on September 16, 1917. However, prior to this they had persuaded fifty people to apply for church membership, and at least twenty-one of these new members attended the second meeting. Although thirty members voted against consolidation, the majority, including the twenty-one new members, espoused the motion and voted Izumida out from both offices, as church president and minister. But for the addition of these new members, neither the proposal for consolidation nor the one to remove Izumida would have passed, since the church by-laws stated that the president, Izumida himself, had to first approve new membership applications.[14] Despite this conspiracy, the Executive Council dismissed Izumida from his two positions and ordered him to leave his residence and return to Japan.

Izumida had his own reasons for protesting Sonoda: Izumida had formed the Rafu Bukkyōkai before the Nishi headquarters recognized it; the headquarters had never appointed him as its minister; he continued conducting religious services even after his dismissal by the Executive Council because the by-laws of the Rafu Bukkyōkai did not specify its exact relationship with the Nishi Honganji; he was clearly sympathetic toward the members who opposed consolidation; and finally, he did not take any money from the church. Izumida, who disagreed with Sonoda's decision, reluctantly admitted that he was disobeying orders from the headquarters and would await a reprimand.[15]

Because of Izumida's refusal to step down, those in favor of consolidation took legal action. The anti-Izumida group filed a petition for an injunction on October 4, 1917, to stop him from continuing as a minister of the Rafu Bukkyōkai and as president of the organization. The next day, the court issued a temporary restraining order against Izumida, based on an affidavit from T. Hirata, who complained that Izumida was still conducting services and receiving money even after his dismissal, as well as causing great embarrassment to the church and the Japanese community as a whole. However, the court later rescinded this order on October 16, 1917, after Izumida provided evidence that he had never been under the jurisdiction of the Nishi Honganji.[16]

After several court sessions, the case went to trial (the jury was waived), and Judge L. N. Valentine rendered a decision on October 4, 1918. He found that neither Izumida nor the Rafu Bukkyōkai was under the jurisdiction of the Nishi Honganji; therefore, the Executive Council could not remove him as minister of the church or president of the organization. The court also found that Izumida did not act in a manner to cause embarrassment to the church or to the Japanese community and ruled in his favor, awarding him all but $3.00 of his requested court costs of $148.10.[17]

In the meantime, on December 7, 1917, Izumida countersued for defamation of character.[18] The public debasement of Izumida in the Los Angeles Japanese press began with the headline "Reverend Izumida [I]s a Traitor" in the *Rafu Shimpo* on September 11, 1917. The newspaper went on to chronicle Izumida's protest of the consolidation of the three churches in Los Angeles with such inflammatory headlines as "Clean Up the Place Where a Demon Hides: Throw out Izumida Junjō . . . Save The Buddhist Mission of Los Angeles," "Advice to Reverend Izumida," and "Izumida Junjō: Reverend of Traitors and Lost Faith."[19]

In addition, on September 15, 1917, the *Rafu Asahi Shinbun* (*Los Angeles Morning Sun*) reported on the efforts to consolidate the three Buddhist churches in Los Angeles, stating that there were good reasons for doing so, despite Izumida and his followers' opposition. The article referred to the opposition as the "pro-Izumida gang" and cited Izumida's dishonesty as the basis for his opposing consolidation. It further accused him of embezzling funds and labeled him a person of low repute and character. The article went on to say that "no further statement is necessary; to be guided by a person with such a character probably there will be no way but to be led to hell."[20] Izumida sued the *Rafu Asahi Shinbun* and its editor, Tanaka, on December 7, 1917, in the Los Angeles Superior Court and contended that the article not only ruined his reputation but also led people to discredit him. He asked for $30,000 in compensatory damages and $20,000 in punitive damages. Tanaka and the *Rafu Asahi Shinbun* denied that the statements were defamatory.[21]

From June 26 to August 15, 1918, Judge Hewitt examined the case, which also involved the controversial handling of offerings. Embezzlement was described as the cause of the contention between Izumida and Ryūun Asayoshi, which was the cause of the latter's leaving the Rafu Bukkyōkai to establish the Nanka Bukkyōkai. On August 16, the *Rafu Shimpo* reported on the last debate between the attorneys of both parties. The respondent's counsel pointed to Izumida's unfair practices and criticized the way he had borrowed money to finance the church, as this did not follow the guidelines of nonprofit organizations. But the plaintiff's counsel argued that financial problems were common for a start-up church in need of operational expenses, and that Izumida used the money for "debit and credit" and not for his personal gain.[22]

After the trial, Judge Hewitt sided with Izumida, recognizing that the Rafu Bukkyōkai was "the largest and most influential and best known Buddhist Mission in the State of California, having a very large congregation and membership composed of persons from the City of Los Angeles,

County of Los Angeles, and other surrounding counties, and from other districts throughout Southern California." Thus, the flagrant remarks concerning Izumida's mishandling of offerings had caused substantial harm to him. On September 24, 1918, Hewitt awarded Izumida $300 in compensatory damages and $279 in court costs.[23]

Although Izumida survived these two *causes célèbres*, the Nishi Honganji headquarters was unsatisfied with the verdicts and decided to defrock him. It twice ordered him to appear before the Kyoto headquarters, but he refused to appear. Without his presence, the headquarters held an internal investigation on December 12, 1918, and went ahead with its decision to disrobe him.[24] In August 1919, the *Rafu Shimpo* reported that Izumida was no longer a Nishi Honganji minister, quoting from the Reports of "Internal Circulation" (*honzan rokuji*) issued on June 30.[25] Izumida was reprimanded under Article 7, Section 1, and Article 13, Section 6, of the "Regulations of Disciplinary Punishment" (*chōkai jōki*), which the headquarters applied to a minister who was disrespectful to the Dharma and dealt with defrocking. Under Chapter 12, Articles 35 and 36, of the "Constitution of Nishi Honganji's Detailed Rules" (*jihō saisoku*), however, the headquarters could reduce sentence and exonerate a minister if he regretted his wrongdoing. In other words, the headquarters did consider reinstating Izumida. Later, Tokumei Inoue, Director of the Propagation Department (Fukyō-bu) at headquarters, sent a letter to Kenju Masuyama, the sixth bishop of the BMNA, on January 16, 1931, mentioning Izumida's possible return to the Nishi Honganji.[26]

Not all the ministers were against Izumida. Gendō Nakai, who had served as resident minister of the Seattle Buddhist Church from 1902 to 1907, sent a letter of protest to the headquarters, while at the same time advising Izumida to accept punishment and wait for exoneration.[27] The two men had known each other before coming to the United States. Izumida had taught at the Bungaku-ryō when Nakai was the student editor of the Buddhist journal *Hansei zasshi* (or *Hanseikai zasshi*). Nakai once wrote an article attacking Kyoto City officials for not tightening the control of prostitution. In response, they indicted Izumida because he was the editorial supervisor. Luckily, Izumida's attorney succeeded in defending him against the charge.[28] Because of Izumida's involvement in the case, Nakai felt indebted to him. But Nakai's protest did not make much of a difference at headquarters. After his excommunication from the Nishi Honganji, Izumida contacted a Higashi Honganji priest. His memoirs describe the entire affair in Los Angeles, and include his final thoughts on the matter:

Although the punishment of the Nishi Honganji headquarters was not just, I avoided further contention. For the propagation of Buddhism, I decided to become independent, as Shinran Shōnin had demonstrated being "neither monk nor layman." Nevertheless, by the request of the members and in my own interest, we asked Fujimoto, a Higashi Honganji priest, to take all the judicial records to the Higashi Honganji headquarters. Then we made a formal request to Higashi Honganji to hire me as its minister, if they found no fault on my side. After evaluation, the headquarters sent me a telegram permitting me to set up a Higashi Honganji propagation center (*fukyōsho*) in the Rafu Bukkyōkai.[29]

Izumida took consolation in regarding his situation as similar to Shinran's exile. It is unclear who was the person named Fujimoto, when and how Izumida contacted him, or what drew Izumida's interest to the Higashi Honganji. At any rate, the Rafu Bukkyōkai became affiliated with the Higashi Honganji in December 1919.[30] In June 1920, Higashi headquarters sent Genryō Abe (who would later serve as the second president of Kōka Joshi Daigaku, or Kōka Women's University, in Kyoto) to the Rafu Bukkyōkai. His records state:

> In the autumn of 1919, Fujimoto conveyed Izumida's message to the Higashi Honganji headquarters. Izumida showed his desire to join our order because he had been defrocked by Nishi. Ōtani Eijō, our chief administrator at that time, accepted his offer and decided to mark Izumida's affiliation as the beginning of the Higashi Honganji propagation in North America. In the following year, I was appointed as minister serving in North America and left Japan at the end of June. After arriving in San Francisco, I met with the bishop of the BMNA, Uchida Kōyū, Izumida's brother-in-law, and heard his side of the story, then I moved to the Rafu Bukkyōkai.[31]

Abe's mission was to supervise the set-up of a Higashi Honganji propagation center at the Rafu Bukkyōkai and recognize Izumida's transfer from the Nishi to the Higashi; however, the nature of the exchange between Abe and Uchida remains unknown.

The Higashi Honganji headquarters moved swiftly to affiliate Izumida with its order. It ordained him (*tokudo*) on May 27, 1921, after registering him at Tokushōji in Kyoto. Izumida became a full-fledged minister (*kyōshi*) on June 1, 1921.[32] The Rafu Bukkyōkai was renamed the Higashi Honganji Los Angeles Betsuin on March 20, 1921, and the Superior Court of Los Angeles County recognized it on October 4 in the same year.[33] The headquarters appointed Izumida as *rinban* of the *betsuin* on May 25, 1922, and Ejō Kurita and Shōsetsu Tsufura began their ministerial service in Southern California.[34] Izumida, representing the Rafu Bukkyōkai, and Esui Abe, the chief administrator representing the headquarters, exchanged signatures of agreement with the establishment of the Higashi Honganji Los Angeles Betsuin and its by-laws. From that time on, the property of the Rafu Bukkyōkai was placed under the authority of the abbot of the Higashi Honganji in Japan. On August 25, 1922, Izumida became the first bishop of the Higashi Honganji Mission in North America.[35]

While the Higashi Honganji began propagation in Los Angeles, the Nishi Honganji completed its consolidation. The merger between the Nanka Bukkyōkai and the anti-Izumida group at the Rafu Bukkyōkai led to the birth of the Nishi Honganji Bukkyōkai in December 1917.[36] The ministers, including Uchida, Jisōji, and Asayoshi, who had led the effort to remove Izumida, placed a statue of Amida Buddha in the building and officiated at the inauguration service. The Chūō Bukkyōkai, which remained independent, received an image of Amida Buddha from the Kyoto headquarters and organized its own women's association sometime in 1919,[37] though it later joined the Nishi Honganji Bukkyōkai. After witnessing the emergence of the Higashi Honganji Los Angeles Betsuin, Uchida asked his headquarters on November 10, 1922, to elevate his *bukkyōkai* in Los Angeles to *betsuin* status. In September 1931, his request was granted.[38]

Conflict over the Americanization and Japanization of Temple Management

The attempts to consolidate three Japanese Buddhist churches in Los Angeles illustrate the democratization of a Buddhist institution in the United States; they also simultaneously reveal the headquarters' desire to Japanize them. The failure to consolidate not only represented a shift in authority within a Japanese Buddhist organization in the United States but also demonstrated the impossibility of applying Japanese customs to the American legal system. In Japan, the headquarters of a Buddhist organization (*honzan*) held power over its affiliating temples and could suppress heretics (*ianjin*), often with the threat of legal action backed up by the judicial system. The Nishi headquarters seemed to have applied this Japanese custom in the United States, although Izumida was merely disloyal to the headquarters and not a heretic.[39] But the headquarters failed to understand how legal authority functioned in the United States.

According to the by-laws of the Rafu Bukkyōkai in English (amended in January 1917), the president was defined as "chief missionary" (Article VII). There was no reference to the name "Nishi Honganji" at all. However, in the Japanese edition of these by-laws (*Rafu Bukkyōkai kaisoku*), the *kaikyōshi*, indicating a minister appointed by the headquarters, was regarded as the president. Though neither the Kyoto headquarters nor the BMNA office directly took Izumida to court, their reputation was damaged, because Uchida had backed the anti-Izumida group headed by Tetsugai Jisōji. The BMNA reported the lawsuit in the *Beikoku bukkyō*, its monthly journal, and justified the headquarters' position by denouncing Izumida's misconduct.

> This incident was caused by the Rafu Bukkyōkai itself, thus, it had nothing to do with the Kyoto headquarters and the Department of the Superintendent (the BMNA's bishop's office). During the reviewing process in court, however, the relationship between Izumida and the headquarters/Department of Superintendent was questioned, and chancellor Sonoda and superintendent [bishop] Uchida were summoned to appear. Unfortunately, because of their involvement, this event was seen as contention between Izumida and headquarters. . . .[40]

While accusing Izumida and his alleged mismanagement of the Rafu Bukkyōkai, the BMNA denied the involvement of its headquarters in the lawsuit. But Uchida was inconsistent in his treatment of Izumida and Shinjō Haraguchi, who was dismissed but not defrocked. In court, when Izumida's counsel asked Uchida why Haraguchi was still working in the same capacity as before at the Chūō Bukkyōkai, Uchida could not give a definitive response.[41]

The consolidation of the three churches also suggests a debate over the authority of the board of trustees. As mentioned earlier, at the BMNA Ministers' Meeting on August 13, 1917, Sonoda and Uchida came up with the idea of terminating the board system and giving more power to the ministers as presidents of the churches. The headquarters attempted to bring to the United States the Japanese style of temple management, in which resident ministers had much more authority.

On the other hand, the by-laws of the Rafu Bukkyōkai stated: "Directors and Representatives shall supervise this institution and decide on important matters of this institution" (Article VIII). It is, however, unclear how much Izumida understood the significance of the board system, since there seem to be other factors that explain the collisions between Izumida and Sonoda and Uchida.

Izumida's excommunication was based on his conduct and had nothing to do with his understanding of doctrine. First, Izumida held double standards regarding his relationship with the Nishi Honganji headquarters and the BMNA. When he came to San Francisco in 1902, Izumida worked for the BMNA. The youth group and women's association of the San Francisco church welcomed him as a *kaikyōshi*. In 1903, he became the chief editor of the *Beikoku bukkyō,* and also often contributed articles.[42] After returning to Japan in 1904, Izumida proposed the establishment of a Los Angeles propagation center to Nishi Honganji administrators. The headquarters, however, could not appoint him as *kaikyōshi* at the time because of the need for more priests on the Asian continent and to support the Japanese army during the Russo-Japanese War. Thus, Izumida came to California without official assignment (he was officially given the title of *kaikyōshi* in 1908).[43]

In Los Angeles, Izumida showed an ambivalent attitude toward the BMNA office. On one hand, he continued to report his activities in the *Beikoku bukkyō,* right up to the time of the Rafu Bukkyōkai's split. He also participated in the BMNA Ministers' Meeting as late as July 1914. In the meantime, the BMNA office paid him a monthly stipend of $25 for two years, in exchange for his reports on the activities of the Buddhist churches in Southern California. His stipend was afterward reduced to $17.50 a month and eventually stopped altogether. Izumida was said to donate all the money he had received from the BMNA office to the Rafu Bukkyōkai.[44]

Despite his involvement with the BMNA, Izumida avoided establishing a Buddhist church affiliated with the Nishi Honganji in Los Angeles. At the turn of the twentieth century, there was no Japanese Buddhist organization in Southern California. If the temple's denomination had been strictly defined, it would have prevented Izumida from pursuing his objectives, namely to serve all immigrants, regardless of their affiliations with other Buddhist sects in Japan.

The second factor that caused Izumida to collide with Sonoda, Uchida, and Jisōji was the differences between them in regard to their commitment to the propagation of Buddhism in the United States. Because of Izumida's decision to settle permanently in Los Angeles, he might have become conservative concerning his local position as president of the Rafu Bukkyōkai and in negotiations with the Executive Council. Izumida died in Los Angeles in 1951, while the other ministers, who had graduated from prestigious universities in Japan, stayed in the United States only for a while, then returned home and became elite ministers. In other words, coming to the United States had paved their way to the top of the administrative echelon. Sonoda became head of the Bungaku-ryō (present-day Ryūkoku University) in 1905 and held the position of *kangaku* in 1911. Uchida stepped down as bishop in 1923 because of ill health, but served as the Director of Education and the Director of Propagation at the Kyoto headquarters from 1925 to 1935. Jisōji resigned from the BMNA in 1919 and later became a professor at Ryūkoku University.[45]

Third, Izumida's personality might have been a factor in the arising of internal rivalries. Records show that the Rafu Bukkyōkai's split had something to do with Izumida's character. He rarely got along well with the other ministers, and he also lacked social skills and rarely complimented anyone.[46] Shōsetsu Tsufura, who later worked at the Higashi Honganji Los Angeles Betsuin, also had a difficult time with him.[47] On the other hand, immigrants from Saga prefecture supported Izumida, because he had also come from Saga. When various newspapers made derogatory statements about him, Honkō Matsumoto and other Issei pioneers from Saga stood by him.[48]

Although the evaluation of his character varied among his detractors and supporters, Izumida tried to avoid legal action. On the advice of Sei Fujii, president of the *Kashū Mainichi Shinbun* (*California Daily Newspaper*), who supported him during the lawsuit, Izumida visited the plaintiffs and asked them to nullify the court action.[49] Contrary to the less than salutary accounts in the *Rafu Shimpo* and the *Los Angeles Morning Sun,* Fujii offered a different image of Izumida in his eulogy published in the *Kashū Mainichi:*

> Old master Izumida finally passed away at county hospital. He came to Los Angeles fifty years ago and started organizing a Buddhist gathering. On East Second Street, Mr. Kunita from Hiroshima had a restaurant where about ten elderly immigrants gathered and listened to Izumida's hopes for propagating Buddhism in America. This was the beginning of the Rafu Bukkyōkai. They still remember that the first small building was built on East Fourth Street, which was later moved to Boyd Street. A couple years later, a bigger church hall was built between South Savannah and Second Street. While attending college, I often helped Izumida with translating Caucasian's lectures. The present Higashi Honganji Betsuin was founded much later. A carpenter from Saga was very kind to Izumida, and built the magnificent building at a low price, to which many of us gave him thanks. Through the years, the old master Izumida had a difficult life and I felt sorry for him. I knew for a long time that he couldn't buy food or take the train. Being at the age of eighty, he still suffered a lot from not having the daily necessities. Tears often blurred my eyes when I thought of him on a rainy morning or stormy evening. The achievements of the old master were never recognized and he died as if forgotten at county hospital. However, I should be happy for him because he fulfilled his life. . . .[50]

Fujii was the one who advised Izumida to affiliate the Rafu Bukkyōkai with the Higashi Honganji, so his perception of Izumida may reflect a favorable bias.

The clash between the authority of American legal institutions and that of the Nishi Honganji headquarters led to the establishment of the Higashi

Honganji on the mainland. After breaking away from the Nishi Honganji, Izumida sought affiliation with the Higashi Honganji, because it was difficult for the Rafu Bukkyōkai to remain completely nonsectarian. By that time, other Japanese Buddhist schools had started propagation in Los Angeles. Shutai Aoyama began to propagate Shingon doctrine in fall 1912; Kansei Asahi held the first gathering of Nichiren believers in May 1914; and Hōsen Isobe established the Sōtō Zen mission in May 1922.[51] With all these new organizations maintaining their sectarian affiliations, Izumida must have felt compelled to become part of a denomination, as otherwise the Rafu Bukkyōkai would not have been able to survive.[52] Therefore, the opportunity for the eastward transmission of Jōdo Shinshū came as something of a surprise for the Higashi Honganji, as it had not intended to advance to the mainland United States.

Further Propagation

Propagation on the Mainland

On the mainland, the Higashi Honganji's development primarily depended on Izumida's efforts. He established Higashi propagation centers in Northern and Central California, and in Vancouver. None of these, however, started out being affiliated with the Higashi. In 1926, Izumida recognized the affiliation of a group that had split off from the Berkeley Buddhist Church, a Nishi Honganji *bukkyōkai*. In 1925, Kōgen Masuda, resident minister of this church, attempted to create a language school run by the *bukkyōkai*, in addition to the one (Berkeley Nihon Gakuen) that the Berkeley Nikkei community had established, which was at the time temporarily closed. Although the church's board of directors approved his proposal, he faced opposition from a group that called a special church meeting. The board, in the name of the Berkeley Bukkyōkai, negotiated with the members of the opposing group twice, with the help of a BMNA adviser, Giyū Tōfuku. According to the arbitration proposal, the Berkeley Buddhist Church would postpone its opening of a Japanese language school, and the Buddhist minister would teach Japanese at the other school. The two groups, however, failed to agree when they deviated from the focus of discussion, such as who would actually sign the request for the special church meeting and the amount of compensation Masuda would receive as a Japanese language instructor.[53]

The exchange became disgraceful when local newspapers reported on it. The executives of the Berkeley Bukkyōkai twice issued statements attacking their counterparts, on June 27 and September 15, to which those who had demanded the special meeting responded in kind. The nonexecutive members strongly believed that the final decision had to be made at such a meeting.[54] The congregation gathered on January 30, 1926, and tension between the two groups peaked; the police were on alert in case the meeting got out of hand. As a result, the nonexecutive party of thirty-six members left the *bukkyōkai* and requested the BMNA office to send a new minister. The bishop, however, ignored their demand, so five representatives of the independent group met Izumida in Los Angeles and petitioned him to assign a resident minister. Izumida accepted their request and named the group Wantō Higashi Honganji (Wantō Shin Bukkyōkai). After receiving consent from the Higashi headquarters, he formally began Higashi Honganji propagation in Berkeley on April 11, 1926, with Chijō Suemori as the first resident minister. In 1933, this group was renamed the Hokka Higashi Honganji; in 1965 it adopted its current name, Berkeley Higashi Honganji.[55]

Izumida advanced Higashi propagation in Central California when a Shin Buddhist association in Parlier sought affiliation in August 1931. When Ryūchi Fujii resigned his teaching position at a Japanese language school, about sixty members, who had formed the Parlier branch of the Fresno Buddhist Church, the Parlier Gōshikai, during the 1920s, left the church. They complained that the money they had raised to pay for a mortgage on the Fresno church was used for a different purpose.[56] The Parlier group then requested Bishop Masuyama to send a new minister who could also serve as a Japanese language teacher. On August 23, 1931, the Fresno church held a special meeting to deal with this problem.[57]

The Nishi clergy became upset by the further actions of the Parlier laity. Despite Masuyama's involvement, the Parlier group insisted on independence and asked Izumida to appoint a resident minister. While advising them that he would nullify his decision if the Parlier Gōshikai and the Fresno Buddhist Church were to settle their dispute, Izumida authorized the affiliation of the Parlier group with the Higashi Honganji and transferred Chijō Suemori from Berkeley to Parlier in 1932.[58] The members were free to affiliate with either of the two branches of the Honganji, but the Parlier residents asked Suemori to take over the teaching position at their Japanese language school. For one Nishi minister, this event was humiliating: "[Suemori's taking control of the Parlier Japanese language school represents] nothing but submission of Nishi [to Higashi]."[59] Izumida recognized the Parlier Higashi Honganji in December 1932 and held the inauguration ceremony on April 25, 1933.[60] Shin Buddhist followers in Kingsburg, who had already been Higashi members in Japan, later joined the Parlier church.[61]

Izumida took the opportunity to expand the Higashi Honganji's propagation in Canada when the Buddhist church in Vancouver was divided. On July 13, 1925, a group of people sought to establish the Higashi Honganji Bukkyōkai in Vancouver. Izumida visited them on July 31 and held a series of lectures in Steveston, New Westminster, Vancouver, and other places. It appeared that he even spoke at the Nishi Honganji's West Second Avenue Buddhist Mission. After receiving Izumida's report, the Higashi headquarters sent Kendō Mito to Vancouver on November 10. Izumida and Mito held the inaugural service of the Ōtani-ha (Higashi Honganji) Bukkyōkai on November 15, 1925, at 240 Alexander Street, Vancouver. Competition between the two Honganjis intensified, as just one day after the Higashi's notice in the *Tairiku Nippō* of its gathering, the Honpa Canada Buddhist Mission announced the inaugural service of its Buddhist Women's Association. At the end of November, the BMNA office sent Gijin Taga to the mission and increased its ministerial personnel. The mission held a welcome party for Taga on various occasions and demonstrated its solidarity.[62]

Izumida and Mito planned the propagation systematically. They held meetings of the Buddhist Women's Association on the first Sunday of each month at 2:00 P.M., the YMBA on the second Friday at 7:00 P.M., and the YWBA on the third Sunday at 2:00 P.M. The minister delivered a Shin Buddhist sermon on the second and fourth Sundays at 2:00 P.M., and gave a lecture on basic Buddhism at 7:00 P.M.; held a Shin study session on the third Wednesday at 8:00 P.M.; and the Sunday school, which initially accommodated seventy children, met every Sunday morning at 9:00 A.M.[63]

The Higashi's operation in Vancouver seemed to be successful, but the Ōtani-ha Bukkyōkai closed suddenly at the end of May 1929, for unknown reasons. The church received pictorial scrolls of Shinran and Rennyo from Japan in July 1926, which suggests that the arrangement of the altar had been completed. According to the church meeting held in September, the board discussed the possibility of purchasing land for a new building and having an assistant minister. Soon after, on October 4, 1926, Shinjō Miura arrived in Vancouver to assist Mito. Miura came from Shiga prefecture, from which a large number of residents had immigrated to Canada; the region was a Higashi stronghold. It seemed that the Ōtani-ha Bukkyōkai flourished initially, but three years later it abruptly announced its closure with the statement "Higashi Honganji propagation center will be closed in the end of May [1929] because of its circumstance."[64] Even Izumida was unaware of the Ōtani-ha Bukkyōkai's situation. His letter to Miura suggests only that the church could no longer afford Miura's services.[65]

With the rise of the Higashi Honganji in California, the Nishi Honganji no longer remained the single authority of Shin Buddhism on the mainland. The Nishi headquarters and the BMNA tried to contain Izumida's advance. In 1923, the Nishi Honganji Diet in Kyoto passed a proposal to increase the budget of the BMNA and condemned Izumida's betrayal and the Higashi Honganji's development in Los Angeles.[66] On November 4, 1936, Masuyama granted *betsuin* status to the Fresno church and unified its diocese in Central California in competition with the Parlier Higashi Honganji.

Propagation in Hawaii

In contrast to Izumida's "acquisition" of Nishi Honganji groups on the mainland, the Higashi Honganji headquarters initially purposely sent *kaikyōshi* to Kauai to propagate. In 1899, Shizuka Sazanami and Kenryū Yamada established the first Buddhist mission in Waimea.[67] Although both men later returned to Japan (Sazanami in 1909 and Yamada in 1902), ministers from Kumamoto prefecture took over their enterprise. By 1910, the Higashi had established two more propagation centers on Kauai, at Makaweli and Kekaha. Sueto Satō built an elementary school and dormitory and intended to create a junior high school program.[68] The ministers' prefectural background, however, did not mean that the Higashi propagation was solely in collaboration with immigrants from Kumamoto. The Waimea Higashi Honganji was also supported by Issei pioneers from Hiroshima and Yamaguchi prefectures, both Nishi strongholds.[69]

There was at least one case of competition between the two Honganjis on Kauai. The Nishi advance on that island was slow because of the presence of the Higashi. The HHMH office tried to open branches in Kekaha, Mana, and Waimea, where a large number of Nishi Honganji followers lived. These efforts did not succeed until the end of 1909, when the HHMH finally opened its first propagation center in Kekaha.[70] By 1930, the situation had been reversed. The number of Nishi propagation centers increased to seven, while Chikō Ōdate of the Higashi single-handedly managed its three centers.[71]

The Higashi Honganji's development in Honolulu was much slower than the Nishi's. Shingyō Doi went to Honolulu in 1916 and founded the first propagation center, between Smith and Maunakea streets; it was later moved to North King Street in Palama. The Kyoto headquarters recognized it as the Higashi Honganji Honolulu Betsuin in August 1922, and appointed Kankai Izuhara as the first *rinban* on November 22, 1916. The church organized the first Sunday school in the same year and published its first news bulletin, *Dharma Friend* (*Kyōyū*) in 1924. The Honolulu Betsuin also initiated propagation in Kaneohe in May 1924.[72]

Izuhara's career stretched over three regions: Japan, Hawaii, and California. His family affiliation was with Saikōji, a Nishi temple in Hiroshima, but when Izuhara married he became the son-in-law of the resident minister of Hōshōji, a Higashi temple in the same prefecture. The headquarters of the Higashi Honganji sent him to Honolulu in 1918 and transferred him to Hilo in 1928, where he founded the first Higashi mission on the Big Island. In May 1936, the Kyoto headquarters transferred him again, to the mainland, and appointed him the second bishop and *rinban* of the Higashi Honganji Los Angeles Betsuin, after Izumida retired. Izuhara served in California until he was interned at Heart Mountain, in Wyoming, in December 1941.[73] Izuhara established an amicable relationship with the Nishi clergy and laity in Los Angeles, primarily because he shared their familial roots in Hiroshima.[74] His successful career in Southern California reveals how connection within the same *kenjinkai* (prefectural association) was just as important as one's Buddhist affiliation in the Japanese immigrant community.

The relationship of Hawaii's two Honganji ministers was relatively mild, compared to that of their mainland counterparts. Owing to the trans-sectarian efforts undertaken by Imamura and Hunt, Hawaii's six Buddhist schools celebrated Śākyamuni's birthday together in April 1929.[75] Leaders of the two Honganjis, Shingon, Sōtō, Jōdo, and Nichiren schools also supported the Japanese plantation workers' higher wage movement in 1920 by petitioning the Hawaiian Sugar Planter's Association (HSPA) to recognize their demands. During the 1930s, the Hawaii Federation of Young Buddhist Association, initiated by the Nishi Honganji, also accommodated members from the other five Buddhist schools, including the Higashi Honganji.[76] It seemed that for the laity, denominational competition in North America appeared far less important than it was for the organizational leaders. Two case studies further testify to this phenomenon: Haya Akegarasu's visit to North America and Taigan Hata's activities in Oakland.

Haya Akegarasu and His Influence

Akegarasu was a direct disciple of Kiyozawa and later became a charismatic leader of the Higashi Honganji (appointed Chief Administrator in 1951). He was a sensational priest who insisted on the importance of being honest to one's own innate nature. There were two dimensions to his faith: living by the grace of Amida Buddha and recognizing one's own instincts.[77] In his article "Even Evil Acts Are Embraced by Tathagata's Grace," published in *Seishinkai* in May 1909, Akegarasu writes:

My understanding [of Shin Buddhism] is that both convenient and inconvenient matters are embraced by Tathagata's grace, to which I remain grateful. I feel his grace when I am encouraged and when I am discouraged. I feel his grace when my wallet is full and when my wallet is empty. I feel his grace when I meet with a person I am fond of and when I depart from him. I feel his grace not only over teachers and friends who have guided me but also individuals who have led me to commit evil acts.[78]

For Akegarasu, entrusting in Amida Buddha's Vow (*shinjin*) meant accepting all phenomena without making any judgment. Akegarasu often tested the faith of the youth by engaging in long and difficult religious dialogues with them. This process was called "stripping one's outer shell" (*muku*), meaning breaking apart one's hypocritical appearance and revealing one's true nature. Those who were "stripped," as it were, would face self-criticism and become ashamed of themselves. Some could not tolerate Akegarasu; others even held grudges against him.[79] He also castigated the ways in which devotees understood Shinran's teaching in a traditional way. They would often spend a lot of time memorizing scriptures and demonstrate their knowledge by reciting passages in front of other followers. For Akegarasu, however, recitation or memorization of Rennyo's letters (*Ofumi* or *Gobunshō*) and Shinran's hymns (*Wasan*) were not useful unless one actually lived one's daily life with faith in Amida Buddha. Because of his radical attitudes, senior priests labeled him a heretic for discarding the sacred texts and recognizing even unwholesome acts as the grace of Amida.[80]

Akegarasu, himself, however, came to reveal part of his true nature—his attachment to sexual intimacy. In 1913, his wife died of tuberculosis. While caring for her, he had an affair with a nurse, which was later made public by a journalist from the religious newspaper *Chūgai Nippō*. Four years later, Akegarasu admitted the affair in public by symbolically "confessing" it to his teacher, Kiyozawa (even though Kiyozawa had passed away by that time). By facing and acknowledging his true self, Akegarasu stood up to the public bashing.

I was naive enough to tell my wife that I would never get married again when I stayed over a night by her side. During the third week of my care of her, however, I had an affair with a nurse. Was I corrupt or evil? But how can a lowly person further be degraded, or become more evil? Is it true I who commit this evil act? Am I ashamed of it? Or is it true I who sleep with a woman?.... Why do you call a fire of sexual desire flaring up in my mind corrupt? After all I was born because my parents had such a desire. Why do you call it evil, when such a fire burns my entire body and reveals the naked I? I have no one else to turn to, but this is who I am. My teacher, this is the significance of being on this earth.[81]

Akegarasu expressed regret for his actions but at the same time he accepted his wrongdoing and did not deceive himself. Five months after his wife's death, in 1914, he married again, but from 1920, Akegarasu maintained what he called a "miracle-like love affair of three individuals," as he embraced his own instincts and did not hesitate to boast about who he was.[82] It was at this time that he became really controversial; some of his followers left him, while others appreciated him for his frankness.[83]

Akegarasu made an extended visit to North America in 1929. He had been on a series of world tours since 1925, visiting ancient sites related to Śākyamuni Buddha in India and other sacred places in the Middle East and Egypt. He arrived in Honolulu on April 20, 1929, and toured the Islands. He met Issei pioneers and delivered sermons. He was welcomed by former friends, such as Tamayose in Honolulu and Izuhara in Hilo. Akegarasu left Honolulu on May 18 and arrived in San Francisco a week later. After visiting Taigan Hata in Oakland, he made a transcontinental tour to New York, accompanied by a young man, Masao Kubose, whose spiritual growth had been nurtured by Hata. They arrived in New York on June 8 and visited Joseph Warren Mason, a journalist, philosopher, and scholar of Shintō. Akegarasu also met with Abbot Lawrence Lowell, the president of Harvard University, and various professors. He returned to California on June 30, this time to Los Angeles, and moved north. He visited Kyōgoku in Fresno and extended his trip to Seattle and Vancouver. Akegarasu left for Japan on July 26, 1929; Hata saw him off in tears.[84]

Akegarasu was well received by the members of various Nishi Honganji Buddhist churches.[85] His arrival in Los Angeles was a cultural phenomenon. Five hundred people attended his public lecture held by the Nishi Honganji Los Angeles Buddhist Church. The priests of Daijōkai (Association of Mahāyāna) also welcomed him, and they engaged in a spirited debate that went on until midnight.[86] An Akegarasu Association (Akegarasu Kai), which met once a month to study Buddhism, formed in Los Angeles. The local nursery association in Oakland sponsored one of Akegarasu's public lectures held in the Bay Area.[87] His Dharma sermons were printed in Buddhist journals and published by churches.[88] A Nishi member in Vancouver who heard Akegarasu's sermon was impressed when Akegarasu said that it was Buddhist priests who would corrupt the Buddha's teachings. This anonymous individual later sent a letter to the BMNA office regarding Gijin Tada's misconduct in Vancouver, and made reference to Akegarasu's sermon.[89]

Taigan Hata

A passionate disciple of Akegarasu, Taigan Hata became a controversial figure in Oakland. He had come to San Francisco in September 1913 as a Nishi Honganji *kaikyōshi,* but had returned to Japan to learn more about Shinran's teaching and eventually became Akegarasu's student. He returned to the United States in April 1922 with his wife, and was assigned to the Buddhist Church of Oakland by the BMNA office the following year. Hata promoted Akegarasu's teaching by distributing small pamphlets written by his teacher.[90] The BMNA office swiftly ordered his transfer to Kyoto in April 1926, but Hata ignored the order and remained in Oakland with the support of some church members. Acting Bishop Kusuhara publicly announced Hata's resignation and replaced him with Kenshi Iwao. Hata's supporters, however, requested Kusuhara to withdraw his decision. Fearing physical violence between the two groups, Kusuhara postponed Iwao's appointment and sought reconciliation.[91]

Hata and a small group within the Buddhist Church of Oakland had their own reasons to protest. Dōshun Mizutani, the resident minister at the Oakland church, was supposed to resign sometime before, so Bishop Uchida assigned Hata to the church. At that time, the congregation passed a resolution to build a new church hall with a budget of $30,000. Soon after, however, Mizutani changed his mind and decided to stay on a bit longer. Although his efforts to extend his service failed, three or four of Mizutani's friends blocked Hata's inauguration, pointing to his radical approach to propagation. Hata felt that he had been made the scapegoat for those who sided with Mizutani and objected to the construction of the new hall.[92]

With the intervention of the consul general of Japan and influential people in San Francisco, the dispute at the Buddhist Church of Oakland was resolved in July 1926. Hata was to leave his position, after paying off the debt directly made by the church and selecting committee members to handle other types of liabilities. In return, the church would pay him a reasonable amount as compensation for his previous work. Six members of a reconciliation committee also asked the Nishi headquarters to nullify its decision to transfer Hata to Japan, because they respected his determination to propagate in the United States.[93] Hata eventually established an independent Buddhist association called the Kyūdōkai in Oakland in 1927. In the meantime, the Nishi headquarters continued to demand that he return to Kyoto, but he ignored this. In March 1931, the headquarters stripped him of his qualification to propagate Buddhism (*fukyōshi*), so Hata voluntarily resigned from the BMNA.[94]

This incident has been perceived as "a dispute involving the question of faith." Kōsei Ogura wrote:

> Seven years ago the minister of the Oakland Church began to propound a heterodoxical [sic] creed in defiance to the orthodox Shin belief. The members were divided into two camps, supporting the conflicting views. The dispute lasted a long time. Finally it ended in the withdrawal of the minister from N.A.B.M (BMNA). He conducts his own individual church and continues to preach his heterodoxy.[95]

From Ogura's point of view, Hata, influenced by Akegarasu, was a heretic of orthodox Shin Buddhism. However, this characterization is questionable. Ogura's views on Akegarasu might have had a personal component, since he had been a minister of the BMNA at one point.[96] If the contention had been based on doctrinal differences between the Nishi and the Higashi (as marked by Akegarasu's approach), Hata could have chosen to affiliate with the Higashi. But since he declared his affiliation with the BMNA, he had no relations with the new organization of the Higashi Honganji in Berkeley.[97]

Hata was also supported by a certain number of the laity. For instance, Sawakichi Harada, a member of the Vacaville Buddhist Church, expressed how his understanding of Buddhism had deepened after meeting Hata. Although he had initially avoided Akegarasu in Vacaville, Harada's perception of him changed once Hata explained the Buddhist teachings to him. Harada writes, "If my mind is bad, I see Reverend Hata as an evil person. If my mind is good, I see him as a good man. This is reasonable." He continues, "[F]or those who want to learn the fundamental teachings of Buddhism, why don't you treat Reverend Hata kindly and study his spirit, instead of trusting ministers whose minds are occupied with commercial bargaining?"[98]

Akegarasu's visit to North America and the incident involving Hata demonstrate that denominational differences between the two Honganjis were not greatly significant to most members of the Shin Buddhist congregations. The BMNA office tried to minimize Akegarasu's influence over its ministers, for example, by removing Hata from the Buddhist Church of Oakland, but the laity enjoyed Akegarasu's outspokenness. The schism in the Buddhist churches in Los Angeles, Berkeley, and Parlier also suggests that affiliation with the Higashi Honganji was not due to differences in doctrinal interpretation.[99] Therefore, the Japanization of denominational authorities took a different turn in North America, as the relationship between the two Shin denominations grew more flexible and interactive among local congregations.

The Case Histories
of Three Ministers

As the Higashi Honganji in the United States was relatively free from its headquarters' control, two ministers demonstrated amicable exchanges between the two Shin Buddhist organizations after World War II. Shōsetsu Tsufura (1893–1975) came to the Higashi Honganji Los Angeles Betsuin in 1921 to assist Izumida. In 1937, Izumida transferred him to the Parlier Higashi Honganji (present-day Buddhist Church of Parlier), where he served until his internment at the Gila River Relocation Center, Arizona, in 1942. After the war, Tsufura, accompanied by his wife and one of his three sons, moved to Seabrook, New Jersey, where he laid the foundations for what would become the Nishi Honganji Seabrook Buddhist Temple in 1945. Tsufura gave up hope of ever returning to Parlier when his wife became seriously ill. The Parlier Higashi Honganji, in the meantime, had become affiliated with the Buddhist Churches of America (BCA) in 1947. In January 1960, the BCA bishop recognized Tsufura's voluntary service to the organization.[100]

While Tsufura served the two BCA churches of Seabrook and Cleveland, Ohio, Gyōmei Kubose (1905–2000) founded the nonsectarian Buddhist Temple of Chicago (BTC) on October 8, 1944. After meeting Akegarasu, Kubose entered the University of California, Berkeley, majoring in philosophy. Upon graduation in 1935, he traveled to Japan to study under Akegarasu in Ishikawa prefecture. Kubose was ordained in August 1936 and became a Dharma teacher (*kyōshi*) in December 1937. He returned to the United States in 1941, prior to outbreak of the Pacific War.[101]

Kubose was one of the precursors who propagated Buddhism by distributing Buddhist journals and newsletters in Chicago. After spending two years at the Heart Mountain Relocation Center, he moved to Chicago, where he founded the BTC. By April 1949, he had organized three periodicals: *Lotus Reader,* designed for children, and the monthly *New World Buddhist* and quarterly *Daily Sort* for adults.[102] Although claiming to be nonsectarian, he often promoted the teachings of Kiyozawa and Akegarasu. In 1966, Kubose entered Ōtani University to study Buddhism for three years. Today, he is known as the founder of the American Buddhist Association and the Buddhist Education Center in Chicago. He was well received at various BCA churches, where he gave many lectures.[103]

Unlike Tsufura and Kubose, Enshō Ashikaga (1910–1984) led a transsectarian campaign in academia. He received a degree similar to a Master of Literature, and was asked to study the Abhidharma at the University of

California, Berkeley, by the president of Ōtani University in July 1937. In Berkeley, Ferdinand D. Lessing invited him to teach Japanese Buddhism and graduate language courses. During the Pacific War, Ashikaga taught at the Navy's intensive Japanese language program at the University of Colorado, Boulder. After the war, he returned to Berkeley where he taught Japanese. When the University of California, Los Angeles, established a Department of Oriental Languages in 1947, the new chair, Richard Rudolph, who had known Ashikaga for ten years, invited him to create a Japanese language program. Ashikaga and Rudolph, who was in charge of the Chinese language program, served as department chairs alternatively. While teaching Buddhist Studies and Tibetan at UCLA, Ashikaga expanded its Oriental Library through contributions from the Los Angeles Buddhist Church Federation, with which he had a good relationship.[104]

Ashikaga, in the meantime, dedicated himself to the development of the two Honganjis. He admitted three Nishi ministers to UCLA's graduate program and contributed an article on the concept of nirvana to the *Berkeley Bussei* journal.[105] He also served as the Head of the Department of Rites and Ceremonies at Higashi Honganji headquarters in Kyoto after retiring from the university. He was elected chair of a group of scholars who compiled and edited the *Shinshū sōden gisho,* Shin Buddhist commentaries transmitted by two of Rennyo's sons.[106]

Summary

The history of the Higashi Honganji propagation in North America has been little studied by scholars both in the United States and Japan. It illustrates how internal conflicts, legal contests, denominational competition and rapprochement, and personality differences paved the way for the Higashi Honganji to advance in North America. Although some ministers created problems for themselves, others skillfully bridged denominational differences. The phenomena of simultaneous competition and cooperation were not new in the relationship of the two Honganjis in Japan. However, Issei and Nisei followers tolerated organizational differences more than their counterparts in Japan, because they considered the constraints imposed by the orders to be impractical. Two other factors need to be considered in looking at the absence of denominational characteristics: there were fewer Higashi Honganji churches on the mainland, and its headquarters had less organizational control over its clergy and laity. The reasons for such a loose organizational structure require further investigation.

Chapter Seven

Local and Translocal Activities
of Issei Shin Buddhist Ministers

The acculturation of Shin Buddhism occurred in relation to the development of its organizations in Hawaii and on the mainland. In both regions, changes in organizational style, rituals, and doctrine reflected the processes of Japanization and Americanization, albeit on different levels. This chapter aims to go beyond the organizational settings and examine the sociopolitical implications of acculturation. When Shin ministers responded to the crises of the Nikkei community as a whole, their actions differed in these two regions.

On the mainland, at two major international religious conferences, BMNA leaders appealed to the American public that Buddhism was a religion of peace. Japanese Buddhist leaders organized the International Buddhist Congress in San Francisco in August 1915 in conjunction with the Panama Pacific International Exposition and invited honorary guests from all over the world. After the weeklong conference, the Japanese delegates met with President Woodrow Wilson to petition for the ending of World War I. In August 1933, Shin clergy participated in the World Fellowship of Faiths in Chicago (the so-called Second Parliament of Religions), held in connection with the Second World's Fair.[1] On this occasion, not only Buddhist delegates but also representatives of the so-called New Religions (*shin shūkyō*) of Japan addressed world peace, though they ignored or attempted to justify Japan's military aggression in China. The Japanese delegates were far from harmonious, since the BMNA leaders saw the Shintō groups Tenrikyō and Konkōkyō, which were then emerging in the United States, as their new rivals.[2]

Contrary to the BMNA, the HHMH became locally involved. Shin clergy participated in the 1920 territory-wide sugar plantation strike initiated by Japanese workers and the early legal test case brought about by Issei educators, who questioned the constitutionality of the territorial government ban on Japanese language schools.[3] The HHMH supported the Nikkei grassroots movement mainly because the Japanese were one of the largest ethnic groups in Hawaii and the majority of their congregations worked on the island plantations. The geographical location of Hawaii with its U.S. territorial status also led the Nikkei to voice their demands.

Despite the differences in translocal and local activities, which entailed various processes of Japanization and Americanization, the national identity of the Issei Shin ministers in North America was equivocal. In addition to Hawaii and the mainland United States, the two branches of the Honganji sent priests to Korea, China, the South Pacific, and even the Kuril Islands, north of Hokkaidō, following Japanese immigrants. The globalization of Shin Buddhism linked to Japan's colonialism in Asia suggests the inherent conflict of Issei Shin clerics in North America, where two sets of secular rules to which they were obliged to conform collided with each other. As a result, they became confused with the identification of secular rules as defined in the doctrine of the two truths that needed to be observed. In other words, they had their own reasons for their ambivalence about identity, which paralleled the two-edged nature of Nikkei ethnicity.

The political uncertainty of Shin Buddhists may suggest the limitation of the doctrine of the two truths as a religious ideology of submission. In Japan, citizens submitted themselves to the state and viewed faith as a private matter. As Article 28 of the Constitution of the Empire of Japan indicated, the government would recognize the citizenship of a person and his or her religious freedom, as long as that person maintained peace and order in society and observed his or her duties as the subject of the emperor. But on a religious frontier, where two sets of secular rules, those of the nation-states of Japan and the United States, came into conflict in relation to political contention and racial discrimination against the Nikkei, neither country assured Shin Buddhists of their political status. Since being Japanese in Hawaii and on the mainland was problematic in itself, Shin Buddhists did not benefit from holding their faith only in a private capacity. Given their plight, faith, which primarily dealt with transcendence, could become a means to critique mundane rule. Imamura's action in Hawaii needs to be reconsidered in light of a critical Shin ethos, since Shin Buddhism had nurtured such a tradition.

Translocal Activities Led by BMNA Ministers

The International Buddhist Congress

The BMNA held the International Buddhist Congress August 2–7, 1915. As part of the Panama Pacific International Exposition in San Francisco, which celebrated the opening of the Panama Canal, Shin clergy voluntarily participated in this commemorative event and demonstrated to Americans that Buddhism was a world religion. The congress attracted between one hundred and three hundred Euro-Americans daily. This gathering differed from the World's Parliament of Religions held in Chicago in 1893, as in this case it was Japanese Buddhists who had initiated the congress and invited Buddhists and scholars from other parts of the world such as Siam (Thailand), Tibet, Ceylon (Sri Lanka), India, England, and elsewhere.[4]

The Japanese clergy dominated the proceedings at this event. In addition to local Shin ministers, delegates from five different Buddhist schools in Japan and one representing all other Japanese Buddhist denominations gathered in San Francisco. Dr. Mazzininanda served as president of the congress, and guest speakers from all around the world gave lectures. Despite the international character of the gathering, the Japanese priests spent almost the entire third day giving lectures and holding internal meetings, including presenting reports on Buddhism in the United States and Japan.[5] After these meetings, they came up with a threefold agenda: to improve communication between Buddhist schools in Japan and the United States; to create a unified organization for Japanese and American Buddhists; and to discuss future Buddhist propagation. Later, they modified these goals by removing their national emphasis, focusing instead on advancing communication among Buddhist schools throughout the world and discussing the future orientation of Buddhism in the United States. The seven priests assigned to this task were, however, all Japanese.[6]

At the conclusion to the six-day conference, the delegates made five resolutions. First, the goal of Buddhists was to introduce Eastern civilization to the West and bring all people closer together. Second, the congress would contribute to the improvement of international relations between Japan and the United States. Third, it was incorrect to consider Buddhist propagation a source of anti-Japanese sentiment in the United States; therefore, Buddhists in Japan and the United States needed to work together to remove misconceptions concerning their religion. Fourth, Buddhists throughout the world wished for an immediate truce in World War I. Under the authority of the International Buddhist Congress, delegates would request President Woodrow Wilson to intervene in and halt the warfare. Fifth, for the fulfillment of the fourth resolution, the congress designated Bishop Uchida of the BMNA and Mokusen Hioki, the delegate representing all other Buddhist denominations in Japan, to visit the president and personally submit the resolution to him.[7]

The Japanese delegates met with Wilson at the White House on August 23, 1915. Along with the resolution, Uchida made an official BMNA report intended to obtain Wilson's "very favorable consideration" toward the president's treatment of Buddhism.[8] The draft of the resolution reads:

San Francisco, California, August 6th 1915.

To His Excellency Woodrow Wilson,
President of the United States of America,
Washington, D.C.

Dear Sir:

We, the duly authorized delegates of the International Buddhist Congress, representing over fifty million of Buddhists throughout the world, do most respectfully present to you the following resolution:

The International Buddhist Congress in due session at San Francisco this sixth day of August, 1915, unanimously passed the following resolution, to wit:

That as the present war in Europe is the greatest calamity ever known to the history of mankind, and its prolongation means but the indefinite extension of this most terrible inhuman tragedy, we, [as] the representatives of the International Buddhists in convention, and as followers of our Gospel of Peace and Love, do most earnestly desire the cessation of this cruel and wanton war and the restoration of peace on earth and good will to men at the earliest possible moment.

We most earnestly and respectfully pray His Excellency Woodrow Wilson, President of the United States of America, in the name of the International Buddhist Congress, representing the Buddhists of all races in their convention held in San Francisco, State of California, United States of America, in connection with the Panama Pacific International Exposition, 1915, that he will kindly exercise his most exalted position to influence the minds of the warring nations into the ways of peace in accordance with his high conceptions of humanity's needs.

Thus to you we most respectfully tender our prayers and services, and duly subscribe. International Buddhist Congress,

By its Delegates:[9]

The International Buddhist Congress made a direct appeal to the President of the United States, in which the delegates explained that Buddhism was a religion of peace and love. By doing so, they attempted to rectify anti-Japanese activists' negative views of Buddhism. Mokusen Hioki also asked President Wilson to allow immigration of more Japanese Buddhist priests to the United States and conveyed to him greetings from Shigenobu Okuma (1838–1922), Prime Minister of Japan at that time.[10]

The Shin Buddhist Peace Movement in Japan

The International Buddhist Congress initiated by the BMNA preceded the Buddhist pacifist movement in Japan. During the 1920s, the headquarters of the two Honganjis promoted world peace. Son'yū Ōtani, the fourth son of the twenty-first abbot, who was a brother-in-law of the Emperor and had served as Executive Director of the Nishi Honganji headquarters, and Kōen Ōtani, the twenty-third abbot of the Higashi Honganji, were concerned with the outcome of the Washington Conference after World War I. They addressed the need for spiritual reflection in the diplomats and officials who would be participating in the conference and discussing disarmament. Son'yū Ōtani wrote:

> When the hard shell of the ego, put away and isolated from others, is crushed and merges itself in the oneness of things, that is, in the idea of universal brotherhood, the earth will really become a peaceful, comfortable place of abode.[11]

Ōtani was, however, politically motivated toward Japan's national interests, as he urged Christians to listen to a Buddhist nation's disarmament plans. Kōen Ōtani also attempted to change the false impressions of those who considered Japan to be a "second Germany in the East" and a source of obstruction to peace in the Pacific.[12]

After the Washington Conference in February 1922, the Japanese Buddhist call for world peace seemed to subside, but Son'yū Ōtani continued to advocate reciprocity between Japan and the United States.[13] When he visited Los Angeles in November 1925 to participate in a local Buddhist church's dedication service, he made a speech on the *Times* radio station program. After drawing a correlation between Japanese civilization and Mahayana Buddhism, he said, "Japanese people are trained from childhood to respect the custom of deference, love and industriousness." Japanese were compatible with Americans, who "stand on exactly the same principle [as Japanese do]—a principle of love, trust, justice, humanity and brotherhood."[14] In this simple way, he proposed intellectual and spiritual exchanges between the two nations.

Buddhist Participation in the World Fellowship of Faiths

The collective efforts of Japanese Buddhists to demand peace resumed in the 1930s; their participation in the World Fellowship of Faiths held in

Chicago in 1933 marked one such effort. This event was called the Second Parliament of Religions, supposedly a continuation of the 1893 World's Parliament of Religions. During the forty years between these two gatherings, the position of Japanese Buddhists in the United States had changed drastically. First-generation Japanese immigrants had built many Buddhist churches in their local communities, and the Nisei and Caucasians had begun to learn and understand Śākyamuni's doctrine, though not necessarily the various sectarian teachings.[15] In contrast to the first Parliament, there were three changes in the way Japanese delegates presented themselves at the World Fellowship. First, the Buddhist participants were in disarray. Second, representatives of the New Religions made their world debut, which put the Buddhist representatives on alert about their future expansion. Third, almost all the delegates introduced their own sectarian teaching. Discussion of these features will follow an outline of the World Fellowship.

The National Committee of Three Hundred World Fellowships of Faiths was the organizing body for the Fellowship held from June to November 1933, during the time of the Second World's Fair in Chicago. The committee included the former President Herbert Hoover, as honorary president, and eight vice-presidents, including John Dewey and Bishop Francis J. McConnell. The World Fellowship held sixty sessions with one hundred and eighty-eight speakers representing various religions and races. During the concluding convention, from August 27 to September 17, it hosted an additional fifty sessions with one hundred and thirty-one speakers. The objective of the World Fellowship was to demonstrate "a new spiritual dynamic competent to master and reform the world," as it was necessary to "build bridges of understanding across the chasms of prejudice" for the "realization of peace and brotherhood." Participants included Buddhists, Christians, Confucians, Daoists, Hindus, Jains, Jews, Muslims, Shintōists, Sikhs, and Zoroastrians.[16]

During this period, Japanese delegates were divided into four groups: Buddhists, Christians, Shintō priests (leaders of New Religions), and religious studies scholars. Bishop Masuyama of the BMNA represented the Federation of Buddhist Schools in Japan, while Tansai Terakawa of the BMNA represented the Nishi Honganji. Izumida from Los Angeles represented the Higashi Honganji, and Nitten Ishida served as the representative of the Nichiren school of Japan. Misaki Shimazu was the delegate of Japan's National Christian Conference; Yoshiaki Fukuda of Konkōkyō and Shozen Nakayama of Tenrikyō represented Shintō. Scholars in the field of religious studies included Masaharu Anesaki, from Tokyo Imperial University, and Hideo Kishimoto.[17]

There was evident internal rivalry among the BMNA ministers, Izumida, and the two Shintō priests. Japanese delegates attended the World Fellowship of Faiths in two ways: at the opening session, in which the thirty-six leaders offered greetings; and by giving individual presentations.

In the opening session, delegates from the Federation of Buddhist Schools in Japan, Nishi, Higashi, Nichiren, and Tenrikyō delivered short felicitations. In the individual presentations, representatives from each order (except for the delegates of the Higashi Honganji and the Nichiren school) gave a short lecture on their religion. Though it may have simply been a result of the way the conferences were arranged, there was no evidence of interaction between Izumida and the Nishi delegates. Masuyama later gave reports to his headquarters in Kyoto and the Federation of Buddhist Schools in Japan, in which there was no mention of Izumida at the meeting with other Japanese delegates held on August 30. Nor do Izumida's memoirs record any exchange between the Nishi ministers and himself, though he mentions the Nichirenist.[18]

In his reports, Masuyama describes his encounter with the leaders of the Tenrikyō and Konkōkyō. At the opening session, Masuyama said, "[T]he majority of the people of Japan are Buddhists. Speaking in [on] behalf of all those Buddhists, some forty-one and a half million in number, I have the honour to express our most sincere hope that the World Fellowship of Faiths will accomplish its aim. . . ."[19] He exaggerated the number of Buddhists precisely because the Tenrikyō delegate had inflated the number of their adherents as "six million."[20] Masuyama wanted to let the world know that Japan was a Buddhist country. Astounded by the number, delegates from India requested Masuyama to host the next Convention of World Fellowship in Japan. Masuyama's attitude toward the representatives of Tenrikyō and Konkōkyō was, however, not necessarily hostile. He sincerely praised the efforts of these Shintō priests, who had introduced their beliefs to the world through large expenditures of money and manpower on propagation pamphlets, and asking two Japanese scholars to help translate their doctrines into English.[21]

Masuyama included other observations in his reports to the Nishi headquarters. He was quite disappointed with the chairperson, Bishop Francis J. McConnell, who failed to appear in public, and with the lack of media coverage, especially in Chicago newspapers. The Fellowship seemed to be merely a showcase of races and religions, though Masuyama sympathized with the senior organizers, who had tried to develop the convention into an international religious movement.

Finally, there was a gap between the negative attitudes of attendees, perceived by some as "boring" (*tsumaranu mono*), and the vitality of those who spoke passionately of their own religions. If the rift between these two groups had been bridged, the outcome of the Fellowship would have been remarkable. This, however, would remain the task of future religious conventions.[22]

The Buddhist delegates had lost their motivation because of the absence of a collective effort to present their religions as a whole. In contrast to the World's Parliament of Religions, there were fewer Japanese Buddhist speakers at this conference. The relationship between the two Buddhist schools that sent representatives, Shin and Nichiren, had historically been hostile in Japan. Instead of pursuing a common religious goal, the Buddhist delegates introduced the doctrines of their own founders. In like manner, the Shintō priests focused on the presentation of their own doctrines and traditions, including the life histories of their respective founders. The representative of Japan's National Christian Conference reported on the Kingdom of God Movement (1930–1932) in Japan.

Despite their competitveness and the lack of cohesion and cooperation among themselves, the Japanese delegates did share a common theme of the Fellowship—promotion of world peace. Masuyama asked all the participants to work for a permanent peace and happiness in the world and to improve their own educational systems.[23] Terakawa said, "In doing Amit[ā]bha's Will to perfect ourselves as Himself, we are indicating the simplest and clearest way of life leading to world peace and happiness."[24] Nakayama cited the objectives of Tenrikyō as "the establishment of peace and happiness in this world through the religious ideals which were taught by its Foundress."[25] Fukuda of the Konkōkyō proposed cooperation between Japan and the United States for the promotion of peace in the Pacific region.[26] Some delegates, however, demanded that the audience recognize Japan's geopolitical status; Fukuda pointed out Japan's access to natural resources in Manchuria, and Shiio remarked on its leadership in Asia. Ishida, further, promoted the Constitution of the Empire of Japan and linked it with Nichirenism.[27]

Clearly, the Japanese delegates did not promote peace solely on a spiritual basis.

Local Activities
Led by HHMH Ministers

The 1920 Strike and Buddhism

Contrary to translocal mainland clerics, Shin ministers in Hawaii participated in the Nikkei's local political and economic struggles. The 1920 territory-wide sugar plantation strike first began as a demand for higher wages in 1917. The average monthly salary of a Japanese plantation worker was between $20 to $24, but because of rapid inflation, the Council of Japanese Plantation Laborers demanded $24 for a single man, $46 for a married couple with two children, and $52 for a family with three children.[28] The Young Men's Association (YMA) often appeared to be a medium for organizing the local labor force. In Hilo, delegates of thirty-one YMAs met in October 1919 and discussed the formation of a labor federation.[29] Five YMAs at the Hamakua plantation, also on Hawaii, were the first to form such a union and petition the Hawaiian Sugar Planters' Association (HSPA).[30]

The Waialua Young Men's Buddhist Association (YMBA), on Oahu, took the initiative in bringing together local efforts on October 25. It distributed the demands for higher wages to YMAs throughout the Hawaiian Islands and united local campaigns. The proposal stated:

> It is a miserable fact that since World War I, low-class workers in Hawaii have suffered a lot because of the rise in prices. Look, prices of rice and miso, which are our staple food, have gone up four times higher than before the war, and continue to increase; however, our wages have not grown even a penny. Our hardship is obvious and if we remain silent, we cannot avoid starvation. What is this? This is none other than the problem of our life and death, the problem of existence of our labor force in all the plantations, and a problem of humanity. This is the reason that we stand rightfully and demand the Association of Planters for a higher wage. Planters have their union and can act in unison. To challenge them, we need to initiate a great campaign by connecting workers in each plantation and each island. This is the reason that we urge you to take action with the best effort, for yourself and on the behalf of workers and humanity.[31]

The protest of the Waialua YMBA was brought about by the economic concerns of its members and was unrelated to the Buddhist teachings. It demanded that the HSPA replace the current wage structure of $20 for men and $15 for women on the basis of twenty-six working days per month, with a bonus system consisting of a daily wage of $3 for men and $2.25 for women. It also demanded a reduction of daily working hours to eight, with pay for overtime work; respect for workers' rights; and reasonable prices for merchandise sold on plantations.[32]

The Japanese sugar plantation workers and their supporters established a territory-wide organization, the Federation of Japanese Labor, in Hawaii in January 1920. By that time, Pablo Manlapit had organized the Filipino Labor Union, which shared similar objectives with the Japanese, even though the two ethnic groups worked independently. The Japanese and Filipinos compromised over their demands and asked the HSPA for a wage increase from $0.77 to $1.25 a day, while retaining a bonus system. After the HSPA rejected their proposal in December, the Japanese workers attempted to negotiate for a third time on January 17, but the Filipinos went on strike two days later. The Japanese threatened to initiate an island-wide strike on February 1, though they were still willing to settle on a daily wage of $1. The HSPA made its final counteroffer on January 27, and the Japanese leaders saw no point in further negotiations.[33]

The Japanese went on strike but faced several internal problems. First, there was a lack of adequate funds to support workers and their families during the strike. The Federation had only $160, and Sumitomo Bank refused a loan of $1,800 the strikers had requested. Japanese supporters formed a Strike Supporters' Association on January 28 in Honolulu and stood behind the Federation. Second, the Federation had to accommodate Filipino strikers. While the majority continued to strike, they either found employment outside the plantations or lived in the Japanese strike camps, because they were also short of funds. Third, there were not enough shelters when the HSPA evicted more than twelve thousand workers, more than ten thousand of which were Japanese, and their families, including four thousand one hundred and thirty-seven children, from plantation housing on February 14. Finally, a serious influenza epidemic infected over a thousand people, and fifty-five Japanese died.[34]

The initial impact of the strike was tremendous, though the HSPA recovered its productivity by spring 1920. By mid-February, "some ninety-seven percent of the Japanese workers had walked off the job in company with ninety-two percent of the other nationalities employed on the six struck Oahu plantations."[35] But since the strike took place only on Oahu, the HSPA was able to fill out its workforce. For instance, the HSPA replaced strikers with a labor force of two thousand two hundred strikebreakers of other ethnicities, who were recruited with a daily wage of $3. By the end of April, the level of sugar production had returned nearly to normal, and the HSPA announced the end of the strike.[36]

The Federation of Japanese Labor, however, did not admit defeat until July 1. Because of the surge of anti-Japanese feelings, its leaders changed their name to the Hawaii Laborers' Association on April 20, removing the ethnic designation. They also encouraged other ethnic minorities to participate, though "communists and anarchists" were excluded. By transcending the national boundaries of the immigrants, Japanese strike leaders appealed to both the planters and the government of Hawaii that labor conflicts were not solely a Japanese problem. The resolve of the strikers eventually abated after a prolonged resistance of six months. On July 1, with the intervention of Bishop Hōsen Isobe of Sōtō Zen, strike leaders met with John Waterhouse, the HSPA representative, who still refused their demands for higher wages but promised future negotiations. At this point, the strikers ended their protest.[37]

Several events followed in the aftermath of the strike. In total, the HSPA paid $635,959 to end the strike and claimed a loss of $11,438,358 on crops, while the Japanese collected more than $900,000 from their strike supporters. The HSPA followed the pattern of the 1909 strike and met some of the strikers' demands, for instance, raising the monthly wage to $30 for twenty-six working days per month.[38] However, the HSPA also brought various charges against strike leaders, and the legal control of future strikes grew much tighter, including restrictions on the press, for which legislation was enacted in 1921.[39] The evaluation of Isobe's involvement varied, as those who were dissatisfied with the HSPA's counterproposals needed a scapegoat for ending the strike. The *Chūgai Nippō* alleged that Isobe had taken the opportunity of the strike to increase his influence over the Nikkei community, since HHMH leaders had stayed out of the strike, yet despite his assistance, the HSPA remained hostile toward the Japanese after the strike.[40]

Contrary to the *Chūgai Nippō*'s allegations, the HHMH, led by Imamura, did support the strikers. Local missions provided shelter for the families of those who had been evicted. Imamura, together with other ministers, conducted the funeral service for Etsutarō Inoue, a board member of the Federation of Japanese Labor, who died in the influenza epidemic. His funeral, held on February 24, 1920, was unprecedented in terms of the size of the service and attendance. The HHMH also offered a place for supporters to gather. For instance, in March, a group of *biwa* players performed at a Honganji mission (though the specific location is not known) to comfort the families of evicted strikers.[41]

Prior to the strike, Buddhist leaders had made a trans-sectarian alliance. The bishops of six schools along with Shintō priests sent the HSPA a petition, dated January 22, 1920, requesting the HSPA to meet the demands of the Japanese workers.[42] Louise H. Hunter summarizes the petition:

> Cane workers, burdened throughout the war by a fluctuating economy and unrelieved inflation, were in dire financial straits and were preparing for the worst, the petition warned. The Buddhist clergy thought it unjust to deny a share of the bonus to laborers who could not work a minimum of twenty days of every month. Some persons, they wrote, were legitimately unable to work twenty days out of every month; human beings, after all, were not machines.

Furthermore, the bonus, as high as it was, did not compensate for the accelerated cost of living. As the spiritual leaders of the Japanese community, the priests felt compelled to take a stand for the right, as they saw the right. For years they had dutifully urged their countrymen to render faithful and honest service to the planters, but now the time had come to support the just claims of labor. The letter was signed by Bishop [Emyō] Imamura of Honpa Hongwanji; Eikaku Seki of the Shingon-shū; Bishop Hōsen Isobe of the Sōtō-shū; Acting Bishop Ryōzen Yamada of the Jōdo-shū; Bishop Chōsei Nunome of the Nichiren-shū; and Kankai Izuhara of the Higashi Hongwanji. Chinjirō [Sakaeki], a Shinto priest, and Katsuyoshi Miyaō of the Izumo Taisha also attached their signatures to the letter.[43]

The clergy saw the cause of the strike as economic and stood behind the strikers. But based on a closer reading of the petition written in Japanese, it can be seen that the ministers called for their own introspection concerning their engagement with Issei workers in the past.

> We, men of religion, do not know whether or not compensation that workers have received in the existing bonus system is appropriate, because we are not experts in the science of economics. But, we have witnessed their actual lives, as we visit the plantations and communicate with them. We are absolutely confident, second to none, to say that we know their present circumstances. . . .
>
> The Japanese religious leaders used to urge our workers (*warera rōdōsha*) to be loyal to the planters, but never demanded the planters to recognize the loyalty of the workers or sympathize with their circumstances. It is inevitable that the Japanese religious leaders would become liars, if we calmed down our fellow workers and forced them to be obedient. In the future, we shall be in a difficult position, and lose our credibility in propagation. The life of religious leaders is to express philanthropy and benevolence (*hakuai jijin*). We do not discern capitalists or laborers, but have an aptitude for saving one's mind and body. Therefore, we, religious leaders, stand between the capitalists and workers to avoid a conflict in the paradise of the Pacific. . . .[44]

The strike prompted Buddhist ministers to question the way they had been propagating to the workers. It is unclear who actually wrote this statement, but the ministers' self-examination might have resonated with Imamura's own experiences.

In the past, Imamura had encouraged protesting workers to go back to work, but his attitude changed in 1920. He had succeeded in reconciling the workers and planters in the 1904 Waipahu strike by pacifying the former.[45] But Imamura failed to reach a similar settlement during the 1909 strike. According to Tomoe Moriya, through this failure he might have learned a lesson that he had ignored the suffering of the "true guests of Amida Buddha" (*Amida butsu no shōkyaku*), the way he referred to the plantation workers.[46] In the 1920 petition, Buddhist (and Shintō) leaders regarded themselves on the same level as the workers by using the rhetorical expression *warera rōdōsha* ("we, as laborers").[47]

The different ways Imamura had dealt with the workers during the 1904 and 1909 strikes might also have reflected the common position held by his counterparts in Japan at that time. Some Buddhist priests initiated humanitarian campaigns to help destitute factory workers after the Russo-Japanese War. Their primary objective, however, was to turn the workers' grudges against their employers into a sense of appreciation and seek the "ethics of hierarchical complementarity" based on the Mahayana doctrine of oneness.[48] The clerics likened the relationship of employer and employee to that of parent and son in family-owned businesses, and promoted both employers' benevolence and workers' indebtedness. Through propagation in spinning and silk-reeling factories, the clergy prevented labor unrest before it arose, while at the same time ferreting out and removing socialists and anarchists. Not until 1931 did factory workers begin resisting the priests.[49]

The strategy of "taming" workers did not work during the 1920 strike. Jōshō Enpuku of the Kahuku Honganji Mission pitied his fellow workers, whom the HSPA had evicted and who were forced to live in poverty, so he broke the local strike. But the mission's board members and members of the Federation of Japanese Labor criticized him for not understanding their real suffering and demanded his resignation. Instead of discharging him, Imamura placed Enpuku under his supervision in Honolulu.[50] Records show that in 1920, Imamura made a third financial contribution to the ministers whose missions had been affected by the strike. A total of twenty-six ministers contributed $15 each, and the sum of $390 was divided among the five ministers involved.[51]

Imamura's Involvement in the Initial Test Case

Besides his involvement in the sugar-plantation strike, Imamura participated in the initial test case in which Issei educators questioned the constitutionality of the territorial government ban on Japanese language schools in the early 1920s. The territorial government recognized Act 30 on November 24, 1920. This law cut the operating hours of Japanese language schools, demanded permits for both schools and teachers, and gave the Department of Public Instruction (DPI) absolute authority to oversee the textbooks and curricula of the schools. The government also introduced Act 36 as a companion bill to impose stricter qualifications for teachers at these schools. Further, it transformed the DPI's suggestions into Act 171 in May 1923, in which the DPI banned Nisei children from attending Japanese language school unless they passed the second grade of public school, and levied an annual tax of $1 per student for the DPI to supervise the foreign language schools. Act 171 forced Issei educators to discontinue kindergartens and the first two years of Japanese language school instruction. But before Act 171 came into effect, the Palama Japanese Language School and three others sued the state government of Hawaii on December 28, 1922, questioning the constitutionality of Act 30.[52]

Seven months after the beginning of the legal contest, Palama Gakuen and Fort Gakuen, affiliated with the HHMH, followed suit, and Imamura sought protection under the Constitution. He was initially reluctant to join this test case for two reasons. First, the Honganji's involvement would arouse serious anti-Buddhist feelings among Christians. Second, if the court case were to be lost, Japanese language schools would have to forfeit their property and the HHMH would lose its credibility. Imamura made up his mind to get involved only after consulting with George M. Robertson, a former Supreme Court judge, who not only agreed with the plaintiffs' counsel but also cited various precedent cases to help Imamura make his decision. Imamura did not encourage the teachers at other Japanese language schools affiliated with the HHMH to follow suit, but respected their individual choice of whether or not to join the action. However, his decision, in part, led previously uncommitted educators to take collective legal action.[53]

When the HHMH supported the 1920 strike and Japanese language schools, hostility between Buddhists and Christians grew within the Nikkei community. In contrast to the Buddhist-Shintō alliance, a group of Japanese Christian clerics led by Takie Okumura advised their parishioners to oppose the strike and repay their indebtedness to the planters. Okumura even asked the HSPA personnel to hire his son as a translator.[54] Gary Okihiro writes, "The merging of religious belief with political allegiance by the Christian clergy was in accord with the Americanization movement's claim that Buddhism and other alien ideologies encouraged rebelliousness, while Christianity promoted patriotism."[55] Japanese Buddhist and Christian clergy also competed in the litigation. The Christians saw Buddhist schools as institutions that transformed the Nisei into imperial subjects of Japan. Okumura sided with Vaughan MacCaughey, Hawaii's Superintendent of Public Instruction, who attempted to remove Buddhist influence from Nisei education.[56]

Imamura had his own reasons for supporting the Japanese language schools. As Tomoe Moriya points out, he saw the importance of individuation in American education.[57] Imamura recognized the value of students' creativity and spontaneity, as proposed by "educators in the United States" (*Amerika no kyōikuka*):

> Educators in the United States oppose the concepts of discipline and obedience, as they are despotic and dictatorial in which those in a superior position press those in an inferior position. The educators say, first [priority] is the interest [of the students] and second [priority] is also the interest [of the students]. The democratic education has to be rooted in the principle of curiosity. Hence those who respect pupils, students and scholars should not imitate others, but take initiative in creating a new field.[58]

Imamura saw the importance of independent thinking in education, though his reference to "educators in the United States" is unclear. As a unique way of learning, he supported the Japanese language school system for the Nisei and connected education with the Buddhist teachings.

As can be seen on the mainland and in Hawaii, the Issei Shin Buddhist clergy's sociopolitical engagement demonstrated the intertwining processes of Americanization and Japanization. On the mainland, Shin ministers' pacifist movement echoed the call for international harmony initiated by religious leaders in the United States. In Hawaii, as Tsuyoshi Nakano argues, the Americanization of Shin Buddhism suggested that Issei clergy had incorporated the tenets of America's founding—freedom, equality, and human rights—and they demanded the improvement of workers' conditions based on these principles.[59] At the same time however, the translocal and local activities of such ministers exhibited the aspects of Japanization reflecting their cultural attachment to their homeland. What Duncan Williams calls "complex loyalties" concerning national identity becomes more apparent when considering the activities of the two branches of the Honganji in the rest of the world.[60]

The Globalization of Shin Buddhism and the Creation of Ethnicity

Paralleling the eastward transmission of the Dharma, the two Honganjis propagated their sectarian teaching on the Asian continent, in the South Pacific, and in the Kuril Islands (part of present-day Russia, which Japan still disputes). By 1937, the Nishi Honganji had established nine overseas parochial districts: Formosa (Taiwan), Chōsen (Korea), Manchūkō (Manchuria), China, the South Sea Islands, Hawaii, the United States, and Canada.[61] The Higashi Honganji created its propagation bases in a similar fashion, though it first advanced into China and Korea.[62]

It is widely recognized today that the Buddhist establishment on the Asian continent was in tandem with Japan's military aggression. The Buddhist orders took part in Japan's imperial projects by providing support for soldiers (*gunjin fukyō*) and immigrants and pathfinders (*imin kaitakudan fukyō*). In 1873, two years after Japan signed a treaty of amity with the Qing dynasty (1644–1912), the Higashi Honganji sent Kōchō Ogurusu to Shanghai, China. He believed that Japan would benefit through an East Asia Buddhist alliance with China and Korea. Six months after Japan concluded a treaty of amity with Korea in February 1876, Ogurusu and others founded the Higashi Honganji's first temple in the British settlement of Shanghai. When requested by Toshimichi Ōkubo (Minister of Home Affairs) and Munenori Terashima (Foreign Minister), Gonnyo, the twenty-first abbot of the Higashi, sent Enshin Okumura to Korea to begin propagation in Pusan (southeast part of the Korean peninsula) in September 1877. In Shanghai and Pusan, the clergy set up language schools to prepare priests from Japan for further settlement in the interior.[63] The Nishi Honganji began propagation in the military in Korea in 1894, during the Sino-Japanese War (1894–1895). Both branches of the Honganji advanced into northern China during the Russo-Japanese War.[64]

In Korea, Honganji leaders demonstrated the effectiveness of the doctrine of the two truths. Higashi priests attempted to transform the Korean people into imperial subjects of Japan. When the priests initially propagated their religion however, the sovereignty of secular rules did not relate to the emperor of Japan but to Yi Kojong, emperor of the so-called Great Han Empire (1897–1910) that Japan "protected." Higashi Honganji clergy enshrined the mortuary tablets of Korean imperial ancestors on the altar, won the sympathies of the people, and increased the number of Korean converts. In the case of the Nishi Honganji, propagation to the imperial army in Korea was twofold: performing confirmation services (*kikyō shiki*) for the soldiers and conducting funerary and memorial rites after their deaths. Since a soldier's birth in the Pure Land had already been determined, according to spiritual principles, he could perform his duty on the battlefield based on secular rules.[65]

The Honganjis' attempts to proselytize among the Koreans and Chinese failed, however, and the clergy shifted its mission to providing spiritual support for Japanese residents in Asia. The priests could not overcome the language barrier, and the Koreans and Chinese did not understand Shin Buddhist doctrine, since it had changed drastically from the schools of Buddhism familiar on the Asian continent. The Shin Buddhist effort was also hindered by Christian missionaries, who succeeded in converting the

Chinese through undertaking social work, such as building schools and hospitals.[66] When Japan secured its territory in northern China and Japanese residents immigrated to Manchuria, the number of Honganji propagation centers increased. Before the Manchurian Incident of 1931,[67] the Higashi had served Japanese soldiers and residents through its seventeen propagation facilities. By 1944, the total number of Higashi propagation centers in northern China jumped to eighty. By that time, the Nishi had also established fifty-three.[68]

The two Honganjis also advanced into territory north of Japan. The Nishi began propagation in Vladivostok in 1886, Siberia in 1895, and Sakhalin in 1904, while the Higashi initiated propagation in Ezo (present-day Hokkaidō) in 1870 and in the Kuril Islands in 1899.[69] The 1907 statistics show that more than six thousand nine-hundred Japanese fishermen, mostly from Toyama prefecture, had migrated to the Kuril Islands.[70] The Meiji government encouraged domestic migration to and cultivation of Hokkaidō in order to contain Russia's southern advance and the intrusion of other European nations. (The port of Hakodate was opened for trade with Europe in 1864.) The Higashi abbot took this opportunity to prove his order's loyalty to the Meiji government and increased his influence in Hokkaidō.[71] The Nishi had made preliminary efforts in Ezo as early as 1857 under the supervision of the Tokugawa shogunate and succeeded in sending three hundred and seventy followers from mainland Japan. The Nishi Honganji increased its influence in Hokkaidō and founded two regional branch temples (betsuin) in Otaru and Esashi in 1877.[72]

In Hokkaidō and the Kuril Islands, the two Honganjis propagated their teachings to the indigenous people. The Higashi particularly made strenuous efforts to transform the Ainu of Hokkaidō, who were regarded as "uncivilized," into imperial subjects by converting them to Shin Buddhism. The priests gave the Ainu daily necessities and luxury items such as liquor and tobacco to attract their attention. Despite this hypocritical kindness, however, the Higashi Honganji enterprise failed partly because most Ainu had already converted to the Orthodox Catholic Church.[73]

In addition to these areas in the north of Japan, Shin clergy propagated in the south, in Kagoshima and Okinawa, and went further on into the South Pacific and even to Brazil.[74] When the Japanese army and residents moved into the South Pacific, the two Honganjis followed them, sending priests to the Mariana Islands, Micronesia, the Philippines, and elsewhere. The Higashi established propagation centers in Saipan in 1920, Davao (in the Mindanao Islands) in the 1920s, Palau in 1925, and Rota Island (present-day Commonwealth of the Northern Mariana Islands) in 1936.[75] The

Nishi established two centers in the South Pacific between 1919 and 1930, five between 1931 and 1936, and seven between 1987 and 1945.[76]

Although the official entry of Shin Buddhism into Brazil did not commence until after World War II, several priests from both branches of the Honganji made their own attempts. Brazil did not admit foreign religions at that time, so the Nishi sent one priest as an employee of an overseas corporation (he failed because he did not get along well with his colleagues). In 1933, a Higashi priest tried to immigrate to South America with his family, but a Japanese customs officer prevented him from embarking after discovering that he was carrying a Buddhist statue and scriptures with him.[77]

In addition, the BMNA and the Higashi Honganji Los Angeles Mission expanded their influence into Mexico. In 1930, Bishop Masuyama assigned Shōdō Fujitani to this task and placed him as assistant minister of the El Centro Buddhist Church.[78] Five years earlier, Izumida had visited Mexico to initiate the mission.[79] Its propagation was designed with Japanese immigrants in mind, just as other overseas destinations where clergy were sent.[80]

Only in Western Europe did the Shin Buddhist clergy not follow Japanese labor immigrants. On February 21, 1891, two Nishi priests, at the request of Émile Guimet (1836–1918), officiated at a *Hōonkō* service in France. In April 1901, Shūe Sonoda, a former bishop of the BMNA, and eighteen other Japanese who had studied in Berlin, held *Die Blume Fest* to celebrate Śākyamuni Buddha's birthday, and introduced Mahayana Buddhism to Germans. Later, Buddhists in Japan began to use *Hanamatsuri* as the translation for *Die Blume Fest* ("Bloom Festival") for their annual celebration of Buddha's birthday.[81] Other Japanese Buddhist activities in Western Europe included those of Kentoku Hori, third bishop of the BMNA, who participated in and reported on the Buddhist Association in Germany in 1907; and Shungaku Ōsumi of the Higashi Honganji, who organized the celebration of the Buddha's birthday in Paris on April 8, 1922, with other Japanese residents as a cultural exchange between Japan and France.[82]

The globalization of Shin Buddhism suggests the exchange of priests in various overseas propagation sites and their connection with Japanese nationalism. There were cases of ministerial transfers between North America and Asia. To name just a few, Ryūsei Kusuhara, acting bishop of the BMNA, later became bishop in the Nishi Honganji's Taiwan district in July 1926. Hōshō Sasaki, fifth bishop of the BMNA, was acting *rinban* in Taiwan from 1922 to 1924. Daishō Tana was assigned to Taiwan prior to his transfer to the United States in 1928. He resigned from the BMNA in January 1931 and was sent to Korea in 1934, but he returned to the United

States in 1936.[83] Prior to becoming minister of the HHMH in 1910, Shōen Yasukuni served in Manchuria. Ryōsei Tanima and Yoshio Itō also worked in Manchuria after leaving the HHMH. The fourth bishop, Gikyō Kuchiba, served in Hong Kong and China from 1910 to 1920, and in Taiwan in 1935. Mihō Satō served the BMNA before transferring to the HHMH in 1913, while Tansai Terakawa served the HHMH before his transfer to the BMNA in 1921.[84] Ejō Kurita, a minister of the Higashi Honganji Los Angeles Betsuin during the early 1920s, became the bishop of the Higashi's Korean District in 1929.[85]

There were several cases in which the BMNA made direct contact with Japanese authorities in China. The Southern Manchurian Railway Company exhibited a Japanese-style building, called the Manshūkan, at the Second World's Fair in Chicago in 1933, and after the exhibition Bishop Masuyama asked the president of the company to donate it to the BMNA. When his request was granted, Masuyama asked the Kyoto headquarters to rename the building in June 1934. The structure was moved to Sebastopol, California, remodeled, and given the temple designation of Enmanji.[86] Furthermore, representatives of the BMNA twice visited the Japanese Armed Forces in China. Kōshi Mikami went to Asia in 1938 and Shōzen Naitō resided there from 1939 to 1940. Their tasks included visiting and offering spiritual support to Japanese soldiers in hospitals and making reports to the BMNA office.[87] The BMNA and the Buddhist Mission of Canada (BMC) also held memorial services in 1938 for Japanese imperial soldiers who had died in China and Korea. The BMNA made donations to the headquarters in Japan, and the BMC sent $100 to the military authorities.[88] The Higashi Honganji in Hawaii sent its headquarters several thousand cotton cloths for the purpose of cleaning Buddhist altars. The Higashi administrators in Japan passed some of these on to the imperial army to use as bandages or for cleaning weapons.[89] Such activities demonstrate Issei ministers' tacit support of Japan's imperial government and its war efforts.

A Critical Ethos of Shin Buddhism

As can be seen in the cases of the two Honganjis' overseas propagation, mundane rules superseded spiritual principles in the modern development of Shin Buddhism. The formation of the nation-state of Japan and the presence of the highly institutionalized systems of the two Honganjis overshadowed a tradition of critiquing mundane affairs. However, some Shin Buddhists did maintain a critical ethos in their belief structure.

Studying the lives of Shin devotees (*myōkōnin*) at the end of the Edo period (or Tokugawa period, 1601–1867), Shiki Kodama analyzes the Shin Buddhist ethos of simultaneously submitting to and yet retaining a critical perspective on authority. When *myōkōnin* juxtaposed the compassion of Amida Buddha with the love of one's parents, two kinds of reactions often developed. One group of followers revered their parents' integrity and strove to repay their indebtedness to them, whereas the other lived unreservedly, entrusting themselves completely to their parents. Okaru, a native of Mutsurejima (a small island in the Hibikinada Sea in the Kanmon Straits, near Shimonoseki in Yamaguchi prefecture), expressed the second type of ethos, as a free spirit. She was not concerned with filial piety or mores because, to her mind, Amida did not discriminate among sentient beings. She also demonstrated a sense of transcending mundane values by ignoring, though not overtly challenging, the political authority of the day. Her understanding of Amida's compassion was quite different from that of the former type of devotees, who strove to show appreciation for every aspect of their lives, including the imposition of secular authority, which concealed the socioeconomic problems created by modernity.[90]

Shin "free spirits" who exercised their critical faculties persisted during the Meiji period; there was an instance of a Shin priest protesting against the Meiji government. Recently, Japanese scholars have carefully studied the efforts of Kenmyō Takagi, a Higashi Honganji priest who was involved in the High Treason Incident of 1910.[91] Takagi was born in 1864 in Aichi prefecture and at the age of thirty-five became a priest at Jōsenji in Shingū (Wakayama prefecture). This temple was located in a *buraku,* or outcast community. Witnessing the plight of the outcasts, and as a way to liberate himself from his own discriminatory feelings toward them, he served the community, and also opposed state-sponsored prostitution and the Russo-Japanese War. Other Buddhist priests in the area, however, did not sympathize with him, so Takagi found support from a socialist group formed by Seinosuke Ōishi. His association with the socialists led to his arrest in the High Treason Incident and excommunication from his order. He later committed suicide while in prison in Akita (northern Japan) in 1914.[92]

In "My Socialism" (*Yoga shakai shugi*), Takagi discusses an Amidist's social engagement. He argues that if one's activities grew parallel to Amida's compassion, then it would "bring about 'progress (*kōjō shinpo*)' and 'community (*kyōdō seikatsu*),'" sustained by 'compassion directed equally towards everyone.'" "Progress" refers to opposing war and social inequities, including discrimination. "Community" suggests alleviating physical struggle and the use of labor for maintaining life. Being in such a position, one can pursue a spiritual life without interference.[93]

It is possible to discover a critical ethos in Shin Buddhism as expressed by Okaru, Takagi, and even Kiyozawa (discussed in Chapter Six) in Imamura's actions. Imamura questioned the exclusivist discourse on Americanization from an egalitarian Buddhist point of view and tried to incorporate democratic values as espoused in the United States into his order. Although it is reasonable to think that American principles of freedom and liberty led the Shin ministers in Hawaii to support the 1920 strike and the early legal test case, it is important not to overlook the influence of an analytical ethos unique to the Shin tradition.

Summary

Living with a sense of uncertainty in the two nation-states and under the discriminative racial hierarchy of Anglo-Americans, Issei Shin ministers sought an amicable relationship with their host country without denouncing their cultural allegiance to Japan. On the mainland, Uchida and Masuyama demonstrated that the BMNA was a religious order capable of promoting world peace. In Hawaii, Imamura showed that the HHMH was pursuing the principles of American democracy. At the same time, both institutions were firmly connected with their respective headquarters in Japan.

The ambiguity of the Issei clergy living between the nation-states of Japan and the United States and the rise of ethnic nationalism were critical factors in the acculturation of Shin Buddhism. When one considers the political identity of Shin Buddhists, the process of acculturation seems confusing at first. Imamura held double standards, recognizing the polities of Japan and the United States at the same time. In Japan, the relationship between secular rules and spiritual truth had been quite simple. Honganji leaders used the doctrine of the two truths to transform parishioners into dutiful imperial subjects, while advising them to keep their Buddhist faith to themselves. But in a religious frontier, such as that in Hawaii and on the mainland, application of that doctrine required a new interpretation of it, as the Shin clergy had to take into account the secular laws of the United States, where Japan did not have the same kind of colonial power it wielded on the Asian continent. In this context, Imamura's involvement in the 1920 strike and the lawsuit dealing with Japanese language schools can be seen as attempts to bring the discussion of the doctrine of the two truths to a new level, or perhaps even as experiments, though incomplete, to reverse the priority of spiritual principles over mundane rules.

Conclusion

Rethinking Acculturation
in the Postmodern World

In the *Passages on the Land of Happiness,* Shinran writes:

> I have collected true words to aid others in their practice for attaining birth, in order that the process be made continuous, without end and without interruption, by which those who have been born first guide those who come later, and those who are born later join those who were born before. This is so that the boundless ocean of birth-and-death be exhausted.[1]

During the first half of the twentieth century, Japanese Buddhism established religious frontiers in three places. The present work is intended to contribute to the study of the religious frontier that emerged in North America, where Shin Buddhism became an interstitial religion despite its clergy's efforts to promote the buddhadharma eastward (*bukkyō tōzen*), and discusses how the modernization of Shin Buddhism impacted and paralleled the acculturation of its counterpart in the United States.

Prior to the eastward progression, religious frontiers had appeared within Japan. Both the Nishi Honganji and the Higashi Honganji sought domestic expansion by propagating in Hokkaidō, Kagoshima, Okinoshima (Shimane prefecture), Okinawa, and elsewhere. Japanese Buddhism also encountered Chinese and Korean Buddhism on the Asian continent through participation in Japan's territorial acquisition. The two branches of the Honganji were the major denominations in Manchuria, Korea, and Taiwan. As its dominance in East Asia suggests, Shin Buddhism also had the largest membership of all forms of Japanese ethnic Buddhism in North America.

Immigrants to the Pure Land situates acculturation in two settings. First, it has investigated acculturation as a complex process of the Japanization and Americanization of Shin Buddhist organizations, rituals, and doctrine, inquiring about their relationships with modernity, immigration, and ethnic subculture. Acculturation must be perceived as an extension of the modern development of Japanese Buddhism, but this process simultaneously intersects with the activities and concerns of Shin immigrants as

189

well as of Euro-American sympathizers, in this way diverging from tradition and emerging as a new form of Buddhism in North America.

Second, acculturation appears to be part of the localization, regionalization, nationalization, and globalization of Shin Buddhism. Shin immigrants often built local Buddhist missions or churches with the support of prefectural associations. At the same time, they tried to internalize two incompatible discourses of their host nation-states, while Shin Buddhist priests traveled around the Pacific Rim connecting the overseas operations of both branches of the Honganji. Therefore, the transnational activity of Shin Buddhism was linked to the globalization of polity (i.e., the politics of both Japan and the United States), economy (the plantation economy in the case of Hawaii, the resources of the Honganjis and their overseas allocations, Shin immigrants' remittances to Japan, and so on), and communication (between the homeland and Japanese living in the diaspora, and among the latter themselves).

The organizational amendments, ritual alterations, and doctrinal interpretations of the BMNA and the HHMH are deeply rooted in the forces of globalization. Each mission or church was under the authority of local state law, though the governor of Hawaii initially opposed the incorporation of the HHMH, while the board of the Seattle Bukkyōkai and the Buddhist group in Raymond, Canada, first registered their organizations as nonreligious associations in conformity with local state regulations. At the same time, Shin clergy—in particular, the heads of the BMNA and the HHMH—maintained close relations with their regional Japanese consuls, who often helped them mediate the breakup of a local *bukkyōkai.* Shin Buddhist members not only bore the expenses of their local mission or church, including the minister's stipend, but also contributed financially to the two organizations. Members' incomes were affected by local markets (plantations, agriculture, fisheries, or small businesses), the national economy (the fluctuation of sugar and wholesale prices), and global financial factors such as the Great Depression.

Shin clergy included imperial ideologies in the liturgy. In the period of early propagation, Shin ministers read the Imperial Rescript on Education at Japanese language schools, performed rituals honoring Japanese emperors (as was the practice in Japan), and observed imperial holidays. After the anti-Japanese movement began to intensify, they ceased these practices. In the case of the HHMH, Imamura recommended that Nisei members study the major speeches of former U.S. presidents and documents such as the Declaration of Independence. However, as late as the 1930s, Shin Buddhists observed memorial services for Japanese soldiers who had died in battle.

The resemblance of Shin rituals to Christianity needs to be reevaluated, as it represents the Shin clergy's arbitrary adaptive strategy. Christianity, being the dominant religion of America and connected to Western colonial power, certainly affected the liturgy of ethnic Buddhism. However, since all rituals provided revenue for missions and churches, it was important for Shin ministers to cater to attendees' requests to some degree. They simplified worship, as requested by Nisei members who did not comprehend ceremonies conducted in Japanese, and, to meet Euro-American sympathizers' interest in basic Buddhism, encouraged Shin clergy to endorse Theravadin teachings and ceremonies. As Chapter Four suggests, the interior and exterior design of worship halls reflected the financial resources and practicality of Issei immigrants and the modernization of Buddhist architecture that had taken place in Japan, in addition to pressure from non-Buddhist communities.

The case study of three Shin thinkers has demonstrated different types of reactions to state ideologies. Despite his pragmatic interpretation of Shin Buddhism, Takeichi Takahashi avoided critiquing the political structures of the two nations. For Ituzō Kyōgoku, one's Buddhist faith was to be kept to oneself. By keeping religious beliefs and practices private, Shin followers avoided resisting anti-Japanese activists and state authority, which discriminated against the Nikkei population. On the other hand, Emyō Imamura attempted to relativize the autocratic system of Japan and the democractic system of the United States from a Buddhist viewpoint. But his efforts appeared to be contradictory, reflecting his roles as both an influential leader of the Nikkei community in Hawaii and head of the HHMH and as an independent liberal thinker. None of these men, however, taught Issei, Nisei, and Caucasians that Shin Buddhism was a religion of worldly benefit, with prayers for gaining good luck and dispelling bad luck. Kyōgoku and Imamura rejected the commercialization of Buddhist faith and religious consumerism. Rather, a type of Shin ethos—namely, striving to repay one's indebtedness to Amida—appears to have persisted among Issei Jōdo Shinshū members, taking the form of devotion to local missions and churches and support for their growth.[2]

Transformation of organizational structure, ritual practice, and hermeneutics occurred through multiple channels of communication. The HHMH and BMNA offices received various types of information from the Kyoto headquarters (transnational), other Buddhist denominations and religious organizations (territorial or national), and local missions and churches (interisland or intercontinental). Some information must have overlapped and/or conflicted, making it difficult for Imamura, Uchida, and Masuyama to decide on the proper action to take. As Niklas Luhmann suggests, social systems, including institutions, construct themselves by communicating binary concepts, such as ownership against nonownership (economy), true versus false (science), and legal as opposed to non-legal (law). The course of communication progresses from selecting information to imparting it and understanding it; thus communication also includes a process of exclusion.[3] At the crossroads of the discourses of the two nation-states, the theory of the two truths, the habits and requests of Shin immigrants, and the motivations of local missions and churches, which were not always harmonious, Shin leaders made choices concerning the adaptation of Jōdo Shinshū in North America at the beginning of the global era. The local and translocal activities of Shin Buddhists, discussed in Chapter Seven, thus demonstrate different adaptive strategies.

Shin Buddhism today continues to be an international religion, albeit with different levels of relationships to the aforementioned forces of globalization. After World War II, the position of Nikkei Buddhists in the United States changed dramatically. According to Michael Masatsugu, they made "significant modifications to Buddhist institutions and to the external practice of Buddhism in response to shifting forms of racialization."[4] Their status altered mainly due to the creation of a politico-economic partnership between the United States and Japan and the disappearance of anti-Japanese activism in North America. Although purportedly positive, for Shin Buddhists in the United States these changes conceal one serious concern. The acceptance of Shin Buddhism in the United States ironically suggests that it is becoming part of world hegemony.

In this situation, unlike during the prewar and internment periods, the followers of American Shin Buddhism can easily conform to the singular secular authority. With the decline of the Issei generation, so-called complex loyalties are no longer an issue. The bilateral relationship between the two countries seems to secure the basis for the future growth of Shin Buddhism in the United States. There is no need for third- and fourth-generation Japanese American Shin Buddhists to worry about a confrontation between their homeland and the country to which their ancestors had immigrated. While existing in something of a "comfort zone," given that the United States is the most powerful nation-state in the world, it is easier for twenty-first-century America Shin Buddhists to turn inward and avoid looking beyond (or beneath) the immediate problems that personally concern them.

Separating the public and private spheres is, however, only one aspect of Shin Buddhist discourse. As Chapters Five and Seven suggest, Shinran's teaching can be made to serve as a basis for its adherents to relativize mundane rules. This analytical attitude may correspond to postmodern critics. Mark Unno argues that when a religion is subsumed under the dominant ideology, it can trigger two reactions. The sacredness manifested in the texts of any religion can be commodified, or a certain amount of detachment can be maintained within its particular cultural discourse. American Shin Buddhists are able to redefine the sacred quality of their texts and provide a spiritual alternative in today's society, where problems of modernization still linger and prevail, because they are in a unique position, sharing the prewar experiences of their ancestors. Unno further proposes that Shin Buddhists in the United States should regain spiritual insight as a form of "resistance against the negative aspects of the global economy."[5]

> In a hegemonic system, those at the bottom of the oppressive hierarchy are often the ones who most clearly see and feel the depths of the hegemonic structure. They are therefore in an advantageous position to catalyze resistance against the commodification of all life, including that of religion. Shin Buddhist religious thought and the experience of Japanese American Shin Buddhists offer possible venues for the articulation of this hegemony, of reading into the depths of the global economy and of evoking the voices of the sacred that originate beyond this world.
>
> Yet, while this potentiality may exist within the sacred texts of Shin Buddhism, and may be inscribed in the bodies of Japanese American Shin Buddhists through such experiences as internment, many Shin Buddhists have turned away from this dimension of their religious lives in order to seek assimilation into the dominant mainstream American culture, the culture that is most deeply implicated in the problematic aspects of the global economy. Japanese Americans inherit the legacy of the two most powerful, and thus potentially most oppressive, economies in the world.[6]

The Issei Shin Buddhist experience is now a thing of the past, but the cultural heritage that their descendants have received can possibly awaken them to the various kinds of contradictions that the United States has created in the era of global economy.

For American Shin Buddhists today, the process of Japanization is no longer an issue. They have sought more independence from the head temples in Japan and have abandoned cultural elements unfit for the religious landscape of the United States. And over time, the Kyoto headquarters of the two branches of the Honganji have become less involved with the operations of their affiliated organizations in North America. The language barrier and differences between the two cultures have separated them. As a result, Shin Buddhism in the United States has a chance to develop a distinctive character, though it may be simultaneously isolated from other

Shin communities in the world and may fail to provide spiritual insights into the crises of the global economy.

As a concluding remark, this book makes two suggestions regarding the future development of a vital Shin Buddhism in the twenty-first century. First, concerning how to recover the critical ethos as found in the tradition, the efforts of Imamura and Kyōgoku will be worth retracing. The combination of a critical spirit and the circular movement of self-power and other-power offers the possibility of searching for a postmodern interpretation of Shin Buddhist doctrine, although it is beyond the objectives of this present study to examine such implications.

Second, as an attempt to relativize secular authority, Shin Buddhism could provide an alternative perspective that goes beyond the national interests of a single nation. Instead of supporting either side of an argument, Buddhist non-attachment can offer a third way. Such an example is found in one Japanese Shin Buddhist's response to the use of the atomic bomb. In his soteriology, Shigenobu Kōji, a Jōdo Shinshū priest in Hiroshima, himself a victim of the bombing, proposes a middle path transcending the polarities of either blaming the United States for using the atomic bomb to attain victory or of criticizing Japan for making the mistake of initiating the Pacific War. For him, the disaster of the atomic bomb represents collective human karma and the weakness of man's moral capacity.[7] In the *Tannishō,* Shinran points out the uncertainty of an individual's actions depending on his or her causes and conditions: "If the karmic cause so prompts us, we will commit any kind of act." Kōji speculates along this line of Shinran's thought. Yuki Miyamoto, in the introduction to Kōji, writes:

> Kōji hypothesizes that he might have been born in the United States during the war, [and] he might have been the pilot in charge of pressing the button [to release] the bomb. He was born into the Kōji family by mere chance, but the same "chance" could have [caused] him [to be] born as an American pilot. If he [had been] a pilot at the time, confesses Kōji, he would, for sure, have pressed the button.[8]

For Kōji, the invention of the atomic bomb does not show scientific superiority but relates to the wonder of birth, the unpredictability of human behavior, and the limitation of individual choices.[9] Understanding the vulnerability of human life, therefore, may lead to the discovery of the importance of spiritual principles over mundane rules. Certainly, as Miyamoto points out, religious ideas alone do not provide any solution to complex political conflicts.[10] However, since Shin Buddhism has become a global religion, it needs to be equipped with a vision that can evaluate "pro" or "con" sociopolitical debates from a different standpoint.

Notes

Translation of Terms

1   Shin'ya Yasutomi, "Daihi no kaishaku gaku: Suzuki Daisetsu yaku Kyōgyō-shinshō shiken," *Gendai to shinran* 10 (2006): pp. 122–23. In the prewar period, D. T. Suzuki, with others, published at least five books or articles in English concerning Jōdo Shinshū: *Principal Teachings of the True Sect of Pure Land* (Kyoto: Higashi Honganji, 1910); *The Life of the Shonin Shinran*, translated in collaboration with Gesshō Sasaki (Tokyo: The Buddhist Text Translation Society, 1911); "The Development of the Pure Land Doctrine in Buddhism," *The Eastern Buddhist* 3, no. 4 (1926): pp. 285–326; *From the Shin Sect* (Kyoto: The Eastern Buddhist Society, 1937); and "The Shin Sect of Buddhism," *The Eastern Buddhist* 7, no. 3/4 (1939): pp. 227–84.

2   There are two aspects (*nishu jinshin*) in this concept:

> One is to believe deeply and decidedly that you are a foolish being of karmic evil caught in birth-and-death, ever sinking and ever wandering in transmigration from innumerable kalpas in the past, with never a condition that would lead to emancipation. The second is to believe deeply and decidedly that Amida Buddha's Forty-eight Vows grasp sentient beings, and that allowing yourself to be carried by the power of the Vow without any doubt or apprehension, you will attain birth.

Dennis Hirota et al., eds., *The Collected Works of Shinran* (*CWS*), 2 vols. (Kyoto: Jōdo Shinshū Hongwanji-ha, 1997), vol. 1, p. 85. "Deep mind" indicates the process of introspection: to question one's existence, through which one encounters Amida's vows.

3   Ryūkichi Mori, *Honganji* (Tokyo: San'ichi shobō, 1973), pp. 209–210.

4   Mori, *Honganji*, pp. 209–210.

Introduction

1   Kōkun Sonoda, ed., *Sonoda Shūe: Beikoku kaikyō nisshi* (Kyoto: Hōzōkan, 1975), p. 10.

2   Robert Spencer, "Japanese Buddhism in the United States: A Study in Acculturation," Ph.D. dissertation (University of California, Berkeley, 1937), pp. 75–78, 81–82; and William C. Rust, "The Shin Sect of Buddhism in America: Its Antecedents, Beliefs, and Present Condition," Ph.D. dissertation (University of Southern California, 1951), p. 163. In this book, Christianity, particularly American Protestantism, is treated as a whole, since it is less likely that Shin

ministers were able to conceptualize denominational differences of Christianity and plurality of its practices.

3   For instance, priests in Japan are self-employed and hold hereditary positions. Their counterparts in the United States, however, are hired by the Buddhist churches (*bukkyōkai*) and are in charge of religious matters and secular activities. Tetsuden Kashima, *Buddhism in America: The Social Organization of an Ethnic Religious Institution* (Westport, CT: Greenwood Press, 1977), pp. 24, 76, 78.

4   Kashima, *Buddhism in America*, pp. 20–21, 29, 37.

5   Kashima, *Buddhism in America*, p. 179.

6   See George J. Tanabe, "Grafting Identity: The Hawaiian Branches of the Bodhi Tree," in *Buddhist Missionaries in the Era of Globalization*, ed. Linda Learman (Honolulu: University of Hawai'i Press, 2005), pp. 77–100.

7   See Tomoe Moriya, *Amerika bukkyō no tanjō: Nijū seiki shotō ni okeru nikkei shūkyō no bunka henyō* (Tokyo: Gendai shiryō shuppan, 2001).

8   Masako Iino, "Bukkyōkai and the Japanese Canadian Community in British Columbia," paper presented at the Issei Buddhism Conference, University of California, Irvine, September 2004; originally published as "BC shū no bukkyō-kai to nikkei kanadajin community," *Tokyo daigaku amerika taiheiyō kenkyū* 2 (2002): pp. 45–61.

9   See Lori Pierce, "Constructing American Buddhisms: Discourse of Race and Religion in Territorial Hawai'i," Ph.D. dissertation (University of Hawai'i, 2000).

10 See Michael Masatsugu, "Reorienting the Pure Land: Japanese-Americans, The Beats, and the Making of American Buddhism, 1941–1966," Ph.D. dissertation (University of California, Irvine, 2004).

11 For instance, David Yoo demonstrates the ways in which Nisei Buddhists negotiated their position with Euro-Americans by pointing to the freedom of religion laid down in the Constitution of the United States. Some even challenged the idea that being a true American meant being Christian. *Growing Up Nisei: Race, Generation, and Culture among Japanese Americans of California, 1924–1949* (Urbana, IL: University of Illinois Press, 2000), pp. 46–54. Valerie Matsumoto discusses the relationship between Buddhists and Christians in the town of Cortez, California, in *Farming the Home Place: A Japanese American Community in California 1919-1982* (Ithaca, NY: Cornell University Press, 1993), pp. 53–54, 168–69, 206–207. Yoo also mentions how Buddhist Women's Associations (*fujinkai*) contributed to the development of the social network of their churches. Although women remained in the domestic sphere, churches could not function without them: they prepared food and refreshments after the services and organized temple bazaars and fundraising programs. *Growing Up Nisei*, p. 43. According to Eiichirō Azuma, the Buddhist Women's Association in California also provided humanitarian aid to Japanese soldiers stationed in

Manchuria. *Between Two Empires: Race, History, and Transnationalism in Japanese America* (New York: Oxford University Press, 2005), p. 165. Eileen Tamura refers to Imamura's Buddhist democracy in her discussion of Nisei identity. *Americanization, Acculturation, and Ethnic Identity: The Nisei Generation in Hawaii* (Urbana, IL: University of Illinois Press, 1994), p. 204. Gary Okihiro mentions that Buddhists in Hawaii initially critiqued the territorial government ban on Japanese language schools and participated in the 1920 sugar plantation strike. *Cane Fires: The Anti-Japanese Movement in Hawaii 1865–1945* (Philadelphia: Temple University Press, 1991), pp. 68, 154. Brian Hayashi reveals that some Buddhist leaders during the internment period encouraged their followers to avoid camp politics and to remain neutral in discussions regarding the progress of the war. *Democratizing the Enemy: The Japanese American Internment* (Princeton, NJ: Princeton University Press, 2004), pp. 169–70.

12 Studies of transnational Buddhism have been conducted by Thomas Tweed and Richard Jaffe. In his recent book, *Crossing and Dwelling: A Theory of Religion* (Cambridge, MA: Harvard University Press, 2006), Tweed explores a theory of religion through the religious activities of transnational immigrants and addresses three points: movement, relation, and position. He also goes beyond the concept of a transnational religious history and uses the term "translocative history." See "American Occultism and Japanese Buddhism," *Japanese Journal of Religious Studies* 32, no. 2 (2005): p. 269. Richard Jaffe investigates the modern development of Japanese Buddhism through an interaction between Japan and the Asian continent. See "Seeking Sakyamuni: Travel and the Reconstruction of Japanese Buddhism," *Journal of Japanese Studies* 30 (2004): pp. 65–96.

13 Eileen Tamura differentiates acculturation from Americanization:

> Acculturation refers to the adaptation of a group to American middle-class norms and assumes that the process entails the persistence of ethnic identity. Americanization, on the other hand, refers to the organized effort during and the following World War I to compel immigrants and their children to adopt certain Anglo-American ways while remaining at the bottom of socioeconomic strata of American society.

Americanization, Acculturation, and Ethnic Identity, p. 52. Karl-Josef Kuschel refers inculturation to a receiver's perspective in the transmission of Christianity, and Emi Mase-Hasegawa applies his idea to her analysis of Shūsaku Endō's work in Japan. *Spirit of Christ Inculturated: A Theological Theme Implicit in Shusaku Endo's Literary Works* (Lund, Germany: Lund University, 2004), p. 12. James H. Grayson defines emplantation as "the rooting of a new religious tradition in the soil of a culture alien to its place of origin" and points out three phases of "contact and explication," "penetration," and "expansion." "Ch'udo yebae: A Case Study in the Early Emplantation of Protestant Christianity in Korea," *The Journal of Asian Studies* 68, no. 2 (2009): p. 413.

14 Among the Euro-Americans who advocated Americanization, not all were exclusionists driven by racial ideologies and fears of immigrants' economic

success. For a discussion of the exclusive and inclusive aspects of Americanization, see John Higham, *Strangers in the Land: Patterns of American Nativism, 1860–1925* (1955) (New Brunswick, NJ: Rutgers University Press, 2004, reprint), pp. 1–11, 19–23.

15 David Chidester, *Savage Systems: Colonialism and Comparative Religion in Southern Africa* (Charlottesville, VA: University Press of Virginia, 1996), p. 254. Also, for the examination of the frontier between Japan and the outside world, Bruce L. Batten's discussion of "border," "boundary," and "frontier" is useful, although his study focuses on the medieval and early modern periods based on secular worldviews. See *To the Ends of Japan: Premodern Frontiers, Boundaries, and Interactions* (Honolulu: University of Hawai'i Press, 2003).

16 With the benefit of hindsight, I find Wendy Cadge's analytical approach relevant to my study. She discusses the conceptualization of Theravada Buddhism on micro and macro levels as a way to

> distinguish between all of the ideas and material objects that relate to religious tradition generally in a culture and the specific ideas, teachings, and practices that matter to individual practitioners in that culture. This distinction further allows me to distinguish between all of the items that are part of Theravada Buddhism in Thailand and those items from Thailand that made it to the United States along one of several global routes.

Heartwood: The First Generation of Theravada Buddhism in America (Chicago: University of Chicago Press, 2005), pp. 13–14.

17 Japanese scholars have already indicated this difference in the orientation of Shin propagation, but they have not explained why or how it came about. See, for example, Kiyomi Morioka, *Shinshū kyōdan to ie seido* (Tokyo: Sōbunsha, 1962), p. 632.

18 Michel Mohr, Introduction to "Feature: Buddhist and Non-Buddhist Trends Towards Religious Unity in Meiji Japan," *The Eastern Buddhist* 37, nos. 1/2 (2005): p. 2.

19 American scholars' interest in Japanese Pure Land Buddhism has been scanty when compared to the attention given to Zen or Tibetan Buddhism. Galen Amstutz points to Buddhologists' tendency to overlook the social history of Shin Buddhism; social scientists' lack of interest in Shin Buddhist hermeneutics in relation to the institutionalization of the politics and economics of Japan; Japanese scholars' tendency to ignore Jōdo Shinshū in the discussion of contemporary religious identities in Japan; Shin Buddhist scholars' inability to engage themselves in a meaningful crosscultural dialogue; and so on. He then argues that Jōdo Shinshū was the least appealing because the Victorian Transcendentalists had become interested in any tradition that was

> a metaphysical monism (a transcendentalist theism) combined with a liberal, individualistic humanistic self-effort theory (not a "grace" theory) and an elitist hostility to religious organizations (antisectarianism).

Interpreting Amida: History and Orientalism in the Study of Pure Land Buddhism (Albany, NY: State University of New York, 1997), pp. 67, 107–108.

20   However, there are several monographs and Ph.D. dissertations that have been recently published. For instance, Elizabetta Porcu, *Pure Land in Modern Japanese Culture* (Leiden, The Netherlands: Brill, 2008); Ugo Dessi, *Ethics and Society in Contemporary Shin Buddhism* (Münster, Germany: Lit Verlag, 2008); and Jessica Main, "Ethics in the Modern History of Shin Buddhism: Human Rights, Discrimination, the Ōtani-ha, and the Burakumin, 1860–1980," Ph.D. dissertation (McGill University, 2010).

Chapter One: The Modern Development of Shin Buddhism

1   Mori, *Honganji,* p. 137.

2   James C. Dobbins, *Jōdoshinshū: Shin Buddhism in Medieval Japan* (Bloomington, IN: Indiana University Press, 1989), p. 2.

3   Between 1861 and 1868, the Nishi Honganji made a total contribution of 124,000 *ryō* and the Higashi Honganji a total of 25,000 *ryō,* together with 4,000 straw bags of rice, to the royalists who eventually formed the Meiji government (Mori, *Honganji,* p. 189). It is also said that the Higashi donated 100,000 *ryō* during the first ten years of the Meiji period and spent 250,000 *ryō* in order to develop Hokkaidō. An accurate conversion of the value of *ryō* into present-day currency is challenging, as there are many ways of doing the calculation; inflation also must be taken into account. For example, *ryō* became yen (¥) in the fourth year of Meiji (1871), and one *koku* of rice was valued at ¥6.74 during the same period. One hundred thousand *ryō* would equate to 14,836 *koku,* or, after conversion, approximately ¥830 million. Another way of calculating the value of *ryō* is based on the ratio of price increase to the cost of rice. Since it had risen three thousandfold by the time of the Meiji Restoration, 100,000 *ryō* could be calculated as approximately ¥3 billion (Akeshi Kiba, personal correspondence with the author, March 7, 2001).

4   For accounts of Shinran's early life, see Yoshifumi Ueda and Dennis Hirota, *Shinran: An Introduction to His Thought* (Kyoto: Hongwanji International Center, 1989), pp. 23–24; Dobbins, *Jōdoshinshū,* pp. 22–23; and Alfred Bloom, *Shinran's Gospel of Pure Grace* (1965) (Ann Arbor, MI: Association for Asian Studies, 1999, reprint), p. x. For a translation and discussion of the *Letters* of Eshinni, Shinran's wife, see James C. Dobbins, *Letters of the Nun Eshinni: Images of Pure Land Buddhism in Medieval Japan* (Honolulu: University of Hawai'i Press, 2004).

5   Ueda and Hirota, *Shinran,* pp. 27–28; Dobbins, *Jōdoshinshū,* pp. 23–24; and Bloom, *Shinran's Gospel of Pure Grace,* pp. x–xi.

6   The title translation comes from the *Collected Works of Shinran* (*CWS*).

7   *CWS,* vol. 1, p. 290.

8   Hisao Inagaki, *The Three Pure Land Sutras: A Study and Translation* (Kyoto: Nagata bunshodō, 1994), p. 107; and *Hōnen's Senchakushū: Passages on the Selection of the Nembutsu in the Original Vow,* ed. The Senchakushū English Translation Project (Honolulu: University of Hawai'i Press, 1998), p. 41.

9   Luis O. Gómez, *The Land of Bliss. The Paradise of the Buddha of Measureless Light: Sanskrit and Chinese Versions of the Sukhāvatīvyūha Sutras* (Honolulu: University of Hawai'i Press, 1996), p. 167.

10 The last Dharma age (Skt. *saddharma viparopa;* Ch. *mofa;* Jpn. *mappō*) refers to a concept in Buddhist thought that originated in Indian cosmological notions of successive stages of flourishing, decadence, and decline. Beginning in Chinese Pure Land thought, the belief was that in the third of three five hundred-year stages of the Buddhist teaching, the last is a period in which the Dharma has decayed into merely a verbal expression, and the spiritual capacities of human beings are so diminished that invocation of Amida's name (Ch. *nianfo;* Jpn. *nenbutsu*) is the only viable practice.

11 *Hōnen's Senchakushū,* pp. 8, 36–37. For a detailed discussion of Hōnen in English, see Sōhō Machida, *Renegade Monk: Hōnen and Japanese Pure Land Buddhism* (Berkeley: University of California Press, 1999); and Mark Blum, *The Origins and Development of Pure Land Buddhism: A Study and Translation of Gyōnen's Jōdo Hōmon Genrushō* (New York: Oxford University Press, 2002).

12 *Hōnen's Senchakushū,* p. 18.

13 *CWS,* vol. 1, p. 289.

14 Ueda and Hirota, *Shinran,* p. 32.

15 Ueda and Hirota, *Shinran,* p. 35.

16 Bloom, *Shinran's Gospel of Pure Grace,* pp. xi–xii.

17 *CWS,* vol. 1, p. 459. According to Shinran, "hunters and peddlers" are "foolish beings in bondage"; they represent those who are considered spiritually hopeless, bound by unwholesome karma since they "earn their living by killing" and as "wine dealers who . . . make and sell liquor," respectively (*CWS,* vol. 1, p. 110).

18 *CWS,* vol. 1, pp. 459–60.

19 Dobbins, *Jōdoshinshū,* p. 38.

20 Ueda and Hirota, *Shinran,* pp. 38–42.

21 For a detailed discussion of these monks as seen through Shinran's eyes, see Inagaki, *The Three Pure Land Sutras,* pp. 59–78, 83–93, 106–114, 158–163, 173–180; and Bloom, *Shinran's Gospel of Pure Grace,* pp. 7–27. For a discussion of Tanluan's work and a translation of the *Commentary,* see Hisao Inagaki, *T'an-luan's Commentary on Vasubandhu's Discourse on the Pure Land* (Kyoto: Nagata bunshodō, 1998). For a discussion of Shandao, though not through Shinran's perception, see Julian Pas, *Visions of Sukhāvatī: Shandao's Commentary on the Kuan Wu-Liang-Shou-Fo Ching* (Albany, NY: State University of New York Press, 1995).

22 *Tannishō,* chap. 12, in *CWS,* vol. 1, p. 668.

23 The original word for *shinjin* is the Sanskrit *citta-prasāda.* "*Citta* indicates one's heart and mind, while *prasāda* means that joy arises in the mind when it becomes pure and clear." Takamaro Shigaraki, "The Problem of the True and the False in Contemporary Shin Buddhist Studies: True Shin Buddhism and False Shin Buddhism," *Pacific World,* 3rd ser., no. 3 (2001): p. 36.

24 Ueda and Hirota, *Shinran,* pp. 144–46; Bloom, *Shinran's Gospel of Pure Grace,* pp. 30–31.

25 Taitetsu Unno, "The Practice of Jodo-shinshu," in *Living in Amida's Universal Vow: Essays in Shin Buddhism,* ed. Alfred Bloom (Bloomington, IN: World Wisdom, 2004), p. 66.

26 Gilbert L. Johnston, "Kiyozawa Manshi's Buddhist Faith and Its Relation to Modern Japanese Society," Ph.D. dissertation (Harvard University, 1972), p. 138.

27 *CWS,* vol. 1, p. 455.

28 For further explanations of "nonretrogression" and "blind passions," see *CWS,* vol. 2, pp. 172, 196.

29 Shigaraki, "The Problem of the True and the False in Contemporary Shin Buddhist Studies," pp. 36–37.

30 *CWS,* vol. 1, p. 406.

31 Medieval Japanese wished for a better afterlife. In *The Tale of Heike* (*Heike monogatari*), there are many descriptions of warriors longing for birth in the Pure Land before dying. For instance, see "The Death of Tadanori" (pp. 315–16), "The Suicide of Koremori" (pp. 348–50), and "The Execution of Shigehara" (pp. 397–400) in *The Tale of the Heike,* trans. Helen Craig McCullough (Stanford, CA: Stanford University Press, 1988).

32 *A Record in Lament of Divergences: A Translation of the Tannishō* (Kyoto: Honganji International Center, 1995), pp. 7–8.

33 For instance, see Minor L. Rogers, "Rennyo Shōnin 1415–1499: A Transformation in Shin Buddhist Piety," Ph.D. dissertation (Harvard University, 1972); Ira M. Solomon, "Rennyo and the Rise of Honganji in Muromachi Japan," Ph.D. dissertation (Columbia University, 1972); Stanley Weinstein, "Rennyo and the Shinshū Revival," in *Japan in the Muromachi Age,* ed. John W. Hall and Toyoda Takeshi (Berkeley: University of California Press, 1977), pp. 331–58; Minor L. Rogers and Ann T. Rogers, *Rennyo: The Second Founder of Shin Buddhism* (Berkeley, CA: Asian Humanities Press, 1991); and Mark L. Blum and Shin'ya Yasutomi, eds., *Rennyo and the Roots of Modern Japanese Buddhism* (New York: Oxford University Press, 2006).

34 Blum and Yasutomi, *Rennyo and the Roots of Modern Japanese Buddhism,* p. 12.

35 Stanley Weinstein, "Continuity and Change in the Thought of Rennyo," in Blum and Yasutomi, *Rennyo and the Roots of Modern Japanese Buddhism,* p. 51.

36 The theory of the two truths is a core teaching in Mahayana Buddhism, through which Nāgārjuna explained the doctrine of emptiness and interaction between *loka-saṃvṛti-satya* (conventional truth) and *paramārtha-satya* (ultimate truth). Without the mediation of language, ultimate truth expressed by Śākyamuni, such as the teaching of dependent origination, could never have been grasped. At the same time, through the working of ultimate truth, one is able to come to see that all objects lack inherent existence. However, these two truths do not oppose one another but rather are reciprocal. For instance, Paul Williams writes that "the ultimate, emptiness, is what is ultimately the case concerning the object under investigation," *Mahayana Buddhism: The Doctrinal Foundations* (New York: Routledge, 1989), pp. 69-71. Bernard Faure writes:

> It (i.e., the doctrine of two truths) provides a convenient hermeneutical device, allowing us to explain all apparent doctrinal contradictions as the result of a shift between the levels of ultimate and conventional truths. It affirms ontological duality only to negate it. . . . The reverse, however, is equally true: by negating duality, it has already acknowledged it and contributed to its preservation.

Faure, *The Rhetoric of Immediacy: A Cultural Critique of Chan/Zen Buddhism* (Princeton, NJ: Princeton University Press, 1991), p. 56.

37 *CWS*, vol. 1, p. 29. Translation is modified.

38 Weinstein, "Continuity and Change," p. 55. Brackets are in the original.

39 Weinstein, "Continuity and Change," p. 53.

40 Weinstein, "Continuity and Change," p. 55. For a detailed discussion of the Shin Buddhist interpretation of the theory of the two truths, see Rogers and Rogers, *Rennyo: The Second Founder of Shin Buddhism*, pp. 307-315; and Michio Tokunaga and Alfred Bloom, "Toward a Pro-Active Engaged Shin Buddhism: A Reconsideration of the Teaching of the Two Truths (*shinzoku-nitai*)," *Pacific World*, 3rd ser., no. 2 (2003): pp. 191-206.

41 Weinstein, "Continuity and Change," pp. 55-56. For Rennyo's use of a strong rhetoric of salvation connected to the afterlife, see, for instance, *The Letters* (*Ofumi* or *Gobunshō*) V-1:

> Lay men and women, lacking wisdom in the last age, [should realize that] sentient beings who rely deeply and with singleness of mind on Amida Buddha and entrust themselves single-heartedly and steadfastly (without ever turning their minds in any other direction) to the Buddha to save them are unfailingly saved by Amida Tathāgata, even if their evil karma is deep and heavy.

The Letters V-3 states:

> Women who have renounced the world while remaining in lay life and ordinary women as well should realize and have absolutely no doubt whatsoever that there is deliverance for all those who simply rely deeply (single-heartedly and steadfastly) on Amida Buddha and entrust themselves to [the Buddha] to save them, [bringing them to buddhahood] in the afterlife. This is the Primal Vow of Other Power, the Vow of Amida Tathāgata.

Once [they have realized] this, when they then feel the thankfulness and joy of being saved in [regard to] the afterlife, they should simply repeat "Namu-amida-butsu, Namu-amida-butsu."

Rogers and Rogers, *Rennyo: The Second Founder of Shin Buddhism,* pp. 242, 244.

42 There was, however, an internal conflict within the Honganji itself at the Battle of Ishiyama with Nobunaga Oda's army in 1580, when the eleventh abbot, Kennyo (1543–1592), and his son, Kyōnyo (1558–1614), disagreed over the Honganji's truce with him. In 1592, Kennyo passed away. Although Hideyoshi Toyotomi suggested Kyōnyo as the twelfth abbot, Nyoshun-ni, Kennyo's wife, requested Hideyoshi to nominate Junnyo, their third son, as successor. Owing to a further internal conflict, Hideyoshi consented. Soon after, Kyōnyo started developing relations with Ieyasu Tokugawa and, at the establishment of the Tokugawa *bakufu,* Ieyasu granted Kyōnyo an estate in Karasuma, Kyoto. From that time on, Junnyo's temple in Horikawa was recognized as the Nishi Honganji, while Kyōnyo's was regarded as the Higashi Honganji (Tatsurō Fujishima, *Honbyō monogatari: Higashi honganji no rekishi* [Kyoto: Shinshū Ōtani-ha, 1999], pp. 87–98, 93–95).

43 This was especially true for Shin Buddhists in outcast communities (*hisabetsu buraku*).

44 Takamoro Shigaraki, ed., *Kindai shinshū kyōdanshi kenkyū* (Kyoto: Hōzōkan, 1987), pp. 10–12.

45 National teaching refers to the one national doctrine marked by the "Three Standards of Instruction" promulgated by the government in 1872, and later along with the "Eleven Themes" and "Seventeen Themes." The "Three Standards of Instruction" refer to 1) understanding the importance of honoring the *kami* (gods) and love for one's nation; 2) clarifying the principle of Heaven and the way of human beings; and 3) serving the emperor and the government.

46 James E. Ketelaar, *Of Heretics and Martyrs in Meiji Japan: Buddhism and Its Persecution* (Princeton, NJ: Princeton University Press, 1990), pp. 95–96, 99, 105–111, 125–130.

47 Tatsuya Naramoto and Meiji Momose, *Meiji ishin no higashi honganji* (Tokyo: Kawade shobō shinsha, 1987), pp. 279–80, 282–83, 302–303. The Ministry of Doctrine recognized Kōshōji's independence in September 1876. Arinori Mori, Japan's first envoy to Washington, particularly opposed the attempt to establish a state religion by proposing "Religious Freedom in Japan" (*nihon ni okeru shinkyō no jiyū ni tsuite*) in 1872.

48 Toshimaro Ama, *Why Are the Japanese Non-Religious? Japanese Spirituality: Being Non-Religious in a Religious Culture,* trans. Michihiro Ama (Lanham, MD: University Press of America, 2004), pp. 35–38; and Kanryū Fukushima, "Teikoku shugi seiritsuki no bukkyō: seishin shugi to shin bukkyō to," in *Bukkyō shigaku ronshū,* ed. Futaba hakase kanreki kinen kai (Kyoto: Nagata bunshodō, 1977), p. 481.

49 Yoshio Yasumaru and Masato Miyachi, eds., *Shūkyō to kokka* (Tokyo: Iwanami shoten, 1992), pp. 229–230. For the Shin Buddhist debate and resistance regarding the acceptance of shrine talismans, see also pp. 184–91.

50 Shigaraki, *Kindai shinshū kyōdanshi kenkyū*, p. 14.

51 Masaharu Hishiki, *Jōdoshinshū no sensō sekinin* (Tokyo: Iwanami, 1993, booklet), pp. 39–40.

52 Shigaraki, *Kindai shinshū kyōdanshi kenkyū*, pp. 17–18.

53 Shigaraki, *Kindai shinshū kyōdanshi kenkyū*, p. 15. The honorary titles were also given to the founders of other Buddhist schools, namely to Dōgen in 1878, Shinsei (founder of Tendaishū Shinsei-ha) and Shunjō (abbot of Shingonshū Sennyūji) in 1883, Ippen in 1886, Hōnen in 1911, Ingen (founder of Ōbakushū) in 1917, and Nichiren in 1922 (Mitsugu Kōmoto, ed. *Ronshū nihon bukkyōshi*, vol. 9: *Taishō shōwa jidai* [Tokyo: Yūzankaku, 1988], p. 17).

54 Fujishima, *Honbyō monogatari*, p. 117.

55 Toshimaro Ama, "Towards a Shin Buddhist Social Ethics," *The Eastern Buddhist* (n.s.), 33, no. 2 (2001): pp. 40–41; and see Chapter Six, note 83.

56 Naramoto and Momose, *Meiji ishin no higashi honganji*, pp. 209–214.

57 Yūsen Kashiwahara, *Kindai Ōtani-ha no kyōdan: Meiji ikō shūseishi* (Kyoto: Shinshū Ōtani-ha, 1986), p. 11. For a discussion of the Religions Bill, see Sheldon M. Garon, "State and Religion in Imperial Japan, 1912–1945," *Journal of Japanese Studies* 12, no. 2 (1986): pp. 280–84.

58 Kōchō Fukuma, "Nishi honganji kyōdan ni okeru kōsen gikai no seiritsu ni tsuite," in *Bukkyō shigaku ronshū*, ed. Futaba hakase kanreki kinen kai (Kyoto: Nagata bunshodō, 1977), p. 420.

59 Fukuma, "Nishi honganji kyōdan," pp. 421–22.

60 Fukuma, "Nishi honganji kyōdan," pp. 424, 432–34.

61 Fukuma, "Nishi honganji kyōdan," pp. 454–56. For a discussion of the Nishi Honganji's constitution and representative assembly plan, see pp. 460–74.

62 Hisashi Mizutani, *Meiji ishin no higashi honganji*, pp. 160–64; "Meiji ishin igo ni okeru Ōtani-ha shūsei no hensen (3)," *Shinshū* (June 1932): p. 5; and "Meiji ishin igo ni okeru Ōtani-ha shūsei no hensen (9)," *Shinshū* (July 1933): pp. 6–8. For a discussion of these topics in English, see Ketelaar, *Of Heretics and Martyrs*, pp. 69, 71–72, 81.

63 In 1896, Kiyozawa, while living in Shirakawa, Kyoto, published a periodical called *Kyōkai jigen* (*Timely Words for the Religious World*) to appeal for reform. The present halls of the Higashi Honganji were completed in 1895; the Founder's Hall is one of the largest wooden buildings in the world.

64 Kashiwahara, *Kindai Ōtani-ha no kyōdan*, pp. 52, 58, 116–18. For a discussion of the modern development of the Higashi Honganji in English, see Notto R.

Thelle, "Power Struggle in Shin Buddhism: Between Feudalism and Democracy," *Japanese Religions* 9, no. 2 (1976): pp. 64–75.

65 Shiki Kodama, *Kinsei shinshū to chiiki shakai* (Kyoto: Hōzōkan, 2005), p. 294. Kodama refers to Machiko Kagotani, "Shūso gōtan'e seiritsu no keii," in *Chiba Jōryū hakase kanreki kinen ronshū Nihon no shakai to shūkyō* (Kyoto: Dōbōsha, 1981). Also see *Honganjishi,* vol. 3, p. 527.

66 *Shūhō* 114 (March 1911): pp. 8–13. Reprint, *Shūhō,* vol. 6, pp. 252–57.

67 Studies on the systematization of Buddhist songs (*bukkyō shōka,* or later *bukkyō sanka*) with Western melodies are lacking in English. The government promoted music education (*shōka,* later *ongaku*) in elementary schools after 1872. Buddhist leaders took this opportunity to modernize their religion and propagated Buddhism to the youth. The introduction of Christian psalms also stimulated the Buddhist clergy. In 1889, Chikai Iwai of Jōdoshū formed a group to study Buddhist hymns, and other priests, such as Seiran Ōuchi and Haya Akegarasu, promoted Buddhist songs accompanied by the organ. While priests in Kantō (eastern part of Japan) enjoyed singing united Buddhist themes, their counterparts in Kansai (western part of Japan), led by Shin Buddhists, produced hymns of their own denominations. When the Young Buddhist Association (YBA) was organized at the national level (Dainihon Bukkyō Seinenkai) in 1892, young priests celebrated the birth of Śākyamuni Buddha as a transsectarian event. With the growth of the Sunday school, singing Buddhist songs became an established practice. Seijin Nomura and Kōsaku Yamada are well known for their arrangements of Buddhist verses to Western music (Kanritsu Asuka, *Sorewa bukkyō shōka kara hajimatta* [Tokyo: Junshinsha, 1999], pp. 21–22, 27–30, 33–36, 44–45). Recent scholars, however, are cautious about the preceding narrative. Yasuyuki Fukumoto argues that Buddhists initially "did not sing" the hymns but merely "listened" to the Western music performed as a type of dedication or entertainment at large-scale Buddhist gatherings. At these occasions, military bands often played the music, as they were the first group of people in Japan to study Western music. The military bands played music that had nothing to do with Buddhist themes, including the Japanese national anthem. Fukumoto also demonstrates that the leaders of the Buddhist Women's Association (BWA) encouraged their members to sing Buddhist songs as one of the "accomplishments of sophisticated women." Therefore, singing was not necessarily designed specifically for children and the younger generation (Fukumoto, "Initial Acceptance of the Western Music in the Japanese Buddhism [Buddhist] Community: Focusing on the Positioning of the Western Music," *Journal of Handai Music Studies* 2 [March 2004]: pp. 150, 153–54, 164–65). Other scholars point to a complex process of composition and argue that in the beginning Buddhist songs were not always accompanied by Western instruments. In the late nineteenth century, there were many Japanese-style melodies with lyrics, which sounded like Japan's folk ballads

(*minyō*) and court music (*gagaku*), with the fourth and seventh notes often missing in the scale (Joaquim M. Benitez and Shiho Jidoi, "A Study of the Seven Collections of Bukkyō Shōka ["Buddhist Songs"] Published with Music between 1889 and 1907," *Elisabeth University of Music Research Bulletin* 21 [2001]: pp. 49, 58–59).

68 Asuka, *Sorewa bukkyō shōka kara hajimatta,* pp. 33, 35.

69 *Shūhō* 195 (December 1917): p. 10. Reprint, *Shūhō,* vol. 9, p. 708.

70 Shigaraki, *Kindai shinshū kyōdanshi kenkyū,* pp. 26–27; and Kyūichi Yoshida, *Nihon kindai bukkyōshi kenkyū* (Tokyo: Yoshikawa kōbunsho, 1964), pp. 12–13.

71 Itō was supported by Roka Tokutomi, Shusui Kōtoku, and Toshihiko Sakai. Furukawa was one of the members who started the journal *Hanseikai zasshi,* later known as *Chūō kōron,* which published the essays of Shōyō Tsubouchi, Shiki Masaoka, Doppo Kunikida, Rohan Kōda, Tōsan Shimasaki, and others (Shigaraki, *Kindai shinshū kyōdanshi kenkyū,* pp. 21, 27).

72 *Shūhō* 281 (March 1925): 7-8. Reprint, *Shūhō,* vol. 13, pp. 489–90.

73 Judith Snodgrass, *Presenting Japanese Buddhism to the West: Orientalism, Occidentalism, and the Columbian Exposition* (Chapel Hill, NC: University of North Carolina Press, 2003), p. 178. Renjō Akamatsu was one of the earliest priests who envisaged introducing Shin Buddhism in English (Amstutz, *Interpreting Amida,* pp. 62–63, 206).

74 Another example of an earlier translation is *The Life of the Shonin Shinran,* trans. D. T. Suzuki and Gesshō Sasaki (Tokyo: The Buddhist Text Translation Society, 1911).

75 For a list of Sasaki's translations, see Amstutz, *Interpreting Amida,* p. 168. Transliteration of other Japanese Buddhist schools include, for instance, an English translation of a pictorial biography of Hōnen (*Hōnen shōnin gyōjō ezu*) by Ryūgaku Ishizuka, a Jōdoshū priest, in September 1925, with the help of a European scholar, Harper Havelock Coates; and an English translation of *Mandala* by Chokuei Iwano, a Nichirenist, in 1926 ("Eiyaku sareta Mandala," *Tairiku Nippō,* June 24, 1926). As a trans-sectarian project, D. T. Suzuki initiated the Buddhist journal *The Eastern Buddhist* in 1921; and Junjirō Takakusu started *The Young East* in 1925.

76 Shigaraki, *Kindai shinshū kyōdanshi kenkyū,* p. 30.

77 The two aspects of entrusting mind (or deep mind) are cited from *CWS,* vol. 1, p. 85.

78 Shigaraki, *Kindai shinshū kyōdanshi kenkyū,* pp. 31–32; Kanae Tada, "Jōdokyō hihan eno hihan," *Shūhō* 76 (October 1924): p. 5. Reprint, *Shūhō,* vol. 13, pp. 317–20.

79 Hataya's entry on Daiei Kaneko, in Shōjun Bandō, Emyō Ito, and Akira Hataya,

Jōdo bukkyō no shisō, vol. 15: *Suzuki Daisetsu, Soga Ryōjin, and Kaneko Daiei* (Tokyo: Kōdansha, 1993), pp. 286–87.

80 Shigaraki, *Kindai shinshū kyōdanshi kenkyū*, pp. 32–33. Soga compared the three aspects of entrusting mind with the three types of mind, or consciousness, in the *ālaya-vijñāna:* entrusting mind (*shingyō*) with Bodhisattva Dharmākara's self-realization; sincere mind (*shishin*) with the effective stage of his experience, and aspiration for birth in the Pure Land (*yokushō*) as the causal stage of his experience (Bandō, Ito, and Hataya, *Jōdo bukkyō no shisō*, pp. 194, 242). Soga also writes: "Dharmākara Bodhisattva is no ancient myth; he is a reality of present faith. If we conceive of him apart from the one-moment of faith, he becomes a mere mythological figure...." "A Savior on Earth: The Meaning of Dharmākara Bodhisattva's Advent," trans. Jan Van Bragt, in *An Anthology of Modern Shin Buddhist Writings: Kiyozawa Manshi, Soga Ryōjin, Kaneko Daiei and Yasuda Rijin* (Kyoto: Ōtani University, 2001), p. 56.

81 Masahiko Okada, "Revitalization versus Unification," *The Eastern Buddhist* (n.s.), 37, nos. 1/2 (2005): pp. 31–32. This volume features Senshō Murakami and his scholarship.

82 Bandō, Ito, and Hataya, *Jōdo bukkyō no shisō*, pp. 286–88.

83 Kyōka kenkyūsho, ed., *Shinshū Ōtani-ha kyōgaku kenkyū*, vol. 1, 92/93 (1986): pp. 154–55; and Jōryū Chiba, ed., *Honganji shūkai hyakunenshi, shiryōhen* (Kyoto: Jōdoshinshū Hongwanji-ha shūkai, 1983), pp. 351–52. Even a group of Shintō scholars planned to honor Shōtoku Taishi by founding a Shintō shrine to him. In the 1,300th-year commemoration of his passing, a party of modern artists held an exhibition of paintings on the theme of his celebration (*Shūhō* 217 [October 1919]: p. 6. Reprint, *Shūhō*, vol. 10, p. 660).

84 In 1872, the two branches of the Honganji marked the year 1224, when Shinran had supposedly compiled the *Kyōgyōshinshō*, as the time of the foundation of their denominations. Concerning the commemorative ceremony, see the special feature volume of *Shūhō* 258/259 (April/May 1923). Reprint, *Shūhō*, vol. 12.

85 *Shūhō* 250 (August, 1922): p. 11. Reprint, *Shūhō*, vol. 12, p. 223. The Federation consisted of the Honganji-ha (Nishi Honganji), the Ōtani-ha (Higashi Honganji), the Bukkōji-ha, the Kōshō-ha, the Takada-ha, the Kibe-ha, the Sammonto-ha, the Yamamoto-ha, the Izumoji-ha, and the Jōshōji-ha. The last four were the four branches in Echizen (present-day Fukui prefecture), and the Meiji government recognized their independence in 1878 (Nishū Utsuki, *The Shin Sect, A School of Mahayana Buddhism: Its Teaching, Brief History, and Present-day Conditions* [Kyoto: Publication Bureau of Buddhist Books Hompa Hongwanji, 1937], pp. ii, 37–38).

86 *Shūhō* 268 (February 1924): p. 28. Reprint, *Shūhō*, vol. 13, pp. 72, 194.

87 Petitions submitted to and approved by the representative assembly in 1921 and 1937 (*Honganji shūkai hyakunenshi, shiryōhen*, pp. 352, 416–17).

Chapter Two: Changes in Organizational Style

1   Masaru Kojima and Akeshi Kiba, eds., *Asia no kaikyō to kyōiku* (Kyoto: Hōzōkan, 1992), p. 14.

2   Kojima and Kiba, eds., *Asia no kaikyō to kyōiku,* pp. 10–14; and Kōnen Tsunemitsu, *Hawai bukkyō shiwa: Nihon bukkyō no tōzen* (Tokyo: Bukkyō dendō kyōkai, 1971), pp. 111, 129. Prior to official engagement, Okabe Gakuō had voluntarily started Jōdoshū propagation in 1894. For the initial propagation of Jōdoshū in Hawaii, see Gidō Shinbo, *Hawai kaikyō kyūjūnenshi* (Tokyo: Sankibō busshorin, 1987), pp. 91–111.

3   It was only after 1900 that the Myōshinji-ha (part of the Rinzai school of Zen), the Nichiren sect, and the Sōtō sect of Zen sent *ryūgakusō* (priests studying abroad) to the United States (*Zensō ryūgaku kotohajime* [Kyoto: Zen bunka kenkyūsho, 1990], pp. 2, 316).

4   Okihiro, *Cane Fires,* p. 27.

5   Yukiko Kimura, *Issei: Japanese Immigrants in Hawaii* (Honolulu: University of Hawai'i Press, 1988), p. 22.

6   Okihiro, *Cane Fires,* pp. 23–24; 281, n. 18.

7   Okihiro, *Cane Fires,* p. 27.

8   Kimura cites *Hawaii Nihonjin Iminshi: Hawaii Kanyaku Imin 75-nen Kinen* (Honolulu: United Japanese Society of Hawaii, 1964), p. 314.

9   The term Aki *monto* began to prevail after 1903. The Nishi Honganji characterized such people as devout; they not only saved money for their temples but also worked night shifts in order to be able to make donations to the head temple in Kyoto (Shigekuni Kumata, *Kindai shinshū no tenkai to aki monto* [Hiroshima: Hiroshima joshi daigaku, 1983], pp. 150–51).

10 Tsunemitsu, *Hawai bukkyō shiwa,* pp. 33–34, 137–38 (Tsunemitsu cites Sōryū Kagahi's *Hawai kikō,* published in 1890); and Rick Fields, *How the Swans Came to the Lake: A Narrative History of Buddhism in America* (Boston: Shambhala Publications, 1981), p. 79.

11 Louise H. Hunter, *Buddhism in Hawaii: Its Impact on a Yankee Community* (Honolulu: University of Hawai'i Press, 1971), pp. 42–45, 49; Tsunemitsu, *Hawai bukkyō shiwa,* pp. 49, 51, 54–57; and Fields, *How the Swans Came to the Lake,* p. 80. According to Tsunemitsu, Kagahi spoke of his aspirations in Kyoto. First, he wanted to establish a permanent office for propagation in Honolulu, and he had already collected $4,000 and purchased a site. Kagahi also planned to set up nine branch temples throughout the Hawaiian Islands, including the one in Hilo that he had just organized. Expanding the Buddhist front was necessary, as 20,000 to 30,000 Japanese had immigrated and immigrants stayed in Hawaii for three years, during which time they would be exposed to Christianity and possibly bring the Christian religion back to Japan (Tsunemitsu, *Hawai bukkyō shiwa,* pp. 52–53).

12 Tsunemitsu, *Hawai bukkyō shiwa,* pp. 57–62; and Emyō Imamura, *Hompa hong-wanji hawai kaikyōshi* (Honolulu: Hompa Hongwanji Mission, 1931), p. 29. According to Tsunemitsu's evaluation, priests such as Tokurō Nishizawa, Ungai Gamō, Tokuo Himeji, and Gyōren Ogino were serious about their Buddhist activities in Hawaii. But it is also said that Himeji and Ogino returned to Japan with money they had collected in Hilo (Yoshio Yamamoto, *Hawai niokeru bukkyō no yōran jidai* [Honolulu: privately printed, n.d.], p. 9).

13 The early Shin Buddhist priests after Kagahi included Ungai (or Yukinari) Gamō, Kakujo Kuwahara, Dōrō Nishizawa, Tokuo Himeji, and Gyōun Hagino. Those recognized by Miyamoto were Gyoshin Satō and Sanju Kaneyasu. Tsunemitsu, *Hawai bukkyō shiwa,* pp. 70–75. See also *A Grateful Past, A Promising Future: The First 100 years of Honpa Hongwanji in Hawaii* (Honolulu: Honpa Hong-wanji Mission, 1989), pp. 9–14; and Barbara Hotta, "Ordeals of First Japanese Immigrants Retold in Buddhist Publication," *The Hawaii Herald,* July 10, 1969. For Hawaii's petition, see Hunter, *Buddhism in Hawaii,* pp. 61–62.

14 *Honganjishi,* ed. Honganji Shiryō Kenkyūsho, 3 vols. (Kyoto: Jōdoshinshū Hong-wanji-ha, 1961–1969), vol. 3, pp. 13–18. The scholar-priests' advancement in the United States seemed to occur during the time of the student-laborers' immigration, before a full-scale labor settlement came into effect on the Pacific Coast. The student immigration prevailed because enlightened thinkers such as Yukichi Fukuzawa encouraged the youth to study in the United States and Western Europe; the Meiji government introduced a mili-tary draft system in 1883 from which only those who studied abroad were ex-empted; and students who were active in the People's Rights Movement and suppressed by the government fled to the U.S. mainland (Yasuo Sakata, "Taiheiyō o matagu kita amerika e no ijū: Teijū o mezasu gyakkyō deno kutō," in *Nikkei Amerikajin no ayumi to genzai,* ed. Harumi Befu [Kyoto: Jinbun shoin, 2002], pp. 29–30; and Yūji Ichioka, *The Issei: The World of the First Generation Japanese Immigrants 1885–1924* [New York: Free Press, 1988], pp. 7–16).

15 *Buddhist Churches of America 75-year History 1899–1974,* vol. 1, pp. 45–46; *Buddhist Churches of America: A Legacy of the First 100 Years,* p. ii; Kōnen Tsunemitsu, *Hoku-bei bukkyō shiwa: Nihon bukkyō no tōzen* (Tokyo: Bukkyō dendō kyōkai, 1973), pp. 61–63; Fields, *How the Swans Came to the Lake,* pp. 143–44; and Rust, "The Shin Sect of Buddhism in America," p. 141.

16 Rust, "The Shin Sect of Buddhism in America," pp. 141–42. The YMBA later moved it to 532 Stevenson Street in April 1899 to accommodate more members.

17 Tsunemitsu, *Hawai bukkyō shiwa,* pp. 65–66; and Kashima, *Buddhism in America,* pp. 14–15.

18 *San Francisco Chronicle,* September 13, 1899; and *Buddhist Churches of America 75-year History,* vol. 1, p. 47.

19 By 1906, the laity had raised more than $5,600 for the establishment of the church (equivalent to $100,000 today). The government of British Columbia

recognized the *bukkyōkai* on April 21, 1909. For descriptions of the early es-
tablishment of Shin Buddhism in Canada, see Terry Watada, *Bukkyo Tozen: A
History of Jodo Shinshu Buddhism in Canada 1905–1995* (Toronto: HpF Press and the
Toronto Buddhist Church, 1996), pp. 36–39; Ken Adachi, *The Enemy That Never
Was* (Toronto: McClelland and Stewart Inc., 1991), pp. 109–116; Charles H.
Young and Helen R. Y. Reid, *The Japanese Canadians* (Toronto: University of
Toronto Press, 1938), pp. 95–107; and Masako Iino, "BC shū no bukkyōkai to
nikkei canadajin community BC," p. 51.

20   Toshiji Sasaki, *Nihonjin kanada iminshi* (Tokyo: Fuji shuppan, 1999), pp. 70, 92.
In Shiga prefecture, two villages were particularly known for sending immi-
grants: Hatsusaka-mura and Mitsuya-mura (present-day Hikone City). In
Wakayama prefecture, Mio-mura is especially known as an "Amerika-mura":
about half of its residents immigrated to the Pacific Coast of Canada. For a
detailed study of these villages and the immigration, see vols. 10 and 11 of
Toshiji Sasaki and Tsuneharu Gonnami, eds., *Kanada iminshi shiryō*, 11 vols.
(Tokyo: Fuji shuppan, 2000).

21   Moriya, *Amerika bukkyō no tanjō*, pp. 28, 101, 233; and *A Grateful Past, A Promising
Future*, p. 15.

22   Tsunemitsu, *Hokubei bukkyō shiwa*, pp. 205–206, 209–210.

23   Tsunemitsu, *Hokubei bukkyō shiwa*, p. 75. Emyō Imamura completed his education at Keiō Gijuku, present-day Keio University, in December 1893 (Moriya,
Amerika bukkyō no tanjō, p. 35).

24   Kojima and Kiba, eds., *Asia no kaikyō to kyōiku*, p. 15.

25   In fact, when Hawaii became part of the United States in 1897, people in Japan
called the U.S. territory of Hawaii *Hawai-ken* ("Hawaii prefecture") (Tsunemitsu,
Hawai bukkyō shiwa, p. 5).

26   Tsunemitsu, *Hawai bukkyō shiwa*, p. 78; Hunter, *Buddhism in Hawaii*, pp. 62–64;
and Pierce, "Constructing American Buddhisms," p. 107. Imamura and Yamada nurtured their friendship for over twenty years after working together in
Hawaii. Imamura wrote the Foreword to Yamada's book, *Megumi no seikatsu*
(Kyoto: Dōbōsha, 1928).

27   Moriya, *Amerika bukkyō no tanjō*, pp. 101; 244, n. 1.

28   Tsunemitsu, *Hawai bukkyō shiwa*, p. 153.

29   Data on the number of temples and the years of their establishment vary slight-
ly. According to the Kyoto headquarters, thirty-seven temples had been built by
1924, including ten on Oahu, twelve on Hawaii (Big Island), eight on Kauai, six
on Maui, and one on Lanai. One temple was founded in Molokai in 1931 (*Honganjishi*, vol. 3, pp. 428–30). According to the HHMH, thirty-three temples had been
built by 1924, including nine on Oahu, ten on Hawaii, seven on Kauai, six on
Maui, and one on Lanai. Jikōen was then founded in 1938. Tsunemitsu, *Hokubei
bukkyō shiwa*, pp. 87–89, in which he cites *Hawai hompa hongwanji kyōdan*

enkakushi, ed. Hawai hompa hongwanji kyōdan (Honolulu: Hompa Hongwanji, 1954). According to Hunter, by the end of 1906 more than thirty stations had been built, and the figure increased to seventy-one stations and temples by the end of the 1920s (*Buddhism in Hawaii,* pp. 70, 129, 150). According to Paul Tajima, as of 1935, thirty-six temples existed in addition to thirty-two stations ("Japanese Buddhism in Hawaii: Its Background, Origin, and Adaptation to Local Conditions," Master's thesis [University of Hawai'i, 1935], p. 29).

30 *Buddhist Churches of America: A Legacy of the First 100 Years,* p. 1.

31 Tsunemitsu, *Hokubei bukkyō shiwa,* pp. 92–94. Tsunemitsu cites Hōkō Terakawa, *Hokubei kaikyō enkakushi* (San Francisco: Hongwanji hokubei kaikyō honbu, 1936); and Manimai Ratanamani, "History of Shin Buddhism in the United States," Master's thesis (College of the Pacific, 1960), p. 27.

32 Watada, *Bukkyo Tozen,* pp. 74, 97. According to a 1940 survey of the Buddhist Mission of Canada, the Vancouver Bukkyōkai had three branches: Kitsilano, Kelowna, and Skeena. The Maple Ridge Bukkyōkai had two: Whonnock and Mission. In addition, Buddhist churches existed in Fairview, Steveston, New Westminster, Royston, and Raymond (Yūtetsu Kawamura, *Kanada bukkyō shi,* [1936–1985] [Kyoto: Dōbōsha, 1988, reprint], pp. 19–21).

33 *Honganjishi,* vol. 3, p. 428.

34 Kōyū Uchida, *Fushi no jinpō* (n.p., 1957), pp. 5–6.

35 Tsunemitsu, *Hokubei bukkyō shiwa,* p. 76; *Hawai bukkyō shiwa,* p. 87.

36 *Honganjishi,* vol. 3, p. 432.

37 Fields, *How the Swans Came to the Lake,* p. 145; and Tsunemitsu, *Hokubei bukkyō shiwa,* pp. 70–71.

38 "Constitution and By-Laws of The Dharma Sangha of Buddha," p. 1 (BCA Archives, Chronological Files, Box No. 1.01.01, Folder 1900).

39 "Constitution and By-Laws of The Dharma Sangha of Buddha," p. 8.

40 Terakawa, *Hokubei kaikyō enkakushi,* pp. 5–7; Tsunemitsu, *Hokubei bukkyō shiwa,* pp. 70–71; and Fields, *How the Swans Came to the Lake,* p. 145.

41 Terakawa, *Hokubei kaikyō enkakushi,* pp. 5–7; Tsunemitsu, *Hokubei bukkyō shiwa,* pp. 70–71; and Fields, *How the Swans Came to the Lake,* p. 145.

42 Tsunemitsu, *Hawai bukkyō shiwa,* pp. 85–86; and Moriya, *Amerika bukkyō no tanjō,* p. 115.

43 Moriya, *Amerika bukkyō no tanjō,* pp. 114; 247, n. 39. Tsunoda later contributed to the development of Asian studies at Columbia University, where he became a lecturer of Japanese cultural history and curator of the Japanese collection (Tsunemitsu, *Hokubei bukkyō shiwa,* pp. 146–47; and http://www.columbia .edu/cu/alumni/Magazine/Spring2002/AsianStudies.html). For Tsunoda's activities in Hawaii, see Utsumi Takashi, "Tsunoda Ryūsaku no hawai jidai: 1909 nen no tofu zengo o megutte," *Waseda daigakushi kiyō* 30 (1998): pp. 121–74;

and "Tsunoda Ryūsaku no hawai jidai sairon: 1909–1917 nen no taizai kikan o chūshin ni shite," *Waseda daigakushi kiyō* 31 (1999): pp. 91–124.

44   "The Constitution and By-laws of the Honpa Hongwanji Mission of Hawaii" (Hawaii Department of Commerce and Consumer Affairs, Business Registration Division Records, Exhibit C, October 1, 1907. File No. 662 D2).

45   Tsunemitsu, *Hawai bukkyō shiwa*, p. 87. However, this excludes Jikōen, founded in 1938.

46   *A Grateful Past, A Promising Future*, p. 34.

47   *A Grateful Past, A Promising Future*, pp. 35–58.

48   *Sacramento Betsuin 70th Anniversary 1899–1969.*

49   "The Articles of Incorporation of the Buddhist Church of San Francisco, July 9, 1913" (Secretary of State, California State Archives Records, File No. 73813). The Articles of Incorporation of the Buddhist Church of Santa Barbara in 1922 state:

> [T]he purposes for which it is formed are: (a) The spreading and propagating of the fundamental principles of Truth as inculcated and taught in the Buddha Dharma.

The Fresno Buddhist Church's Articles of Incorporation in 1922 state:

> [T]o establish a Church in Fresno, County of Fresno, State of California, and in connection therewith suitable and customary organizations, for the purpose of public worship and religious training, according to the rules and discipline of the Buddhist Church, to take charge of the church building, estate and property, and the affairs of the temporalities thereof.

BCA Archives, Subject Files, Box No. 1.03.08, Folder 1905, 1913, 1919, 1922–23, 1925.

50   *Beikoku bukkyō* 19, no. 6 (June 1918): p. 25.

51   *Buddhist Churches of America 75-year History*, vol. 1, p. 49; and Tsunemitsu, *Hokubei bukkyō shiwa*, p. 76. There were exceptions, however. For instance, the Articles of Incorporation of the Buddhist Temple of Berkeley, with the seal of the Notary Public C. H. Henderson, dated May 18, 1925, state:

> [P]ublic worship and religious training according to and in conformity with the religious teachings and doctrines of Buddha, subject to the rule, jurisdiction and control of the Hongwanji Sect of Buddhists.

According to the Articles of Incorporation of the Honganji Buddhist Church of El Centro endorsed by the deputy clerk on July 16, 1913, members of the El Centro and Stockton temples initially called their groups "Honganji Buddhist Church" (BCA Archives, Subject Files, Box No. 1.03.08, Folder 1905, 1913, 1919, 1922–23, 1925). The tendency to emphasize Śākyamuni's teachings appeared on the letterheads of various Buddhist churches. When corresponding with the BMNA office, local priests used letterheads of their own Buddhist associations, such as the Intermountain Buddhist Church in Utah, the Watsonville Buddhist Church, and the Portland Buddhist Church. At the same time, there were also letterheads from the Honganji Buddhist Church of Brawley, the

Honganji Buddhist Church of Oxnard, and the San Diego Honganji Buddhist Temple. See, for instance, BCA Archives, Correspondence Files, Box No. 1.02.01, Folder 1924–1925. Those churches that had initially included the title "Honganji" in their names, however, eventually dropped it.

52　Ronald E. Madgen, "Buddhism Comes to Seattle," in *More Voices, New Stories: King County, Washington's First 150 Years,* ed. Mary C. Wright (Seattle: Pacific Northwest Historians Guild, 2002), pp. 178–179; and *Furusato: Tacoma-Pierce County Japanese 1888-1899* (Tacoma, WA: Nikkeijinkai Tacoma Japanese Community Service, 1998), p. 195, n. 20. See also *Seattle Betsuin 75th Anniversary,* p. 23.

53　From a handwritten copy of the Articles possessed by Ellen Hale, a member of the Seattle Buddhist Church.

54　Leslie Kawamura, "The Historical Development of the Buddhist Churches in Southern Alberta," in *Religion and Culture in Canada,* ed. Peter Slater (Waterloo, Ontario: Wilfred Laurier University Press, 1977), p. 498.

55　*Raymond bukkyōkaishi,* ed. Raymond Bukkyōkai (Kyoto: Dōbōsha, 1970), p. 21.

56　Sasaki and Gonnami, eds., *Kanada iminshi shiryō,* vol. 8, p. 1302.

57　Tsuyoshi Nakano, "Hawai shū no seikyō kankei to hōseido," in *Hawai nikkeijin shakai to nihon shūkyō: Hawai nikkeijin shūkyō chōsa hōkokusho,* ed. Keiichi Yanagawa and Kiyomi Morioka (Tokyo: Tokyo daigaku shūkyōgaku kenkyūshitsu, 1981), pp. 83, 89; and Spencer, "Japanese Buddhism in the United States," pp. 75–76, 81.

58　Ratanamani, "History of Shin Buddhism in the United States," p. 31.

59　Utsuki, *The Shin Sect,* p. 40.

60　Tsunemitsu, *Hawai bukkyō shiwa,* p. 91; and *A Grateful Past, A Promising Future,* pp. 41, 60. The total number of lay delegates from each island was twenty in 1923 (Emyō Imamura, *Hompa hongwanji hawai kaikyō sanjūgonen kiyō* [Honolulu: Hompa Hongwanji Mission, 1931], p. 40). The by-laws of the Honpa Honganji Mission of Hawaii were later modified and according to Article V, the convention (*giseikai*) was defined as:

> 5. The convention of the ministers and delegates (Giseikai) shall constitute the general meeting of the Mission. . . . 8. The membership of the convention shall consist of all the ministers present thereat and lay delegates accredited thereto. There shall be sixty-two (62) lay delegates as follows: thirty (30) from Honolulu, eight (8) from rural Oahu, five (5) from Kauai, six (6) from Maui and thirteen (13) from Hawaii, and in addition thereto there shall be six (6) delegates representing the Hawaii Federation of Young Buddhist Associations.

This version of the by-laws of the Honpa Honganji Mission of Hawaii is cited in Yanagawa and Morioka, eds., *Hawai nikkei shūkyō no tenkai to genkyō: Hawai nikkeijin shūkyō chōsa hōkokusho* (Tokyo: Tokyo daigaku shūkyōgaku kenkyūshitsu, 1979), pp. 236–37. On the mainland, an annual conference of ministers and lay delegates began in 1914 (Tsunemitsu, *Hokubei bukkyō shiwa,* p. 80).

61 Kazuko Tsurumi, "Sōsestu," in *Sōgō kōza nihon no shakai bunkashi,* vol. 3: *Dochakuka to gairaika,* ed. Kazuko Tsurumi (Tokyo: Kōdansha, 1973), pp. 28–30.

62 Kenshi Kusano, *Sengokuki honganji kyōdanshi no kenkyū* (Kyoto: Hōzōkan, 2004), pp. 352, 357. Kusano cites Kazuo Kasahara, *Ikkō ikki no kenkyū* (Tokyo: Yamagawa shuppan sha, 1962).

63 *Dōbō* 10, no. 11 (November 1909): p. 30. These confraternities were known as *shinyū-kō* (friends of *shinjin*), *hōshin-kō* (mind of Dharma), *tenshin-kō* (gratitude for receiving *shinjin*), *shūon-kō* (paying indebtedness), and *sūshin-kō* (revering *shinjin*).

64 Imamura, *Hompa hongwanji hawai kaikyōshi,* p. 29.

65 *A Grateful Past, A Promising Future,* p. 17. Hōsui Takeshima also had similar experiences in Hilo (*Tōko: Takeshima Hōsui-shi gofusai keigyō tsuitōshi,* ed. Tōko henshū iinkai [Hiroshima: Shinkōji bukkyōkai, 1968], pp. 375–76).

66 Hunter, *Buddhism in Hawaii,* pp. 81–82.

67 Tsunemitsu, *Hawai bukkyō shiwa,* pp. 142–43; and *A Grateful Past, A Promising Future,* p. 19.

68 Hawaii Honolulu Hongwanji, ed., *Chōshōin ibunshū* (Honolulu: Hawaii Honolulu Hongwanji, 1937), p. 160. This translation is found in Kimura, *Issei: Japanese Immigrants in Hawaii,* p. 155.

69 *Dōbō* 5, no. 1 (January 1904): pp. 28–29; and *Dōbō* 7, no. 8 (August 1906): p. 27. Soyoku Fujimura also attempted to end a strike in Kahuku, which began in May 1909, but he died before it was settled (*A Grateful Past, A Promising Future,* p. 149).

70 *Dōbō* 10, no. 2 (February 1909): p. 31.

71 *A Grateful Past, A Promising Future,* p. 41.

72 Moriya, *Amerika bukkyō no tanjō,* pp. 113–14.

73 For records of this organization, see *Shinshū Kyōkai Mission of Hawaii, 1914-1984: A Legacy of Seventy Years* (Honolulu: Shinshū Kyōkai Mission of Hawaii, 1985).

74 Kimura, *Issei: Japanese Immigrants in Hawaii,* p. 80.

75 Imamura's letter sent to Masuyama dated March 14 (BCA Archives, Correspondence Files, Box No. 1.02.06, Folder 1932 Communications from District Temples, H-O).

76 *Hokubei kaikyō enkakushi,* p. 101.

77 Tsunemitsu, *Hokubei bukkyō shiwa,* pp. 109–110.

78 Ratanamani, "History of Shin Buddhism in the United States," p. 24.

79 Terakawa, *Hokubei kaikyō enkakushi,* pp. 192, 249; and Kashima, *Buddhism in America,* p. 21.

80 Matsumoto, *Farming the Home Place,* pp. 53–54.

81 Rust, "The Shin Sect of Buddhism in America," p. 155. Rust cites Dōsetsu Takeuchi, "The Religious Life of Japanese Children in America," Master's thesis (University of Southern California, 1935), pp. 64–65.

82 Rintarō Hayashi, "Kuroshio no hateni," in Sasaki and Gonnami, eds., *Kanada iminshi shiryō,* vol. 11, pp. 329, 333.

83 Iino, "BC shū no bukkyōkai to nikkei Canadajin community," pp. 54–55. Iino cites Audrey Kobayashi, "The Early History of Japanese Canadians," in *Spirit of Redress: Japanese Canadians in Conference,* ed. Cassandra Kobayashi and Roy Miki (Vancouver: JC Publications, 1989), p. 83.

84 Iino, "BC shū no bukkyōkai to nikkei Canadajin community," p. 56. Iino cites Adachi, *The Enemy That Never Was,* p. 114.

85 Kōnen Tsunemitsu, *Nihon bukkyō tobeishi* (Tokyo: Bukkyō Times, 1964), pp. 313–14; Terakawa, *Hokubei kaikyō enkakushi,* pp. 451–53.

86 David Iwaasa, "Canadian Japanese in South Alberta: 1905–1945," in *Two Monographs on Japanese Canadians,* pp. 40, 49 (Iwaasa cites *A History of Forty Years of the Raymond Buddhist Church,* ed. Raymond Buddhist Church [Raymond, Canada: Raymond Buddhist Church, 1970]); and Tadamasa Murai, "Dainiji sekai taisenmae no minami alberta nikkei shakai: Sono seisei to hatten no kiseki," *Imin kenkyū nenpō* 4 (1998): pp. 57–58 (Murai cites *Raymond bukkyōkaishi*).

87 Kashima, *Buddhism in America,* p. 17.

88 Terakawa, *Hokubei kaikyō enkakushi,* pp. 293, 314, 332–33, 387–89.

89 Magden, "Buddhism Comes to Seattle," p. 183.

90 Terakawa, *Hokubei kaikyō enkakushi,* pp. 237, 347; Kashima, *Buddhism in America,* p. 20; and Mitsuru Shinpo, *Kanada imin haisekishi: Nihon no gyogyō imin* (Tokyo: Miraisha, 1996), p. 180.

91 Kōsei Ogura, "A Sociological Study of Buddhism in North America with a Case Study of Gardena, California Congregation," Master's thesis (University of Southern California, 1932), pp. 85–86. A similar view is also shared by Rust ("The Shin Sect of Buddhism in America," p. 162).

92 Ogura, "A Sociological Study of Buddhism in North America," p. 32.

93 Ogura, "A Sociological Study of Buddhism in North America," p. 32.

94 It is unclear whether or not earlier Shin ministers in North America received the same degree of harassment that Imamura and other ministers in Hawaii encountered. No descriptions of such incidents are found in Sonoda's "Beikoku kaikyō nisshi" ("Diary in the Propagation of North America"; see Notes to Introduction, n. 1) or in Izumida's "Zaibei gojūnen no kaiko" ("Memoirs of Fifty Years in the United States").

95 Letter dated February 12 (BCA Archives, Correspondence Files, Box No. 1.02.08, Folder 1934). Kitarō Hayashi, in "Po shi bussei no bunri ni tsuite,"

compares the personalities of the two priests (BCA Archives, Correspondence Files, Box No. 1.02.08, Folder 1934).

96   Letter from board president Denjirō Kawamura to Kazuo Sasaki, BMNA executive secretary, dated July 11, 1929. The dispute at the church was fueled by the involvement of two Japanese language schools located in Holtville and Calexico (BCA Archives, Correspondence Files, Box No. 1.02.04, Folder 1929). Also, "Sawada kaikyōshi no jinin no shinsō" was serialized in the *Rafu Shinpō* on July 4, July 6, July 7, and July 10 in 1929. According to Tsuneharu Sugimoto's letter addressed to Masuyama on April 1 (year unknown), Sawada, after his resignation in 1929, continued to disturb the church by visiting those who had supported him (BCA Archives, Correspondence Files, Box No. 1.02.06, Folder 1931 A-J).

97   Masuyama's correspondence to the Kyoto headquarters dated January 21, 1931 (BCA Archives, Correspondence Files, Box No. 1.02.06, Folder 1931), and Kyōgoku's letter to the BMNA office dated March 26, 1930 (BCA Archives, Subject Files, Box No. 1.03.09, Folder 1923–1931).

98   Tsunemitsu, *Hokubei bukkyō shiwa,* pp. 175–80; Watada, *Bukkyo Tozen,* pp. 54–57; and Terakawa, *Hokubei kaikyō enkakushi,* pp. 425–27.

99   Tsunemitsu, *Hokubei bukkyō shiwa,* pp. 180–82.

100 Watada, *Bukkyo Tozen,* p. 64.

101 Taga's letter to the BMNA office dated June 10, 1929 (BCA Archives, Correspondence Files, Box No. 1.02.04). Also Izumida's progress in Vancouver is reported in "Izumida junjō-shi no Vancouver iri," *Chūgai Nippō,* September 19, 1925.

102 Shinjō Ikuta, *Kanada bukkyōkai enkakushi* (Toronto: Buddhist Churches of Canada, 1981), p. 58.

103 Yutaka Yasunaka's letter to the BMNA office (BCA Archives, Chronological Files, Box No. 1.01.02, Folder 1926–1931).

104 The first letter was issued by Eikichi Kagetsu and others (BCA Archives, Chronological Files, Box No. 1.01.02), while the second was by Kagetsu himself (BCA Archives, Correspondence Files, Box No. 1.02.04). Kagetsu, a native of Wakayama prefecture, was a successful entrepreneur who founded the Deep Bay Logging Company in 1923 and also served as president of the Canadian Japanese Association (Toyo Takata, *Nikkei Legacy: The Story of Japanese Canadians from Settlement to Today* [Toronto: NC Press, 1983], pp. 84–85).

105 BCA Archives, Correspondence Files, Box No. 1.02.04, Folder 1929.

106 Watada, *Bukkyo Tozen,* pp. 55, 58, 65; Ikuta, *Kanada bukkyōkai enkakushi,* p. 38; and Sasaki and Gonnami, eds., *Kanada iminshi shiryō,* vol. 8, p. 1320.

107 BCA Archives, Correspondence Files, Box No. 1.02.05, Folder Communication 1930 from District Temples K-S.

108 Terakawa, *Hokubei kaikyō enkakushi,* p. 481.

109 The agreement was exchanged between Kannosuke (or Hironosuke) Uenishi and Shintarō Toda, the board presidents of the Honpa Canada Bukkyōkai and the New Westminster Bukkyōkai respectively (BCA Archives, Correspondence Files, Box No. 1.02.06, Folder 1931 Communications from Districts T-Z).

110 The letter was signed and sent by Uenishi (BCA Archives, Correspondence Files, Box No. 1.02.07, Folder 1932).

111 The pact was exchanged between Uenishi and Yosaku Yamashita (BCA Archives, Correspondence Files, Box No. 1.02.07, Folder 1932). It is unclear whether or not territorial disputes were unique to the Buddhist churches in the Vancouver area. At least one record shows that the laity of the Berkeley Buddhist Church, concerned about defining the propagation zone (*fukyō kuiki*), requested at the BMNA Ministers' Meeting in 1926 that this matter be taken up. According to a proposal submitted by the Berkeley Bukkyōkai on January 10, 1926, it defined its propagation zone from the city of Berkeley to Contra Costa County (BCA Archives, Correspondence Files, Box No. 1.02.05, Folder 1926 2B).

112 Uenishi sent a petition (*shinseisho*) to Masuyama on January 25, 1932 (BCA Archives, Correspondence Files, Box No. 1.02.07, Folder 1932).

113 Terakawa, *Hokubei kaikyō enkakushi*, pp. 421–22.

114 Masuyama's correspondence to Eikichi Kagetsu dated July 30, 1933 (BCA Archives, Correspondence Files, Box No. 1.02.07, Folder 1932–1933). There might have been other causes that triggered the inauguration of an independent administrative office in Canada, such as the Canadian government's stricter enforcement of immigration law on Buddhist clergy. For instance, in his correspondence to the Kyoto headquarters on October 17, 1933, Masuyama reported that nonimmigrants in Canada could stay only one year, with a maximum renewal of three years, thus making it inconvenient for ministers to propagate unless they decided to settle permanently. He asked the headquarters to contact the Ministry of Foreign Affairs in Japan and amend the conditions of ministers' visas in Canada (BCA Archives, Correspondence Files, Box No. 1.02.07, Folder 1933–1934).

115 Tsunemitsu, *Hokubei bukkyō shiwa*, p. 183. However, Aoki resigned in June 1941 after which Bishop Matsukage of the BMNA served concurrently as bishop of Canada (Kawamura, *Kanada bukkyō shi*, pp. 21–22).

116 *Buddhist Churches of America: A Legacy of the First 100 Years*, p. 239; and "Honpa saisho no hokubei betsuin ga dekiru," *Chūgai Nippō*, October 9, 1931.

117 "Suggestions to Propagation in North America" (*Hokubei gasshūkoku kaikyō ni kansuru ikensho*), sent to the Kyoto headquarters from BMNA officials on May 4, 1928. The name of the author of this document is not recorded (BCA Archives, Correspondence Files, Box No. 1.02.04, Folder 1928).

118 Immense debts brought about by the Honganji Buddhist Church of Los Angeles were a serious problem to the entire operation of the BMNA.

Eventually Kyoto headquarters gave half toward an unpaid bill of $20,000. To solve this problem, former bishop Hōshō Sasaki, who had returned to Japan in 1928, was reassigned to Los Angeles in 1933 ("Honpa rafu betsuin no fusai mondai kaiketsu," *Bunka Jihō,* July 27, 1935; and "Rafu mondai mo junchō ni susumu: Sasaki rinban kinin," *Bunka Jihō,* August 17, 1935).

119 BCA Archives, Correspondence Files, Box No. 1.02.06, Folder 1931. Also for the dispute between the Gardena and Los Angeles churches, see Ratanamani, "History of Shin Buddhism in the United States," pp. 23–24.

120 Letter dated November 5, 1931 (BCA Archives, Correspondence Files, Box No. 1.02.06, Folder 1931 T–Z).

121 Petition for *betsuin* status by the Fresno Buddhist Church (BCA Archives, Correspondence Files, Box No. 1.02.09, Folder 1935–1936; and Correspondence Files, Box No. 1.02.08, Folder 1933–1935).

122 Terakawa, *Hokubei kaikyō enkakushi,* pp. 102–103.

123 *Beikoku bukkyō* 10, no. 4 (April 1909): pp. 15, 34.

124 *Beikoku bukkyō* 18, no. 10 (October 1909): p. 18.

125 For instance, there was the oath signed by Kizu Kakujō on July 10, 1932 (BCA Archives, Chronological Files, Box No. 1.01.01, Folder 1917–1919/1922–1924). No such oath was found during previous bishops' tenures.

126 *Buddhist Churches of America: A Legacy of the First 100 Years,* pp. vi, 306. *Time* magazine covered the event in which Masuyama received the relics of the Buddha in Siam. See "Bones of Buddha," *Time* (September 1935): p. 53.

127 Through the unification of the two organizations, the BMNA office tried to invoke a sense of commitment among its members and elevate the status of the Buddhist Church of San Francisco (Sōkō bukkyōkai shōkaku hokubei honganji gōdō riyūsho, BCA Archives, Chronological Files, Box No. 1.01.06, Folder 1941, 1942). Several priests also submitted tentative plans for unification (BCA Archives, Choronological Files, Box No.1.01.05, Folder 1940–1942).

128 Response by a special meeting of the Buddhist Church of San Francisco (San Francisco bukkyōkai rinji sōkai no iken, BCA Archives, Chronological Files, Box No. 1.01.06, Folder 1941, 1942). After a series of discussions between the two parties, a final decision was made: 1) the BMNA and the Buddhist Church of San Francisco would construct the building as a joint venture; 2) the Buddhist Church of San Francisco would donate its property (valued at $5,000) to the project; 3) the committee would purchase the vacant lot on the corner of Octavia and Pine streets; 4) the building of the Buddhist Church of San Francisco would be demolished and a new one built on the two lots; and 5) construction would cost $78,000 with the donated land valued at $5,000 (*Buddhist Churches of America 75-year History,* vol. 1, p. 57).

129 Watada, *Bukkyo Tozen,* p. 65.

130 Ichirō Hori, *Nihon shūkyō no shakaiteki yakuwari* (Tokyo: Miraisha, 1962), pp. 129, 154–55.

131 Kodama, *Kinsei shinshū to chiiki shakai,* pp. 78–79.

132 For instance, the proposal for rebuilding the facility of the Stockton Buddhist Church testifies to the combination of Shin Buddhist practice and ancestor worship: "real happiness is gained by having *shinjin.* Those who have *shinjin* are happy, even though poor" (Su shi bukkyōkai honkai kaidō saikon shushisho, 1–2). It further states, "[O]nce the Buddhist shrine is set up and our ancestor's souls are enshrined here, the foreign land turns into our fondly-remembered land (homeland)" (Su shi bukkyōkai honkai kaidō saikon shushisho, p. 8). This proposal is kept at the BCA Archives, Subject Files, Box No. 1.03.09, File 1923–1931. Even in places like Steveston, where immigrants did not come from Shin Buddhist strongholds, religious practices included ancestral worship and Shin practice. From Mio-mura in Wakayama prefecture, the village locally known as "Amerika-mura," about half the residents immigrated to Canada, and most settled in Steveston. According to a survey conducted in this village in 1951, the majority of its residents appeared to ignore denominational differences such as Jōdoshū, Jōdo Shinshū, Shingonshū, Tenrikyō, Konkonkyō, etc. This survey, which included interviews from those who had once lived in Steveston but had returned to Mio-mura, summarizes the religious climate of Steveston as follows:

> The religious environment between Mio-mura and Steveston is almost the same, since there is a tendency to fulfill all kinds of religious needs in both places; There is no Shintō shrine, which locally connects (*jien kankei*) the immigrants [to Mio-mura], but a Buddhist temple, which signifies one's family affiliation (*ketsuen kankei*), and the immigrants maintain rituals related to Buddhism in their daily lives, including ancestor worship; and the immigrants do not accept Christianity.

"Kaigai imin ga boson ni oyoboshita eikyō: Wakayama-ken hitaka-gun mio-mura jittai chōsa," in Sasaki and Gonnami, eds., *Kanada iminshi shiryō,* vol. 10, p. 309. The Steveston Buddhist Church promoted Buddhism as a family religion, but there were groups of devout Shin Buddhists there and others who affiliated with the Nishi Honganji after moving to Steveston. According to an interview with a local Shin priest in Mio-mura, which was included in the same survey, those who had immigrated to Steveston and returned to the village were more informed of the Shin Buddhist doctrine than villagers who had never traveled abroad (*Kanada iminshi shiryō,* vol. 10, p. 306).

133 Sasaki and Gonnami, eds., *Kanada iminshi shiryō,* vol. 10, p. 232.

134 "Kotō imin mura no kenkyū," *Ritsumeikan daigaku jinbun kagaku kenkyū kiyō* 14 (1964), which is included in Sasaki and Gonnami, eds., *Kanada iminshi shiryō,* vol. 11, p. 162. According to Sasaki, the Shiga prefectural association in Vancouver was also divided into two groups in the late 1900s (Sasaki, *Nihonjin kanada iminshi,* p. 208).

135 Adachi states in *The Enemy That Never Was* (p. 122):

> In the matter of a few decades, then, the Japanese built up a vast complex of associations and clubs, involving at least 230 units of secular and religious associations in British Columbia, of which 84 functioned in the Vancouver colony which contained, by the 1930s, nearly one-third of the province's Japanese population.

136 David K. Yoo, *Growing Up Nisei: Race, Generation, and Culture among Japanese Americans of California, 1924-1949* (Urbana, IL: University of Illinois Press, 2000), p. 5. Yoo cites "The Nisei Population in California, 1900–1940," a source from Dorothy Swaine Thomas, Charles Kikuchi, and James Sakoda, *Japanese American Evacuation and Resettlement: The Salvage* (Berkeley: University of California Press, 1952), pp. 575–79.

137 Kashima, *Buddhism in America*, p. 39.

138 Tamura, *Americanization, Acculturation, and Ethnic Identity*, p. 146; and Hunter, *Buddhism in Hawaii*, p. 129.

139 According to previous studies, there were relatively few Japanese language schools affiliated with Buddhist churches on the mainland. For instance, during the 1920s, sixty-one Japanese language schools were established in Northern California and sixty in Southern California, but the number of schools affiliated with *bukkyōkai* was six and nine respectively. In the 1930s, the total number rose to one hundred and fourteen and eighty-two in those respective areas, with the establishment of Buddhist ones only two and five respectively (Tomoe Moriya, "California shū ni okeru bukkyōkai fuzoku nihongo gakkō no seikaku," in *A History of Transnational Education [Ekkyō Kyōiku] of the Japanese Immigrants in the U.S., 1877-1945*, ed. Ryō Yoshida [Tokyo: Nihon tosho center, 2005], p. 117). Information drawn from Ken Ishikawa, *Beikoku kashū nihongo gakuen ni kansuru kenkyū* (Privately printed, 1923); Toyotomi Morimoto, *Japanese Americans and Cultural Continuity: Maintaining Language and Heritage* (New York: Garland Publishing, 1997); and *Buddhist Churches of America: A Legacy of the First 100 Years.* However, it is possible that these data are incorrect. According to the *Hokubei kaikyō enkakushi,* published in 1936, almost every Buddhist church in California had a Japanese language school. Also, in Central California, the Fresno Buddhist Church was affiliated with more than thirty such schools (*Fresno Betsuin Buddhist Temple Centennial 1901–2001*, p. 17).

140 Moriya, "California shū ni okeru bukkyōkai," p. 117; and Frank Miyamoto, *Social Solidarity Among the Japanese in Seattle* (1939) (Seattle: University of Washington Press, 1981, reprint), p. 47.

141 Tamura, *Americanization, Acculturation, and Ethnic Identity*, p. 155.

142 Moriya, "California shū ni okeru bukkyōkai," p. 124; and Okihiro, *Cane Fires,* pp. 151–55.

143 Morioka, *Shinshū kyōdan to ie seido*, p. 633; and Utsuki, *The Shin Sect*, p. 40.

144 Tsunemitsu, *Nihon bukkyō tobeishi,* p. 346.

145 *Tōko: Takeshima Hōsui-shi gofusai keigyō tsuitōshi,* pp. 387–88.

146 On January 31, 1928, in the presence of several witnesses, the two parties agreed that the church would no longer be held responsible for the management of the Japanese language school (oath between the Oakland Bukkyōkai and the Wantō Gakuen, BCA Archives, Correspondence Files, Box No. 1.02.03, Folder 1927–1928).

147 BCA Archives, Correspondence Files, Box No. 1.02.08, Folder 1934.

148 BCA Archives, Correspondence Files, Box No. 1.02.09, Folder 1922–1936.

149 BCA Archives, Subject Files, Box No. 1.03.08, Folder 1936-1937.

150 Yukuji Okita, *Hawai nikkei imin no kyōikushi: Nichibei bunka sono deai to sōkoku* (Kyoto: Minerva shobō, 1997), pp. 121–25. Okita discusses the management of the Papaikou Japanese elementary school as a case in point, pp. 125–33.

151 Hunter, *Buddhism in Hawaii,* p. 99; and *Chōshōin ibunshū,* pp. 139–40.

152 Moriya, "California shū ni okeru bukkyōkai," pp. 122, 134.

153 Moriya, "California shū ni okeru bukkyōkai," pp. 128–29.

154 Report on the resolution of the Ministers' Meeting, held between February 25 and 27, 1936 (BCA Archives, Subject Files, Box No. 1.03.03, Folder 1940).

Chapter Three: The Development of Shin Buddhist Ministries

1 "Watashi no hakujin kyōka no hōshin," *Bunka Jihō,* April 9, 1935.

2 An Issei minister was simply defined as a priest from Japan; however, there were several cases in California where a small number of Issei who had immigrated to the United States entered the priesthood. Ministers such as Inshu Yonemura and Taiken Masunaga were ordained when Son'yū Ōtani visited the United States in fall 1925 (Records of the request for ordination, BCA Archives, Chronological Files, Box No. 1.01.01, Folder 1925–1926).

3 Imamura, *Hompa hongwanji hawai kaikyōshi,* p. 553.

4 Morioka, *Shinshū kyōdan to ie seido,* pp. 632–33.

5 Tsunemitsu, *Hokubei bukkyō shiwa,* p. 116.

6 Possibly in Canadian dollars, but this is uncertain.

7 Correspondence from the acting bishop, Ryūsei Kusuhara, to the board president of the Honpa Canada Buddhist Mission, dated March 3, 1926 (BCA Archives, Correspondence Files, Box No. 1.02.01, Folder 1926 1B).

8 BCA Archives, Correspondence Files, Box No. 1.02.02. In the prewar period, the yen/dollar exchange rate was approximately ¥100 to $49–$50, based on the gold standard. Even when the ban on gold was removed, the same rate was maintained in 1930 (Momose Takashi, *Jiten: Shōwa senzenki no nihon*

[Tokyo: Yoshikawa kōbunkan, 1990], p. 206). Therefore, the bishop received approximately $2,500 annually and his secretary received $1,200.

9   Ogura, "A Sociological Study of Buddhism in North America," p. 35.

10   Record of the HHMH Ministers' Meeting, p. 145.

11   *Buddhist Churches of America 75-year History,* vol. 1, p. 55.

> In a period like this, the biggest headache was the early disposition of the Los Angeles Betsuin mortgage and the financial controversy of the Fresno Buddhist Church. These problems seemed to have affected the entire Buddhist Mission of North America and even the Honzan officials were quite concerned. This seemed to have influenced their selection of the Bishop, as the appointment was made with the hope that the Bishop can arrive at an early solution to these problems.

> Cited from the *Wheel of Dharma* (February 23, 1973).

12   Interview with Marii Hasegawa April 3, 2004; and *Buddhist Churches of America: A Legacy of the First 100 Years,* p. 71.

13   Correspondence from Bishop Hōshō Sasaki to the Kyoto headquarters dated January 20, 1927 (BCA Archives, Chronological Files, Box No. 1.01.02, Folder 1926–1931; and Chronological Files, Box No. 1.01.02, Folder 1926–1931).

14   Terakawa, *Hokubei kaikyō enkakushi,* p. 251.

15   Correspondence from Kakujō Kizu to Bishop Masuyama dated September 15, 1932 (BCA Archives, Correspondence Files, Box No. 1.02.06, Folder 1932 Communications from Districts A–G).

16   Yūtetsu Kawamura, *Kanada alberta shū cowboy song no sato* (Kyoto: Dōbōsha, pp. 2–8.

17   Imamura, *Hompa hongwanji hawai kaikyōshi,* pp. 559–61.

18   Watada, *Bukkyo Tozen,* p. 41.

19   *A Grateful Past, A Promising Future,* p. 21; and *Dōbō* 4, no. 10 (October 1903): p. 4. In Honolulu, as of 1902, eighty Japanese immigrants were attending English school every night; the classes were divided into four and taught by six teachers. *Dōbō* 3, no. 7 (July 1902): p. 31.

20   Rust, "The Shin Sect of Buddhism in America," p. 145; *Beikoku bukkyō* 3, no. 7 (July 1902): p. 25; *Beikoku bukkyō* 4, no. 5 (May 1903): p. 27; *Beikoku bukkyō* 12, no. 2 (February 1911): p. 17; and *Beikoku bukkyō* 13, no. 6 (June 1912): p. 40.

21   Emyō Imamura, *Hawai kaikyō shiyō* (Honolulu: Hompa Hongwanji Mission, 1918), pp. 25–28.

22   The Petition for Resident Minister signed by Yosaku Yamashita and five counselors of the *bukkyōkai* (BCA Archives, Correspondence Files, Box No. 1.02.07, Folder 1932 Communications from District Temples T–Z).

23   According to the prospectus of the *bukkyōkai* attached to this petition, the total number of laity was three hundred and twenty-four; the annual budget

was approximately $1,000; annual religious events included the *Hōonkō* (commemoration of Shinran's passing), the *Ohigan* or *Higan-e* (two services held during the weeks of the spring and fall equinoxes), the *Eitaikyō* (celebrating the temple's perpetual existence), and celebrations of Śākyamuni Buddha's and Shinran's birthdays, in addition to regular Sunday services; the number of annual wedding services were three or four and that of funerals eight or nine; and the number of annual memorial services were one hundred and twenty to one hundred and thirty, from which donations received by the minister were written into the church's accounts.

24 Shinpo, *Kanada imin haisekishi*, p. 180.

25 Shinpo, *Kanada imin haisekishi*, pp. 179–82.

26 Correspondence from Yoichi Hironaka to Bishop Masuyama (BCA Archives, Correspondence Files, Box No. 1.02.07, Folder 1933 Communications from Districts L–R). For the activities of Hironaka, who contributed tremendously to the Raymond Buddhist Mission, see Kawamura, *Kanada alberta shū cowboy song no sato*, pp. 20-25, 156–61.

27 Kawamura, *Kanada alberta shū cowboy song no sato*, pp. 20-25, 156–61.

28 Correspondence of Sasaki's report to the Kyoto headquarters dated June 20, 1927 (BCA Archives, Correspondence Files, Box No. 1.02.02, Folder 1926–1927 2A).

29 Tamura, *Americanization, Acculturation, and Ethnic Identity*, p. 203; and Okihiro, *Cane Fires*, p. 67.

30 Tamura, *Americanization, Acculturation, and Ethnic Identity*, p. 205.

31 Rust, "The Shin Sect of Buddhism in America," p. 160; Tsunemitsu, *Nihon bukkyō tobeishi*, p. 310; and "Tenth Anniversary Conference of the North American Federation of the YWBA Leagues, July 21–25, 1936," *The New Canadians*, May 27, 1939.

32 The formation of the YWBA was triggered by Son'yū Ōtani's visit to the United States in 1925, when he made a donation of $50 to its foundation. But there had been a grassroots movement to form such a group before his visit (Yoo, *Growing Up Nisei*, p. 46; and Moriya, "California shū ni okeru bukkyōkai," p. 129).

33 "Canada Young Buddhist League," *The New Canadians*, May 27, 1939; "Bussei, Carry on! National Meet Impresses Localites," *The New Canadians*, May 2, 1941; and Tsunemitsu, *Nihon bukkyō tobeishi*, pp. 109–111. David Yoo has studied the ideas of the Nisei Buddhist laity in the United States who assumed leadership at YBA meetings. For instance, Masao Kubose, who was later ordained at the Higashi Honganji and founded the Buddhist Temple of Chicago in 1944, strongly believed that the Nisei were capable of bridging the gap between Japan and the United States in the coming Pacific era. Manabu Fukuda stated that the Land of Buddha would serve as an alternative for those who could not be recognized in either Japan or the United States (Yoo, *Growing Up Nisei*, pp. 49–50).

34 Imamura, *Hompa hongwanji hawai kaikyō sanjūgonen kiyō*, p. 14; Hunter, *Buddhism in Hawaii*, p. 163; and "Hawai no ryūgakusei," *Chūgai Nippō*, April 9, 1927.

35 "Hawai ryūgakusei no tokudo," *Chūgai Nippō*, October 8, 1931; and *A Grateful Past, A Promising Future*, p. 62.

36 "Nikkei beijin ya minkokujin ga honpa sōryo ni naru benpō no naiki ga dekiru," *Chūgai Nippō*, October 10, 1931.

37 *Buddhist Churches of America: A Legacy of the First 100 Years*, p. 120.

38 Masatsugu, "Reorienting the Pure Land," pp. 165–67, 174–80; and Fields, *How the Swans Came to the Lake*, pp. 214–215.

39 *Buddhist Churches of America 75-year History*, vol. 1, p. 53.

40 Letter of recommendation written by Tairyō Sawada dated May 21, 1931 (BCA Archives, Correspondence Files, Box No. 1.02.05, Folder 1928 K–S).

41 Correspondence from Bishop Masuyama to the Kyoto headquarters dated May 14, 1931 (BCA Archives, Correspondence Files, Box No. 1.02.06, Folder 1931).

42 *Buddhist Churches of America: A Legacy of the First 100 Years*, p. 117.

43 Terakawa, *Hokubei kaikyō enkakushi*, pp. 519–20.

44 *Buddhist Churches of America: A Legacy of the First 100 Years*, p. vi.

45 *Buddhist Churches of America: A Legacy of the First 100 Years*, pp. 118–21. The BMNA also sent Yoshihiko Fujimoto and Akio Ōshima in fall 1941. Fujimoto returned to the United States after the war as a minister; there is no information available on Ōshima (BCA Archives, Correspondence Files Box No. 1.02.12, Folder 1940 Communication from Headquarters).

46 Watada, *Bukkyo Tozen*, pp. 83, 100–103; Ikuta, *Kanada bukkyōkai enkakushi*, p. 83; Kawamura, *Kanada alberta shū cowboy song no sato*, pp. 13, 18, 22; "Nisei Priest is Welcomed at Banquet," *The New Canadians*, November 7, 1941; and "Nisei Priest at Hompa Service," *The New Canadians*, November 21, 1941.

47 *Buddhist Churches of America: A Legacy of the First 100 Years*, p. 1.

48 Noboru Tsunoda, "The Reason Why I Wish to Study Buddhism as My Life Work," a clipping from an unidentified newspaper (BCA Archives, Correspondence Files, Box No. 1.02.06, Folder 1931); and Rust, "The Shin Sect of Buddhism in America," pp. 165–66.

49 *Bussei* (Seattle: Seattle Betsuin, 1941), p. 1. Tsunoda and Tsuji later explore Shinran's teaching; for instance, see Shōdō Tsunoda, "Freedom of Choice," *Tri-Ratna* 7, no. 2 (March/April 1953): pp. 3–7; and Takashi Tsuji, "Freedom," *Tri-Ratna* 6, no. 4 (July/August 1952): pp. 5–7.

50 The commitment of the Nisei laity to Shin Buddhism was much more vague. Hunter observes a Nisei Buddhist, Katsumi C. Yamasaki, who critiqued the ways in which ministers had taught Buddhism in Hawaii. Yamasaki complained that not all fairy tales were necessarily tied to Buddhist moral teachings; the

clergy needed to demonstrate the real relevance of Buddhism and its applications to the Nisei; an English-speaking Buddhist, not necessarily a minister, should teach Buddhism; and all sectarian barriers were useless (*Buddhism in Hawaii*, pp. 162–63; Hunter cites Yamasaki's "Thoughts of a Hawaiian-born Buddhist"). Further, one YBMA leader on the mainland explicitly stated: "It is true that there are more than 2,000 second[-]generation members who call themselves Buddhists, but how many of them are true Buddhists who have unfaltering faith in Amida?" (Rust, "The Shin Sect of *Buddhism in America*," p. 171. Rust cites Y. H. Secon, "A Study of the Religious Organizations in Japanese Communities in America," unpublished report presented to the University of Southern California, 1945, pp. 199–200). In Canada, the YBA held annual oratorical contests from the mid-1920s. The majority of representatives, whose speeches were transcribed in *Otakebi* (published by the Fairview YBA as a special edition in 1930 to celebrate its ten-year anniversary) and *Butsuda* (published by the Kitsilano YBA in 1935 for the same occasion) were concerned with preserving the Nisei's ethnic identity, including *yamato damashii* as a cultural ethos inherited from Japan. In other words, they hardly discussed their understanding of Shinran or Śākyamuni's teachings, except for Hatsue Nishisaki's expression of joy of having faith in Shin Buddhism (*Butsuda*, p. 35) and Sutekichi Nishikawa's explanation of self-introspection (*Otakebi*, pp. 93–99).

51 Kirby was ordained on April 3, 1920, as Sogaku (or Sōgaku). Robert S. Clarke and Alice J. Clarke were ordained on September 21, 1920, with the Dharma names of Kokyo (or Kōkyō) and Myoyu (or Myōyū), respectively (*Buddhist Churches of America: A Legacy of the First 100 Years*, pp. 171, 174, 304). The certificates for the Clarkes are found in the BCA Archives, Chronological Files, Box No. 1.01.01, Folder 1920.

52 Sasaki and Gonnami, eds. *Kanada iminshi shiryō*, vol. 8, pp. 1287, 1305–1306, 1318–19.

53 As a resident staff member of the BMNA, Kirby used to lecture in Fresno on the first Sunday of each month, San Francisco on the second Sunday, and Sacramento on the fourth Sunday. On the third and fifth (if any) Sundays, he would visit other Buddhist churches upon request (Resolution 3 in the Minutes of the 1920 Ministers' Meeting. BCA Archives, Subject Files, Box No. 1.03.01, Folder 1914–1925). Svami Mazzininanda, a doctoral scholar from India, often assisted in the English services at Watsonville, Sacramento, San Francisco, and Fresno in the 1900s (*Beikoku bukkyō* 9, no. 5 [May 1908]: pp. 34–35; *Beikoku bukkyō* 10, no. 5 [May 1909]: p. 13; *Beikoku bukkyō* 11, no. 4 [April 1910]: p. 22; and *Beikoku bukkyō* 12, no. 3 [March 1911]: p. 34). Mazzininanda was abbot of the Udana Karana Order of the Jain Sect, located in Los Angeles (*The Light of Dharma* 6, no. 3 [December 1907]: pp. 31, 33–34).

54 The English section of the Buddhist Church of San Francisco might have been

called the American Buddhist Organizations, as the letter of appointment dated June 1, 1922, states:

> This is to certify that we have appointed the Rev. Dr. Robert Clarke (Kokyo Shaku) and Rev. Dr. Alice Clarke (Myoyu Shaku) to the full and entire charge of the American Buddhist Organizations that is now or may be brought into form, in San Francisco, Oakland, and all the towns and cities known as the Bay Cities.

BCA Archives, Chronological Files, Box No. 1.01.01, Folder 1920.

55 J. M. Hayes was ordained on March 10, 1922, and Dr. A. Brodbeck on June 1, 1922, with the Dharma name of Kakudo (or Kakudō) (BCA Archives, Chronological Files, Box No. 1.01.01, Folder 1920).

56 Hunter, *Buddhism in Hawaii*, pp. 132–34. Cited by Moriya, *Amerika bukkyō no tanjō*, pp. 124–25; and Pierce, "Constructing American Buddhisms," pp. 201–202.

57 Hunter, *Buddhism in Hawaii*, pp. 152–53; and *Hawai honpa hongwanji kyōdan enkakushi*, ed. Hawai honpa hongwanji kyōdan (Honolulu: Hompa Hongwanji, 1954), p. 30. Before officiating at the ordination of Hunt and his wife, Imamura asked Bishop Uchida of the BMNA for the English-language procedure, since Uchida had already done it on the mainland. Imamura was aware that Kirby had created a short program, starting with the Three Refuges, followed by a Confession, Invocation, Burning of Incense, and a Second Invocation. (BCA Archive, Correspondence, Box No. 1.02.01, Folder 1912–1922.) This demonstrates that the ritual format for Caucasian ordinations was first created by the BMNA. Since Imamura did not carry out any other similar ordination after Hunt and his wife, the HHMH lost a chance to develop its own program. At one point, BMNA ministers tried to work with the HHMH to propagate in English, but the collaboration did not expand during the prewar period (Resolution 7 in the Minutes of the 1920 Ministers' Meeting. BCA Archives, Subject Files, Box No. 1.03.01, Folder 1914–1925).

58 In Hawaii, the activities of Ernest Hunt were prominent, but there were precursors who had sought Buddhism before him. Lillian Shrewsbury Mesick and Barber, who taught English to Issei immigrants at the HHMH, had expressed their Buddhist faith as early as 1901. Especially Barber, who was a member of the Theosophical Society, appeared to have understood part of Shinran's teaching. She considered him somewhat similar to Martin Luther of the Reformation, because Shinran had made complex Buddhist philosophies available to the laity. Unfortunately, Barber died on August 15, 1903, in San Francisco, after leaving Honolulu for medical treatment. See Lillian Shrewsbury Mesick, "Koto wa shōmei ni ari," *Dōbō* 1, no. 13 (September 1901): pp. 5–9; and Barber, "Hijiri, Shinran," *Dōbō* 1, no. 10 (June 1901): pp. 13–15. These articles were based on their speeches and translated into Japanese—the former on the occasion of the first anniversary of the YBA in Hawaii and the latter at the time of commemorating Shinran's 729th birthday. For the death of Barber, see *Dōbō* 4, no. 10. (October 1903): pp. 6–7.

59   Imamura, *Hompa hongwanji hawai kaikyō sanjūgonen kiyō*, pp. 14–15; Pierce, "Constructing American Buddhisms," pp. 1–2; *A Grateful Past, A Promising Future*, p. 63; and Hunter, *Buddhism in Hawaii*, p. 154.

60   Hunter, *Buddhism in Hawaii*, p. 163.

61   Imamura, *Hompa hongwanji hawai kaikyō sanjūgonen kiyō*, p. 17.

62   Imamura, *Hompa hongwanji hawai kaikyō sanjūgonen kiyō*, p. 16; Moriya, *Amerika bukkyō no tanjō*, pp. 125–27; Pierce, "Constructing American Buddhisms," pp. 174–76; and Hunter, *Buddhism in Hawaii*, p. 164. In the case of the Issei ministers, Takahiko Matsuda was the first to initiate a prison program in Honolulu in 1935 ("Honpa hawai kyōdan de keimu kyōkai jigyō," *Bunka Jihō*, December 17, 1935).

63   Imamura, *Hompa hongwanji hawai kaikyō sanjūgonen kiyō*, pp. 17–18.

64   Imamura, *Hompa hongwanji hawai kaikyō sanjūgonen kiyō*, p. 17.

65   Tanabe, "Grafting Identity," p. 90. The relationship between cosmopolitan Buddhism in Hawaii and united Buddhism in Japan needs further research. The Meiji Buddhist clergy created the notion of *tsū bukkyō* in order to demonstrate the commonalities of the sectarian teachings of Mahayana Buddhism. It also constructed a modern Japanese Buddhist history and promoted so-called Eastern Buddhism to the West. It is unknown whether or not Imamura incorporated these aspects of a united Buddhism into his order.

66   Moriya, *Amerika bukkyō no tanjō*, p. 123.

67   "Hawai nishihonganji kyōdan Imamura sochō no ato," *Chūgai Nippō*, January 22, 1933.

68   Amstutz, *Interpreting Amida*, p. 81; and Hunter, *Buddhism in Hawaii*, p. 171.

69   Interview with Bishop Yosemori, January 30, 2007.

70   *A Grateful Past, A Promising Future*, pp. 73–74.

71   *A Grateful Past, A Promising Future*, p. 72; and Moriya, *Amerika bukkyō no tanjō*, p. 219.

72   Tsunemitsu, *Hokubei bukkyō shiwa*, p. 12.

73   *Buddhist Churches of America: A Legacy of the First 100 Years*, pp. 171, 172, 177. Francis G. Geske and Richard K. Prosser were initiated on February 12, 1933, with the Dharma names of Jikai and Chisen, respectively. Robert S. Clifton was initiated on October 19 as Rigen.

74   Correspondence from Masuyama, November 19, 1933 (BCA Archives, Correspondence Files, Box No. 1.02.07, Folder 1933).

75   Correspondence from Masuyama to the Kyoto headquarters dated July 7 and 8, 1934 (BCA Archives, Correspondence Files, Box No. 1.02.08, Folder 1933–1934).

76   BCA Archives, Chronological Files, Box No. 1.01.03, Folder 1934.

77   *Buddhist Churches of America: A Legacy of the First 100 Years*, pp. 119, 149, 178.

78   *Buddhist Churches of America: A Legacy of the First 100 Years*, p. 171.

79 *Buddhist Churches of America: A Legacy of the First 100 Years,* pp. 119, 172, 177.

80 Julius Goldwater received the Dharma name of Jukō (*Buddhist Churches of America: A Legacy of the First 100 Years,* p. 172).

81 BCA Archives, Chronological Files, Box No. 1.01.01, Folder 1920.

82 *Why I Became a Buddhist* (San Francisco: The Kyōdan Times of the BMNA, n.d.), pp. 3–16.

83 Translation by Hirota et al., *CWS,* vol. 1, p. 289.

84 "Buddhists Ordain American S. A. Goldwaite [*sic*] Enters Priesthood Here," *Los Angeles Times,* June 18, 1934, Part II, p. 5.

85 "Conversion Work of Yakima Man," *The Yakima Daily Republic,* May 2, 1936.

86 For instance, "Buddhist Service," *Los Angeles Times,* March 24, 1935; "Buddhist Service," *Los Angeles Times,* September 30, 1934; and "Beijin tachi ga otera e sankei," *Kashū Mainichi Shinbun,* February 16, 1935.

87 The source of this information comes from an unidentified newspaper. The article, entitled "American Priest Holds Classes," was clipped and pasted onto a thick piece of paper without identification of the source. It reads:

> Rev. Julius A. Goldwater of the Nishi Hongwanji Betsuin is planning to leave for the Orient for the deeper and further study of Buddhism. But before his departure he wishes to spend the remaining eight or nine weeks in giving a simple exposition of St. Shinran's teaching the Jyodo [*sic*] Shin Shu Sect, from the Tannisho.

Los Angeles Honpa Honganji Buddhist Temple Archives, Folder Goldwater.

88 *Time* magazine ran a feature article on Pratt, "Teiun" (Pratt's Dharma name), in May 1936. See also "To Be First Buddhist Priestess," *The Tacoma Times,* April 22, 1936.

89 Sunya N. Pratt, "The Faith Aspect in Buddhism (Repress Doubting until Results Show Themselves)," *Bussei* (Seattle: Seattle Betsuin, 1941), p. 47. Pratt briefly discussed the *Kyōgyōshinshō* in "Doctrine, Practice, Faith, Attainment," *Tri-Ratna* 6, no. 2 (March/April 1952): pp. 8–11.

90 For Nakai's propagation activities in Seattle, see Magden, "Buddhism Comes to Seattle," pp. 175–81.

91 BCA Archives, Chronological Files, Box No. 1.01.04, Folder 1938–1939.

92 *Buddhist Churches of America: A Legacy of the First 100 Years,* p. 149.

93 Correspondence from Goldwater to Bishop Matsukage dated July 30, 1939 (BCA Archives, Chronological Files, Box No. 1.01.04, Folder 1938–1939).

94 Correspondence from Pratt to the BMNA English Department dated February 16, 2503 (probably 1938) (BCA Archives, Chronological Files, Box No. 1.01.04, Folder 1938–1939).

95 For instance, two people were admitted in February 2504 (probably 1938) and

another two in May of the same year (BCA Archives, Chronological Files, Box No. 1.01.04, Folder 1938–1939).

96 BCA Archives, Subject Files, Box No. 1.03.09, Folder 1925–1937.

97 The Japanese translation of his petition is found in the BCA Archives, Correspondence Files, Box No. 1.02.08, Folder 1933–1935, though the original document is missing.

98 Terakawa's correspondence to Kumata dated April 6, 1942, and Kumata's correspondence to the FBI on April 13, 1942 (BCA Archives, Chronological Files, Box No. 1.01.06, Folder 1942).

99 *Buddhist Churches of America: A Legacy of the First 100 Years,* p. 171.

100 Correspondence from S. Alex White to Bishop Matsukage dated May 19, 1941 (BCA Archives, Chronological Files, Box No. 1.01.05, Folder 1941).

101 Correspondence from White to Bishop Matsukage dated May 19, 1941.

102 Correspondence from Pratt on May 25, 2505 (probably 1939) (BCA Archives, Chronological Files, Box No. 1.01.04, Folder 1938–1939). However, the article in *The Tacoma Times* has not yet been found.

103 The date of this letter is unknown, but it was placed in Folder 1933–1934 of the BCA Archives, Chronological Files, Box No. 1.01.03.

104 Terakawa, *Hokubei kaikyō enkakushi,* p. 521. It is important to note that a few Euro-American ministers showed their dedication to the BMNA by serving as church caretakers during the internment period. Goldwater took care of the Los Angeles Betsuin, the Gardena Buddhist Church, and the Senshin Buddhist Church, and he visited several relocation and internment camps to assist Japanese internees. Udale held Buddhist services at the Tanforan Assembly Center in California in 1942 and conducted services for non-Japanese at the Buddhist Church of San Francisco between 1942 and 1945. Pratt was permitted by the War Relocation Authority to serve the Buddhists at Camp Harmony (Puyallup, Washington) and teach in the Sunday school until the U.S. government relocated internees again to permanent camps (Kashima, *Buddhism in America,* p. 53; *Buddhist Churches of America: A Legacy of the First 100 Years,* pp. 172, 178; and the Tacoma Buddhist Temple website: www.tacomabt.org). In Hawaii, Hunt played a significant role in reactivating several of the Shin Buddhist missions closed by the military authorities. He directly appealed to the military governor, General Emmons, to grant him permission to restart Buddhist services, assuring him that he would speak only of religious matters. He and his wife were active in the mission on Makiki Street, Honolulu, and the one in Hilo. He also officiated services at Jikōen, a Shin Buddhist temple founded by Okinawans (interview with Rev. H. Hunt by Mrs. Culver, File "Buddhist," Hawaii War Records Depository; and interview with Bishop Yosemori Chikai, January 30, 2007).

105 "An American, Who Studied Buddhism in a Tibetan Lamasery, Priest in S.D. Temple," *The San Diego Sun,* July 5, 1936.

106 Correspondence from Masuyama to the Kyoto headquarters, regarding the proposal for the founding of a *bukkyōkai* in New York, dated December 9, 1935 (BCA Archives, Correspondence Files, Box No. 1.02.09, Folder 1935).

107 Hōzen Seki's record of comforting Japanese immigrants in Mexico dated May 27, 1932 (BCA Archives, Correspondence Files, Box No. 1.02.06, Folder 1932 H–O).

108 For instance, correspondence from the San Francisco branch of Mitsubishi Shōji Kaisha, Ltd., to its New York branch, entitled "Introducing Reverend Hōzen Seki," dated September 14, 1936 (BCA Archives, Correspondence Files, Box No. 1.02.09, Folder 1935); correspondence from the director of the Japanese Business Association in San Francisco to the president of a Japanese newspaper company in New York, September 16, 1936, and "New York bukkyōkai sōritsu kinen, tōbu dendō daihikō" (BCA Archives, Correspondence Files, Box No. 1.02.09, Folder 1935). Also Tsunemitsu, *Hokubei bukkyō shiwa,* p. 125; and "Zaibei bukkyō no nade bussho zōtei," *Rafu Shimpo,* September 12, 1936; "Bonsan to kisha o nose demo hikō," *Rafu Shimpo,* September 17, 1936; "Butsu no jihi o nosete heiwagō sōte e," *Rafu Shimpo,* September 18, 1936; and "Chojin-Takemoto Plane Leaves on Flight to East," *Rafu Shimpo,* September 19, 1936.

109 Correspondence from Masuyama to the Kyoto headquarters, regarding the establishment of the New York Bukkyōkai, October 27, 1936 (BCA Archives, Correspondence Files, Box No. 1.02.10, Folder July 1936–April 1937).

110 For instance, a BWA was founded in Honolulu in 1898, in San Francisco in 1901, in Fresno in 1904, in Seattle in 1908, and in Los Angeles in 1918 (Terakawa, *Hokubei kaikyō enkakushi,* pp. 44, 78, 94, 160).

111 Aya Honda, "The Social Solidarity of the Seattle, Washington, Bukkyō Fujinkai: 1908-1942," paper presented at the Issei Buddhism Conference, University of California, Irvine, September 2004, pp. 6–7.

112 Honda, "The Social Solidarity of the Seattle, Washington, Bukkyō Fujinkai," p. 9.

113 Honda, "The Social Solidarity of the Seattle, Washington, Bukkyō Fujinkai," pp. 3, 9.

114 Kumata, *Kindai shinshū no tenkai to aki monto,* p. 220.

115 Ogura, "A Sociological Study of Buddhism in North America," pp. 22–23, 79; and Azuma, *Between Two Empires,* p. 165. Buddhist women in Hawaii and Canada also contributed in similar ways. For material on their activities, see Imamura, *Hompa hongwanji hawai kaikyō sanjūgonen kiyō,* p. 22; and Ikuta, *Kanada bukkyōkai enkakushi,* p. 80.

116 Report from the 1933 Meeting of Ministers' and Representatives of Lay Members (BCA Archives, Subject Files, Box No. 1.03.01, Folders 1927–1928, 1930–1938).

117 "Concerning the examination for female teachers" (BCA Archives, Correspondence Files, Box No. 1.02.01, Folder 1925 Outgoing and Correspondence Files; and Box No. 1.02.02, Folder 1926–1927 2B). Those who took the examination were Chiharu Aida, Asako Shirota (or Shiroda), and Tome Yoshida (BCA Archives, Chronological Files, Box No. 1.01.01, Folder 1925–1926).

118 "Nishi Honganji no kyōshi seido," *Shūhō* 97 (October 1909): pp. 17–18. Reprint, *Shūhō*, vol. 5, pp. 353–54.

119 *Seattle Betsuin 75th Anniversary*, p. 25.

120 *Buddhist Churches of America: A Legacy of the First 100 Years*, p. 106.

121 *A Grateful Past, A Promising Future*, pp. 62–63, 69.

122 *Biographical History of Hawaii Hongwanji Ministers* (Honolulu: Honpa Hongwanji Mission of Hawaii, 1991), pp. 40, 42, 46, 48. Among them, Kinu Hirasa, Mitsue Hamada, and Tomiko Ōhara took over the Honolulu Betsuin's administrative and ceremonial affairs during the war years, and Yoshiko Shimabukuro took care of the missions on Kauai.

123 The Kyoto headquarters paid the BMNA bishop's salary. In addition, BMNA officials paid him $150. Correspondence from the Kyoto headquarters to the BMNA office dated June 17, 1930 (BCA Archives, Correspondence Files, Box No. 1.02.04, Folder 1929–1930). The aims of the foundation were to train the laity, promote propagation on a firm financial basis, and provide social help to those in need (Rust, "The Shin Sect of Buddhism in America," pp. 161–62).

124 Correspondence from Masuyama to the Kyoto headquarters dated July 30, 1933 (BCA Archives 34, Correspondence Files, Box No. 1.02.07, Folder 1932–1933).

125 Award requests in 1931 and 1932 (BCA Archives, Chronological Files, Box No. 1.01.02, Folders 1931 and 1932).

126 Correspondence from Masuyama to the Kyoto headquarters dated January 4, 1932 (BCA Archives, Correspondence Files, Box No. 1.02.06, Folder 1932).

127 Tajima, "Japanese Buddhism in Hawaii," p. 45.

128 "Nishi-ha beikoku senden no tōitsu," *Chūgai Nippō*, September 4, 1920.

129 Moriya, *Amerika bukkyō no tanjō*, pp. 186, 206. Also, see the records of the HHMH Ministers' Meeting for a discussion on the exchanges between the HHMH and the BMNA.

130 Resolution 14 in the 1938 Ministers' Meeting (BCA Archives, Subject Files, Box No. 1.03.01, Folders 1927–1928 and 1930–1938).

131 For instance, on January 10 and February 1, 1928, Sasaki requested Imamura to send Takeko Kujō, who was to visit Hawaii, to North America and make arrangements for her stopover (BCA Archives, Correspondence Files, Box No. 1.02.03, Folder 1927–1928, 16A). On October 5, 1929, Imamura recommended Kazuo Sasaki, the executive secretary of the BMNA office, to invite Kōnen Tsunemitsu and Rokō Adachi, a *biwa* (traditional Japanese string instrument)

player, to North America, as both were visiting Honolulu at the time (BCA Archives, Correspondence Files, Box No. 1.02.04, Folder 1929 #15). At one point, Imamura explained the taxation system of ministers in Hawaii, including the exemption of personal tax, to Kusuhara (BCA Archives, Correspondence Files, Box No. 1.02.02, Folder 1926 2A).

132 Uchida stopped over at the Hawaii Betsuin in November 1909 and August 1916, Sonoda in June 1917, Kusuhara in March 1927, Masuyama in June 1936 and February 1938, and Matsukage in February 1938 (*Hawai honpa hongwanji kyōdan enkakushi*, pp. 21, 26–27, 32, 39–40).

133 *A Grateful Past, A Promising Future*, p. 76. Cited by Alfred Bloom, "Shin Buddhism in America: A Social Perspective," in *The Faces of Buddhism in America*, ed. Charles S. Prebish and Kenneth K. Tanaka (Berkeley: University of California Press, 1998), p. 34.

Chapter Four: The Transformation of Shin Buddhist Rituals

1 Victor Turner, *The Anthropology of Performance* (New York: PAJ Publications, 1988), p. 158. Turner also defines ritual as "a transformative performance revealing major classifications, categories, and contradictions of cultural processes" (p. 157).

2 Carl Becker, "Japanese Pure Land Buddhism in Christian America," *Buddhist-Christian Studies* 10 (1990): p. 148.

3 Becker, "Japanese Pure Land Buddhism," p. 149.

4 Ogura, "A Sociological Study of Buddhism in North America," p. 58.

5 The advertisement section of the *Beikoku bukkyō*. See *Beikoku bukkyō* 10, no. 4 (April 1909), and *Beikoku bukkyō* 11, no. 10 (October 1910).

6 Isao Horinouchi, "Americanized Buddhism: A Sociological Analysis of a Protestantized Japanese Religion," Ph.D. dissertation (University of California, Davis, 1973), p. 143. Issei merchants in Seattle usually closed their businesses at 7:30 P.M. on Sundays (Magden, "Buddhism Comes to Seattle," p. 174).

7 An advertisement for a propagation guide (*fukyō no an'nai*) in *Dōbō* 4, no. 9 (September 1903); and *Dōbō* 8, no. 5 (May 1907).

8 At the Buddhist Church of San Francisco, Shin Buddhist sermons were given on Saturday nights and trans-sectarian sermons on Sunday nights. See the advertisement in *Beikoku bukkyō* 7, no. 1 (January 1906). At the Los Angeles Rafu Bukkyōkai, trans-sectarian sermons were given on Sunday nights and Shin Buddhist sermons on the first Saturday night of each month. See the advertisement in *Rafu bukkyō* 1, no. 8 (October 1907).

9 Horinouchi, "Americanized Buddhism," p. 146. As a reference to the size of the congregation, a total of one thousand six hundred laypeople attended twenty-one regular services and six special services in 1932 at the Gardena Buddhist Church (Ogura, "A Sociological Study of Buddhism," p. 58).

10 For instance, see the inauguration ceremony of the Pearl City elementary school, *Dōbō* 8, no.10 (October 1907): p. 36; the opening of the Honganji Hawaii junior high school, *Dōbō* 8, no. 11 (November 1907): p. 30; and the inauguration ceremony of the Waipahu elementary school, *Dōbō* 9, no. 4 (April 1908): pp. 28–29.

11 *Beikoku bukkyō* 9, no. 5 (May 1908): pp. 34–35.

12 *Beikoku bukkyō* 17, no. 6 (June 1916): pp. 19–20; and "Commemorate Buddha's Day," *Los Angeles Times,* May 20, 1916, part L.

13 Hunter, *Buddhism in Hawaii,* pp. 131–34; and Tajima, "Japanese Buddhism in Hawaii," p. 49. Cited by Horinouchi, "Americanized Buddhism," pp. 100, 161–62.

14 Horinouchi, "Americanized Buddhism," pp. 163–64.

15 *Shūhō* 159 (December 1914): p. 8. Reprint, *Shūhō,* vol. 8, p. 202; and *Shūhō* 263 (September 1923): pp. 14–15. Reprint, *Shūhō,* vol. 12, pp. 612–13. See also see Tsutomu Ema, *Kekkon no rekishi: Nihon ni okeru konreishiki no keitai to hatten* (Tokyo: Yūzankaku, 1971), pp. 181–86.

16 Horinouchi, "Americanized Buddhism," p. 161.

17 According to Yukiko Kimura, "Japan took the initiative to restrict emigration by not issuing passports to prospective emigrants except the close kin and picture brides of those already in the United States and its territories." *Issei: Japanese Immigrants in Hawaii,* p. 15.

18 Magden, "Buddhism Comes to Seattle," p. 181.

19 *Dōbō* 10, no. 2 (February 1909): p. 31; *Hawai honpa hongwanji kyōdan enkakushi,* p. 31; and "Honganji betsuin de eidoku dōmei no kekkonshiki," *Hawai Hōchi,* October 16, 1925.

20 On June 25, 1918, Shutai Aoyama of the Shingon sect officiated at the first Shingon marriage ceremony in the United States, creating a new program because his Japanese counterparts had not yet systematized such a procedure (Richard K. Payne, "Hiding in Plain Sight: The Invisibility of the Shingon Mission to the United States," in *Buddhist Missionaries in the Era of Globalization,* ed. Linda Learman [Honolulu: University of Hawai'i Press, 2005], pp. 106–107).

21 There were three types of Buddhist wedding ceremonies practiced in Hawaii. The first included a performance with musical instruments and a wedding reception at the *betsuin.* The second type, which was the most popular, reflected the wedding services recommended by the Kyoto headquarters. The third style was a simplification of the second type. *Hawai bukkyō tokuhon* (*Hawai Buddhist Reader*) (Honolulu: Jikōen, 1939), pp. 119–22.

22 Horinouchi, "Americanized Buddhism," p. 163. Robert Spencer also points out that Nikkei couples refrained from kissing in public (Spencer, "Japanese Buddhism in the United States," p. 108).

23 Terakawa, *Hokubei kaikyō enkakushi,* pp. 527–31.

24 Toshimi Yoshinaga, "Japanese Buddhist Temples in Honolulu," *Social Process in Hawaii* 3 (1937): pp. 36–37.

25 Yoshinaga, "Japanese Buddhist Temples in Honolulu," pp. **532**–34.

26 "Dress Code," *Honpa hōki* (Kyoto: Honpa Hongwanji, 1921), pp. 241–42; *Honganji shūkai hyakunenshi, shiryōhen*, p. 390. The dress code of priests working at the temple administration office was set up in 1934. See the Nishi Honganji's internal circular, *Honzan rokuji* (September 1934), p. 7.

27 "Shinan no kokudō fuku de sonyū-shi ga teitōshiki," *Tairiku Nippō*, October 8, 1925.

28 Keiko Wells, "Shin Buddhist Song Lyrics Sung in the United States: Their History and Expressed Buddhist Images (1) 1898–1939," *Tokyo daigaku amerika taiheiyō kenkyū* 2 (2002): p. 77. Wells actually describes two more stages, the composition of children's *gathas* in English by Nisei and new English songs produced by Caucasians and Sansei. Most likely these developments happened after World War II.

29 Wells, "Shin Buddhist Song Lyrics" (1), pp. 78, 82, 84.

30 Asuka, *Sorewa bukkyō shōka kara hajimatta,* pp. 68, 81–82.

31 Wells, "Shin Buddhist Song Lyrics" (1), p. 88; and George J. Tanabe, Jr., "Glorious Gathas: Americanization and Japanization in Honganji Hymns," in *Engaged Pure Land Buddhism: Essays in Honor of Professor Alfred Bloom*, ed. Kenneth K. Tanaka and Eishō Nasu (Berkeley, CA: WisdomOcean Publications, 1998), pp. 223–24. Wells counts one hundred and thirty-eight songs, and Tanabe counts one hundred and fourteen songs.

32 Wells, "Shin Buddhist Song Lyrics" (1), pp. 88–93; Tanabe, "Glorious Gathas," p. 227.

33 Utsuki, "Introduction" to *Standard Buddhist Gathas and Services.* Cited by Keiko Wells, "Shin Buddhist Song Lyrics Sung in the United States: Their History and Expressed Buddhist Images (2) 1936–2001," *Tokyo daigaku amerika taiheiyō kenkyū* 3 (2003), p. 43.

34 Tanabe, "Glorious Gathas," pp. 224–25.

35 Wells, "Shin Buddhist Song Lyrics" (2), p. 43.

36 Utsuki, "Introduction" to *Standard Buddhist Gathas and Services.*

37 Tanabe, "Glorious Gathas," pp. 225–26.

38 Tanabe, "Glorious Gathas," pp. 227, 229.

39 Wells, "Shin Buddhist Song Lyrics" (2), pp. 41–42.

40 Resolution 12 of the 1932 Ministers' Meeting (BCA Archives, Subject Files, Box No. 1.03.01, Folders 1927–1928 and 1930–1938).

41 Resolution of the 1933 Ministers' and Lay Delegates' Meeting (BCA Archives, Subject Files, Box No. 1.03.01, Folders 1927–1928 and 1930–1938).

42   According to the 33rd notice from the BMNA office to ministers dated December 25, 1938, there is a list of English textbooks translated and printed by the Publication Bureau of Buddhist Books of the Nishi Honganji. At the end, it states that the BMNA service book was also available (BCA Archives, Chronological Files, Box No. 1.01.04, Folder 1938).

43   Keiko Wells, "'Fall, Make Yourself Fall': A Continuity of Shin Buddhist Spirituality in Hawaii: How It was Passed from Issei and Was Acculturated," paper presented at the Issei Buddhism Conference, University of California, Irvine, September 2004. Wells covers the period between 1930 and 1950, and also discusses the characteristics of poems composed by Issei Shin female followers during World War II.

44   Wells, "'Fall, Make Yourself Fall,'" pp. 1–4.

45   Wells, "'Fall, Make Yourself Fall,'" pp. 7–8.

46   "Bukkyō shinshū shōkai sho," *Chūgai Nippō*, January 8, 1933; "Hakujin ni yomaseru eiyaku no seiten kankō," *Bunka Jihō,* May 3, 1935; "Gaijin ni bukkyō o rikai saseru tame konponteki na bussho honyaku ni jōshutsu su," *Bunka Jihō,* May 9, 1935; and "Seiten honyaku no jigyō ni tōkyoku mo ryōkai sareta," *Bunka Jihō,* May 18, 1935.

47   33rd notice from the BMNA office to ministers, dated December 25, 1938 (BCA Archives, Chronological Files, Box No. 1.01.04, Folder 1938).

48   "Dendō seishin no ketsunyo ga gaijin dendō fushin no geiin," *Chūgai Nippō,* July 26, 1925.

49   Refuges and Precepts for Initiation of Lay Members (BCA Archives, Correspondence Files, Box No. 1.02.07, Folder 1933).

50   BCA Archives, Correspondence Files, Box No. 1.02.07, Folder 1933.

51   "Buddhists Ordain American, S. A. Goldwaite [*sic*] Enters Priesthood Here," *Los Angeles Times,* June 18, 1934, Part II. The article states that the event marked "the first initiation and the first Buddhist ordination in Los Angles."

52   According to Shandao, the standing figure indicates Amida Buddha's gesture of approaching sentient beings, when they recite his name and wish for salvation immediately. "Jūryū kūchū," *Shinshū shin jiten* (Kyoto: Hōzōkan, 1992), p. 243.

53   BMNA officials considered changing the rituals not only for Caucasians but also for adult Nisei laity. At the third national Bussei conference, held in 1941, delegates proposed that ministers should present the Buddhist scriptures to the Nisei congregation in more comprehensive ways and design easier services, including marriage and funerary rites ("Bussei Conference," *The New Canadians,* October 31, 1941). It was not until after World War II that their demands caught the attention of Issei ministers. The ministers taught the Nisei laity that the purpose of services was to "practice indebtedness" (*hōongyō*) and honor the virtue of Amida Buddha (as a response to some YBA members

who ignored the importance of sutra chanting). But the ministers simplified daily rituals, as well as all-night vigils for the dead, funerary rites, and memorial services, responding to the "demands of the day" (Report on the First Meeting of the Propagation Study, dated August 30, 1947, and Report on the Second Meeting of the Propagation Study, which was held August 3–5, 1948. These reports are found in the Los Angeles Honpa Honganji Buddhist Temple Archives, Folders 1947 and 1948).

54   Horinouchi, "Americanized Buddhism," p. 117; and *A Grateful Past, A Promising Future*, pp. 52, 64. The temple gong was first installed at the Kahuku Honganji Mission. See *Dōbō* 10, no. 3 (March 1909): p. 31.

55   Horinouchi, "Americanized Buddhism," pp. 115–16.

56   For studies of the modernization of Japanese Buddhist art and architecture, see Richard Jaffe, "Buddhist Material Culture, 'Indianism,' and the Construction of Pan-Asian Buddhism in Prewar Japan," *Material Religion: The Journal of Objects, Art and Belief* 2, no. 3 (2005): pp. 266–92.

57   Lorraine Reiko Minatoshi Palumbo, "The Process of Transformation of the Buddhist Temple Architecture of the Japanese Society of Hawaii," Dissertation for the Doctorate of Engineering (Waseda University, 1999), pp. 40, 44–45.

58   Palumbo, "The Process of Transformation of the Buddhist Temple Architecture," pp. 51–53, 68.

59   Palumbo, "The Process of Transformation of the Buddhist Temple Architecture," pp. 74–76.

60   Palumbo, "The Process of Transformation of the Buddhist Temple Architecture," pp. 71–72.

61   Palumbo, "The Process of Transformation of the Buddhist Temple Architecture," pp. 107–109.

62   Palumbo, "The Process of Transformation of the Buddhist Temple Architecture," p. 110.

63   Palumbo, "The Process of Transformation of the Buddhist Temple Architecture," p. 110.

64   Translated and quoted by Palumbo, "The Process of Transformation of the Buddhist Temple Architecture," p. 125.

65   Palumbo, "The Process of Transformation of the Buddhist Temple Architecture," pp. 125–26.

66   Jaffe, "Buddhist Material Culture," p. 281.

67   Moriya, *Amerika bukkyō no tanjō*," p. 189.

68   Palumbo, "The Process of Transformation of the Buddhist Temple Architecture," p. 126.

69   Tsunemitsu, *Hokubei bukkyō shiwa*, p. 103; and *Fresno Betsuin Buddhist Temple Centennial*, pp. 13-17.

70   Yukiko Yanagida McCarty, "Nihonmachi, Reminiscent of 1950s Japan, San Jose Buddhist Church Betsuin (1937–)," *The East* 41, no. 3 (2005): pp. 19–20. In 1911 the Nishiura brothers built the first temple at 523 North Sixth Street in San Jose, but it was gutted by fire in 1925 (*San Jose Buddhist Church Betsuin 1902–2002*, pp. 7, 10).

71   Yukiko Yanagida McCarty, "Little Tokyo and Its Buddhist Temple, National Center for the Preservation of Democracy (Former Nishi Hongwanji Buddhist Temple building 1925–)," *The East* 41, no. 5 (2006): pp. 18–19. The Islamic style of architecture was also observed in the main building of the Jōdo Mission in Honolulu (Becker, "Japanese Pure Land Buddhism in Christian America," p. 145; and Shinbo, *Hawai kaikyō kyūjūnenshi*, p. 187).

Chapter Five: Shin Buddhist Doctrine Reconstructed

1   Nishi Honganji priests submitted the following M.A. theses: Kenjō Kurokawa, "History and Present Status of the Vacation Religious Day School" (University of Southern California, 1923); Toryū Kudara, "The Influence of the Namu Amida Butsu in Japan" (University of Southern California, 1924); Ryūchi Fujii, "The Conception of Personality in a System of Absolute Idealism" (University of Southern California, 1924); and Tansai Terakawa, "A Critical Exposition of J. M. Guyau's the Non-Religious of the Future" (Stanford University, 1927). Ryūgyō Fujimoto and Nishū Utsuki, who attended the University of Southern California in the 1920s, later published books in English from the Honpa Honganji. Fujimoto published *An Outline of the Triple Sutra of Shin Buddhism, Volume 1: The Sutra on the Eternal Buddha* (Kyoto: Honpa Hongwanji, 1955), and *An Outline of the Triple Sutra of Shin Buddhism, Volume 2: The Sutra of Meditation on the Eternal Buddha* (Kyoto: Hyakka-en, 1960). Before World War II, Utsuki published *The Shin Sect, A School of Mahayana Buddhism: Its Teaching, Brief History, and Present-Day Conditions* (Kyoto: Publication Bureau of Buddhist Books, Hompa Hongwanji, 1937); *History of Honganji* (Buddhist Churches of America, n.d.); and *The Seven Spiritual Fathers* (Kyoto: Honpa Hongwanji, 1938). Three Higashi clerics also received their M.A. degrees: Aihō Suehiro, "A Study of Culture of Ainos (Ainu), with Special Reference to Their Religious Life" (University of Southern California, 1928); Kendō Mito, "Character Education through Religious Dramatization" (University of Southern California, 1931); and Shūken Yamanouchi, "The Japanese in California: The Development of the Japanese Communities in California" (Boston University, 1933).

2   Imamura mentioned pragmatism as the mode of intellectual thinking developed in the United States. See Imamura, "Beikoku oyobi beikokujin" in *Chōshōin ibunshū*, pp. 127–28. Ryūsaku Tsunoda contributed the article "James kyōju no seikyo" to *Dōbō*, the journal published by Hawaii's YBA. See *Dōbō* 11, no. 11 (November 1910): pp. 2–7.

3   Takeichi Takahashi and Junjō Izumida, *Shinranism in Mahayana Buddhism and the Modern World* (Los Angeles: Higashi Hongwanji, 1932), p. i.

4   Michihiro Ama, "Analysis of 'Shinranism in Mahayana Buddhism and the Modern World,'" *The Pure Land* 18–19 (2002): pp. 72–88; and "The Early History of the Americanization of Shin Buddhism: The Case of Kyōgoku Itsuzō," paper submitted to the Issei Buddhism Conference, University of California, Irvine, September, 2004.

5   Matriculation No. 93187, Office of the Recorder, University of Chicago.

6   Junjō Izumida, "Zaibei gojūnen no kaiko 83," *Kashū Mainichi Shinbun,* July 14, 1949; and Takahashi and Izumida, *Shinranism,* inside back cover.

7   John Dewey, "The Pragmatic Acquiescence," *The Essential Dewey,* vol. 1: *Pragmatism, Education, Democracy,* ed. Larry A. Hickman and Thomas M. Alexander (Bloomington, IN: Indiana University Press, 1998), p. 36.

8   John Dewey, *Reconstruction in Philosophy* (1920) (New York: Mentor Books, 1950, reprint), p. 10.

9   Takeichi Takahashi, "The Symptomatic Function and Value of Synthetic Moral Judgment," Ph.D. dissertation (University of Chicago, 1927), pp. 106–107.

10 John Dewey, *A Common Faith* (New Haven, CT: Yale University Press, 1934), pp. 39, 42, 54, 114.

11 Takahashi and Izumida, *Shinranism,* p. i.

12 Takahashi and Izumida, *Shinranism,* pp. v–vi.

13 Takahashi and Izumida, *Shinranism,* p. 57.

14 Takahashi and Izumida, *Shinranism,* p. 72.

15 Takahashi and Izumida, *Shinranism,* p. 1.

16 Takahashi and Izumida, *Shinranism,* p. iv.

17 Takahashi and Izumida, *Shinranism,* p. 204.

18 Takahashi and Izumida, *Shinranism,* pp. 3, 7, 9.

19 Takahashi and Izumida, *Shinranism,* pp. 33, 56, 125, 177–78, 211.

20 Shinran's statement in the Postscript to the *Tannishō:* "When I consider deeply the Vow of Amida, which arose from five *kalpas* of profound thought, I realize that it was entirely for the sake of myself alone!" (*CWS,* vol. 1, p. 679).

21 Takahashi and Izumida, *Shinranism,* pp. 55, 120, 150, 188, 196.

22 Takahashi and Izumida, *Shinranism,* pp. 64, 80–81. Takahashi's analysis of faith is still relevant today. In 1981, when the Nishi Honganji Translation Committee began to translate the collected works of Shinran, Japanese and American scholars debated whether or not it was appropriate to translate *shinjin* as "faith." According to Yoshifumi Ueda, "[T]he fundamental difference between *shinjin* and faith is that while the concept of faith stands in the duality of God (creator) and man (created), *shinjin* is the oneness of Buddha and man, or man's becoming a Buddha," and "[for Shinran,] *shinjin* is not a means to salvation but salvation itself" (Ueda, "Response to Thomas P.

Kasulis's Review of 'Letter of Shinran.'" *Philosophy East and West* 31, no. 4 [1981]: p. 507). When *The Collected Works of Shinran* (*CWS*) was finally published in 1997, for the first time the word *shinjin* was left untranslated in the texts themselves.

23 Takahashi and Izumida, *Shinranism*, pp. 64, 70.

24 Takahashi and Izumida, *Shinranism*, p. 120.

25 Takahashi and Izumida, *Shinranism*, pp. 106–107, 116, 120–21.

26 Nishū Utsuki elaborated on the two buddha-body theory by introducing the concept of "three bodies of the Buddha" in English: scholars regarded the Dharma as the *dharmakāya* ("Dharma body") and its activity as *nirmāṇakāya* ("manifested body") and placed the accommodated law-body known as *saṃbhogakāya* ("reward body") between these two. The first body suggests Buddha's wisdom, such as the law of dependent co-arising and the doctrine of emptiness. From this oneness, the second body arises, manifesting itself as the form of Bodhisattva Dharmākara, who becomes enlightened as Amida Buddha upon fulfillment of his forty-eight vows. In essence, the *saṃbhogakāya* is known as the "reward body." This body is further reincarnated as Śākyamuni (as *nirmāṇakāya*), who demonstrates the attributes of Amida. While Amida represents "mercy" (compassion), Śākyamuni symbolizes the concrete activity of the Dharma (Utsuki, *The Shin Sect*, pp. 8–11). By explaining the theory of the Buddha's three bodies, Utsuki tried to clarify Christians' misconception in labeling Shin Amidists as "idol worshipers." However, it only served to generate further confusion, since the concept was somewhat similar to the Christian doctrine of the Trinity (*A Grateful Past, A Promising Future*, pp. 74–5). In other words, the metaphysical relationship between Amida and Śākyamuni remained unclear to non-Buddhists during the prewar period. For further clarification of the theory of the three bodies of Buddha, see Gajin Nagao, "On the Theory of Buddha-body," *The Eastern Buddhist* (n.s.) 6, no. 1 (1973): pp. 25–53.

27 Takahashi and Izumida, *Shinranism*, pp. 160, 179.

28 Takahashi and Izumida, *Shinranism*, pp. 208–209.

29 Itsuzō Kyōgoku, ed., *Akarui bukkyō* (Fresno, CA: Maha Maya Society, 1954), pp. 257–58.

30 *Tri-Ratna* 5, no. 1 (April 1951): pp. 14–16.

31 Saburōji Suzuki, ed., *Sotsugyōsha meibo* (Tokyo: Tokyo Teikoku daigaku bungakubu gakuyūkai, 1936), p. 55.

32 Enryō Sasaki, "Atogaki," in *Akarui bukkyō*, ed. Kyōgoku, pp. 259–61.

33 Letter dated November 18 (year unknown). Since Kyōgoku was already living in Fresno in December 1921, it is likely that the letter was written that year. BCA Archives, Chronological Files, Box No. 1.01.01, Folder 1917–1919/1922–1924.

34 In 1934, both the Los Angeles and Fresno churches had five ministers. The former had one thousand five hundred members and the latter had seven hundred, the largest and second largest membership of all churches. Terakawa, *Hokubei kaikyō enkakushi,* pp. 583–84.

35 *Buddhist Churches of America: A Legacy of the First 100 Years,* p. 71.

36 Correspondence from the Kyoto headquarters dated September 21, 1929 (BCA Archives, Correspondence Files, Box No. 1.02.05, Folder 1931).

37 This document was originally found in the BCA Archives, Box 34, A1P21, Folder 10. According to the new classification at the BCA Archives, it is possibly located in Chronological Files, Box No. 1.01.02, Folders 1929 and 1931.

38 Correspondence from the Kyoto headquarters dated December 26, 1925 (BCA Archives, Correspondence Files, Box No. 1.02.01, Folder 1925 Outgoing).

39 Terakawa, *Hokubei kaikyō enkakushi,* pp. 567–69.

40 Setsugo Sakamoto, "Chōji," *Jikishin* 9, no. 3 (1953): p. 16; and *Fresno Betsuin Buddhist Temple Centennial,* p. 18.

41 Letter from Marii Hasegawa, Kyōgoku's second daughter, to the author, received January 2004.

42 After World War II, when Kyōgoku was still ill, YBA members provided his family with housing. Kiyo Kyōgoku, "Anotoki konotoki," *Jikishin* 9, no. 3 (1953): pp. 56–60.

43 Ryō Munekata mentioned Kyōgoku's lay speaker program. Interviewed March 29, 2004.

44 *Fresno Betsuin Buddhist Temple Centennial,* pp. 17–18.

45 Interview with Marii Hasegawa, April 3, 2004.

46 Masuyama was concerned about Kyōgoku's situation and discussed his withdrawal with Tokurei Inoue, Chief of the Propagation Department in Kyoto. According to their correspondence, they thought about securing a position for Kyōgoku in Japan, but because of his extraordinary talent it was difficult to implement their plan at that time. Correspondence to Bishop Masuyama dated November 16, 1931 (BCA Archives, Correspondence Files, Box No. 1.02.05, Folder 1931).

47 Sasaki, "Atogaki," p. 260.

48 Tatsuya Ichikawa, "Kanzen hōwa," *Jikishin* 9, no. 3 (1953): pp. 18–19, 52.

49 Itsuzō Kyōgoku, "Jikishin kyō ni narumade," *Jikishin* 4, no. 2 (1948): pp. 17–18.

50 Articles included 1) Buddhists of other traditions, scholars, and various professions, such as D. T. Suzuki, Bensaburō Kato (Ph.D. in Chemistry), Masaki Iwamoto (professor at the Medical School of Tōhoku University), Alan Watts, Dr. G. P. Malalasekera (President of the World Fellowship of Buddhists and Dean of the University of Ceylon), James U. W. Thompson (Sōtō Zen lay missionary and

a member of the Council of the Western Buddhist Order), Marie Byles (attorney and writer), and so on; 2) Euro-American BMNA ministers, including Sunya Pratt, Robert Clifton, Philip Eidmann, Frank Udale, and Ernest Hunt of the HHMH; 3) Manshi Kiyozawa, translated by Kunji Tajima and Floyd Shacklock; 4) Kyōgoku's fellow and junior ministers, including Ryūgyō Fujimoto, Kanmo Imamura, Arthur Yamabe, Arthur Takemoto; and 5) members of the YBA.

51   Sasaki, "Atogaki," p. 259.

52   Interview with George Teraoka, November 6, 2001.

53   Saburō Ienaga, "Japan's Modernization and Buddhism," *Contemporary Religions in Japan* 6 (March 1965): p. 25; and Johnston, "Kiyozawa Manshi's Buddhist Faith," pp. 1–2. Johnston quotes Joseph Kitagawa, *Religion in Japanese History* (New York: Columbia University Press, 1966), p. 288.

54   Nobuo Haneda, trans., *December Fan: The Buddhist Essays of Manshi Kiyozawa* (Kyoto: Shinshū Ōtani-ha, 1984), p. 1.

55   Johnston, "Kiyozawa Manshi's Buddhist Faith," pp. 152–53. American academics have begun to study Kiyozawa's thought, and Japanese scholars' articles on him have been translated, e.g., Shunshō Terakawa, "Shin Buddhism in Modern Japan: An Examination of the Thought of Kiyozawa Manshi," in *Studies in History of Buddhism,* ed. A. K. Narain (Delhi: B. R. Publishing Corporation, 1980); and Mark L. Blum, "Kiyozawa Manshi and the Meaning of Buddhist Ethics," *The Eastern Buddhist* (n.s.) 21, no. 1 (1988): pp. 61–81. There is a featured volume on Kiyozawa, entitled "Kiyozawa Manshi Centennial," in *The Eastern Buddhist* (n.s.) 35, nos. 1/2 (2003), which includes articles by Alfred Bloom, "Kiyozawa Manshi and the Revitalization of Buddhism" (pp. 1–5); Mineo Hashimoto, "Two Models of the Modernization of Japanese Buddhism: Kiyozawa Manshi and D. T. Suzuki" (pp. 6–41); Mark L. Blum, "Truth in Need: Kiyozawa Manshi and Søren Kierkegaard" (pp. 57–101); and Shin'ya Yasutomi, "The Way of Introspection: Kiyozawa Manshi's Methodology" (pp. 102–114).

56   Yūsen Kashiwahara, "Kiyozawa Manshi," in *Shapers of Japanese Buddhism,* ed. Yūsen Kashiwahara and Kōyū Sonoda (Tokyo: Kōsei Publishing Co., 1994), pp. 231–34.

57   Kashiwahara, "Kiyozawa Manshi," pp. 234–38. Also, for an introduction to Kiyozawa's life, see Alfred Bloom, "Kiyozawa Manshi and the Path to the Revitalization of Buddhism," *Pacific World,* 3rd ser., no. 5 (2003): pp. 21–24.

58   *Skeleton of a Philosophy of Religion* was translated by Zenshirō Noguchi and submitted to the World's Parliament of Religions in Chicago in 1893.

59   Johnston, "Kiyozawa Manshi's Buddhist Faith," pp. 112–13, 196.

60   For a discussion of "dependent co-arising" and "the trichiliocosm in a moment of consciousness," see, for instance, Paul L. Swanson, *Foundations of T'ien-T'ai Philosophy: The Flowering of the Two Truths Theory in Chinese Buddhism* (Berkeley, CA: Asian Humanities Press, 1989), pp. 4–5, 12–13.

61 Kiyozawa's philosophy was inclusive of all religions, and he avoided participating in other Buddhist leaders' anti-Christianity campaigns during the Meiji
period (Johnston, "Kiyozawa Manshi's Buddhist Faith," p. 7).

62 Johnston, "Kiyozawa Manshi's Buddhist Faith," pp. 126–27.

63 Hashimoto, "Two Models of the Modernization of Japanese Buddhism," pp.
30–31.

64 Hashimoto, "Two Models of the Modernization of Japanese Buddhism," pp.
29–30.

65 Yasutomi, "The Way of Introspection: Kiyozawa Manshi's Methodology," p. 102.

66 Haneda, trans., *December Fan*, p. 3.

67 Manshi Kiyozawa, "The Nature of My Faith," in *An Anthology of Modern Shin
Buddhist Writings: Kiyozawa Manshi, Soga Ryōjin, Kaneko Daiei and Yasuda Rijin,*
trans. Mark L. Blum (Kyoto: Ōtani University, 2001), p. 38. A two-member team
translated some of Kiyozawa's writings as early as 1936. See Kunji Tajima and
Floyd Shacklock, trans., *Selected Essays of Manshi Kiyozawa* (Kyoto: The Bukkyō
Bunka Society, 1936).

68 Johnston, "Kiyozawa Manshi's Buddhist Faith," p. 144.

69 Bloom, "Kiyozawa Manshi and the Path to the Revitalization of Buddhism," p. 28.

70 Johnston, "Kiyozawa Manshi's Buddhist Faith," pp. 150–52, 201. Kiyozawa also
writes, "Our true self is nothing but this: committing our total existence to the
wondrous working of the Infinite, then settling down just as we are in our
present situation" (Haneda, trans., *December Fan*, p. 25). Kiyozawa further
writes:

> We simply are to depend on the Absolute Infinity. The matter of life and death is not
> worth worrying about, let alone the following matters: excommunication is accept-
> able, imprisonment bearable, and slander, exclusion and all kinds of insults are not
> minded at all. Rather, we shall entirely enjoy what is given by the Absolute Infinity.

Quoted by Hashimoto, "Two Models of the Modernization of Japanese
Buddhism," p. 29.

71 Yoshida, *Nihon kindai bukkyōshi kenkyū,* p. 312.

72 Kiyozawa, "Discourse on Religious Morality and Common Morality," pp. 30–31.

73 For instance, see Kyōgoku's articles "Kaga tayori," *Seishinkai* 9, no. 11 (November 1909): pp. 63–64; and "Tsuneni dai issen ni," *Seishinkai* 14, no. 1 (April
1914): pp. 54–55.

74 Shōichi Matsuda, *Akegarasu Haya: Yo to tomo ni yo o koen,* 2 vols. (Kanazawa:
Kitagui shinbunsha, 1998), vol. 2, pp. 2, 18.

75 Kyōgoku, "Dedicated Words" and "Preface" in *Akarui bukkyō.*

76 Masaharu Nagata, "Topaz no omoide," *Jikishin* 3, no. 3 (1947): pp. 40–41. Kyōgoku's visit is also recorded in the Berkeley Higashi Honganji Temple records.

77 Kyōgoku, "Tsuneni dai issen ni," pp. 54–55. The *Tannishō* is a well-known Shin Buddhist text that uses Shinran's own words as recorded by Yuien, who lamented how Shinran's teaching was misinterpreted by his later followers, and he therefore urged them to listen to what Shinran had actually said. The *Goichidai kikigaki* is a compilation of the dialogues of the eighth abbot of the Honganji, Rennyo. Kyōgoku also expressed undergoing a similar struggle to Akegarasu on October 25, 1913 (*Akegarasu Haya zenshū*, vol. 3, no. 2, p. 76).

78 In the Mahayana tradition the six *pāramitās* ("perfections") are virtues to be perfected by a bodhisattva on the path toward buddhahood: generosity or giving (*dāna*), morality or ethical behavior (*śīla*), forbearance or patience (*kṣānti*), energy or effort (*vīrya*), meditation (*dhyāna*), and wisdom (*prajñā*). (Adapted from *The Encyclopedia of Eastern Philosophy and Religion* [Boston: Shambhala, 1994], p. 267.)

79 Kyōgoku, "Direct and Indirect Understanding," *Tri-Ratna* 6, no. 1 (January/ February 1952): pp. 15–16.

80 Kyōgoku, *Akarui bukkyō*, pp. 52–56.

81 Manshi Kiyozawa, *Shūkyō teki dōtoku (zokutai) to futsū dōtoku to no kōshō* (*Discourse on Religious Morality and Common Morality*), trans. Mark Blum, in *An Anthology of Modern Shin Buddhist Writing*, pp. 26–28. Brackets appear as in the translation.

82 Kiyozawa, *Shūkyō teki dōtoku (zokutai) to futsū dōtoku to no kōshō*, p. 27.

83 Hitoshi Imamura, *Gendaigo yaku: Kiyozawa Manshi goroku* (Tokyo: Iwanami gendai bunko, 2001), pp. 482–83.

84 Yasutomi, "The Way of Introspection: Kiyozawa Manshi's Methodology," p. 106.

85 Kyōgoku, *Akarui bukkyō*, pp. 153, 216–18; Toshimaro Ama, "Shin Buddhism and Economic Ethics," *The Eastern Buddhist* (n.s.) 34, no. 2 (2002): pp. 39–40.

86 Partly because of Hamako Watanabe's popular song, "Ah, the Night Is Deep in Monten Lupa," the lives of war criminals, including those awaiting execution without any valid charges, came to be known to people in Japan (John Dower, *Embracing Defeat* [New York: W. W. Norton & Co., 2000], pp. 514–15).

87 Gibun Kimura, "Kyōgoku sensei to Monten Lupa no senpansha," *Jikishin* 9, no. 3 (1953): pp. 35–39. The correspondence between Kyōgoku and Kagao was also recorded in *Jikishin* 8, no. 1 (1952): pp. 16–22; and *Jikishin* 8, no. 2 (1952): pp. 22–28. Kagao later sent a petition to various organizations in the Philippines, requesting a halt to the executions. Concerning his activities, see Shūnin Kagao, *Monten Lupa ni inoru*, ed. Takeshi Yamashita (Tokyo: Kokusho kankōkai, 1982).

88 Kyōgoku, "Buddhism as a Whole, Not as a Sect," *Bhratri* 2, no. 2 (July 1934): p. 87.

89 Kyōgoku, "Buddhism as a Whole, Not as a Sect," p. 87.

90 Kikuo Taira, "Reverend Kyogoku, in Remembrance," *Tri-Ratna* 7, nos. 5/6 (September/October–November/December, 1953): p. 21. The Sunday School Department had six sub-departments: cards, stories, music, material, research,

and slides. Kyōgoku divided this two-course curriculum into three levels according to age group. The theme of Course One was "The Life of Buddha," consisting of twenty lessons: 1) Birth of Buddha, 2) Boyhood, 3) Youth, 4) Marriage, 5) Renunciation, 6) Ascetic Practice, 7) Enlightenment, 8) First Sermon, 9) Sangha, 10) Sariputta and Moggallana, 11) Jotavana Vihara, 12) Visiting Homes, 13) Abolishment of Castes, 14) Divine Vows, 15) Miracles Forbidden, 16) Devadatta, 17) Tragedy at Rajagaha, 18) Sermon on the Pure Land, 19) Death of the Buddha, and 20) Dividing the Relics. Course Two dealt with "The Teaching of Buddha," consisting of twenty-five lessons: 1) Causation, 2) Karma, 3) Buddha Nature, 4) Right View, 5) Right Thought, 6) Right Speech, 7) Right Conduct, 8) Right Livelihood, 9) Right Effort, 10) Right Mindfulness, 11) Right Meditation, 12) Dana-Giving, 13) Benevolence, 14) Sympathy, 15) Tenderness, 16) Filial Piety, 17) Duty, 18) Brotherhood, 19) Reflection and Confession, 20) Buddha's Compassion, 21) Liberation, 22) Entrusting, 23) Thankfulness, 24) Namu Amida Butsu, and 25) Enlightenment (Rust, "The Shin Sect of Buddhism in America," pp. 215–16, 221–22).

91 Sasaki, "Atogaki," in *Akarui bukkyō;* "Nikkō card no nihon shinshutsu," *Jikishin* 4, no. 4 (1948): p. 21; and Setsugo Sakamoto, "Chōji," *Jikishin* 9, no. 3 (1953): p. 14. The Sunday school program was not a Buddhist phenomenon unique to the United States. Kyōgoku's wife, Kiyo, recalled, "I was disappointed in the first Sunday school session I attended on my arrival [in California] forty years ago. It consisted of practicing a few secular songs and listening to fairy tales" (*Buddhist Churches of America 75-year History,* vol. 1, p. 101). At the beginning of the Meiji period, priests in the Aki district of Hiroshima opened a Sunday school, and Akegarasu also did so in Ishikawa in 1899. Later, the Nishi Honganji headquarters in Kyoto issued the Regulation of Buddhist Sunday Schools in 1915 (Matsuda, *Akegarasu Haya: Yo to tomo ni yo o koen,* vol. 1, 1998, pp. 250–57; and Kumata, *Kindai shinshū no tenkai to aki monto,* pp. 228–29). Initially, the BMNA used lesson cards from Japan, but as Nisei Buddhists grew up, Kyōgoku and others created new cards in English in 1946 (*Buddhist Churches of America 75-year History,* vol. 1, pp. 102–103).

92 *Buddhist Churches of America 75-year History,* vol. 1, p. 101.

93 Fifth Bishop Hōshō Sasaki's correspondence to Gendō Nakai dated January 21, either 1926 or 1927 (BCA Archives, Correspondence Files, Box No. 1.02.02, Folder 1926–1927, 2A). In the letter, Sasaki writes:

> [F]or my ideal, I want to teach Jōdo [S]hinshū to [N]isei/[S]ansei and Caucasians. It would be difficult for them to understand the teaching of *tariki* through *tsū bukkyō.* As our study group is vigorous now, I want to let them understand the significance of the Primal Vow first. Instead of using *dana* of Buddha as translation, I suggest you to translate *Namu Amida Butsu* as it is.

94 Interview with the late Reverend Arthur Takemoto, October 16, 2001.

95 Masahiro Shimoda differentiates between Kiyozawa's activities and other

Japanese Buddhologists, who were influenced by Orientalists (Shimoda, "Kindai bukkyōgaku no tenkai to asia ninshiki: tasha toshiteno bukkyō," in *Iwanami kōza: Teikoku nihon no gakuchi,* vol. 3, ed. Mio Kishimoto [Tokyo: Iwanami shoten, 2006], p. 201).

96 Tsunemitsu, *Nihon bukkyō tobeishi,* p. 500. Also, when a nursery school was established at the Fresno Buddhist Church, Kyōgoku named the boys' club the Four L[s] Club (*Fresno Betsuin Buddhist Temple Centennial,* p. 7).

97 Yoshida, *Nihon kindai bukkyōshi kenkyū,* pp. 324–26.

98 Ama, *Why Are the Japanese Non-Religious?,* p. 44.

99 Moriya, *Amerika bukkyō no tanjō,* p. 127.

100 Emyō Imamura, *Beikoku no seishin to shūkyō no jiyū* (Honolulu: Honpa Hongwanji Hawai kaikyō kyōmusho, 1920), p. 28.

101 Moriya, *Amerika bukkyō no tanjō,* pp. 19–21.

102 Moriya, *Amerika bukkyō no tanjō,* pp. 26, 28, 30–33.

103 Moriya, *Amerika bukkyō no tanjō,* pp. 25, 35–37.

104 In *The Letters* III-12, Rennyo writes:

> When we consider presenting our tradition's Other-Power faith, we must first distinguish between the people who have good from the past and those who lack good from the past. For however long ago a person may have listed his name as a participant in this [tradition], it will be difficult for one who lacks good from the past to attain faith. Indeed, faith (*shin*) will of itself be decisively settled in the person for whom past good has unfolded. And so, when we discuss the two [kinds of] practice—right and sundry—in the presence of people who lack good from the past, this may lay the foundation for slander, contrary to what one would expect. To teach extensively in the presence of ordinary people without understanding this principle of the presence or absence of good from the past is in total opposition to our tradition's rules of conduct.

> Rogers and Rogers, *Rennyo: The Second Founder of Shin Buddhism,* pp. 214–15.

105 Moriya, *Amerika bukkyō no tanjō,* pp. 34–35, 61–62, 64–67, 70. Moriya cites Masao Maruyama, "Fukuzawa Yukichi no tetsugaku: toku ni sono jiji hihan tono kanren," *Kokka gakkai zasshi* 61, no. 3 (1947): p. 21.

106 Moriya, *Amerika bukkyō no tanjō,* pp. 72, 85–91.

107 Moriya, *Amerika bukkyō no tanjō,* pp. 86, 98–99.

108 Moriya, *Amerika bukkyō no tanjō,* p. 99. Although the explicit relationship between Kiyozawa and Imamura is unknown, *Seishinkai* was published by Kiyozawa and circulated in the HHMH, and when Kiyozawa died his obituary was printed in *Dōbō,* a Buddhist journal published by the YBA of the HHMH. At the same time, a series of *Dōbō* journals was kept at Ōtani University, of which Kiyozawa served as the first president (Moriya, *Amerika bukkyō no tanjō,* pp. 61–62).

109 *Chōshōin ibunshū,* pp. 299, 305.

110 *Chōshōin ibunshū,* p. 16.

111 Imamura writes:

> [I]f one attaches oneself to worldly affairs, one cannot live one's life actively and joy-fully. People feel shackled and freedom seems limited, if they take their matters too serious[ly]. It is important to take worldly affairs lightly. While involved in them, one's mind remains like a moving cloud under the moon. Things come around if they do, and things go around if they do. Everything is just like that. Therefore when worldly matters are taken lightly, one can become active and real courage arises. There is no need to get depressed.

> *Chōshōin ibunshū*, pp. 18–19.

112 Imamura also published *Beikoku no seshin o ronsu* in 1921 (Moriya, *Amerika bukkyō no tanjō*, pp. 282, 285).

113 Imamura, *Democracy According to the Buddhist Viewpoint* (*Bukkyō yori mitaru min-pon shugi*) (Honolulu: The Publishing Bureau of Hongwanji Mission, 1918), p. 8. Victor S. Hori is careful about connecting the early sangha with modern American democracy. Instead of applying Buddhist principles, the early sangha in India operated as a tribal council, derived from the Śākyas (Hori, "Japanese Zen in America: Americanizing the Face in the Mirror," in *The Faces of Buddhism in America,* ed. Charles S. Prebish and Kenneth K. Tanaka [Berkeley: University of California Press, 1998], p. 64). Hori cites Sukumar Dutt, *Buddhist Monks and Monasteries of India* (London: George Allen and Unwin, 1962), pp. 86–87; and Trevor Ling, *The Buddha. Buddhist Civilization in India and Ceylon* (New York: Scribner's and Sons, 1973), pp. 130–31.

114 Imamura, *Democracy According to the Buddhist Viewpoint*, p. 10.

115 Imamura, *Democracy According to the Buddhist Viewpoint*, p. 11.

116 Imamura, *Democracy According to the Buddhist Viewpoint*, pp. 4, 18–19.

117 Imamura, *Democracy According to the Buddhist Viewpoint*, pp. 26, 28–29.

118 Moriya, *Amerika bukkyō no tanjō*, pp. 175–78.

119 Alexis de Tocqueville, *Democracy in America,* trans. George Lawrence, ed. J. P. Mayer (New York: Doubleday, 1969), p. 252.

120 de Tocqueville, *Democracy in America* (Chicago: University of Chicago Press, 2000), p. 298.

121 Moriya, *Amerika bukkyō no tanjō*, pp. 186–87.

122 Imamura, *Beikoku no seishin to shūkyō no jiyū,* p. 32.

123 In *Beikoku no seishin o ronsu,* Imamura makes a survey of "Beikoku oyobi beikokujin" ("America and American people").

124 Imamura, *Beikoku no seishin o ronsu,* pp. 15–17, 22.

125 Imamura, *Beikoku no seishin o ronsu,* pp. 12–13.

126 Imamura, *Beikoku no seishin o ronsu,* pp. 58–61.

127 Imamura, *Beikoku no seishin o ronsu,* pp. 65–67, 69.

128 Imamura, *Democracy According to the Buddhist Viewpoint,* p. 23.

129 Imamura, *Democracy According to the Buddhist Viewpoint,* pp. 23–24.

130 Moriya, *Amerika bukkyō no tanjō,* p. 183. Imamura was more explicit about his efforts to transform this world into the Pure Land in an article, "Nipu jiji ichiman gō o shukushi shinbun honshitsu ron ni oyobi: shakai kyōiku kikan to shiteno sekimu," in *Nippu jiji,* October 4, 1929.

131 Moriya, *Amerika bukkyō no tanjō,* p. 69.

132 Emyō Imamura, Preface to *Five Appeals to American Patriotism* (Honolulu: The Publishing Bureau of the Hongwanji Mission, 1917).

133 Amstutz, *Interpreting Amida,* p. 80.

134 Moriya's interview with Imamura's third daughter, Kazuko Imamura (Moriya, *Amerika bukkyō no tanjō,* p. 229).

135 Imamura, *Beikoku no seishin to shūkyō no jiyū,* p. 30.

136 Higham, *Strangers in the Land,* p. 235.

137 Higham, *Strangers in the Land,* p. 237.

138 Randolph Bourne, "Trans-National America," in *Randolph Bourne: The Radical Will, Selected Writings 1911-1918,* ed. Olaf Hansen (New York: Urizen Books, 1977), p. 262.

139 Christopher Lasch, Preface to *Randolph Bourne: The Radical Will,* p. 11.

140 Dewey, *Democracy and Education,* p. 83.

141 For Bourne's critique of Dewey and their differences, see Olaf Hansen, Introduction to *Randolph Bourne: The Radical Will,* pp. 52–54.

142 Dewey, *Reconstruction in Philosophy,* p. 147.

143 For a critique of and an evaluation on Dewey's concept of education, see Richard Hofstadter, *Anti-Intellectualism in American Life* (New York: Vintage Books, 1963), pp. 359–92.

144 Regarding the anti-Chinese campaign in the 1880s, Higham writes:

> Americans have never maintained that every European endangers American civilization; attacks have centered on the 'scum' or 'dregs' of Europe, thereby allowing for at least some implicit exceptions. But opponents of Oriental folk have tended to reject them one and all.

Strangers in the Land, p. 25.

145 For instance, a pro-Japanese Christian missionary, Sidney L. Gulick, opposed anti-Japanese immigration laws and proposed a new immigration statute to Congress (Moriya, *Amerika bukkyō no tanjō,* pp. 140–44).

146 Masaji Marumoto became an associate justice of the Supreme Court of Hawaii, and Wilfred Chōmatsu Tsukiyama became the chief justice in 1959. They are said to have received scholarships from the HHMH and studied on the mainland

(interview with Bishop Yosemori, January 30, 2007). The two men also played significant roles in Hawaii's YMBA. Marumoto was determined not to surrender to an authority linked to false democracy and nationalism (Tomoe Moriya, *Yemyo Imamura: Pioneer American Buddhist*, trans. Tsuneichi Takeshita, ed. Alfred Bloom and Ruth Tabrah [Honolulu: Buddhist Study Center Press, 2000], pp. 54–55, 66–67). How Shin Buddhist teaching was incorporated into their careers and practice of law is a topic that needs further study.

147 Kashima, *Buddhism in America*, p. 32. After Senator Phelan stated in the *San Francisco Examiner* that Japanese Buddhist churches fostered "Mikadoism," Uchida and Kirby sent a letter of protest to the Committee on Immigration and Naturalization in Sacramento, California, on July 14, 1920, to defend the BMNA. They explained that all churches affiliated with the BMNA were religious congregations in accordance with the Constitution and state laws; thus, they were legitimate religious orders in the United States. Uchida further wrote:

> We wish to strongly emphasize that our churches have nothing to do what so ever with Shintoism, politics or Imperialistic policy formulated by the Japanese government. Our Mission is to elevate the spiritual life, not to dictate politics or policies of any government. We should also like to point out that Buddhism is democratic, an ideal long held by the citizens of the United States of America. . . .

Uchida's petition dated July 14, 1920 (BCA Archives, Chronological Files, Box No. 1.01.01, Folder 1920).

148 There were articles about native Hawaiians in *Dōbō*, but they were merely introductory descriptions of their lives and customs. See, for instance, *Dōbō* 4, no. 3 (March 1903): p. 3; *Dōbō* 4, no. 8 (August 1903): pp. 9, 18; and *Dōbō* 4, no. 12 (December 1903): p. 12.

Chapter Six: A History of the Higashi Honganji

1 Tajima, "Japanese Buddhism in Hawaii," pp. 29–30. Tajima cites the *Hawaii Japanese Annual and Directory, 1933–1934.*

2 Kyojirō Takahashi, "A Social Study of the Japanese Shinto and Buddhism in Los Angeles," Master's thesis (University of Southern California, 1937), pp. 122–23.

3 The ministers sent to Hawaii were Kenryū Yamada, Shizuka Sazanami, Matsuto Satō, Yuijō Kai, Hōden Mashita, Ryōshō Kumabe (1913–1914), Kankai Izuhara (1918–1936), Shingyō Doi (1915–1920), Kenjirō Hamada (1919–?), Tenran Mōri (1920–1981, died in Hawaii), Hōun Tamayose (1920–1955, died in Hawaii), Tatsuo Sawai (1923–1933), Tsukumo Fukaoku (1925–1931), Chikō Ōdate, Shizuo Misumi (1928–?), Kanryō Sekito (1930–1933), Yū Matsudaira (1932–1937), Chōei Ichijō (1933), Takeo Akegarasu (1933–1942 and 1950–1955), Hōryū Akita (1932–1935), Keisei Kuroda (1935–1942), Daiyū Tachibana (1936–1938, died in Hawaii), Hōkō Okichi (1938–1941), and Kakushin Kusuda (1941–1943). Dates in parentheses show their respective periods of service in Hawaii. The ministers

sent to continental North America were Shōsetsu Tsufura (1920–1975, died in New Jersey), Manabu Fujimura (1920–1934), Ejō Kurita (1921–1923), Kendō Mito (1925–1930), Yoshimaro Atsumi (1926–1927), Shinjō Miura (1926–?), Shūken Yamanouchi (1929–?), Tokumei Satō (1932–1934), Kazuo Fujimoto (1926–?), Chijō Suemori (1926–1936), Hideo Ogasawara (1934–1940), Shōdō Yoshigami (1933–1950), and Nobuo Matsumoto (1940–1947). Dates in parentheses show the ministers' respective periods of service on the mainland. Izuhara and Ōdate were transferred to Los Angeles, while Matsumoto moved to Kaneohe after the war. Information from *Sixty-Seven Years' History of the Higashi Honganji Mission of Hawaii* and *Shūmon kaikyō nenpyō* (Kyoto: Higashi Honganji, 1969), passim (this document for internal circulation only).

4 Kimura, *Issei: Japanese Immigrants in Hawaii,* p. 81.

5 This section, "Buddhist Disputes over the Applicability of Japanese Practices to the American Legal System," pp. 147–54, and the next section, "Conflict over the Americanization and Japanization of Temple Management," pp. 154–58, are adapted from Duncan Williams and Tomoe Moriya, *Issei Buddhism in the Americas* (Urbana: University of Illinois Press, 2010), pp. 65–81.

6 Izumida, "Zaibei gojūnen no kaiko 1," *Kashū Mainichi Shinbun,* April 8, 1949; "Zaibei gojūnen no kaiko 2," *Kashū Mainichi Shinbun,* April 9, 1949; and "Zaibei gojūnen no kaiko 3," *Kashū Mainichi Shinbun,* April 11, 1949.

7 According to Izumida's memoirs, the first gathering was held at a Japanese restaurant on 115 East Second Street in early August 1904 ("Zaibei gojūnen no kaiko 4," *Kashū Mainichi Shinbun,* April 12, 1949). In January 1907, plans were made to purchase land and build a temple with a budget of $25,000 ("Zaibei gojūnen no kaiko 28," *Kashū Mainichi Shinbun,* May 10, 1949). The temple's inauguration ceremony was held July 3–4, 1911, on South Savannah Street ("Zaibei gojūnen no kaiko 46," *Kashū Mainichi Shinbun,* June 1, 1949).

8 *Honpa Hongwanji Los Angeles Betsuin 1905–1980* (Los Angeles: Honpa Hongwanji Los Angeles Betsuin, 1980), pp. 37–38; *Minami kashū nihonjin nanajūnenshi: A History of 70 Years* (Los Angeles: Japanese Chamber of Commerce of Southern California, 1960), p. 242; and *Buddhist Churches of America: A Legacy of the First 100 Years,* p. 239.

9 "Ranbō rōzeki naru rafu *bukkyōkai* yakuin kai," *Rafu Shimpo,* September 19, 1916; "Rafu bukkyōkai no chōsa," *Rafu Shimpo,* September 22, 1916; "Bukkyō-kai soshō jiken chōtei," *Rafu Shimpo,* September 27, 1916; and "Bukkyōkai soshō iyoiyo rakuchaku," *Rafu Shimpo,* September 29, 1916.

10 "Gōdō ni kanshite," *Rafu Shimpo,* August 25, 1917.

11 "Shinshū shozoku san bukkyōkai gōdō kettei," *Rafu Shimpo,* September 5, 1917. However, the Chūō Bukkyōkai was reluctant to consolidate ("Chūbutsu no rinji sōkai," *Rafu Shimpo,* August 14, 1917), though the Rafu Bukkyōkai accepted the proposal ("Sanbutsu gōdō mondai," *Rafu Shimpo,* August 21, 1917).

The following week, the Nanka Bukkyōkai also agreed, though not unanimously ("Nanbukkai no sōkai," *Rafu Shimpo*, August 28, 1917).

12 The minutes of the 1917 Ministers' Meeting was initially found in P3 Box 4. According to the new classification at the BCA Archives, the minutes are most likely found in Subject Files, Box No. 1.03.01, which contains the minutes of the annual ministers' meetings.

13 The Rafu Bukkyōkai dispute was brought to the Los Angeles Superior Court in two cases: *Jisōji v. Izumida* (1918) and *Izumida v. L. A. Morning Sun* (1918). Plaintiffs in the first lawsuit (Case #B55497) were Rev. T. Jisōji, T. Hirata, J. Okamoto, N. Tōyama, Y. Hirai, S. Shigaki, and R. Suenaga. Plaintiffs' counsel was L. V. Stanton and Evans, Abbott & Pearce. The respondent was Izumida, and his counsel was J. Marion Wright. The lawsuit was filed on October 4, 1917, and the trial judge, L. N. Valentine, handed down the verdict exactly one year later.

14 Affidavit of Seidō Chiji'iwa on October 11, 1917.

15 Sonoda's "Records of Izumida's Examination," filed under Case #B55497.

16 The Petition for Writ of Injunction was filed on October 4, 1917. Based on an Affidavit on Application for Injunction Pendente lite made by T. Hirata, the court issued an Order to Show Cause and Interlocutory Injunction on October 5. T. Hirata made an Affidavit upon Application for Order Citing Defendant for Contempt on October 8. He requested the action against Izumida because he continued to perform religious duties. Kiyoshi Ono, one of the Rafu Bukkyōkai board directors, and one of Izumida defenders, made the affidavit on October 10. Izumida's wife, Suma Izumida; Mr. Shirahama, another Rafu Bukkyōkai board director; and Izumida himself made the affidavits on October 11 to verify that Izumida had not acted against the court order issued on October 5. Seidō Chiji'iwa made the affidavit on October 11. Both parties agreed upon the Stipulation to Set for Trial on October 11. The court issued the Vacating Temporary Restraining Order on October 16 to remove the previous order released on October 5, which prohibited Izumida from performing any religious duties. Izumida made the Answer to Respondent to Petition for Writ of Injunction Izumida on October 17. T. Hirata made the Affidavit for Subpoena Duces Tecum on October 29, and submitted financial records and documents, kept during the second general meeting of the Rafu Bukkyōkai, to the court. The original trial date was set for November 8, 1917. In the trial, Sei Fujii, president of the *Kashū Mainichi Shinbun*, made the affidavit on November 19. The plaintiffs made an Amendment to Complaint on March 5, 1918, stating that the Executive Council fired Izumida on September 16, 1917, and in his place, Tetsugai Jisōji had become president of the Rafu Bukkyōkai. The respondent made the Answer to Amendment to Complaint on March 18, and rejected the complaint. The plaintiffs made the Second Amendment to Complaint to Conform to Proof on June 5, 1918, and stated that Izumida lacked the qualities and credibility of a minister; Izumida caused confusion for both

the Rafu Bukkyōkai and the Nishi Honganji headquarters; and the Executive Council had fired Izumida from the presidency of the Rafu Bukkyōkai. The respondent made the Answer to the Second Amendment to Complaint on June 7 and rejected the amendment, since Izumida had not been under the authority of the Nishi headquarters. The Los Angeles Superior Court made the final judgment on October 4, 1918, but the *Rafu Shimpo* ran a headline, "Izumida tachinoki saiban: hikoku shōso to naru," stating that Izumida had won the case, on June 11, 1918.

17 Conclusions of Law, 10.

18 The second lawsuit appears as Case #B57794. The plaintiff was Izumida himself, with counsel J. Marion Wright. The respondent was the *Los Angeles Morning Sun;* Mr. H. Tanaka and his counsel, E. J. Fleming; and B. F. Woodward. Trial judge Leslie R. Hewitt handed down judgment on September 24, 1918.

19 "Negaeri utta izumida junjō-shi," *Rafu Shimpo*, September 11, 1917; "Fukumaden no ōsōji, izumida junjō o hōmure, rafu bukkyōkai o sukue," *Rafu Shimpo*, September, 14, 1917; and "Haitoku fushin no kaikyōshi izumida junjō," and "Izumida-shi ni chūkoku mōsu, *Rafu Shimpo*, September 15, 1917.

20 Quoted from the file of Case #B57794. For a complete translation of the newspaper article, see Findings of Fact, III in Appendix 2, under the heading "Time of the Downfall of the Anti-Consolidation Party."

21 Based on the Summons and Complaint for Libel filed by Izumida against the *Los Angeles Morning Sun* and H. Tanaka, the defendant claimed the Notice of Exception of Sureties and Demand to Justify in December 1917. Tanaka made a contract with a third party in case he would lose the lawsuit and be ordered to pay compensation. The court recognized Tanaka's action on December 24. Both parties agreed upon the Stipulation for the Case to be Set for Trial on January 21, 1918. A Notice of Motion was delivered to Izumida on June 18, 1918, in which the respondent requested the examination of the minutes of Rafu Bukkyōkai board meetings, its financial records and records of death certificates (*kakochō*), and donation envelopes given to Izumida. On the same day, the respondent made an Affidavit Under Section 1000 of the Code of Civil Procedure, stating that the records were necessary to defend himself. The court delivered the Notice of Taking Deposition to Izumida and Shirahama and requested them to report the financial situation of the Rafu Bukkyōkai to the court by June 21, 1918 (Order Directing Subpoenas to Issue).

22 "Ihōsha no songai yōkyū hitoshi," *Rafu Shimpo*, August 16, 1918. The trial was held on June 26, 27, and 28, July 31, and August 1, 2, 5, 6, 12, 13, 14, and 15. Since the process of the trial is not recorded in the file, it is worthwhile to read the articles published in the *Rafu Shimpo.* For instance, Izumida expressed anger toward Asayoshi, who had spread the rumor that Izumida was embezzling offerings ("Izumida hibō saiban," *Rafu Shimpo,* June 29, 1918). The newspaper reported on the testimonies of two individuals, Ono and Yamamoto,

who defended Izumida, saying that there were no guidelines for ministers' receiving offerings ("Gogo kara no higi jiken kōhan," *Rafu Shimpo*, August 2, 1918). In the next day's edition, the *Rafu Shimpo* reported that three individuals—Tanimoto, Shigaki, and Nakamura—testified that Izumida had embezzled the offerings given to Asayoshi, after which Asayoshi decided to start the Nanka Bukkyōkai ("Omoshirokatta gogo no kōhan," *Rafu Shimpo*, August 3, 1918).

23 Findings of Fact, IV in Appendix 2. Jacob M. Wright, who defended Izumida in both cases, was well known as an attorney for Southern California Nikkei plaintiffs and defendants. He was a leader in their quest for civil rights and equality in the United States. For a discussion of his work, see Bruce A. Castleman, "The California Alien Land Laws," Master's thesis (University of San Diego, 1993), p. 57.

24 "Izumida sōseki hakudatsu," *Rafu Shimpo*, January 7, 1919.

25 "Sōseki hakudatsu tsūchō," *Rafu Shimpo*, August 6, 1919.

26 "Chōkaijōki dai shichijō, ichi" and "Chōkaijōki dai jūsanjō, roku," in *Honzan rokuji* (July 15, 1912), pp. 115–16; "Jihō saisoku dai jūni shō dai sanjūgojō/dai sanjūrokujō," in *Honzan rokuji* (April 13, 1898), p. 84; and correspondence to Bishop Masuyama dated November 16, 1931 (BCA Archives, Correspondence Files, Box No. 1.02.05, Folder 1931).

27 "Sonoda shi no hōkoku," *Rafu Shimpo*, February 24, 1918.

28 Izumida, "Zaibei gojūnen no kaiko 43," *Kashū Mainichi Shinbun*, May 27, 1949. Although Nakai returned to Japan because of illness, he helped Issei ministers propagate Buddhism in English. He was outspoken and critical of the headquarters' efforts to transplant the style of Japanese temple management to the BMNA. See Gendō Nakai, "Beikoku bukkyōkai no kiki (1)," *Chūgai Nippō*, September 10, 1925; and "Beikoku bukkyōkai no kiki (2)," *Chūgai Nippō*, September 11, 1925. After World War II, Nakai refused to use the black market, only accepted food as part of the ration system, and subsequently died. *Nembutsu seizan: Oshū nembutsu denpa shōshi,* ed. Kokusai bukkyō bunka kyōkai (Kyoto: Nagata bunshōdo, 2000), p. 17.

29 Izumida, "Zaibei gojūnen no kaiko 74," *Kashū Mainichi Shinbun*, July 2, 1949.

30 "Rabutsu nishi kara higashi e utsuru," *Rafu Shimpo*, December 13, 1919.

31 Higashi Honganji Internal File, "Reports from Overseas Propagation, including China, Taiwan, South Pacific, etc."

32 From the record of Junjō Izumida's registration filed at the Higashi Honganji.

33 Statement attached to the by-laws of the Higashi Honganji Buddhist Church, amended on January 17, 1963.

34 *Shūhō* 235 (May 1921): 8. Reprint, *Shūhō*, vol. 11, p. 464; *Shūhō* 237 (July 1921): 12. Reprint, *Shūhō*, vol. 11, p. 516; and *Shūhō* 248 (June 1922): pp. 10–11. Reprint, *Shūhō*, vol. 12, pp. 164–65.

35   Izumida, "Zaibei gojūnen no kaiko 79," *Kashū Mainichi Shinbun,* July 9, 1949.

36   "Sakan naru honganji bukkyōkai nyūbutsu shiki," *Rafu Shimpo,* December 9,
      1917. In September 1917, the three Buddhist churches (the anti-Izumida group
      was seen as representing the Rafu Bukkyōkai) agreed to consolidate and de-
      cided on the following points: the consolidation committee would announce
      the merger of the three churches and designate the Nanka Bukkyōkai as the
      tentative office of the three; six selected committee members would calcu-
      late the debt owed by the three churches; three committee members and
      Sonoda would draft new by-laws; and Sonoda would have the authority to re-
      locate ministers ("San bukkyōkai gōdō seishiki ni seiritsu su," *Rafu Shimpo,*
      September 30, 1917). However, the members of the Chūō Bukkyōkai sudden-
      ly opposed the plan, though the anti-Izumida group of the Rafu Bukkyōkai
      and the Nanka Bukkyōkai went ahead. The Nishi Honganji headquarters even-
      tually dismissed Haraguchi from the Chūō Bukkyōkai, after attempts at a rec-
      onciliation between the two failed. He also resisted Sonoda's orders to leave
      the church ("Chūō bukkyōkai no gōdō hantai kettei," *Rafu Shimpo,* October 6,
      1917; and "Haraguchi-shi kaishoku saru," *Rafu Shimpo,* October 10, 1917). The
      displacement of Haraguchi from the position of *kaikyōshi* occurred on October
      9, 1917. See *Honzan rokuji* (February 29, 1918), p. 8.

37   "Chūbutsu butsudan tōchaku," *Rafu Shimpo,* March 27, 1918; and "Chūbutsu
      fujin kaigi," *Rafu Shimpo,* May 19, 1918.

38   Quoted from the eight-page letter of request kept in the BCA Archives, P3 Box
      4. At the time of the establishment of the Higashi Betsuin in Los Angeles, on
      February 24, 1919, the Nishi Honganji headquarters sent a letter to Uchida
      encouraging him to expand his propagation territory to compete with Izu-
      mida. This letter was initially found in the BCA Archives, P2 Box1.

39   Within the Nishi Honganji, the incident known as the "Turmoil Over Three
      Kinds of Religious Acts" (*sangō wakuran*) in the late eighteenth and early nine-
      teenth centuries exemplifies the customary practice of its headquarters,
      which shows "overriding concern with social stability and orthodoxy exer-
      cised by both the state and temple authorities during the Tokugawa period
      and the willingness of the temple to employ its bureaucratic apparatus to de-
      termine and suppress dissent" (Dennis Hirota, ed., *Toward a Contemporary
      Understanding of Pure Land Buddhism* [New York: State University of New York
      Press, 2000], p. 12. James Ketelaar describes the incident involving Ohama in
      Mikawa in the early Meiji period. A local Higashi Honganji priest, Tairei
      Ishikawa, was said to have instigated a riot, involving three to four thousand
      peasants and fifty-one priests, by opposing local bureaucrats who forced
      Shintō practices upon Shin Buddhists. Two priests, Ishikawa and his friend
      Hōtaku Hoshikawa, disagreed with the headquarters' suggestion to work with
      the local authorities. Eventually, the headquarters distanced itself from the
      Mikawa priests, and when local authorities suppressed the riot, Ishikawa was

executed. Sixteen years after Ishikawa's execution, both he and Hoshikawa were granted imperial pardons and elevated to the status of martyrs by the headquarters (*Of Heretics and Martyrs*, pp. 77–86).

40 "Rafu Bukkyōkai soshō jiken ryakuhō," *Beikoku bukkyō* 19, no. 7 (1918): p. 17.

41 "Izumida kōhan," *Rafu Shimpo*, June 5, 1918.

42 For instance, "Beikoku bukkyō," *Beikoku bukkyō* 4, no. 5 (1903): p. 21; and "Rafu bukkyōkai kaihō," *Beikoku bukkyō* 12, no. 3 (1911): pp. 28–29.

43 Izumida, "Zaibei gojūnen no kaiko 3," *Kashū Mainichi Shinbun*, April 11, 1949.

44 Izumida had further solicited financial help from headquarters, which instead gave him the honorary title of *shinju santō* on December 9, 1915 (BCA Archives P2 Box1). The affidavit of Kiyoshi Ono, on October 10, 1917, testifies that Izumida came to Los Angeles alone, without a letter of appointment by the Nishi Honganji headquarters. Ono's testimony includes information about Izumida's relationship with the BMNA.

45 Sonoda and Uchida graduated from Tokyo Imperial University (present-day Tokyo University), and Jisōji from Kyoto Imperial University (present-day Kyoto University) (*Buddhist Churches of America: A Legacy of the First 100 Years*, pp. iv–v).

46 Honkō Matsumoto, "Ikeru Izumida Junjō-shi no omoide 3," *Kashū Mainichi Shinbun*, December 4, 1951.

47 Telephone interview with Satoru Tsufura, third son of the late Shōsestu Tsufura, July 11, 2006.

48 Honkō Matsumoto, "Ikeru Izumida Junjō-shi no omoide 2," December 3, 1951, and "Ikeru Izumida Junjō-shi no omoide 3," December 4, 1951, *Kashū Mainichi Shinbun*.

49 Izumida, "Zaibei gojūnen no kaiko 79," *Kashū Mainichi Shinbun*, July 9, 1949.

50 Sei Fujii, "Watashi no ran," *Kashū Mainichi Shinbun*, November 27, 1951.

51 For the early propagation of Shingonshū in Los Angeles, see Payne, "Hiding in Plain Sight," pp. 101–22.

52 This story has been passed down in the Higashi Honganji Los Angeles Betsuin. This account is from the late Tsuyoshi Hirosumi, who served as its minister in Los Angeles for more than forty years.

53 "Kōkaijō," by Berkeley Bukkyōkai, June 27, 1925; "Berkeley bukkyōkai sonogo no keika hōkoku," by Berkeley Bukkyōkai, August 24, 1925; "Berkeley bukkyōkai keika hōkoku ni taisuru benmei," by those who requested the general meeting; "Rinsō yōkyū shuryōren no bakuron o hansu," by Berkeley Bukkyōkai, September 15, 1925; "Berkeley kanburen matohazure no chimayoikoto," by those who requested the general meeting, September 28, 1925; and "Kōkaijō," by the Construction Committee of Berkeley Hall and School, October 6, 1925 (BCA Archives, Subject Files, Box No. 1.03.11, Folder 1925–1926).

54 "Kōkaijō," by Berkeley Bukkyōkai, June 27, 1925; "Berkeley bukkyōkai sonogo no keika hōkoku," by Berkeley Bukkyōkai, August 24, 1925; "Berkeley bukkyōkai keika hōkoku ni taisuru benmei," by those who requested the general meeting; "Rinsō yōkyū shuryōren no bakuron o hansu," by Berkeley Bukkyōkai, September 15, 1925; "Berkeley kanburen matohazure no chimayoikoto," by those who requested the general meeting, September 28, 1925; and "Kōkaijō," by the Construction Committee of Berkeley Hall and School, October 6, 1925 (BCA Archives, Subject Files, Box No. 1.03.11, Folder 1925–1926).

55 Moriya, "California shū ni okeru bukkyōkai," p. 127; and *Berkeley Higashi Honganji 75th Anniversary 1926-2001*, pp. 16–17. For the newspaper accounts: "Berkeley no higashi honganji," *Nichibei Shinbun,* February 20, 1926; "Hokkai-shiki," *Nichibei Shinbun,* April 4, 1926; "Berkeley gakuen mondai," *Shinsekai,* January 31, 1926; "Berkeley bukkyōkai dai funkyū," *Shinsekai,* February 1, 1926; and "Shinbutsu katei shūkai," *Shinsekai,* June 9, 1926.

56 Yorizane Takashi's account, in an interview with two other members, Tadashi Kanemoto and James Goishi, September 23, 2006.

57 "About the separation of the Buddhist group in Parlier from Fresno Buddhist Church," correspondence from Masuyama to the Kyoto headquarters dated August 31, 1931 (BCA Archives, Correspondence Files, Box No. 1.02.06, Folder 1931). Accounts in the *Nichibei Shinbun* include "Nijūmei no iin o erabi sara ni Parlier ni kōshō," *Nichibei Shinbun,* August 25, 1931; "Parlier dokuritsu jiken chōtei iin," *Nichibei Shinbun,* August 26, 1931; "Parlier gawa iin to chōtei iin no kaiken," *Nichibei Shinbun,* August 30, 1931; "Kaikyōshi wa higashi honganji," *Nichibei Shinbun,* August 31, 1931; "Fu bukkai to Parlier to no kōshō danzetsu ni itaru made," *Nichibei Shinbun,* September 1, 1931; "Parlier to kōshō danzetsu," *Nichibei Shinbun,* September 4, 1931; and "Parlier dayori," *Nichibei Shinbun,* September 6, 1931.

58 Izumida's letter to Kiyoko Karaki, November 25, 1931 (BCA Archives, Correspondence Files, Box No. 1.02.06, Folder 1932 H–O).

59 Correspondence from Sasaki to Bishop Masuyama dated August 31 (BCA Archives, Correspondence Files, Box No. 1.02.06, Folder 1932 H–O).

60 "Parlier higashi honganji," *Kashū Mainichi Shinbun,* December 1, 1932; and "Parlier higashi honganji nyūbutsu shiki," *Chūgai Nippō*, March 25, 1933.

61 Yorizane Takashi's account from interview, September 23, 2006.

62 Accounts in the *Tairiku Nippō* include "Higashi honganji bukkyōkai setsuritsu," *Tairiku Nippō,* July 13, 1925; "Izumida-shi kōen," *Tairiku Nippō,* August 1, 1925; "Izumida-shi kōen, nishi dainigai de," *Tairiku Nippō,* August 5, 1925; "Mito kendo-shi," *Tairiku Nippō,* November 11, 1925; "Kinkoku," *Tairiku Nippō,* November 12, 1925; "Kinkoku," *Tairiku Nippō,* November 13, 1925; "Taga kaikyōshi raiban," *Tairiku Nippō,* November 26, 1925; and "Seidai na kangeikai," *Tairiku Nippō,* December 7, 1925.

63 Accounts in the Tairiku Nippō include "Ōtani-ha bukkyōkai," *Tairiku Nippō,* November 16, 1925; and "Ōtani-ha bukkyōkai," *Tairiku Nippō,* November 23, 1925.

64 Accounts in the *Tairiku Nippō* include "Kyōkai tayori," *Tairiku Nippō,* July 17, 1926; "Ōtani bukkyōkai hōe," *Tairiku Nippō,* August 7, 1926; "Ōtani bukkyōkai tayori," *Tairiku Nippō,* September 4, 1926; "Sakujitsu rainin shita Miura Shin kaikyōshi," *Tairiku Nippō,* October 5, 1926; and "Miura-shi sōbetsu kai," *Tairiku Nippō,* May 20, 1929.

65 Correspondence from Izumida to Miura dated May 23, 1929, kept at Ryōtokuji, a Higashi temple in Hikone, Shiga prefecture.

66 Jōryū Chiba, *Honganji shūkai hyakunenshi, shiryōhen,* 3 vols. (Kyoto: Jōdoshinshū Hongwanji-ha shūkai, 1983), vol. 3, pp. 365–56. In November 1930, Izumida established a second propagation center in Los Angeles at 38 Towne Avenue. Takahashi, "A Social Study of the Japanese Shinto and Buddhism," p. 123; and *Shinshū* (December 1930), p. 12. The Higashi headquarters appointed Shūken Yamanouchi to the propagation center on Towne Avenue in January 1931. He had been propagating in Denver ("Ōtani-ha no Denver shinshutsu," *Chūgai Nippō,* April 17, 1929). Yamanouchi later studied at Boston University and received an M.A. in 1933.

67 Hunter, *Buddhism in Hawaii,* p. 70; Tsunemitsu, *Hawai bukkyō shiwa,* pp. 124–25; and *Waimea Higashi Hongwanji Centennial Anniversary 1899-1999.*

68 Three priests from Kumamoto prefecture continued propagation in Kauai: Sueto Satō (1901–1910), Yuijō Kai (August 1909–April/May 1921), and Hōden Mashita (November 1910 or possibly May 1911–November 1928). Kai took charge of Makaweli, succeeding Sazanami, while Mashita supervised Waimea, taking over from Satō. *Shūmon kaikyō nenpyō,* pp. 27, 30, 37, 40, 67; and *Waimea Higashi Hongwanji Centennial Anniversary 1899-1999.* Also see *Shūhō* 92 (May 1909): p. 17. Reprint, *Shūhō,* vol. 5, p. 247; *Shūhō* 96 (September 1909): p. 28. Reprint, *Shūhō,* vol. 5, p. 326; *Shūhō* 107 (August 1910): p. 18. Reprint, *Shūhō,* vol. 6, p. 74; and *Shūhō* 236 (June 1921): p. 8. Reprint, *Shūhō,* vol. 11, p. 488.

69 A list of those who donated money for the temple bell in 1910 testifies to the diversity of the Waimea Higashi Honganji membership (*Waimea Higashi Hongwanji Centennial Anniversary 1899-1999*).

70 *Dōbō* 10, no. 12 (December 1909): p. 30.

71 Correspondence from Ōdate to Shimotsuma, Head of the Doctrinal Department of the Higashi Honganji headquarters, dated February 6, 1930. In the letter, Ōdate reported that the Makaweli propagation facility was rebuilt after a sugar company offered $5,000 for repairs. But the pressure from the Nishi was too strong for the Higashi ministers in that region to expand their territory. Ōdate's letter, kept at Tashiro Bunko, Ōtani University.

72 The Higashi expanded its operations with the arrival of two more ministers, Tenran Mōri and Hōun Tamayose, in 1920. Mōri resided at the Moiliili propagation

center (established in 1922), and later moved it to Palolo. Tamayose moved the Smith-Maunakea propagation center to 2132 Fern Street, Honolulu, and founded the McCully Higashi Honganji in 1936.

73 *Shūmon kaikyō nenpyō*, pp. 57, 119; and *Hilo Higashi Hongwanji Mission 75th Anniversary 1928-2003*.

74 Interview with Ryūken Izuhara and his wife, at Hōshōji, Hiroshima, November 8, 2006.

75 The early development of three of the six Buddhist schools in Hawaii are discussed by Naofumi Annaka, "Nichirenshū Mission in [the] Early Twentieth Century Hawaii: Findings from Its Early Documents in the 1910s"; Yoshifusa Asai, "Sōtōshū in Hawaii in the Early Twentieth Century"; and Joshin Washimi, "The Issei and the Jōdo Denomination in Hawaii during the 1920s: Research from the 'Propagation Records.'" All of these papers were presented at the Issei Buddhism Conference, Irvine, California, September, 2004.

76 Hunter, *Buddhism in Hawaii*, pp. 122, 164; and Yasuo Toda, "Report on the Federation of the YBA in Hawaii" (cited in Tsunemitsu, *Nihon bukkyō tobeishi*, p. 113). Japanese Buddhist clergy in Los Angeles also held trans-sectarian exchanges, though the Nishi Honganji did not take the initiative in these efforts. Leaders of the Sōtō, Nichiren, and Jōdo schools created the Association of Mahāyāna (Daijōkai) in 1924. During the celebration of Śākyamuni Buddha's birthday in 1935, four events were held at the Los Angeles Nishi Honganji Betsuin: a Japanese service, a cultural exhibition for Buddhist children and teenagers, an English service with a lecture and traditional dancing, and a Japanese sermon for adult attendees. It was not until after World War II that the Los Angeles Buddhist Church Federation was formed. See Tsunemitsu, *Nihon bukkyō tobeishi*, pp. 305-306; and the *Hanamatsuri* program dated April 7, 1935 (Los Angeles Honpa Honganji Buddhist Temple Archives, Folder Goldwater).

77 Matsuda, *Akegarasu Haya: Yo to tomo ni yo o koen*, vol. 1, pp. 15-16.

78 Matsuda, *Akegarasu Haya: Yo to tomo ni yo o koen*, vol. 1, p. 272.

79 Matsuda, *Akegarasu Haya: Yo to tomo ni yo o koen*, vol. 1, pp. 273-74.

80 Matsuda, *Akegarasu Haya: Yo to tomo ni yo o koen*, vol. 1, pp. 278-82.

81 Matsuda, *Akegarasu Haya: Yo to tomo ni yo o koen*, vol. 1, pp. 15-16.

82 Matsuda, *Akegarasu Haya: Yo to tomo ni yo o koen*, vol. 1, p. 17.

83 Matsuda, *Akegarasu Haya: Yo to tomo ni yo o koen*, vol. 2, pp. 21-24. Akegarasu's denial of morality reflected the finite nature of ethics as pointed out by Kiyozawa. Contrary to his own religious ideals, however, Kiyozawa was still a man of the Meiji era and respected Confucian ethics (Yoshida, *Nihon kindai bukkyōshi kenkyū*, pp. 312-13, 330-31). Akegarasu internalized faith by keeping it to himself and compromised spiritual principles with mundane rules. When the Ashio copper mine affair in Tochigi prefecture became a social

problem in the 1890s, he wrote an essay on the peasants who were suing the mining company:

> I met with Mr. Tanaka Shōzō and sympathized with him over the problem of contamination. I was however bothered when he said it took about five years for the victims to understand the concept of human rights. What I wanted to tell them was to give up their rights and be obedient. I don't understand why Mr. Tanaka and others explained the concept of human rights to them. As far as I'm concerned, suffering, whether they suffer or not, is not caused by the copper mine but by the mind of the individual.

Haya Akegarasu, "Fukujūron," *Seishinkai* 2, no. 4 (April 1902). Cited by Yukio Hisaki, *Kenshō Kiyozawa Manshi hihan* (Kyoto: Hōzōkan, 1995), pp. 147–48. Akegarasu passionately supported the Russo-Japanese War. In a "Letter to a Soldier Going Off to the Front Line" he wrote:

> [B]efore you defeat the enemy country, you must defeat the enemy in your heart: the voice that says 'I want to return alive.' You must consider this voice as the devil's temptation.... Please fight courageously and when you return ... come back as white bones.

Akegarasu, "Shussei gunjin ni atauru sho," *Seishinkai* 4, no. 4 (1904). Cited by Ama, "Towards a Shin Buddhist Social Ethics," p. 36.

84 Matsuda, *Akegarasu Haya: Yo to tomo ni yo o koen,* vol. 2, pp. 236–40, 244–48.

85 For instance, when the YMBA and YWBA sponsored Akegarasu's public lecture in Watsonville, approximately a hundred people gathered to listen to his Dharma talk ("Bukkyō shisōkai no shinjin, Akegarasu Haya-shi no kōen," *Nichibei Shinbun,* July 10, 1929). Akegarasu also spoke at the Vacaville Buddhist Church on July 10, the Stockton Buddhist Church on July 12, the Buddhist Temple of Alameda on July 14, and the Buddhist Church of Sacramento on July 17, 1929 ("Akegarasu Haya-shi bukkyō dai kōen," *Nichibei Shinbun,* July 10, 1929; "Akegarasu sensei no dai kōen," *Nichibei Shinbun,* July 13, 1929; and "Shaka wa sekai ichi no binan: Akegarasu Haya-shi no kōen," *Nichibei Shinbun,* July 18, 1929).

86 "Akegarasu-shi to daijōkai ga shinkō mondai de tōron," *Nichibei Shinbun,* July 4, 1929.

87 "Akegarasu-shi no kōenkai," *Nichibei Shinbun,* July 5, 1929; and "Rafu ni dekita Akegarasu kai," *Nichibei Shinbun,* July 7, 1929.

88 For instance, the monthly journal in Japanese published by the Seattle Buddhist Temple, *Butsu no oshie (The Teaching of Buddha)* 10, no. 8 (August 1913): pp. 8–13. For Akegarasu's tour in Hawaii in 1929, see *Hawaii Hōchi,* April 27, 1929; May 13, 1929; May 15, 1929; and May 16, 1929.

89 BCA Archives, Correspondence Files, Box No. 1.02.06, Folder 1932 H–O.

90 Matsuda, *Akegarasu Haya: Yo to tomo ni yo o koen,* vol. 2, pp. 237–38; *Buddhist Churches of America: A Legacy of the First 100 Years,* pp. 63–64; and interview with Akira Hata, April 25, 2006.

91 Kusuhara's report on the settlement of the Oakland Bukkyōkai dispute dated July 24, 1926 (BCA Archives, Correspondence Files, Box No. 1.02.02). The BMNA

office publicized Hata's transfer. "Ōfu bukkyōkai zen kaikyōshi Hata Taigan," *Shinsekai,* June 12, 1926.

92 "Iwayuru aigosha no ōi o hiraku," *Nichibei Shinbun,* June 28, 1926; and "Ofu bukkyōkai no shinsō ni tsuite kaiin shoshi ni tsugu," *Shinsekai,* June 26, 1926. Correspondence from Taigan Hata to the vice president of the BMNA office dated April 19, 1926 (BCA Archives, Chronological Files, Box No. 1.01.01, Folder 1926–1927).

93 "Ōfu bukkyōkai naisō enman ni kaiketsu su," *Nichibei Shinbun,* July 21, 1926.

94 BCA Archives, Correspondence Files, Box No. 1.02.05, Folder 1931.

95 Ogura, "A Sociological Study of Buddhism in North America," pp. 32–33.

96 On December 22, 1925, Ogura, then the resident minister of the Seattle Bukkyōkai, submitted his resignation to Kusuhara. In this correspondence, Ogura admonishes Kusuhara not to replace him with Hata, since Hata was a member of the Akegarasu "cult" and thus unsuitable for Seattle. Ogura actually wrote the name "Hatano," but since there was no minister by that name in the United States at the time, it is highly probable that this refers to Hata. (BCA Archives, Correspondence Files, Box No. 1.02.01, Folder 1925).

97 Correspondence from Taigan Hata to the vice president of the BMNA office dated April 19, 1926 (BCA Archives, Chronological Files, Box No. 1.01.01, Folder 1926–1927).

98 "Kōkoku: bukkyō no shinzui o kenkyū shitai mono wa hatashi no tokoro e ikubeshi," *Nichibei Shinbun,* July 8, 1926.

99 When Eishō Ōtani, a relative of the abbot of the Higashi Honganji, Shōnyo, came to the United States in 1911 to study at the University of Chicago, he visited the Buddhist Church of Sacramento and delivered a sermon on July 30. *Shūhō* 119 (August 1911): p. 11. Reprint, *Shūhō,* vol. 6, p. 481.

100 *Buddhist Churches of America: A Legacy of the First 100 Years,* pp. 177, 282–83. Telephone interview with Satoru Tsufura, July 11, 2006.

101 *Buddhist Churches of America: A Legacy of the First 100 Years,* p. 174. Information on Kubose's entry into the ministry comes from a Higashi Honganji headquarters' internal file.

102 "Chicago-shi chūshin ni eibunsho dendō," *Kashū Mainichi Shinbun,* April 4, 1949.

103 *Buddhist Churches of America: A Legacy of the First 100 Years,* p. 174; and http://www. brightdawn.org/history.htm.

104 In Memoriam, University of California, Los Angeles 1986; and interview with Toshi Ashikaga on March 29, 2006. Pioneer Shin priests had made attempts to found a Japanese library. For instance, books collected by Imamura and other Issei educators in Hawaii were donated to what is known as the "Imamura Bunko" at the University of Hawaii in 1941, though they are neither in one particular location nor extant *in toto* (Moriya, *Amerika bukkyō no tanjō,* pp. 128–29;

250, n. 88). Izumida also attempted to create a Japanese library in Los Angeles (Izumida, "Zaibei gojūnen no kaiko, 98," and "Zaibei gojūnen no kaiko, 99," *Kashū Mainichi Shinbun,* August 1 and August 3, 1949). Yurii Kyōgoku, Itsuzō Kyōgoku's first daughter, donated her father's books to the Ohio State University library (interview with Marii Hasegawa, April 3, 2004).

105 Three Nishi Honganji ministers studied at UCLA under Ashikaga: Arthur Takemoto, Tetsuo Unno, and Chūhō Matsubayashi (interview with Toshi Ashikaga, March 29, 2006). Concerning Ashikaga's article in the *Berkeley Bussei,* see Masatsugu, "Reorienting the Pure Land," pp. 161–62.

106 The *Shinshū sōden gisho* was serialized, and the Higashi Honganji began publishing it in 1978.

Chapter Seven: Local and Translocal Activities

1 In the 1930s, the BMNA participated in two more expositions, one held in San Diego in August 1935 and the 1939 Golden Gate International Exposition in San Francisco.

2 These religious groups, which emerged from the New Religions movement during the nineteenth century, were "all deeply involved in faith healing and the promotion of a very enthusiastic, evangelical spirituality." Helen Hardacre, *Shinto and the State 1868-1968* (Princeton, NJ: Princeton University Press, 1989), p. 71.

3 There might have been other cases in which Shin Buddhists were part of the composition of the Nikkei enclave and joined labor strikes in the mainland United States or Canada. But because of the lack of local records, this possibility has not been explored. It would have hardly been surprising if Shin Buddhists in British Columbia had participated in the series of fishing strikes during the 1920s. In Walnut Grove, California, Japanese immigrants pressed the Japanese Association of the United States to initiate a test case to contest the constitutionality of the Alien Land Laws of 1920 (Azuma, *Between Two Empires,* p. 70). From the early 1900s there were Shin immigrants to Walnut Grove (though the *bukkyōkai* was not formally organized until 1926), so it would be reasonable to speculate that they were involved in this movement.

4 Tsunemitsu, *Nihon bukkyō tobeishi,* pp. 51–52. For the program and a list of participants in the congress, see *Beikoku bukkyō* 16, no. 9 (September 1915): pp. 2–5.

5 There was some dissension between Ernest E. Power (secretary) and Mazzininanda (president) at the commencement of the congress ("Officer Resigns at Buddhist Congress," *San Francisco Chronicle,* August 3, 1915). Other than this, the *Chronicle* carried no other reports on the International Buddhist Congress.

6 *Beikoku bukkyō* 16, no. 9 (September 1915): p. 4.

7 *Beikoku bukkyō* 16, no. 9 (September 1915): pp. 4–5.

8   Official report of the BMNA (BCA Archives, Chronological Files, Box No. 1.01.01, Folder 1920).

9   The words "fifty million of Buddhists throughout the world" are crossed out and a handwritten notation has been inserted, which can be read either as "580" or "180" (BCA Archives, Chronological Files, Box No. 1.01.01, Folder 1920).

10   *Biography of Hioki mokusen* (*Hioki mokusen den*). Cited by Tsunemitsu, *Nihon bukkyō tobeishi,* pp. 64–65.

11   Son'yū Ōtani, "The Washington Conference from the Buddhist Point of View," *The Eastern Buddhist* 1, no. 4 (November/December 1921): pp. 261–62.

12   S. Ōtani, "The Washington Conference from the Buddhist Point of View," p. 263; and Kōen Ōtani, "The First Step Towards the Realization of World-Peace," *The Eastern Buddhist* 1, no. 4 (November/December 1921): p. 255.

13   The conference gave rise to three outcomes: the replacement of the Anglo-Japanese alliance with the recognition of the respective territories of the four world powers in the Pacific region (England, Japan, France, and the United States); Japan's withdrawal from Shandong and Siberia; and a reduction of battleships, including submarines, to a fixed quota over a ten-year period among these four nations plus Italy (Charles A. Beard and Mary R. Beard, *The Rise of American Civilization* [New York: The Macmillan Co., 1946], pp. 689–91). Although the Japanese clergy continued to hold or attend various Buddhist conventions, including ones in Sri Lanka and China, it is unclear whether or not they made urgent pacifist statements in English. For information on other Buddhist conferences, see, for instance, "Dai rokkai seiron bukkyō taikai," *Chūgai Nippō,* March 10, 1925; and "Tōa bukkyō taikai," *Chūgai Nippō,* July 19, 1925. In Japan, the first All-Japan Buddhist Congress was held in Kyoto in November 1928, the Second Congress in Nagoya in November 1929, and the Third Congress in Fukuoka in 1930. "Bukkyō to jūichi gatsu," *Shinshū* (November 1934), p. 15.

14   "Buddhist Extols Amity," *Los Angeles Times,* November 14, 1925.

15   Nisei Shin Buddhists in the Hawaiian Islands organized the first Pan Pacific YMBA Conference in Honolulu in 1930, and based on its resolution, Japanese Buddhists convened the Second Conference in Tokyo in 1934. The significance of these events should be discussed separately, but these conferences were primarily organized for young people, so they were not concerned with representing the affiliated orders. One aim was to remove sectarian barriers among Buddhists in Asia and promote world peace. In the first Pan Pacific YMBA Conference, delegates passed a resolution to spread peace from a Buddhist standpoint by holding lectures, selling books, and promoting through the media; sending Buddhist messages to organizations and conferences that would promote world peace; and establishing a special department designated to advance these plans within the International YBA Alliance (Tsunemitsu, *Nihon bukkyō tobeishi,* p. 85).

16 Honorary presidents were Jane Addams and former president Herbert Hoover. Vice presidents were Newton D. Baker, John Dewey, Glenn Frank, John A. Lapp, R. A. Millikan, Frank Murphy, Chester H. Rowell, and Mary E. Woolley. Presentation themes included "Poverty-amidst-Plenty—How to Cure It?", "The World Crisis and The Way Out," "Men and Machines—Which Shall Be Master?", "Non-Violence—A Key to World Peace," "Racial and Religious Persecution—How to Prevent it?", "How to Expand Patriotism Into World Consciousness," "Peace and Brotherhood as Taught by the World's Faiths," "How Faiths, in Fellowship, May Save Civilization," "How May Man Master Fear?", "Youth and the Future," "Disarmament," "Ideals for a New World Order," "Prohibition as My Faith Sees It," "After Death—What?", "Mahatma Gandhi," "Russia's Soviet Faith," and "How to Realize World Unity" (*A Special Number of Appreciation Magazine of the World Fellowship of Faiths*, pp. 2–3).

17 The Program for World Fellowship of Faiths in the Culminating Convention Period, kept in BCA Archives, Chronological Files, Box No. 1.01.03, Folder 1933. Also, the speeches and presentations of the Japanese delegates are included in *World Fellowship: Addresses and Messages by Leading Spokesmen of All Faiths, Races and Countries,* ed. Charles Frederick Weller (New York: Liveright Publishing, 1933). Three other scholars spoke on Japanese religion: Kenneth J. Saunders; Benkyo Shiio, Dean of Taishō University and professor of Waseda and Nihon Universities; and Ken Nakazawa, University of Southern California, Department of Oriental Culture.

18 Izumida, "Zaibei gojūnen no kaiko 84," *Kashū Mainichi Shinbun,* July 15, 1949.

19 Kenju Masuyama, "From Forty-One Million Buddhists," in *World Fellowship,* ed. Weller, p. 14.

20 Shozen Nakayama, "Six Million Japanese Followers of Tenrikyo," in *World Fellowship,* ed. Weller, p. 18.

21 Masuyama's correspondence to the Nishi Honganji headquarters and the Federation of Buddhist Schools in Japan dated October 8 and October 10, 1931, respectively (BCA Archives, Chronological Files, Box. No. 1.01.03, Folder 1933). In part due to the economic depression at the time and frequent social disturbances after World War I, the New Religions movement emerged in Japan. In 1927, there were sixty-five groups associated with Shintō, twenty-nine with Buddhism, and four with Christianity. The total number of these groups increased to four hundred and fourteen in 1930, and to one thousand and twenty-nine over the next five years. These groups first appeared in rural areas toward the end of the Edo period. However, by the 1930s, they had sprung up in big cities such as Tokyo and Osaka, as more people moved to metropolitan areas to look for jobs. In the case of Tenrikyō, for instance, the number of churches in Tokyo shot up from four hundred and eighteen in 1923 to seven hundred and fifty-four by 1926 (Kōmoto, ed., *Ronshū nihon bukkyōshi*, pp. 24–25).

22 Correspondence from Masuyama to the Nishi Honganji headquarters.

23 Masuyama, "From Forty-One Million Buddhists," p. 16.

24 Tansai Terakawa, "Buddhist Greetings from the West Hongwanji Buddhist Sect in Japan and America," in *World Fellowship,* ed. Weller, p. 31.

25 Nakayama, "Six Million Japanese Followers of Tenrikyo," p. 19.

26 Yoshiaki Fukuda, "Japan A Center of World Peace Problems," in *World Fellowship,* ed. Weller, p. 764.

27 Fukuda, "Japan A Center of World Peace Problems," pp. 768–69; Benkyo Shiio, "How Japan's Buddhism Leads Toward World Recovery," in *World Fellowship,* ed. Weller, p. 758; and Nitten Ishida, "Japan and Ho-Kwe-Kyo Are One," in *World Fellowship,* ed. Weller, p. 23.

28 Takashi Tsutsumi, *Hawai rōdō undōshi* (Honolulu: Hawai rōdō renmeikai honbu, 1921), pp. 60–61.

29 Okihiro, *Cane Fires,* p. 68; and Edward D. Beechert, *Working in Hawaii: A Labor History* (Honolulu: University of Hawai'i Press, 1985), pp. 197–98.

30 Tsutsumi, *Hawai rōdō undōshi,* pp. 10–11, 75–76; and John E. Reinecke, *Feigned Necessity: Hawaii's Attempt to Obtain Chinese Contract Labor, 1921-1923* (San Francisco: Chinese Materials Center, 1979), pp. 97–98. Beechert is mistaken in his monograph, cited by Okihiro, when he writes that the Young Men's Buddhist Association (YMBA) was responsible for the initial higher-wage movement. This should be corrected to "Young Men's Association," according to *The Pacific Commercial Advertiser,* also cited by Beechert. The former states, "The Japanese Young Men's Association is a non-religious organization composed of laborers and its members must be found on practically all island plantations." "Hawaii Japanese Meet to Draft Wage Demands," *The Pacific Commercial Advertiser,* October 19, 1919. Reinecke and Tsutsumi also point to the YMA, rather than the YMBA, in this higher-wage movement.

31 Tsutsumi, *Hawai rōdō undōshi,* p. 76.

32 Tsutsumi, *Hawai rōdō undōshi,* pp. 77–78.

33 Reinecke, *Feigned Necessity,* pp. 101–106.

34 Reinecke, *Feigned Necessity,* p. 106–110; Beechert, *Working in Hawaii,* pp. 201–204.

35 Beechert, *Working in Hawaii,* p. 204.

36 Reinecke, *Feigned Necessity,* p. 115.

37 Okihiro, *Cane Fires,* pp. 74–75.

38 Reinecke, *Feigned Necessity,* pp. 117, 137.

39 Beechert, *Working in Hawaii,* pp. 209, 214–15.

40 "Hawai rōdō mondai no kaiketsu, dekasegi konjō ga wazawai suru bukkyō no zento," *Chūgai Nippō,* August 21, 1920.

41 *A Grateful Past, A Promising Future,* pp. 46–47; Tsutsumi, *Hawai rōdō undōshi,* pp. 350–53, 388–89, 400; and Reinecke, *Feigned Necessity,* p. 133.

42   The Association of Japanese Christian Ministers petitioned the HSPA to make a positive reply to the workers on January 12, 1920. Both Buddhist and Christian clergy on Kauai sent a petition, dated January 29, 1921, to the HSPA and to Curtis Piehu Iaukea, Acting Governor (Tsutsumi, *Hawai rōdō undōshi*, pp. 244, 290–91).

43   Hunter, *Buddhism in Hawaii*, pp. 121–22.

44   Tsutsumi, *Hawai rōdō undōshi*, pp. 245–46. The statement was translated into English by Tsutsumi and published ("Priests Say Japanese to Strike," *The Pacific Commercial Advertiser*, January 24, 1920).

45   Kimura, *Issei: Japanese Immigrants in Hawaii*, p. 155.

46   Moriya, *Amerika bukkyō no tanjō*, pp. 118–119. The translation "true guests of Amida Buddha" comes from Noriko Asato, *Teaching Mikadoism: The Attack on Japanese Language Schools in Hawaii, California, and Washington, 1919-1924* (Honolulu: University of Hawai'i Press, 2005), p. 7.

47   This rhetoric is similar to the way in which Shinran identified himself with people in the lower levels of the social hierarchy, though the connection between those drafters of the petition and Shinran is unclear. Shinran writes, "Such peddlers, hunters, and others are none other than we, who are like stone and tiles and pebbles" (*CWS*, vol. 1, p. 459).

48   Winston Davis, *Japanese Religion and Society: Paradigms of Structure and Change* (Albany, NY: State University of New York Press, 1992), pp. 176–77.

49   Davis, *Japanese Religion and Society*, pp. 176–77. Also, Kyūichi Yoshida, *Nihon no kindai shakai to bukkyō* (Tokyo: Hyōronsha, 1970), pp. 212–15.

50   Moriya, *Amerika bukkyō no tanjō*, p. 119. For Enpuku's act of breaking the strike, see "Strike Situation Plainly Worries Japanese Press," *The Pacific Commercial Advertiser*, March 2, 1920; "Stern Measures Threatened for Strike Traitors," *The Pacific Commercial Advertiser*, March 3, 1920; and "Japanese Gather to Talk Strike," *The Pacific Commercial Advertiser*, March 8, 1920.

51   Record of the HHMH Ministers' Meeting, pp. 75–76.

52   Asato, *Teaching Mikadoism*, pp. 101–102.

53   Hawaii Hōchi, ed., *Hawai no nihongo gakuen ni kansuru shiso oyobi futai jiken* (Honolulu: Hawaii Hōchi, 1926), pp. 48–49. For G. M. Roberston, see John M. Van Dyke, *Who Owns the Crown Lands of Hawai'i?* (Honolulu: University of Hawai'i Press, 2007), pp. 79–84.

54   Okihiro, *Cane Fires*, pp. 130–31.

55   Okihiro, *Cane Fires*, pp. 133–34.

56   Asato, *Teaching Mikadoism*, p. 28.

57   Moriya, *Amerika bukkyō no tanjō*, pp. 192–93.

58   Imamura, *Beikoku no seishin to shūkyō no jiyū*, p. 34.

59　Tsuyoshi Nakano, "Hawai nikkei kyōdan no keisei to henyō," *Shūkyō kenkyū* 55 (1981): p. 61.

60　See Duncan R. Williams, "Complex Loyalties: Issei Buddhist Ministers during the Wartime Incarceration," *Pacific World,* 3rd ser., no. 5 (2003): pp. 255–74.

61　Utsuki, *The Shin Sect,* p. 40.

62　The Higashi Honganji had sided with the Tokugawa shogunate before the Meiji Restoration (1868); Kaishū Katsu, the *bakufu's* statesman, advocated Japan's alliance with Korea and China. In the meantime, the leaders of the Nishi Honganji cooperated with politicians from Chōshū domain (Yamaguchi prefecture), such as Takayoshi Kido, who stressed the development of domestic affairs (Akeshi Kiba and Atsuyoshi Keika, "Higashi honganji chūgoku fukkyōshi no kisoteki kenkyū," *Ōtani daigaku shinshū sōgō kenkyūsho kiyō* 5 [1987]: pp. 10–11).

63　Akeshi Kiba, "Manshū ni okeru Ōtani-ha kaikyō," in Kojima and Kiba, eds., *Asia no kaikyō to kyōiku,* pp. 90–93, 134.

64　Masaru Kojima, "Chōsen ni okeru kaikyō, Honganji-ha chōsen kaikyō eno hottan," in Kojima and Kiba, eds., *Asia no kaikyō to kyōiku,* pp. 149, 151; "Kaigai kaikyō to kyōiku jigyō," in Kojima and Kiba, eds., *Asia no kaikyō to kyōiku,* p. 15; and Kiba, "Manshū ni okeru Ōtani-ha kaikyō," p. 92.

65　Masaru Takahashi, "Chōsen ni okeru kaikyō, meiji ni okeru kaikyō to shūkyō seisaku—Ōtani-ha o chūshin toshite, " in Kojima and Kiba, eds., *Asia no kaikyō to kyōiku,* pp. 137–40; and Masaru Kojima, "Chōsen ni okeru kaikyō, Honganji-ha chōsen kaikyō eno hottan," in Kojima and Kiba, eds., *Asia no kaikyō to kyōiku,* pp. 51–53.

66　Kiba and Keika, *Ōtani daigaku shinshū sōgō kenkyūsho kiyō* 5 (1987): pp. 4, 22–23.

67　Staff officers led by Kanji Ishihara of the Kwangtung Army, stationed in southern Manchuria, plotted to take over China's three northeastern provinces (commonly known as Manchuria) by military force. This incident led to the beginning of Japan's Fifteen-Year War, including the China War (1937–1945) and the Pacific War (1941–1945). Wm. Theodore de Barry, Carol Gluck, and Arthur E. Tiedemann, eds., *Sources of Japanese Tradition 1600 to 2000,* vol. 2: *1868 to 2000* (New York: Columbia University Press, 2005), p. 294; W. Miles Fletcher III, "The Fifteen-Year War, " in *A Companion to Japanese History,* ed. William M. Tsutsui (Hoboken, NJ: Wiley-Blackwell, 2009), p. 241.

68　Akeshi Kiba, "Kaikyō: Kokui kakuchō ni taiō shita kaigai kaikyō jigyō," in *Shūmon kindaishi no kenshō* (Kyoto: Shinshū Ōtani-ha, 2003), pp. 145–46, 151. By 1944, Shingonshū had established forty propagation centers in northern China, Sōtōshū had thirty-seven, Nichirenshū had thirty-four, and Jōdoshū had twenty-eight.

69　Kojima, "Kaigai kaikyō to kyōiku jigyō," p. 15; Michiko Hattori, "Hokkaidō kaitaku to higashi honganji: fukyōken no kakuritsu o motomete," *Shindō* 8

(1989): p. 77; and Akeshi Kiba, "Shinshū no hoppō kaikyō: Kuriru (Chishima) chiiki ni okeru shinshū ōtani-ha no kōdō," *Indo tetsugaku bukkyōgaku* 8 (1993): p. 275.

70 Masao Arimoto, *Shinshū no shūkyō shakaishi* (Tokyo: Yoshikawa kōbundō, 1995), pp. 255–56.

71 Hattori, "Hokkaidō kaitaku to higashi honganji," pp. 79, 104.

72 *Honganjishi,* vol. 3, pp. 359–61.

73 Kiba, "Shinshū no hoppō kaikyō," pp. 283–85. Ketelaar also mentions Higashi Honganji's propagation in Hokkaidō (*Of Heretics and Martyrs,* pp. 68–69).

74 The Meiji government lifted the ban on the propagation of Shin Buddhism in Kagoshima in 1876 (propagation had been proscribed by the Satsuma domain). *Honganjishi,* vol. 3, p. 355.

75 *Shūmon kaikyō nenpyō,* pp. 58, 68, 72, 76, 94.

76 Kojima, "Kaigai kaikyō to kyōiku jigyō," p. 15.

77 "Nishi honganji no nanbei kaikyō shippai," *Chūgai Nippō,* August 20, 1925; and "Butsuzō to kyōten shoji no tameni nanbei imin tokō kinshi," *Chūgai Nippō,* August 22, 1933.

78 Correspondence from Masuyama to the Kyoto headquarters dated December 8, 1930 (BCA Archives, Correspondence Files, Box No. 1.02.04, Folder 1930).

79 Izumida, "Zaibei gojūnen no kaiko 82," *Kashū Mainichi Shinbun,* July 13, 1949.

80 For instance, Seki wrote a record concerning providing support for his countrymen in Mexico, dated May 27, 1921 (BCA Archives, Correspondence Files, Box No. 1.02.06, Folder 1932 H–O).

81 *Nembutsu seizan: Oshū nembutsu denpa shōshi,* ed. Kokusai bukkyō bunka kyōkai (Kyoto: Nagata bunshodō, 2000), pp. 6, 10. Guimet was known for collecting Japanese art, such as *ukiyoe,* which is now kept at Musée Guimet in Paris.

82 Kentoku Hori, "Buddhist Association in Germany," *The Light of Dharma* 6, no. 1 (January 1907): pp. 16–19. Concerning Ōsumi, see *Shūhō* 248 (June 1922): p. 17. Reprint, *Shūhō,* vol. 12, p. 171.

83 *Buddhist Churches of America: A Legacy of the First 100 Years,* pp. 84–85, 88.

84 *Biographical History of Hawaii Hongwanji Ministers,* pp. 15, 18, 20, 25.

85 *Shūmon kaikyō nenpyō,* p. 92.

86 Correspondence from Masuyama to the president of the Southern Manchurian Railway Company dated October 28, 1933; correspondence from Masuyama to the Kyoto headquarters dated June 8, 1934; and correspondence from Masuyama to the president of the Southern Manchurian Railway Company dated January 12, 1934 (BCA Archives, Correspondence Files, Box No. 1.02.09, Folder 1933–1934).

87   Documents regarding Mikami's visit (BCA Archives, Chronological Files, Box No. 1.01.04, Folder 1938); and the record of sending Shōzen Naitō to China (BCA Archives, Chronological Files, Box No. 1.01.04, Folder 1939). See also *Buddhist Churches of America: A Legacy of the First 100 Years,* pp. 95, 102.

88   BCA Archives, Chronological Files, Box No. 1.01.04, Folder 1938, 1939; and Ikuta, *Kanada bukkyōkai enkakushi,* p. 80.

89   *Shinshū* (November 1937): p. 11; and *Shinshū* (January 1941): p. 17.

90   Kodama, *Kinsei shinshū to chiiki shakai,* pp. 162–69, 174–75.

91   Shigeki Izumi's study led to Takagi's reinstatement after more than eighty years of excommunication.

92   Kōshō Bekki, "Rekishi no yami o mitsumete: Taigyaku jiken to bukkyōsha tachi," *Shindō* 17 (1998): pp. 136–38; and Shigeki Izumi, "Takagi Kenmyō to buraku sabetsu mondai (1): Shōsestu kano sō ni mirareru Kenmyō no hisa-betsu buraku kan," *Ōtani Gakuhō,* no. 1 (1999): pp. 22–23. A group of Buddhists were rounded up and executed in a government conspiracy aimed at elimi-nating socialists. They were Gudō Uchiyama of the Sōtōshū, Setsudō Mineo of the Rinzaishū Myōshinji-ha, and Heishirō Naruishi, a Shin Buddhist layman. Uchiyama and Naruishi were executed along with Shusui Kōtoku and others, and the three Buddhist orders to which they belonged defrocked them (Bekki, "Rekishi no yami o mitsumete," pp. 136–38).

93   Ama, "Towards a Shin Buddhist Social Ethics," p. 50.

Conclusion: Rethinking Acculturation

1   Shinran, *Kyōgyōshinshō,* in *CWS,* vol. 1, p. 291.

2   For the discussion of the economic ethics of Shin Buddhist merchants, see Robert N. Bellah, *Tokugawa Religion: The Cultural Roots of Modern Japan* (1957) (New York: The Free Press, 1985, reprint), pp. 117–26.

3   Cited and discussed by John H. Simpson, "Religion as Identity and Contesta-tion," in *Religion, Globalization, and Culture,* ed. Peter Beyer and Lori Beaman (Leiden, The Netherlands: Brill, 2007), pp. 122, 135. Simpson does not quote from Luhmann. He writes:

> But communication according to Luhmann is not simply the transmission and receipt of a message, a gesture or linguistic event that evokes a response. Communication is a process of selection and, thereby, a process of rejection or leaving something (known or unknown) aside.

In the footnote, Simpson refers to Niklas Luhmann's *Social Systems* (Stanford, CA: Stanford University Press, 1995), pp. 137–75.

4   Michael Masatsugu, "Reorienting the Pure Land," p. 1.

5   Mark T. Unno, "The Voice of Sacred Texts in the Ocean of Compassion: The Case of Shin Buddhism in America," *Pacific World,* 3rd ser., no. 5 (2003): pp. 301, 303.

6   Unno, "The Voice of Sacred Texts in the Ocean of Compassion," pp. 304–305.

7   Yuki Miyamoto, "Rebirth in the Pure Land or God's Sacrificial Lambs? Religious Interpretations of the Atomic Bombings in Hiroshima and Nagasaki," *Japanese Journal of Religious Studies* 32, no. 1 (2005): pp. 153–54.

8   *Tannishō,* in *CWS,* vol. 1, p. 671. In the thirteenth chapter of the *Tannishō* (pp. 670–71), Shinran and Yuien, one of his closest followers, have the following exchange:

> Further, the Master once asked, "Yuien-bō, do you accept all that I say?"
>
> "Yes, I do," I answered.
>
> "Then will you not deviate from whatever I tell you?" he repeated. I humbly affirmed this.
>
> Thereupon he said, "Now, I want you to kill a thousand people. If you do, you will definitely attain birth."
>
> I responded, "Though you instruct me thus, I'm afraid it is not in my power to kill even one person."
>
> "Then why did you say that you would follow whatever I told you?"
>
> He continued, "By this you should realize that if we could always act as we wished, then when I told you to kill a thousand people in order to attain birth, you should have immediately done so. But since you lack the karmic cause inducing you to kill even a single person, you do not kill. It is not that you do not kill because your heart is good. In the same way, a person may wish not to harm anyone and yet end up killing a hundred or a thousand people."

9   Miyamoto, "Rebirth in the Pure Land or God's Sacrificial Lambs?", p. 153.

10   Miyamoto, "Rebirth in the Pure Land or God's Sacrificial Lambs?", p. 153.

References

Unpublished Sources

Manuscript Materials

Japanese American National Museum, Los Angeles
    BCA Archives, Record Group 1 Buddhist Mission of North America, 1899–1944

Series 1: Chronological Files (Boxes 1.01.01–1.01.08)
    Undated (1 folder)
    1900–1919 (3 folders)
    1920s (15 folders)
    1930s (32 folders)
    1940s (52 folders)

Series 2: Correspondence (Boxes 1.02.01–1.02.12)
    1900–1919 (2 folders)
    1920s (30 folders)
    1930s (64 folders)
    1940s (23 folders)

Series 3: Subject Files (Boxes 1.03.01–1.03.14)
    Commission of Immigration (4 folders)
    Diaries and Records of Communication (1 oversize box)
    Gojikai (2 folders and 1 oversize box)
    Meetings and Conferences (33 folders)
    Ohtani family (6 folders)
    Special Dharma Lecture Tour (4 folders)
    Stupa (12 folders)
    Sunday School (19 folders)
    Temple by-laws (1 folder)
    Temple rosters (4 folders)
    Temple status reports (19 folders)

Series 4: Financial Records (Boxes 1.04)

Series 5: Publications (Boxes 1.05)
    Buddhism in America
    Light of Dharma (Box 1.05.01)
        vol. 1, nos. 1–6 1901–1902 (bimonthly)
        vol. 2, nos. 1–6 1902–1903 (bimonthly)
        vol. 3, nos. 1–4 1903–1904 (quarterly)

vol. 4, nos. 1–4 1904–1905 (quarterly)

vol. 5, nos. 1–4 1905–1906 (quarterly)

vol. 6, nos. 1–3 1907 (quarterly)

Collected Publications

Los Angeles Honpa Hongwanji Buddhist Temple Archives
Folders 1947 and 1948
Goldwater (1 folder)

Ōtani University, Tashiro Bunko

Seattle Betsuin Buddhist Temple Archives
Cross-indexed Card Files

Special Collections

Center for Labor Education and Research, University of Hawai'i—West Oahu
Waialua Strike File

Japanese American Research Project Collections, University of California, Los
Angeles

Collection 2010, Box 295 and Other type Oversize Package No. 91, "III. Organizational Records and Papers; D. Prewar Japanese Religious Organizations;
2. Publications By or Relating to Prewar Religious Organizations; 2.2 Books,
booklets, and pamphlets published by or relating to religious organizations."

Collection 2010, Box 329, "IV. Japanese Language Schools and Education of
the Second Generation; 3. Books Relating to the Japanese Language Schools in
America and the Education of the Second Generation; 3.4."

Japanese Canadian Research Collections, University of British Columbia

Kitsilano bukkyō seinenkai. *Butsuda sōritsu jisshūnen kinen tokushūgō.* Vancouver:
Kitsilano bukkyō seinenkai, 1935.

Fairview bukkyō seinenkai. *Otakebi.* Vancouver: Uchida shoten, 1930.

Hawaii War Records Depository, Special Collections, University of Hawai'i,
Manoa Library
Interview with Reverend H. Hunt by Mrs. Culver, File "Buddhist."

Tokyo Daigaku Shūkyōgaku kenkyūshitsu
Kaikyōshi kaigi gijiroku. Recorded at Hompa Hongwanji Mission of Hawaii
(copy).

Public Records

Los Angeles Superior Court Archives
Jisōji v. Izumida, Case #B55497 (1918)
Izumida v. L. A. Morning Sun, Case #B57794 (1918)

"The Articles of Incorporation of the Buddhist Church of San Francisco, July 9,
1913." Secretary of State, California State Archives Records, File No. 73813.

"The Constitution and By-laws of the Honpa Hongwanji Mission of Hawaii."
Hawaii Department of Commerce and Consumer Affairs, Business
Registration Division Records, Exhibit C, October 1, 1907. File No. 662 D2.

Author's Interviews

Reverend Arthur Takemoto, October 16, 2001.
George Teraoka, November 6, 2001.
Dr. Ryō Munekata, March 29, 2004.
Mari Hasegawa, April 3, 2004.
Toshi Ashikaga, March 29, 2006.
Reverend Akira Hata, April 25, 2006.
Satoru Tsufura, July 11, 2006.
Takashi Yorizane, September 23, 2006.
Reverend Ryūken Izuhara and Kiko Izuhara, November 8, 2006.
Bishop Chikai Yosemori, January 30, 2007.
Tōmei Akegarasu, February 1, 2007.

Newspapers and Periodicals

Buddhist Journals

Beikoku bukkyō (San Francisco), 1899(?)–1918(?)
Bhratri (San Francisco), 1934(?)–?
Butsu no oshie (*The Teaching of Buddha*), Seattle Buddhist Temple, 1904–1926(?)
Butsuda (Vancouver), 1935
Dōbō (Honolulu), 1901(?)–1912(?)
Jikishin (Fresno), 1945–1953
Light of Dharma (San Francisco), 1901–1907
Otakebi (Vancouver), 1930
Rafu Bukkyō (Los Angeles), 1907–1911(?)
The Eastern Buddhist (Kyoto), 1921–1958 (original series)
The Hawaiian Buddhist Annual (Honolulu), 1930–1932
The Young East (Tokyo), 1925
Tri-Ratna (Fresno), 1945(?)–1953

Time Magazine

"Bones of Buddha" (September 1935).
"Teiun" (May 1936).

Japanese-language Newspapers

Hawai Hōchi (Honolulu), 1925
"Honganji betsuin de eidoku dōmei no kekkonshiki," *Hawai Hōchi,* October 16,
1925.

Kashū Mainichi Shinbun (Los Angeles), 1932, [1935], 1949, 1951
"Beijin tachi ga otera e sankei," *Kashū Mainichi Shinbun,* February 16, 1935.
"Chicago-shi chūshin ni eibunsho dendō," *Kashū Mainichi Shinbun,* April 4, 1949.
Fujii, Sei. "Watashi no ran," *Kashū Mainichi Shinbun,* November 27, 1951.
Izumida, Junjō. "Zaibei gojūnen no kaiko" ("The Memoirs of Fifty Years in the
United States"), serialized in 137 parts in *Kashū Mainichi Shinbun,* April 8–
September 17, 1949. (See also Izumida under Selected Primary Sources.)
Matsumoto, Honkō. "Ikeru Izumida Junjō-shi no omoide 2" and "Ikeru
Izumida Junjō-shi no omoide 3,"*Kashū Mainichi Shinbun,* December 3, 1951.
"Parlier higashi honganji," *Kashū Mainichi Shinbun,* December 1, 1932.

Nichibei Shinbun (San Francisco), 1926, 1929, 1931
"Akegarasu Haya-shi bukkyō dai kōen," *Nichibei Shinbun,* July 10, 1929.
"Akegarasu sensei no dai kōen," *Nichibei Shinbun,* July 13, 1929.
"Akegarasu-shi no kōenkai," *Nichibei Shinbun,* July 5, 1929.
"Akegarasu-shi to daijōkai ga shinkō mondai de tōron," *Nichibei Shinbun,* July
4, 1929.
"Berkeley no higashi honganji," *Nichibei Shinbun,* February 20, 1926.
"Bukkyō shisōkai no shinjin, Akegarasu Haya-shi no kōen," *Nichibei Shinbun,*
July 10, 1929.
"Fu bukkai to Parlier to no kōshō danzetsu ni itaru made," *Nichibei Shinbun,*
September 1, 1931.
"Hokkaishiki," *Nichibei Shinbun,* April 4, 1926.
"Iwayuru aigosha no ōi o hiraku," *Nichibei Shinbun,* June 28, 1926.
"Kaikyōshi wa higashi honganji," *Nichibei Shinbun,* August 31, 1931.
"Kōkoku: bukkyō no shinzui o kenkyū shitai mono wa hatashi no tokoro e
ikubeshi," *Nichibei Shinbun,* July 8, 1926.
"Nijūmei no iin o erabi sara ni Parlier ni kōshō," *Nichibei Shinbun,* August 25, 1931.
"Ōfu bukkyōkai naisō enman ni kaiketsu su," *Nichibei Shinbun,* July 21, 1926.
"Parlier dayori," *Nichibei Shinbun,* September 6, 1931.
"Parlier dokuritsu jiken chōtei iin," *Nichibei Shinbun,* August 26, 1931.
"Parlier gawa iin to chōtei iin no kaiken," *Nichibei Shinbun,* August 30, 1931.
"Parlier to kōshō danzetsu," *Nichibei Shinbun,* September 4, 1931.
"Rafu ni dekita Akegarasu kai," *Nichibei Shinbun,* July 7, 1929.
"Shaka wa sekai ichi no binan: Akegarasu Haya-shi no kōen," *Nichibei Shinbun,*
July 18, 1929.

Rafu Shimpo (Los Angeles), 1916–1919, 1929, 1936
"Bonsan to kisha o nose demo hikō," *Rafu Shimpo,* September 17, 1936.
"Bukkyōkai soshō iyoiyo rakuchaku," *Rafu Shimpo,* September 29, 1916.
"Bukkyōkai soshō jiken chōtei," *Rafu Shimpo,* September 27, 1916.
"Butsu no jihi o nosete heiwagō sōte e," *Rafu Shimpo,* September 18, 1936.
"Chojin-Takemoto Plane Leaves on Flight to East," *Rafu Shimpo,* September 19, 1936.
"Chūbutsu butsudan tōchaku," *Rafu Shimpo,* March 27, 1918.
"Chūbutsu fujin kaigi," *Rafu Shimpo,* May 19, 1918.

"Chūbutsu no rinji sōkai," *Rafu Shimpo,* August 14, 1917.

"Chūō bukkyōkai no gōdō hantai kettei," *Rafu Shimpo,* October 6, 1917.

"Fukumaden no ōsōji, izumida junjō o hōmure, rafu bukkyōkai o sukue," *Rafu Shimpo,* September, 14, 1917.

"Gōdō ni kanshite," *Rafu Shimpo,* August 25, 1917.

"Gogo kara no higi jiken kōhan," *Rafu Shimpo,* August 2, 1918.

"Haitoku fushin no kaikyōshi izumida junjō," *Rafu Shimpo,* September 15, 1917.

"Haraguchi-shi kaishoku saru," *Rafu Shimpo,* October 10, 1917.

"Ihōsha no songai yōkyū hitoshi," *Rafu Shimpo,* August 16, 1918.

"Izumida hibō saiban," *Rafu Shimpo,* June 29, 1918.

"Izumida kōhan," *Rafu Shimpo,* June 5, 1918.

"Izumida-shi ni chūkoku mōsu, *Rafu Shimpo,* September 15, 1917.

"Izumida sōseki hakudatsu," *Rafu Shimpo,* January 7, 1919.

"Izumida tachinoki saiban: hikoku shōso to naru," *Rafu Shimpo,* June 11, 1918.

"Nanbukkai no sōkai," *Rafu Shimpo,* August 28, 1917.

"Negaeri utta izumida junjō-shi," *Rafu Shimpo,* September 11, 1917.

"Omoshirokatta gogo no kōhan," *Rafu Shimpo,* August 3, 1918.

"Rabutsu nishi kara higashi e utsuru," *Rafu Shimpo,* December 13, 1919.

"Rafu bukkyōkai no chōsa," *Rafu Shimpo,* September 22, 1916.

"Ranbō rōzeki naru rafu bukkyōkai yakuin kai," *Rafu Shimpo,* September 19, 1916.

"Sakan naru honganji bukkyōkai nyūbutsu shiki," *Rafu Shimpo,* December 9, 1917.

"San bukkyōkai gōdō seishiki ni seiritsu su," *Rafu Shimpo,* September 30, 1917.

"Sanbutsu gōdō mondai," *Rafu Shimpo,* August 21, 1917.

"Sawada kaikyōshi no jinin no shinsō," *Rafu Shimpo,* July 4, July 6, July 7, and July 10, 1929.

"Shinshū shozoku san bukkyōkai gōdō kettei," *Rafu Shimpo,* September 5, 1917.

"Sonoda shi no hōkoku," *Rafu Shimpo,* February 24, 1918.

"Sōseki hakudatsu tsūchō," *Rafu Shimpo,* August 6, 1919.

"Zaibei bukkyō no nade bussho zōtei," *Rafu Shimpo,* September 12, 1936.

Shinsekai (San Francisco), 1926

"Berkeley bukkyōkai dai funkyū," *Shinsekai,* February 1, 1926.

"Berkeley gakuen mondai," *Shinsekai,* January 31, 1926.

"Ōfu bukkyōkai no shinsō ni tsuite kaiin shoshi ni tsugu," *Shinsekai,* June 26, 1926.

"Ōfu bukkyōkai zen kaikyōshi Hata Taigan," *Shinsekai,* June 12, 1926.

"Shinbutsu katei shūkai," *Shinsekai,* June 9, 1926.

Tairiku Nippō (Vancouver), 1925, 1926, 1929

"Eiyaku sareta Mandala," *Tairiku Nippō,* June 24, 1926.

"Higashi honganji bukkyōkai setsuritsu," *Tairiku Nippō,* July 13, 1925.

"Izumida-shi kōen," *Tairiku Nippō,* August 1, 1925.

"Izumida-shi kōen, nishi dainigai de," *Tairiku Nippō,* August 5, 1925.

"Kinkoku," *Tairiku Nippō,* November 12, 1925.

"Kinkoku," *Tairiku Nippō,* November 13, 1925.

"Kyōkai tayori," *Tairiku Nippō,* July 17, 1926.

"Mito kendo-shi," *Tairiku Nippō,* November 11, 1925.

"Miura-shi sōbetsu kai," *Tairiku Nippō,* May 20, 1929.

"Ōtani bukkyōkai hōe," *Tairiku Nippō,* August 7, 1926.

"Ōtani bukkyōkai tayori," *Tairiku Nippō,* September 4, 1926.

"Ōtani-ha bukkyōkai," *Tairiku Nippō,* November 16, 1925.

"Ōtani-ha bukkyōkai," *Tairiku Nippō,* November 23, 1925.

"Sakujitsu rainin shita Miura Shin kaikyōshi," *Tairiku Nippō,* October 5, 1926.

"Seidai na kangeikai," *Tairiku Nippō,* December 7, 1925.

"Shinan no kokudō fuku de sonyū-shi ga teitōshiki," *Tairiku Nippō,* October 8, 1925.

"Taga kaikyōshi raiban," *Tairiku Nippō,* November 26, 1925.

English-language Newspapers

Los Angeles Times, 1916, 1925, 1934, 1935

"Buddhist Extols Amity," *Los Angeles Times,* November 14, 1925.

"Buddhist Service," *Los Angeles Times,* September 30, 1934.

"Buddhist Service," *Los Angeles Times,* March 24, 1935.

"Buddhists Ordain American S. A. Goldwaite [*sic*] Enters Priesthood Here,"
Los Angeles Times, June 18, 1934, Part II.

"Commemorate Buddha's Day," *Los Angeles Times,* May 20, 1916, part L.

San Francisco Chronicle, 1899, 1915

"Missionaries of the Buddhist Faith. Two Representatives of the Ancient Creed Are
in San Francisco to Proselyte [*sic*]," *San Francisco Chronicle,* September 13, 1899.

"Officer Resigns at Buddhist Congress," *San Francisco Chronicle,* August 3, 1915.

"They Teach the Buddhist Faith," *San Francisco Chronicle,* September 12, 1899.

The Hawaii Herald, 1969

Hotta, Barbara. "Ordeals of First Japanese Immigrants Retold in Buddhist
Publication," July 10, 1969.

The New Canadians, 1939, 1941

"Bussei, Carry on! National Meet Impresses Localites," *The New Canadians,*
May 2, 1941.

"Bussei Conference," *The New Canadians,* October 31, 1941.

"Canada Young Buddhist League," *The New Canadians,* May 27, 1939.

"Nisei Priest at Hompa Service," *The New Canadians,* November 21, 1941.

"Nisei Priest is Welcomed at Banquet," *The New Canadians,* November 7, 1941.

"Tenth Anniversary Conference of the North American Federation of the
YWBA Leagues, July 21–25, 1936," *The New Canadians,* May 27, 1939.

The Pacific Commercial Advertiser, 1919, 1920

"Hawaii Japanese Meet to Draft Wage Demands," *The Pacific Commercial
Advertiser,* October 19, 1919.

"Japanese Gather to Talk Strike," *The Pacific Commercial Advertiser,* March 8, 1920.

"Priests Say Japanese to Strike," *The Pacific Commercial Advertiser,* January 24,
1920.

"Stern Measures Threatened for Strike Traitors," *The Pacific Commercial Advertiser,* March 3, 1920.

"Strike Situation Plainly Worries Japanese Press," *The Pacific Commercial Advertiser,* March 2, 1920.

The San Diego Sun, 1936

"An American, Who Studied Buddhism in a Tibetan Lamasery, Priest in S.D. Temple," *The San Diego Sun,* July 5, 1936.

The Tacoma Times, 1936

"To Be First Buddhist Priestess," *The Tacoma Times,* April 22, 1936.

The Yakima Daily Republic (Washington), 1936

"Conversion Work of Yakima Man," *The Yakima Daily Republic,* May 2, 1936.

Newspapers Published in Japan

Bunka Jihō, 1935

"Gaijin ni bukkyō o rikai saseru tame konponteki na bussho honyaku ni jōshutsu su," *Bunka Jihō,* May 9, 1935.

"Hakujin ni yomaseru eiyaku no seiten kankō," *Bunka Jihō,* May 3, 1935.

"Honpa hawai kyōdan de keimu kyōkai jigyō," *Bunka Jihō,* December 17, 1935.

"Honpa rafu betsuin no fusai mondai kaiketsu," *Bunka Jihō,* July 27, 1935.

"Rafu mondai mo junchō ni susumu: Sasaki rinban kinin," *Bunka Jihō,* August 17, 1935.

"Seiten honyaku no jigyō ni tōkyoku mo ryōkai sareta," *Bunka Jihō,* May 18, 1935.

"Watashi no hakujin kyōka no hōshin," *Bunka Jihō,* April 9, 1935.

Chūgai Nippō (Kyoto), 1920, 1925, [1927,] 1929, 1931, 1933

"Bukkyō shinshū shōkai sho," *Chūgai Nippō,* January 8, 1933.

"Butsuzō to kyōten shoji no tameni nanbei imin tokō kinshi," *Chūgai Nippō,* August 22, 1933.

"Dai rokkai seiron bukkyō taikai," *Chūgai Nippō,* March 10, 1925.

"Dendō seishin no ketsunyo ga gaijin dendō fushin no geiin," *Chūgai Nippō,* July 26, 1925.

"Hawai nishihonganji kyōdan Imamura sochō no ato," *Chūgai Nippō,* January 22, 1933.

"Hawai no ryūgakusei," *Chūgai Nippō,* April 9, 1927.

"Hawai rōdō mondai no kaiketsu, dekasegi konjō ga wazawai suru bukkyō no zento," *Chūgai Nippō,* August 21, 1920.

"Hawai ryūgakusei no tokudo," *Chūgai Nippō,* October 8, 1931.

"Honpa saisho no hokubei betsuin ga dekiru," *Chūgai Nippō,* October 9, 1931.

"Izumida junjō-shi no Vancouver iri," *Chūgai Nippō,* September 19, 1925.

Nakai, Gendō. "Beikoku bukkyōkai no kiki (1)" and "Beikoku bukkyōkai no kiki (2)," *Chūgai Nippō,* September 10–11, 1925.

"Nikkei beijin ya minkokujin ga honpa sōryo ni naru benpō no naiki ga dekiru," *Chūgai Nippō,* October 10, 1931.

"Nishi-ha beikoku senden no tōitsu," *Chūgai Nippō*, September 4, 1920.

"Nishi honganji no nanbei kaikyō shippai," *Chūgai Nippō*, August 20, 1925.

"Ōtani-ha no Denver shinshutsu," *Chūgai Nippō*, April 17, 1929.

"Parlier higashi honganji nyūbutsu shiki," *Chūgai Nippō*, March 25, 1933.

"Tōa bukkyō taikai," *Chūgai Nippō*, July 19, 1925.

Internal Bulletins

Shinshū Ōtani-ha (Higashi Honganji)

Shinshū, 1930, 1932–1934, 1937, 1941

"Bukkyō to jūichi gatsu," *Shinshū* (November 1934): pp. 15–18.

Mizutani, Hisashi. "Meiji ishin igo ni okeru Ōtani-ha shūsei no hensen (3)," *Shinshū* (December 1932): pp. 5–8.

———. "Meiji ishin igo ni okeru Ōtani-ha shūsei no hensen (9)," *Shinshū* (July 1933): pp. 5–8.

Shinshū (December 1930): p. 12.

Shinshū (November 1937): p. 11.

Shinshū (January 1941): p. 17.

Shūhō, 1909–1911, 1914, 1917, 1919, 1921–1925

Reprint, *Shūhō tō kikanshi fukkokuban*, vols. 5–6, 8–13

"Nishi Honganji no kyōshi seido," *Shūhō* 97 (October 1909): pp. 17–18. Reprint, *Shūhō*, vol. 5, pp. 353–54.

Shūhō 92 (May 1909): p. 17. Reprint, *Shūhō*, vol. 5, p. 247.

Shūhō 96 (September 1909): p. 28. Reprint, *Shūhō*, vol. 5, p. 326.

Shūhō 107 (August 1910): p. 18. Reprint, *Shūhō*, vol. 6, p. 74.

Shūhō 114 (March 1911): pp. 8–13. Reprint, *Shūhō*, vol. 6, pp. 252–57.

Shūhō 119 (August 1911): p. 11. Reprint, *Shūhō*, vol. 6, p. 481.

Shūhō 159 (December 1914): p. 8. Reprint, *Shūhō*, vol. 8, p. 202.

Shūhō 195 (December 1917): p. 10. Reprint, *Shūhō*, vol. 9, p. 708.

Shūhō 217 (October 1919): p. 6. Reprint, *Shūhō*, vol. 10, p. 660.

Shūhō 235 (May 1921): 8. Reprint, *Shūhō*, vol. 11, p. 464.

Shūhō 236 (June 1921): p. 8. Reprint, *Shūhō*, vol. 11, p. 488.

Shūhō 237 (July 1921): 12. Reprint, *Shūhō*, vol. 11, p. 516.

Shūhō 248 (June 1922): pp. 10–11. Reprint, *Shūhō*, vol. 12, pp. 164–65.

Shūhō 248 (June 1922): p. 17. Reprint, *Shūhō*, vol. 12, p. 171.

Shūhō 250 (August, 1922): p. 11. Reprint, *Shūhō*, vol. 12, p. 223.

Shūhō 258/259 (April/May 1923), pp. 14–32. Reprint, *Shūhō*, vol. 12, pp. 474–92.

Shūhō 263 (September 1923): pp. 14–15. Reprint, *Shūhō*, vol. 12, pp. 612–13.

Shūhō 268 (February 1924): p. 28. Reprint, *Shūhō*, vol. 13, pp. 72, 194.

Shūhō 281 (March 1925): 7–8. Reprint, *Shūhō*, vol. 13, pp. 489–90.

Tada, Kanae. "Jōdokyō hihan eno hihan," *Shūhō* 76 (October 1924): p. 5. Reprint, *Shūhō*, vol. 13, pp. 317–20.

Jōdoshinshū Hongwanji-ha (Nishi Honganji)

Honzan rokuji, 1898, 1912, 1918

"Chōkaijōki dai jūsanjō, roku," *Honzan rokuji* (July 15, 1912): p. 116.

"Chōkaijōki dai shichijō, ichi," *Honzan rokuji* (July 15, 1912): p. 115.

"Jihō saisoku dai jūni shō dai sanjūgojō/dai sanjūrokujō," *Honzan rokuji* (April 13, 1898): p. 84.

"Kyōgaku Kiji," *Honzan rokuji* (February 29, 1918): pp. 8–9.

Anniversary Publications

A Grateful Past, A Promising Future: The First 100 years of Honpa Hongwanji in Hawaii. Honolulu: Honpa Hongwanji Mission, 1989.

Biographical History of Hawaii Hongwanji Ministers. Honolulu: Honpa Hongwanji Mission of Hawaii, 1991.

Berkeley Higashi Honganji 75th Anniversary 1926-2001.

Buddhist Churches of America 75-year History 1899-1974, 2 vols.

Buddhist Churches of America: A Legacy of the First 100 Years.

Buddhist Churches of Canada Centennial Celebration.

Buddhist Church of Parlier 60th Anniversary 1931-1991.

Butsuda. Special 10th Anniversary Edition. Kitsilano YBA, 1935.

Embraced in the Light of the Dharma 100 Years, Buddhist Churches of Oakland 1901-2001.

Fresno Betsuin Buddhist Temple Centennial 1901-2001.

Hawaii Nihonjin Iminshi: Hawaii Kanyaku Imin 75-nen Kinen. Honolulu: United Japanese Society of Hawaii, 1964.

Hilo Higashi Hongwanji Mission 75th Anniversary 1928-2003.

Hompa Hongwanji Los Angeles Betsuin 1905-1980. Los Angeles: Honpa Hongwanji Los Angeles Betsuin, 1980.

Kaneohe Higashi Honganji 25th Dedication and 65th Anniversary Commemoration.

Minami kashū nihonjin nanajūnenshi: A History of 70 Years. Los Angeles: Japanese Chamber of Commerce of Southern California, 1960.

Oregon Buddhist Church 1903-1983.

Otakebi. Special 10th Anniversary Edition. Fairview YBA, 1930.

Raymond Buddhist Church, ed. *A History of Forty Years of the Raymond Buddhist Church.* Raymond, Canada: Raymond Buddhist Church, 1970.

Sacramento Betsuin 70th Anniversary 1899-1969.

San Jose Buddhist Church Betsuin 1902-2002.

Santō Sanshū Bukkyōkai gojūnenshi.

Seattle Betsuin 1954.

Seattle Betsuin 75th Anniversary.

Shinshū Kyōkai Mission of Hawaii 1914-1984: A Legacy of Seventy Years. Honolulu: Shinshū Kyōkai Mission of Hawaii, 1985.

Sixty-Seven Years' History of the Higashi Hongwanji Mission of Hawaii.

Vancouver Buddhist Church Centennial Celebration 1904-2004.

Waimea Higashi Hongwanji Centennial Anniversary 1899–1999.

Waimea Higashi Hongwanji Dedication Ceremony, July 13, 1996.

Selected Primary Sources

Hawai bukkyō tokuhon. Honolulu: Jikōen, 1939.

Hawaii Hōchi, ed. *Hawai no nihongo gakuen ni kansuru shiso oyobi futai jiken.* Honolulu: Hawai Hōchi, 1926.

Hawaii Honolulu Hongwanji, ed. *Chōshōin ibunshū.* Honolulu: Hawaii Honolulu Hongwanji, 1937.

Imamura, Emyō. *Beikoku no seishin o ronzu.* Tokyo: Kaneo bun'endō, 1921.

———. *Beikoku no seishin to shūkyō no jiyū.* Honolulu: Hompa Hongwanji Hawai Kaikyō Kyōmusho, 1920.

———. *Democracy According to the Buddhist Viewpoint* (Bukkyō yori mitaru minpon shugi). Honolulu: The Publishing Bureau of Hongwanji Mission, 1918.

———. *Hawai kaikyō shiyō.* Honolulu: Hompa Hongwanji Mission, 1918.

———. *Hompa Hongwanji Hawai kaikyōshi.* Honolulu: Hompa Hongwanji Mission, 1918.

———. *Hompa Hongwanji Hawai kaikyō sanjūgonen kiyō.* Honolulu: Hompa Hongwanji Mission, 1931.

Izumida, Junjō. "Zaibei gojūnen no kaiko" ("The Memoirs of Fifty Years in the United States"), serialized in 137 parts in the *Kashū Mainichi Shinbun,* April 8–September 17, 1949.
"Zaibei gojūnen no kaiko 1," *Kashū Mainichi Shinbun,* April 8, 1949.
"Zaibei gojūnen no kaiko 2," *Kashū Mainichi Shinbun,* April 9,1949.
"Zaibei gojūnen no kaiko 3," *Kashū Mainichi Shinbun,* April 11, 1949.
"Zaibei gojūnen no kaiko 4," *Kashū Mainichi Shinbun,* April 12, 1949.
"Zaibei gojūnen no kaiko 28," *Kashū Mainichi Shinbun,* May 10, 1949.
"Zaibei gojūnen no kaiko 43," *Kashū Mainichi Shinbun,* May 27, 1949.
"Zaibei gojūnen no kaiko 46," *Kashū Mainichi Shinbun,* June 1, 1949.
"Zaibei gojūnen no kaiko 74," *Kashū Mainichi Shinbun,* July 2, 1949.
"Zaibei gojūnen no kaiko 79," *Kashū Mainichi Shinbun,* July 9, 1949.
"Zaibei gojūnen no kaiko 82," *Kashū Mainichi Shinbun,* July 13, 1949.
"Zaibei gojūnen no kaiko 83," *Kashū Mainichi Shinbun,* July 14, 1949.
"Zaibei gojūnen no kaiko 84," *Kashū Mainichi Shinbun,* July 15, 1949.
"Zaibei gojūnen no kaiko 98," *Kashū Mainichi Shinbun,* August 1, 1949.
"Zaibei gojūnen no kaiko 99," *Kashū Mainichi Shinbun,* August 3, 1949.

Jōdoshinshū Hongwanji-ha. *Hompa hōki.* Kyoto: Hompa Hongwanji, 1921.

Kyōgoku, Itsuzō, ed. *Akarui bukkyō.* Fresno, CA: Maha Maya Society, 1954.

———. "Kaga tayori," *Seishinkai* 9, no. 11 (1909): pp. 63–64.

———. "Tsuneni dai issen ni," *Seishinkai* 14, no. 1 (1914): pp. 54–55.

Takahashi, Takeichi, and Junjō Izumida. *Shinranism in Mahayana Buddhism and the Modern World.* Los Angeles: Higashi Hongwanji, 1932.

Tsutsumi, Takashi. *Hawai rōdō undōshi.* Honolulu: Hawai rōdō renmeikai honbu, 1921.

Secondary Sources

A Special Number of Appreciation Magazine of the World Fellowship of Faiths. Pamphlet, 1933.

Adachi, Ken. "A History of the Japanese Canadians in British Columbia, 1877– 1958." In *Two Monographs on Japanese Canadians,* ed. Roger Daniels, pp. 1–43. New York: Arno Press, 1978.

———. *The Enemy That Never Was.* Toronto: McClelland and Stewart Inc., 1991.

Akegarasu, Haya. "Amerika ryoko." In *Akegarasu Haya zenshū,* ed. Akegarasu Haya zenshū kankōkai, Bekkan, vol. 23, pp. 291–415. Kanazawa: Ryōfū gakusha, 1976.

Ama, Michihiro. "Analysis of 'Shinranism in Mahayana Buddhism and the Modern World,'" *The Pure Land* 18–19 (2002): pp. 72–88.

———. "The Early History of the Americanization of Shin Buddhism: The Case of Kyōgoku Itsuzō." Paper submitted to the Issei Buddhism Conference, University of California, Irvine, September 2004.

Ama, Toshimaro. "Shin Buddhism and Economic Ethics," *The Eastern Buddhist* (n.s.) 34, no. 2 (2002): pp. 25–50.

———. "Towards a Shin Buddhist Social Ethics," *The Eastern Buddhist* (n.s.) 33, no. 2 (2001): pp. 35–53.

———. *Why Are the Japanese Non-Religious? Japanese Spirituality: Being Non-Religious in a Religious Culture,* trans. Michihiro Ama. Lanham, MD: University Press of America, 2004.

Amstutz, Galen. *Interpreting Amida: History and Orientalism in the Study of Pure Land Buddhism.* Albany, NY: State University of New York Press, 1997.

Annaka, Naofumi. "Nichirenshū Mission in Early Twentieth Century Hawaii: Findings from Its Early Documents in the 1910s." Paper presented at the Issei Buddhism Conference, University of California, Irvine, September 2004.

Arimoto, Masao. *Shinshū no shūkyō shakaishi.* Tokyo: Yoshikawa kōbundō, 1995.

Asai, Yoshifusa. "Sōtōshū in Hawaii in the Early Twentieth Century." Paper presented at the Issei Buddhism Conference, University of California, Irvine, September 2004.

Asato, Noriko. *Teaching Mikadoism: The Attack on Japanese Language Schools in Hawaii, California, and Washington, 1919-1924.* Honolulu: University of Hawai'i Press, 2005.

Ashikaga, Enshō. *Shinshū sōden gisho.* Kyoto: Shinshū Ōtani-ha, 1978–1984.

Asuka, Kanritsu. *Sorewa bukkyō shōka kara hajimatta.* Tokyo: Junshinsha, 1999.

Azuma, Eiichirō. *Between Two Empires: Race, History, and Transnationalism in Japanese America.* New York: Oxford University Press, 2005.

Bandō, Shōjun, Emyō Ito, and Akira Hataya. *Jōdo bukkyō no shisō, Volume 15: Suzuki Daisetsu, Soga Ryōjin, and Kaneko Daiei.* Tokyo: Kōdansha, 1993.

Barrett, Timothy. "History." In *Critical Terms for the Study of Buddhism,* ed. Donald S. Lopez Jr., pp. 124–42. Chicago: University of Chicago Press, 2005.

Batten, Bruce L. *To the Ends of Japan: Premodern Frontiers, Boundaries, and Interactions.* Honolulu: University of Hawai'i Press, 2003.

Beard, Charles A., and Mary R. Beard. *The Rise of American Civilization.* New York: The Macmillan Co., 1946.

Becker, Carl. "Japanese Pure Land Buddhism in Christian America," *Buddhist-Christian Studies* 10 (1990): pp. 143–56.

Beechert, Edward D. *Working in Hawaii: A Labor History.* Honolulu: University of Hawai'i Press, 1985.

Bekki, Kōshō. "Rekishi no yami o mitsumete: Taigyaku jiken to bukkyōsha tachi," *Shindō* 17 (1998): pp. 132–49.

Bellah, Robert N. *Tokugawa Religion: The Cultural Roots of Modern Japan* (1957). New York: The Free Press, 1985, reprint.

Benitez, Joaquim M., and Shiho Jidoi. "A Study of the Seven Collections of Bukkyō Shōka ("Buddhist Songs") Published with Music between 1889 and 1907," *Elisabeth University of Music Research Bulletin* 21 (2001): pp. 49–61.

Biography of Hioki mokusen (Hioki mokusen den). Tokyo: Daihōrinkaku, 1962.

Bloom, Alfred. "Kiyozawa Manshi and the Path to the Revitalization of Buddhism," *Pacific World,* 3rd ser. 5 (2003): pp. 19–34.

———. "Kiyozawa Manshi and the Revitalization of Buddhism," *The Eastern Buddhist* (n.s.) 35, nos. 1/2 (2003): pp. 1–5.

———, ed. *Living in Amida's Universal Vow: Essays in Shin Buddhism.* Bloomington, IN: Worlds Wisdom, 2004.

———. "Shin Buddhism in America: A Social Perspective." In *The Faces of Buddhism in America,* ed. Charles S. Prebish and Kenneth K. Tanaka, pp. 31–47. Berkeley: University of California Press, 1998.

———. *Shinran's Gospel of Pure Grace* (1965). Ann Arbor, MI: Association for Asian Studies, 1999, reprint.

Blum, Mark L. "Kiyozawa Manshi and the Meaning of Buddhist Ethics," *The Eastern Buddhist* (n.s.) 21, no. 1 (1988): pp. 61–81.

———. *The Origins and Development of Pure Land Buddhism: A Study and Translation of Gyōnen's Jōdo Hōmon Genrushō.* New York: Oxford University Press, 2002.

———. "Truth in Need: Kiyozawa Manshi and Søren Kierkegaard," *The Eastern Buddhist* (n.s.) 35, nos. 1/2 (2003): pp. 57–101.

Blum, Mark L., and Shin'ya Yasutomi, eds. *Rennyo and the Roots of Modern Japanese Buddhism.* New York: Oxford University Press, 2006.

Bourne, Randolph. "Trans-National America." In *Randolph Bourne: The Radical Will, Selected Writings 1911–1918,* ed. Olaf Hansen, pp. 248–64. New York: Urizen Books, 1977.

Cadge, Wendy. *Heartwood: The First Generation of Theravada Buddhism in America.* Chicago: University of Chicago Press, 2005.

Carnes, Tony, and Fenggang Yang, eds. *Asian American Religions: The Making and Remaking of Borders and Boundaries.* New York: New York University Press, 2004.

Castleman, Bruce A. "The California Alien Land Laws," Master's thesis. University of San Diego, 1993.

Chen, Carolyn. *Getting Saved in America: Taiwanese Immigration and Religious Experience.* Princeton, NJ: Princeton University Press, 2008.

Chiba, Jōryū, ed. *Honganji shūkai hyakunenshi, shiryōhen,* 3 vols. Kyoto: Jōdoshinshū Hongwanji-ha shūkai, 1983.

Chidester, David. *Savage Systems: Colonialism and Comparative Religion in Southern Africa.* Charlottesville, VA: University Press of Virginia, 1996.

Coates, Harper Havelock, and Ryūgaku Ishizuka. *Honen the Buddhist Saint: His Life and Teaching.* Kyoto: Chion'in, 1925.

Cooke, Gerald. "A New Life-Stage in the Otani Denomination," *Japanese Religions* 15 (January 1989): pp. 69–73.

Daniels, Roger. *The Politics of Prejudice: The Anti-Japanese Movement in California and the Struggle for Japanese Exclusion.* Berkeley: University of California Press, 1962.

Davis, Winston. *Japanese Religion and Society: Paradigms of Structure and Change.* Albany, NY: State University of New York Press, 1992.

Dessi, Ugo. *Ethics and Society in Contemporary Shin Buddhism.* Münster, Germany: Lit Verlag, 2008.

Dewey, John. *A Common Faith.* New Haven, CT: Yale University Press, 1934.

———. *Democracy and Education* (1916). New York: Dover Publications, 2004, reprint.

———. *Reconstruction in Philosophy* (1920). New York: Mentor Books, 1950, reprint.

———. "The Pragmatic Acquiescence." In *The Essential Dewey Volume 1: Pragmatism, Education, Democracy,* ed. Larry A. Hickman and Thomas M. Alexander, pp. 33–36. Bloomington, IN: Indiana University Press, 1998.

Dobbins, James C. *Jōdoshinshū: Shin Buddhism in Medieval Japan.* Bloomington, IN: Indiana University Press, 1989.

———. *Letters of the Nun Eshinni: Images of Pure Land Buddhism in Medieval Japan.* Honolulu: University of Hawai'i Press, 2004.

Dower, John. *Embracing Defeat: Japan in the Wake of World War II.* New York: W. W. Norton & Co., 2000.

"Dress Code." *Honpa hōki,* pp. 241–42. Kyoto: Honpa Hongwanji, 1921.

Edwards, Walter. *Modern Japan Through Its Weddings: Gender, Person, and Society in Ritual Portrayal.* Stanford, CA: Stanford University Press, 1989.

Ema, Tsutomu. *Kekkon no rekishi: Nihon ni okeru konreishiki no keitai to hatten.* Tokyo: Yūzankaku, 1971.

Faure, Bernard. *The Rhetoric of Immediacy: A Cultural Critique of Chan/Zen Buddhism.* Princeton, NJ: Princeton University Press, 1991.

Fields, Rick. *How the Swans Came to the Lake: A Narrative History of Buddhism in America.* Boston: Shambhala Publications, 1981.

Fitzgerald, Timothy. *The Ideology of Religious Studies.* New York: Oxford University Press, 2000.

Fujii, Ryūchi. "The Conception of Personality in a System of Absolute Idealism," Master's thesis. University of Southern California, 1924.

Fujii, Takeshi. "Meiji shoki ni okeru shinshū no shintōkan: Shimaji Mokurai to Nanjō Shinkō no baai," *Tokyo gakugei daigaku kiyō* 39 (1988): pp. 147–56.

Fujimoto, Ryūkyō. *An Outline of the Triple Sutra of Shin Buddhism, Volume 1: The Sutra on the Eternal Buddha.* Kyoto: Honpa Hongwanji, 1955.

———. *An Outline of the Triple Sutra of Shin Buddhism, Volume 2: The Sutra of Meditation on the Eternal Buddha.* Kyoto: Hyakka-en, 1960.

Fujishima, Tatsurō. *Honbyō monogatari: Higashi honganji no rekish.* Kyoto: Shinshū Ōtani-ha, 1999.

Fukuda, Yoshiaki. "Japan a Center of World Peace Problems." In *World Fellowship: Addresses and Messages by Leading Spokesmen of All Faiths, Races and Countries,* ed. Charles F. Weller, pp. 207–11, 763–70. New York: Liveright Publishing Co., 1935.

Fukuma, Kōchō. "Nishi honganji kyōdan ni okeru kōsen gikai no seiritsu ni tsuite." In *Bukkyō shigaku ronshū,* ed. Futaba hakase kanreki kinen kai, pp. 417–78. Kyoto: Nagata bunshodō, 1977.

Fukumoto, Yasuyuki. "Initial Acceptance of the Western Music in the Japanese Buddhism [Buddhist] Community: Focusing on the Positioning of the Western Music," *Journal of Handai Music Studies* 2 (March 2004): pp. 150–66.

Fukushima, Kanryū. "Teikoku shugi seiritsuki no bukkyō: seishin shugi to shin bukkyō to." In *Bukkyō shigaku ronshū,* ed. Futaba hakase kanreki kinen kai, pp. 479–517. Kyoto: Nagata bunshodō, 1977.

Futaba, Kenkō. "Shinshū kyōdan kindaika no dōkō: fukyōken no kaifuku to mat-suji byōdōka shikō." In *Zoku kokka to bukkyō: Kinsei kindai-hen,* ed. Futaba Kenkō, pp. 63–86. Kyoto: Nagata bunshodō, 1981.

Garon, Sheldon M. "State and Religion in Imperial Japan, 1912–1945," *Journal of Japanese Studies* 12, no. 2 (1986): pp. 273–302.

Glenn, Evelyn Nakano. *Issei, Nisei, War Bride: Three Generations of Japanese American Women in Domestic Service.* Philadelphia: Temple University Press, 1986.

Goa, David J., and Harold G. Coward. "Sacred Ritual, Sacred Language: Jodo Shinshu Religious Forms in Transition," *Studies in Religion* 12, no. 4 (1983): pp. 363–79.

Gómez, Luis O. *The Land of Bliss. The Paradise of the Buddha of Measureless Light: Sanskrit and Chinese Versions of the Sukhavativyuha Sutras.* Honolulu: University of Hawai'i Press, 1996.

Gonnami, Tsunemaru. "The Perception Gap: A Case Study of Japanese-Canadians." Paper presented at the "Communication among Japanese-Canadians: The Role of Non-Profit and For-Profit Organizations in Media and Education Service Industries" conference, British Columbia, Canada, 2005.

Grayson, James H. "Ch'udo yebae: A Case Study in the Early Emplantation of Protestant Christianity in Korea," *The Journal of Asian Studies* 68, no. 2 (2009): pp. 413–34.

Haneda, Nobuo, trans. *December Fan: The Buddhist Essays of Manshi Kiyozawa.* Kyoto: Shinshū Ōtani-ha, 1984.

Hansen, Olaf. Introduction to *Randolph Bourne: The Radical Will, Selected Writings 1911–1918,* ed. Olaf Hansen, pp. 17–62. New York: Urizen Books, 1977.

———, ed. *Randolph Bourne: The Radical Will, Selected Writings 1911–1918.* New York: Urizen Books, 1977.

Hardacre, Helen. *Shinto and the State 1868–1988.* Princeton, NJ: Princeton University Press, 1989.

Hashimoto, Mineo. "Two Models of the Modernization of Japanese Buddhism: Kiyozawa Manshi and D. T. Suzuki," *The Eastern Buddhist* (n.s.) 35, nos. 1/2 (2003): pp. 6–41.

Hattori, Michiko. "Hokkaidō kaitaku to higashi honganji: fukyōken no kakuritsu o motomete," *Shindō* 8 (1989): pp. 77–107.

Hawai hompa hongwanji kyōdan, ed. *Hawai hompa hongwanji kyōdan enkakushi.* Honolulu: Hompa Hongwanji, 1954.

Hawaii Hōchi, ed. *Hawai no nihongo gakuen ni kansuru shiso oyobi futai jiken.* Honolulu: Hawaii Hōchi, 1926.

Hayashi, Brian M. *Democratizing the Enemy: The Japanese American Internment.* Princeton, NJ: Princeton University Press, 2004.

———. *For the Sake of Our Japanese Brethren: Assimilation, Nationalism, and Protestantism Among the Japanese of Los Angeles, 1895–1942.* Stanford, CA: Stanford University Press, 1995.

Hickman, Larry A., and Thomas M. Alexander, eds. *The Essential Dewey, Volume 1: Pragmatism, Education, Democracy.* Bloomington, IN: Indiana University Press, 1998.

Higham, John. *Strangers in the Land: Patterns of American Nativism 1860-1925* (1955). New Brunswick, NJ: Rutgers University Press, 2004, reprint.

Hirota, Dennis, ed. *Toward a Contemporary Understanding of Pure Land Buddhism.* New York: State University of New York Press, 2000.

Hirota, Dennis, et al., trans. *The Collected Works of Shinran,* 2 vols. Kyoto: Jōdo Shinshū Hongwanji-ha, 1997.

Hisaki, Yukio. *Kenshō Kiyozawa Manshi hihan.* Kyoto: Hōzōkan, 1995.

Hishiki, Masaharu. *Jōdoshinshū no sensō sekinin.* Tokyo: Iwanami, 1993, booklet.

Hofstadter, Richard. *Anti-Intellectualism in American Life.* New York: Vintage Books, 1963.

Honda, Aya. "The Social Solidarity of the Seattle, Washington, Bukkyō Fujinkai: 1908-1942." Paper presented at the Issei Buddhism Conference, University of California, Irvine, September 2004.

Honganji Shiryō Kenkyūsho, ed. *Honganjishi, shiryō hen,* 3 vols. Kyoto: Jōdo-shinshū Hongwanji-ha, 1961-1969.

Hori, Ichirō. *Nihon shūkyō no shakaiteki yakuwari.* Tokyo: Miraisha, 1962.

Hori, Kentoku. "Buddhist Association in Germany," *The Light of Dharma* 6, no. 1 (January 1907): pp. 16-19.

Hori, Victor S. "Japanese Zen in America: Americanizing the Face in the Mirror." In *The Faces of Buddhism in America,* ed. Charles S. Prebish and Kenneth K. Tanaka, pp. 49-78. Berkeley: University of California Press, 1998.

Horinouchi, Isao. "Americanized Buddhism: A Sociological Analysis of a Protestantized Japanese Religion," Ph.D. dissertation. University of California, Davis, 1973.

Hunter, Louise H. *Buddhism in Hawaii: Its Impact on a Yankee Community.* Honolulu: University of Hawai'i Press, 1971.

Ichikawa, Tatsuya. "Kanzen hōwa," *Jikishin* 9, no. 3 (1953): pp. 18-19.

Ichioka, Yūji. *Before Internment: Essays in Prewar Japanese American History,* ed. Gordon H. Chang and Eiichirō Azuma. Stanford, CA: Stanford University Press, 2006.

———. *The Issei: The World of the First Generation Japanese Immigrants 1885-1924.* New York: Free Press, 1988.

Ienaga, Saburō. "Japan's Modernization and Buddhism," *Contemporary Religions in Japan* 6, no. 1 (1965): pp. 1-41.

Iino, Masako. "BC shū no bukkyōkai to nikkei canadajin community BC," *Tokyo daigaku amerika taiheiyō kenkyū* 2 (2002): pp. 45-61.

———. "Bukkyōkai and the Japanese Canadian Community in British Columbia." Paper presented at the Issei Buddhism Conference, University of California, Irvine, September 2004.

——. "Bukkyōkai to nikkei kanadajin community," *Gakuto* 99, no. 5 (2002): pp. 12–15.

——. "Otakebi to butsuda ni mirareru nikkeijin no ishiki: BC shū no nikkei kanadajin community to bukkyōkai: BC," *Ryūkoku daigaku keieigaku ronshū* 43, no. 1 (2003): pp. 1–14.

Ikeda, Eishun, ed. *Ronshū nihon bukkyōshi,* vol. 8. Tokyo: Yūzankaku, 1987.

Ikuta Shinjō. *Kanada bukkyōkai enkakushi.* Toronto: Buddhist Churches of Canada, 1981.

Imamura, Emyō. "Beikoku oyobi beikokujin." In *Chōshōin ibunshū,* ed. Hawaii Honolulu Hongwanji, pp. 118–35. Honolulu: Hawaii Honolulu Hongwanji, 1937.

——. "Nipu jiji ichiman gō o shukushi honshitsu ron ni oyobu: shakai kyōiku kikan to shiteno sekimu," *Nippu jiji,* October 4, 1929.

——. Preface to *Five Appeals to American Patriotism.* Honolulu: The Publishing Bureau of the Hongwanji Mission, 1917.

Imamura, Hitoshi. *Gendaigo yaku: Kiyozawa Manshi goroku.* Tokyo: Iwanami gendai bunko, 2001.

Inagaki, Hisao, ed. *A Record in Lament of Divergences: A Translation of the Tannishō.* Shin Buddhism Translation Series. Kyoto: Honganji International Center, 1995.

——. *T'an-luan's Commentary on Vasubandhu's Discourse on the Pure Land.* Kyoto: Nagata bunshodō, 1998.

——. *The Three Pure Land Sutras: A Study and Translation.* Kyoto: Nagata bunshodō, 1994.

Inoue, Toshio. *Honganji* (1962). Tokyo: Kōdansha, 2009, reprint.

Ishida, Nitten. "Japan and Ho-Kwe-Kyo Are One." In *World Fellowship: Addresses and Messages by Leading Spokesmen of All Faiths, Races and Countries,* ed. Charles F. Weller, p. 23. New York: Liveright Publishing Co., 1935.

Ishikawa, Ken. *Beikoku kashū nihongo gakuen ni kansuru kenkyū.* Privately printed, 1923.

Isomae, Jun'ichi. "Deconstructing 'Japanese Religion': A Historical Survey," *Japanese Journal of Religious Studies* 33, no. 2 (2005): pp. 235–48.

Iwaasa, David. "Canadian Japanese in South Alberta: 1905–1945." In *Two Monographs on Japanese Canadians,* ed. Roger Daniels, pp. 1–97. New York: Arno Press, 1978.

Izumi, Shigeki. "Takagi Kenmyō to buraku sabetsu mondai (1): Shōsestu kano sō ni mirareru Kenmyō no hisabetsu buraku kan," *Otani Gakuhō,* no. 1 (1999): pp. 13–25.

Jaffe, Richard. "Buddhist Material Culture, 'Indianism,' and the Construction of Pan-Asian Buddhism in Prewar Japan," *Material Religion: The Journal of Objects, Art and Belief* 2, no. 3 (2005): pp. 266–92.

———. *Neither Monk nor Layman: Clerical Marriage in Modern Japanese Buddhism.* Princeton, NJ: Princeton University Press, 2001.

———. "Seeking Sakyamuni: Travel and the Reconstruction of Japanese Buddhism," *Journal of Japanese Studies* 30 (2004): pp. 65–96.

Johnston, Gilbert L. "Kiyozawa Manshi's Buddhist Faith and Its Relation to Modern Japanese Society," Ph.D. dissertation. Harvard University, 1972.

Josephson, Jason A. "When Buddhism Became a 'Religion': Religion and Super-stition in the Writings of Inoue Enryō," *Japanese Journal of Religious Studies* 33, no. 1 (2006): pp. 143–68.

"Jūryū kūchū," *Shinshū shin jiten,* p. 243. Kyoto: Hōzōkan, 1992.

Kagahi, Sōryū. *Hawai kikō.* Ōita: Privately published, 1890.

Kagao, Shūnin. *Monten Lupa ni inoru,* ed. Takashi Yamashita. Tokyo: Kokusho kankōkai, 1982.

Kanda, Shigeo H. "Recovering Cultural Symbols: A Case for Buddhism in the Japanese American Communities," *Journal of the American Academy of Religion* 44, no. 4, supplement A (1978): pp. 445–75.

Kasahara, Kazuo. *Ikkō ikki no kenkyū.* Tokyo: Yamagawa shuppan sha, 1962.

Kashima, Tetsuden. *Buddhism in America: The Social Organization of an Ethnic Religious Institution.* Westport, CT: Greenwood Press, 1977.

Kashiwahara, Yūsen. *Kindai Ōtani-ha no kyōdan: Meiji ikō shūseishi.* Kyoto: Shinshū Ōtani-ha, 1986.

———. "Kiyozawa Manshi." In *Shapers of Japanese Buddhism,* ed. Yūsen Kashiwahara and Kōyū Sonoda, pp. 230–40. Tokyo: Kōsei Publishing Co., 1994.

Kawamura, Leslie. "The Historical Development of the Buddhist Churches in Southern Alberta." In *Religion and Culture in Canada,* ed. Peter Slater, pp. 491–506. Waterloo, Ontario: Wilfred Laurier University Press, 1977.

Kawamura, Yūtetsu. *Chronicles of True Pure Land Buddhism in Canada, 1933-85.* N.p., 1999.

———. *Kanada alberta shū cowboy song no sato.* Kyoto: Dōbōsha, 1988.

———. *Kanada bukkyō shi (1936–1985).* Kyoto: Dōbōsha, 1988, reprint.

———. *The Dharma Survives with the People.* N.p., n.d.

Ketelaar, James E. *Of Heretics and Martyrs in Meiji Japan: Buddhism and Its Persecution.* Princeton, NJ: Princeton University Press, 1990.

Kiba, Akeshi. "Kaikyō: Kokui kakuchō ni taiō shita kaigai kaikyō jigyō." In *Shūmon kindaishi no kenshō,* pp. 133–65. Kyoto: Shinshū Ōtani-ha, 2003.

———. "Manshū ni okeru Ōtani-ha kaikyō." In *Asia no kaikyō to kyōiku,* ed. Masaru Kojima and Akeshi Kiba, pp. 87–132. Kyoto: Hōzōkan, 1992.

———. "Shinshū no hoppō kaikyō: Kuriru (Chishima) chiiki ni okeru shinshū Ōtani-ha no kōdō," *Indo tetsugaku bukkyōgaku* 8 (1993): pp. 274–95.

Kiba, Akeshi, and Atsuyoshi Keika. "Higashi honganji chūgoku fukkyōshi no kisoteki kenkyū," *Otani daigaku shinshū sōgō kenkyūsho kiyō* 5 (1987): pp. 1–28.

Kiba, Akeshi, and Joi Tei, eds. *Nicchu ryōkoku no shiten kara kataru shokuminchi Manshū no shūkyō.* Tokyo: Kashiwa shobō, 2007.

Kimura, Gibun. "Kyōgoku sensei to Monten Lupa no senpansha," *Jikishin* 9, no. 3 (December 1953): pp. 35–39.

Kimura, Yukiko. *Issei: Japanese Immigrants in Hawaii.* Honolulu: University of Hawai'i Press, 1988.

Kitagawa, Joseph. *Religion in Japanese History.* New York: Columbia University Press, 1966.

Kiyozawa, Manshi. *Kyōkai jigen (Timely Words for the Religious World).* N.p., n.d.
——. *Shūkyō teki dōtoku (zokutai) to futsū dōtoku to no kōshō (Discourse on Religious Morality and Common Morality).* Trans. Mark L. Blum. In *An Anthology of Modern Shin Buddhist Writings: Kiyozawa Manshi, Soga Ryōjin, Kaneko Daiei and Yasuda Rijin,* ed. Shin Buddhist Comprehensive Research Institute, pp. 19–34. Kyoto: Ōtani University, 2001.
——. "The Nature of My Faith." Trans. Mark L. Blum. In *An Anthology of Modern Shin Buddhist Writings: Kiyozawa Manshi, Soga Ryōjin, Kaneko Daiei and Yasuda Rijin,* ed. Shin Buddhist Comprehensive Research Institute, pp. 35–41. Kyoto: Ōtani University, 2001.

Kobayashi, Audrey. "The Early History of Japanese Canadians." In *Spirit of Redress: Japanese Canadian in Conference,* ed. Cassandra Kobayashi and Roy Miki, pp. 81–88. Vancouver: JC Publications, 1989.

Kodama, Shiki. *Kinsei shinshū to chiiki shakai.* Kyoto: Hōzōkan, 2005.
——. "Shimaji Mokurai." In *Shapers of Japanese Buddhism,* ed. Yūsen Kashiwahara and Kōyū Sonoda, pp. 207–18. Tokyo: Kōsei Publishing Co., 1994.

Kojima, Masaru. "Chōsen ni okeru kaikyō, Honganji-ha chōsen kaikyō eno hottan." In *Asia no kaikyō to kyōiku,* ed. Masaru Kojima and Akeshi Kiba, pp. 149–68. Kyoto: Hōzōkan, 1992.
——. "Kaigai kaikyō to kyōiku jigyō." In *Asia no kaikyō to kyōiku,* ed. Masaru Kojima and Akeshi Kiba, pp. 7–20. Kyoto: Hōzōkan, 1992.

Kojima, Masaru, and Akeshi Kiba, ed. *Asia no kaikyō to kyōiku.* Kyoto: Hōzōkan, 1992.

Kokusai bukkyō bunka kyōkai, eds. *Nembutsu seizan: Oshū nembutsu denpa shōshi.* Kyoto: Nagata bunshōdo, 2000.

Kōmoto, Mitsugu, ed. *Ronshū nihon bukkyōshi, Volume 9: Taishō shōwa jidai.* Tokyo: Yūzankaku, 1988.

Kudara, Toryū. "The Influence of the Namu Amida Butsu in Japan," Master's thesis. University of Southern California, 1924.

Kumata, Masaru. "Dedication." In *Bussei,* p. 1. Seattle: Seattle Betsuin, 1941.

Kumata, Shigekuni. *Kindai shinshū no tenkai to aki monto.* Hiroshima: Hiroshima joshi daigaku, 1983.

Kurokawa, Kenjō. "History and Present Status of the Vacation Religious Day School," Master's thesis. University of Southern California, 1923.

Kusano, Kenshi. *Sengokuki honganji kyōdanshi no kenkyū.* Kyoto: Hōzōkan, 2004.

Kyōgoku, Itsuzō. "Buddhism as a Whole, Not as a Sect," *Bhratri* 2, no. 2 (July 1934): p. 87.

——. "Direct and Indirect Understanding," *Tri-Ratna* 6, no. 1 (January/February 1952): pp. 10–16.

——. "Jikishin kyō ni narumade," *Jikishin* 4, no. 2 (1948): pp. 17–22.

Kyōgoku, Kiyo. "Anotoki konotoki," *Jikishin* 9, no. 3 (1953): pp. 56–60.

Lasch, Christopher. Preface to *Randolph Bourne: The Radical Will, Selected Writings 1911-1918,* ed. Olaf Hansen, pp. 9–14. New York: Urizen Books, 1977.

Layman, Emma McCloy. *Buddhism in America.* Chicago: Nelson-Hall, 1978.

Lobreglio, John S. "Unified Buddhism: The Varieties of Tsūbukkyō in Meiji-Taishō Japan and the Case of Takada Dōken," *The Eastern Buddhist* (n.s.) 37, nos. 1/2 (2005): pp. 39–76.

Machida, Sōhō. *Renegade Monk: Hōnen and Japanese Pure Land Buddhism.* Berkeley: University of California Press, 1999.

Maeda, Takakazu. *Hawai no jinjashi.* Tokyo: Taimeidō, 1999.

Maffly-Kipp, Laurie F. "Eastward Ho! American Religion from the Perspective of the Pacific Rim." In *Retelling U.S. Religious History,* ed. Thomas A. Tweed, pp. 127–48. Berkeley: University of California Press, 1997.

Magden, Ronald E. "Buddhism Comes to Seattle." In *More Voices, New Stories: King County, Washington's First 150 Years,* ed. Mary C. Wright, pp. 172–88. Seattle: Pacific Northwest Historians Guild, 2002.

——. *Furusato: Tacoma-Pierce County Japanese 1888-1899.* Tacoma, WA: Nikkeijinkai Tacoma Japanese Community Service, 1998.

Main, Jessica. "Ethics in the Modern History of Shin Buddhism: Human Rights, Discrimination, the Ōtani-ha, and the Burakumin, 1860–1980," Ph.D. dissertation. McGill University, 2010.

Masatsugu, Michael. "Reorienting the Pure Land: Japanese Americans, the Beats, and the Making of American Buddhism, 1941–1966," Ph.D. dissertation. University of California, Irvine, 2004.

Mase-Hasegawa, Emi. *Spirit of Christ Inculturated: A Theological Theme Implicit in Shusaku Endo's Literary Works.* Lund, Germany: Lund University, 2004.

Masuyama, Kenju. "From Forty-One Million Buddhists." In *World Fellowship: Addresses and Messages by Leading Spokesmen of All Faiths, Races and Countries,* ed. Charles F. Weller, pp. 14–16. New York: Liveright Publishing Co., 1935.

Matsuda, Shōichi. *Akegarasu Haya: Yo to tomo ni yo o koen,* 2 vols. Kanazawa: Kitagui shinbunsha, 1998.

Matsumoto, Valerie J. *Farming the Home Place: A Japanese American Community in California 1919-1982.* Ithaca, NY: Cornell University Press, 1993.

McCarty, Yukiko Yanagida. "Little Tokyo and Its Buddhist Temple, National Center for the Preservation of Democracy (Former Nishi Hongwanji Buddhist Temple building 1925-)," *The East* 41, no. 5 (2006): pp. 17–22.

———. "Nihonmachi, Reminiscent of 1950s Japan, San Jose Buddhist Church Betsuin (1937-)," *The East* 41, no. 3 (2005): pp. 17–22.

McCullough, Helen Craig, trans. *The Tale of the Heike.* Stanford, CA: Stanford University Press, 1988.

Min, Pyong Gap, and Jung Ha Kim, eds. *Religions in Asian America: Building Faith Communities.* Walnut Creek, CA: AltaMira Press, 2002.

Mito, Kendō. "Character Education through Religious Dramatization," Master's thesis. University of Southern California, 1931.

Miyamoto, Frank. *Social Solidarity Among the Japanese in Seattle* (1939). Seattle: University of Washington Press, 1981, reprint.

Miyamoto, Yuki. "Rebirth in the Pure Land or God's Sacrificial Lambs? Religious Interpretations of the Atomic Bombings in Hiroshima and Nagasaki," *Japanese Journal of Religious Studies* 32, no. 1 (2005): pp. 131–59.

Modell, John. *The Economics and Politics of Racial Accommodation: The Japanese of Los Angeles, 1900-1942.* Urbana, IL: University of Illinois Press, 1977.

Mohr, Michel. Introduction to "Feature: Buddhist and Non-Buddhist Trends Towards Religious Unity in Meiji Japan," *The Eastern Buddhist* (n.s.) 37, nos. 1/2 (2005): pp. 1–8.

Montero, Darrel. *Japanese Americans: Changing Patterns of Ethnic Affiliation over Three Generations.* Boulder, CO: Westview, 1980.

Mori, Ryūkichi. *Honganji.* Tokyo: San'ichi shobō, 1973.

Morioka, Kiyomi. *Shinshū kyōdan to ie seido.* Tokyo: Sōbunsha, 1962.

Moriya, Tomoe. *Amerika bukkyō no tanjō: Nijū seiki shotō ni okeru nikkei shūkyō no bunnka henyō.* Tokyo: Gendai shiryō shuppan, 2001.

———. "California shū ni okeru bukkyōkai fuzoku nihongo gakkō no seikaku." In *A History of Transnational Education (Ekkyo Kyōiku) of the Japanese Immigrants in the U.S., 1877-1945,* ed. Ryō Yoshida, pp. 113–38. Tokyo: Nihon tosho center, 2005.

———. *Yemyo Imamura: Pioneer American Buddhist,* trans. Tsuneichi Takeshita, ed. Alfred Bloom and Ruth Tabrah. Honolulu: Buddhist Study Center Press, 2000.

Murai, Tadamasa. "Dainiji sekai taisenmae no minami alberta nikkei shakai: Sono seisei to hatten no kiseki," *Imin kenkyū nenpō* 4 (1998): pp. 45–64.

Nagao, Gadjin. "On the Theory of Buddha-body," *The Eastern Buddhist* (n.s.) 6, no. 1 (1973): pp. 25–53.

Nagata, Masaharu. "Topaz no omoide," *Jikishin* 3, no. 3 (1947): pp. 40–41.

Nakai, Gendō. "Beikoku bukkyōkai no kiki (1)," *Chūgai Nippō,* September 10, 1925.

———. "Beikoku bukkyōkai no kiki (2)," *Chūgai Nippō,* September 11, 1925.

Nakanishi, Don Toshiaki. "The Visual Panacea: Japanese Americans in the City of Smog," *Amerasia Journal* 2 (1973): pp. 82–129.

Nakano, Tsuyoshi. "Hawai Nikkei kyōdan no keisei to henyō," *Shūkyō kenkyū* 55 (June 1981): pp. 45–72.

———. "Hawai shū no seikyō kankei to hōseido." In *Hawai nikkeijin shakai to nihon shūkyō: Hawai nikkeijin shūkyō chōsa hōkokusho,* ed. Keiichi Yanagawa and Kiyomi Morioka, pp. 68–95. Tokyo: Tokyo daigaku shūkyōgaku kenkyūshitsu, 1981.

———. "Shūkyō kankei hō." In *Hawai Nikkei shūkyō no tenkai to genkyō: Hawai nikkenjin shūkyō chōsa chūkan hōkoku,* ed. Keiichi Yanagawa and Kiyomi Morioka, pp. 223–40. Tokyo: Tokyo daigaku shūkyōgaku kenkyūshitsu, 1979.

Nakayama, Shozen. "Six Million Japanese Followers of Tenrikyo." In *World Fellowship: Addresses and Messages by Leading Spokesmen of All Faiths, Races and Countries,* ed. Charles F. Weller, pp. 18–19. New York: Liveright Publishing Co., 1935.

Narain, A. K., ed. *Studies in history of Buddhism.* Delhi: B. R. Publishing Corporation, 1980.

Naramoto, Tatsuya, and Meiji Momose, eds. *Meiji ishin no higashi honganji.* Tokyo: Kawade shobō shinsha, 1987.

"Nikkō card no nihon shinshutsu," *Jikishin* 4, no. 4 (1948), pp. 21–22.

Ogawa, Ichijō, et al., eds. *Kiyozawa Manshi zenshū,* 9 vols. Tokyo: Iwanami shoten, 2002–2003.

Ogura, Kōsei. "A Sociological Study of Buddhism in North America with a Case Study of Gardena, California Congregation," Master's thesis. University of Southern California, 1932.

Okada, Masahiko. "Revitalization versus Unification," *The Eastern Buddhist* (n.s.) 37, nos. 1/2 (2005): pp. 28–38.

Okihiro, Gary. *Cane Fires: The Anti-Japanese Movement in Hawaii 1865-1945.* Philadelphia: Temple University Press, 1991.

Okita, Yukuji. *Hawai nikkei imin no kyōikushi: Nichibei bunka sono deai to sōkoku.* Kyoto: Minerva shobō, 1997.

Ōtani, Kōen. "The First Step Towards the Realization of World-Peace," *The Eastern Buddhist* 1, no. 4 (November/December 1921): pp. 253–58.

Ōtani, Son'yū. "The Washington Conference from the Buddhist Point of View," *The Eastern Buddhist* 1, no. 4 (November/December 1921): pp. 259–64.

Palumbo, Lorraine Reiko Minatoshi. "The Process of Transformation of the Buddhist Temple Architecture of the Japanese Society of Hawaii," dissertation for the Doctorate of Engineering. Waseda University, 1999.

Pas, Julian. *Visions of Sukhāvatī: Shandao's Commentary on the Kuan Wu-Liang-Shou-Fo Ching.* Albany, NY: State University of New York Press, 1995.

Payne, Richard K. "Hiding in Plain Sight: The Invisibility of the Shingon Mission to the United States." In *Buddhist Missionaries in the Era of Globalization,* ed. Linda Learman, pp. 101–220. Honolulu: University of Hawai'i Press, 2005.

———, ed. *Shin Buddhism: Historical, Textual, and Interpretive Studies.* Berkeley, CA: Institute of Buddhist Studies and Numata Center for Buddhist Translation and Research, 2007.

Pierce, Lori. "Constructing American Buddhisms: Discourse of Race and Religion in Territorial Hawaii," Ph.D. dissertation. University of Hawai'i, 2000.

Porcu, Elizabetta. *Pure Land in Modern Japanese Culture.* Leiden, The Netherlands: Brill, 2008.

Pratt, Sunya N. "Doctrine, Practice, Faith, Attainment," *Tri-Ratna* 6, no. 2 (March/April 1952): pp. 8–11.

———. "The Faith Aspect in Buddhism (Repress Doubting until Results Show Themselves)." In *Bussei,* pp. 47, 53. Seattle: Seattle Betsuin, 1941.

Ratanamani, Manimai. "History of Shin Buddhism in the United States," Master's thesis. College of the Pacific, 1960.

Raymond bukkyōkaishi, ed. *Raymond bukkyōkai.* Kyoto: Dōbōsha, 1970.

Reinecke, John E. *Feigned Necessity: Hawaii's Attempt to Obtain Chinese Contract Labor, 1921-1923.* San Francisco: Chinese Materials Center, 1979.

Rogers, Minor L. "Rennyo Shōnin 1415–1499: A Transformation in Shin Buddhist Piety," Ph.D. dissertation. Harvard University, 1972.

Rogers, Minor L., and Ann T. Rogers. *Rennyo: The Second Founder of Shin Buddhism.* Berkeley, CA: Asian Humanities Press, 1991.

Roy, Patricia E. *The Oriental Question: Consolidating a White Man's Province, 1914-1941.* Vancouver: University of British Columbia Press, 2003.

———. *White Man's Province: British Columbia Politicians and Chinese and Japanese Immigrants 1858-1914.* Vancouver: University of British Columbia Press, 1989.

Rust, William C. "The Shin Sect of Buddhism in America: Its Antecedents, Beliefs, and Present Condition," Ph.D. dissertation. University of Southern California, 1951.

Sakamoto, Setsugo. "Chōji," *Jikishin* 9, no. 3 (1953): pp. 13–17.

Sakata, Yasuo. "Taiheiyō o matagu kita amerika e no ijū: Teijū o mezasu gyakkyō deno kutō." In *Nikkei Amerikajin no ayumi to genzai,* ed. Harumi Befu, pp. 15–36. Kyoto: Jinbun shoin, 2002.

Sasaki, Enryō. "Atogaki." In *Akarui bukkyō,* ed. Itsuzō Kyōgoku, pp. 258–65. Fresno, CA: Maha Maya Society, 1954.

Sasaki, Gesshō. *A Study of Shin Buddhism* (1925). Whitefish, MT: Kessinger Publishing, 2008, reprint.

Sasaki, Toshiji. *Nihonjin kanada iminshi.* Tokyo: Fuji shuppan, 1999.

Sasaki, Toshiji, and Tsuneharu Gonnami, eds. *Kanada iminshi shiryō,* 11 vols. Tokyo: Fuji shuppan, 2000.

Sawada, Janine Tasca. *Practical Pursuit: Religion, Politics, and Personal Cultivation in Nineteenth-Century Japan.* Honolulu: University of Hawai'i Press, 2004.

Seager, Richard Hughes. *Buddhism in America.* New York: Columbia University Press, 1999.

Secon, Y. H. "A Study of the Religious Organizations in Japanese Communities in America." Unpublished report presented to the University of Southern California, 1945.

Senchakushū English Translation Project, ed. *Hōnen's Senchakushū: Passages on the Selection of the Nembutsu in the Original Vow.* Honolulu: University of Hawai'i Press, 1998.

Sharf, Robert. "The Zen of Japanese Nationalism." In *Curators of the Buddha: The Study of Buddhism under Colonialism,* ed. Donald S. Lopez Jr., pp. 107–160. Chicago: University of Chicago Press, 1995.

Shibutani, Tamotsu. *The Derelicts of Company K.* Berkeley: University of California Press, 1978.

Shigaraki, Takamoro, ed. *Kindai shinshū kyōdanshi kenkyū.* Kyoto: Hōzōkan, 1987.
——. "The Problem of the True and the False in Contemporary Shin Buddhist Studies: True Shin Buddhism and False Shin Buddhism," *Pacific World,* 3rd ser., no. 3 (2001): pp. 27–51.

Shiio, Benkyo. "How Japan's Buddhism Leads Toward World Recovery." In *World Fellowship: Addresses and Messages by Leading Spokesmen of All Faiths, Races and Countries,* ed. Charles F. Weller, pp. 757–63. New York: Liveright Publishing Co., 1935.

Shimoda, Masahiro. "Kindai bukkyōgaku no tenkai to asia ninshiki: tasha toshi-teno bukkyō." In *Iwanami kōza: Teikoku nihon no gakuchi,* ed. Mio Kishimoto, vol. 3, pp. 176–214. Tokyo: Iwanami shoten, 2006.

Shinbo, Gidō. *Hawai kaikyō kyūjūnenshi.* Tokyo: Sankibō busshorin, 1987.

Shinpo, Mitsuru. *Kanada imin haisekishi: Nihon no gyogyō imin.* Tokyo: Miraisha, 1996.

Shinshū Ōtani-ha kyōka kenkyūsho, ed. "Shōtoku taishi sen sanbyaku nenki hōyō ni mukete no kyōji," *Kyōka kenkyū* 92/93 (1986): pp. 154–55.

Simpson, John H. "Religion as Identity and Contestation." In *Religion, Globalization, and Culture,* ed. Peter Beyer and Lori Beaman, pp. 121–44. Leiden, The Netherlands: Brill, 2007.

Snodgrass, Judith. *Presenting Japanese Buddhism to the West: Orientalism, Occidentalism, and the Columbian Exposition.* Chapel Hill, NC: University of North Carolina Press, 2003.

Soga, Ryōjin. "A Savior on Earth: The Meaning of Dharmākara Bodhisattva's Advent." Trans. Jan Van Bragt. In *An Anthology of Modern Shin Buddhist Writings: Kiyozawa Manshi, Soga Ryōjin, Kaneko Daiei and Yasuda Rijin,* ed. Shin Buddhist Comprehensive Research Institute, pp. 45–57. Kyoto: Ōtani University, 2001.

Solomon, Ira M. "Rennyo and the Rise of Honganji in Muromachi Japan," Ph.D. dissertation. Columbia University, 1972.

Sonoda, Kōkun, ed. *Sonoda Shūe: Beikoku kaikyō nisshi.* Kyoto: Hōzōkan, 1975.

Spencer, Robert. "Japanese Buddhism in the United States: A Study in Acculturation," Ph.D. dissertation. University of California, Berkeley, 1937.

Stone, Jackie. "A Vast and Grave Task: Interwar Buddhist Studies as an Expression of Japan's Envisioned Global Role." In *Culture and Identity: Japanese Intellectuals During the Interwar Years,* ed. J. Thomas Rimer, pp. 217–33. Princeton, NJ: Princeton University Press, 1990.

Suehiro, Aihō. "A Study of Culture of Ainos, with Special Reference to Their Religious Life," Master's thesis. University of Southern California, 1928.

Suh, Sharon A. *Being Buddhist in a Christian World: Gender and Community in a Korean American Temple.* Seattle: University of Washington, 2004.

Suzuki, D. T. *From the Shin Sect.* Kyoto: The Eastern Buddhist Society, 1937.

——. *Principal Teachings of the True Sect of Pure Land.* Kyoto: Higashi Honganji, 1910.

——. "The Development of the Pure Land Doctrine in Buddhism," *The Eastern Buddhist* 3, no. 4 (1926): pp. 285–326.

——. "The Shin Sect of Buddhism," *The Eastern Buddhist* 7, nos. 3/4 (1939): pp. 227–84.

Suzuki, D. T., and Gesshō Sasaki, trans. *The Life of the Shonin Shinran.* Tokyo: The Buddhist Text Translation Society, 1911.

Suzuki, Saburōji, ed. *Sotsugyōsha meibo.* Tokyo: Tokyo teikoku daigaku bungakubu gakuyūkai, 1936.

Swanson, Paul L. *Foundations of T'ien-T'ai Philosophy: The Flowering of the Two Truths Theory in Chinese Buddhism.* Berkeley, CA: Asian Humanities Press, 1989.

Tada, Kanae. "Jōdokyō hihan eno hihan," *Shūhō* 76 (October 1924): pp. 5–8. Reprint, *Shūhō,* vol. 13, pp. 317–20.

Tada, Minoru. *Bukkyō tōzen: Taiheiyō o watatta bukkyō.* Kyoto: Zen bunka kenkyūsho, 1990.

Tahara, Yukio. *Soshi ni somuita kyōdan.* Kyoto: Hakubasha, 1997.

Taira, Kikuo. "Reverend Kyogoku, in Remembrance," *Tri-Ratna* 7, nos. 5/6 (September/October–November/December, 1953): pp. 20–24.

Tajima, Kunji, and Floyd Shacklock, trans. *Selected Essays of Manshi Kiyozawa.* Kyoto: The Bukkyō Bunka Society, 1936.

Tajima, Paul J. "Japanese Buddhism in Hawaii: Its Background, Origin, and Adaptation to Local Conditions," Master's thesis. University of Hawai'i, 1935.

Takahashi, Jere. *Nisei/Sansei: Shifting Japanese American Identities and Politics.* Philadelphia: Temple University Press, 1997.

Takahashi, Kyojirō. "A Social Study of the Japanese Shinto and Buddhism in Los Angeles," Master's thesis. University of Southern California, 1937.

Takahashi, Masaru. "Chōsen ni okeru kaikyō, meiji ni okeru kaikyō to shūkyō seisaku—Ōtani-ha o chūshin toshite. " In *Asia no kaikyō to kyōiku,* ed. Masaru Kojima and Akeshi Kiba, pp. 133–49. Kyoto: Hōzōkan, 1992.

Takahashi, Seitsū. *Amerika kaikyō shōwa no mikkyō tōzen.* Osaka: Tōhō shuppan, 1990.

Takahashi, Takeichi. "The Symptomatic Function and Value of Synthetic Moral Judgment," Ph.D. dissertation. University of Chicago, 1927.

Takahatake, Takamichi. *Kanada to jōdoshinshū.* Kyoto: Hyakka-en, 1978.

Takashi, Momose. *Jiten: Shōwa senzenki no nihon.* Tokyo: Yoshikawa kōbunkan, 1990.

Takashi, Utsumi. "Tsunoda Ryūsaku no hawai jidai: 1909 nen no tofu zengo o megutte," *Waseda daigakushi kiyō* 30 (1998): pp. 121–74.

———. "Tsunoda Ryūsaku no hawai jidai sairon: 1909–1917 nen no taizai kikan o chūshin ni shite," *Waseda daigakushi kiyō* 31 (1999): pp. 91–124.

Takata, Toyo. *Nikkei Legacy: The Story of Japanese Canadians from Settlement to Today.* Toronto: NC Press, 1983.

Takeuchi, Dōsetsu. "The Religious Life of Japanese Children in America," Master's thesis. University of Southern California, 1935.

Tamura, Eileen. *Americanization, Acculturation, and Ethnic Identity: The Nisei Generation in Hawaii.* Urbana, IL: University of Illinois Press, 1994.

Tanabe, George J., Jr. "Glorious Gathas: Americanization and Japanization in Honganji Hymns." In *Engaged Pure Land Buddhism: Essays in Honor of Professor Alfred Bloom,* ed. Kenneth K. Tanaka and Eishō Nasu, pp. 221–37. Berkeley, CA: WisdomOcean Publications, 1998.

———. "Grafting Identity: The Hawaiian Branches of the Bodhi Tree." In *Buddhist Missionaries in the Era of Globalization,* ed. Linda Learman, pp. 77–100. Honolulu: University of Hawai'i Press, 2005.

Tanaka, Stephan. *Japan's Orient: Rendering Pasts into History.* Berkeley: University of California Press, 1993.

Terakawa, Hōkō, ed. *Hokubei kaikyō enkakushi.* San Francisco: Hongwanji hokubei kaikyō honbu, 1936.

Terakawa, Tansai. "A Critical Exposition of J. M. Guyau's the Non-Religious of the Future," Master's thesis. Stanford University, 1927.

———. "Buddhist Greetings from the West Hongwanji Buddhist Sect in Japan and America." In *World Fellowship: Addresses and Messages by Leading Spokesmen of*

All Faiths, Races and Countries, ed. Charles F. Weller, pp. 30–32. New York: Liveright Publishing Co., 1935.

Thal, Sarah. *Rearranging the Landscape of Gods: The Politics of a Pilgrimage Site in Japan, 1573–1912.* Chicago: University of Chicago Press, 2005.

Thelle, Notto R. "Power Struggle in Shin Buddhism: Between Feudalism and Democracy," *Japanese Religions* 9, no. 2 (1976): pp. 64–75.

Thomas, Dorothy Swaine, with Charles Kikuchi and James Sakoda. "The Nisei Population in California, 1900–1940." In *The Salvage: Japanese American Evacuation and Resettlement,* pp. 575–79. Berkeley: University of California Press, 1952.

de Tocqueville, Alexis. *Democracy in America.* Trans. George Lawrence, ed. J. P. Mayer. New York: Doubleday, 1969.

——. *Democracy in America.* Chicago: University of Chicago Press, 2000.

Tōko henshū iinkai, ed. *Tōko: Takeshima Hōsui-shi gofusai keigyō tsuitōshi.* Hiroshima: Shinkōji bukkyōkai, 1968.

Tokunaga, Michio, and Alfred Bloom. "Toward a Pro-Active Engaged Shin Buddhism: A Reconsideration of the Teaching of the Two Truths (shinzoku-nitai)," *Pacific World,* 3rd ser., no. 2 (2003): pp. 191–206.

Toyotomi, Morimoto. *Japanese Americans and Cultural Continuity: Maintaining Language and Heritage.* New York: Garland Publishing, 1997.

Tsang, Carol Richmond. *War and Faith: Ikkō Ikki in Late Muromachi Japan.* Cambridge, MA: Harvard University Press, 2009.

Tsuji, Takashi. "Freedom," *Tri-Ratna* 6, no. 4 (July/August 1952): pp. 5–7.

Tsunemitsu, Kōnen. *Hawai bukkyō shiwa: Nihon bukkyō no tōzen.* Tokyo: Bukkyō dendō kyōkai, 1971.

——. *Hokubei bukkyō shiwa: Nihon bukkyō no tōzen.* Tokyo: Bukkyō dendō kyōkai, 1973.

——. *Nihon bukkyō tobeishi.* Tokyo: Bukkyō Times, 1964.

Tsunoda, Noboru. "The Reason Why I Wish to Study Buddhism as My Life Work." N.p., n.d.

Tsunoda, Shōdō. "Freedom of Choice," *Tri-Ratna* 7, no. 2 (March/April 1953): pp. 3–7.

Tsurumi, Kazuko. "Sōsestu." In *Sōgō kōza nihon no shakai bunkashi, Volume 3: Dochakuka to gairaika,* ed. Kazuko Tsurumi, pp. 9–44. Tokyo: Kōdansha, 1973.

Tuck, Donald R. *Buddhist Churches of America Jodo Shinshu.* Lewiston, NY: The Edwin Mellen Press, 1987.

Turner, Victor. *The Anthropology of Performance.* New York: PAJ Publications, 1988.

Tweed, Thomas. "American Occultism and Japanese Buddhism," *Japanese Journal of Religious Studies* 32, no. 2 (2005): pp. 249–81.

———. *Crossing and Dwelling: A Theory of Religion.* Cambridge, MA: Harvard University Press, 2006.

———. *The American Encounter with Buddhism, 1844–1912.* Chapel Hill, NC: University of North Carolina Press, 1992.

Uchida, Kōyū. *Fushi no jinpō.* N.p., 1957.

Ueda, Yoshifuji. "Response to Thomas P. Kasuli's Review of 'Letter of Shinran,'" *Philosophy East and West* 31, no. 4 (1981): pp. 507–511.

Ueda, Yoshifuji, and Dennis Hirota. *Shinran: An Introduction to His Thought.* Kyoto: Hongwanji International Center, 1989.

Unno, Mark T. "The Voice of Sacred Texts in the Ocean of Compassion: The Case of Shin Buddhism in America," *Pacific World,* 3rd ser., no. 5 (2003): pp. 293–307.

Unno, Taitetsu. "The Practice of Jodo-shinshu." In *Living in Amida's Universal Vow: Essays in Shin Buddhism,* ed. Alfred Bloom, pp. 63–71. Bloomington, IN: World Wisdom, 2004.

Utsuki, Nishū. *History of Honganji.* Buddhist Churches of America, n.d.

———. *The Seven Spiritual Fathers.* Kyoto: Honpa Hongwanji, 1938.

———. *The Shin Sect, a School of Mahayana Buddhism: Its Teaching, Brief History, and Present-day Conditions.* Kyoto: Publication Bureau of Buddhist Books Hompa Hongwanji, 1937.

Washimi, Joshin. "The Issei and the Jōdo Denomination in Hawaii during the 1920s: Research from the 'Propagation Records.'" Paper presented at the Issei Buddhism Conference, University of California, Irvine, September 2004.

Watada, Terry. *Bukkyo Tozen: A History of Jodo Shinshu Buddhism in Canada 1905–1995.* Toronto: HpF Press and the Toronto Buddhist Church, 1996.

Weinstein, Stanley. "Continuity and Change in the Thought of Rennyo." In *Rennyo and the Roots of Modern Japanese Buddhism,* ed. Mark L. Blum and Shin'ya Yasutomi, pp. 49–58. New York: Oxford University Press, 2006.

———. "Rennyo and the Shinshū Revival." In *Japan in the Muromachi Age,* ed. John W. Hall and Toyoda Takeshi, pp. 331–58. Berkeley: University of California Press, 1977.

Weller, Charles F., ed. *World Fellowship: Addresses and Messages by Leading Spokesmen of All Faiths, Races and Countries.* New York: Liveright Publishing Co., 1933.

Wells, Keiko. "'Fall, Make Yourself Fall': A Continuity of Shin Buddhist Spirituality in Hawaii: How It Was Passed from Issei and Was Acculturated." Paper presented at the Issei Buddhism Conference, University of California, Irvine, September 2004.

———. "Shin Buddhist Song Lyrics Sung in the United States: Their History and Expressed Buddhist Images (1) 1898–1939." *Tokyo daigaku amerika taiheiyō kenkyū* 2 (2002): pp. 75–99.

———. "Shin Buddhist Song Lyrics Sung in the United States: Their History and Expressed Buddhist Images (2) 1936–2001," *Tokyo daigaku amerika taiheiyō kenkyū* 3 (2003): pp. 41–64.

Westfall, William. "Voices from the Attic: The Canadian Border and the Writing of American Religious History." In *Retelling U.S. Religious History*, ed. Thomas A. Tweed, pp. 181–99. Berkeley: University of California Press, 1997.

Why I Became a Buddhist. San Francisco: The Kyōdan Times of the BMNA, n.d.

Williams, Duncan R. "Complex Loyalties: Issei Buddhist Ministers during the Wartime Incarceration," *Pacific World,* 3rd ser., no. 5 (2003): pp. 255–74.

Williams, Duncan R., and Tomoe Moriya, eds. *Issei Buddhism in the Americas.* Urbana, IL: University of Illinois Press, 2010.

Williams, Paul. *Mahayana Buddhism: The Doctrinal Foundations.* New York: Routledge, 1989.

Yamada, Shōi. *Megumi no seikatsu.* Kyoto: Dōbōsha, 1928.

Yamamoto, Yoshio. *Hawai ni okeru bukkyō no yōran jidai.* Honolulu: Privately printed, n.d.

Yamanouchi, Shūken. "The Japanese in California: The Development of the Japanese Communities in California," Master's thesis. Boston University, 1933.

Yamasaki, Katsumi C. "Thoughts of a Hawaiian-born Buddhist," Okumura papers.

Yamazaki, Shōken. "Meiji ikō no bukkyō ongaku (1)," *Bukkyō Ongaku* 8 (August 1983): pp. 12–13.

———. "Meiji ikō no bukkyō ongaku (2)," *Bukkyō Ongaku* 9 (November 1983): pp. 10–11.

Yanagawa, Keiichi, and Kiyomi Morioka, eds. *Hawai nikkei shūkyō no tenkai to genkyō: Hawai nikkeijin shūkyō chōsa hōkokusho.* Tokyo: Tokyo daigaku shūkyō-gaku kenkyūshitsu, 1979.

Yanagisako, Sylvia Junko. *Transforming the Past: Tradition and Kinship among Japanese Americans.* Stanford, CA: Stanford University Press, 1985.

Yasumaru, Yoshio, and Masato Miyachi, eds. *Shūkyō to kokka.* Tokyo: Iwanami shoten, 1992.

Yasutomi, Shin'ya. "Daihi no kaishaku gaku: Suzuki Daisetsu yaku Kyōgyōshinshō shaken," *Gendai to Shinran* 10 (June 2006): pp. 112–39.

———. "The Way of Introspection: Kiyozawa Manshi's Methodology," *The Eastern Buddhist* (n.s.), 35, nos. 1/2 (2003): pp. 102–114.

Yesaki, Mitsuo. *Sutebusuton: A Japanese Village on the British Columbia Coast.* Vancouver: Peninsula Publishing, 2003.

Yoo, David K. "Enlightened Identities: Buddhism and Japanese Americans of California, 1924–1941," *The Western Historical Quarterly* 27, no. 3 (1996): pp. 281–301.

———. *Growing Up Nisei: Race, Generation, and Culture among Japanese Americans of California, 1924-1949.* Urbana, IL: University of Illinois Press, 2000.

———, ed. *New Spiritual Home: Religion and Asian Americans.* Honolulu: University of Hawai'i Press, 1999.

Yoshida, Kyūichi. *Nihon kindai bukkyōshi kenkyū.* Tokyo: Yoshikawa kōbunsho, 1964.

———. *Nihon no kindai shakai to bukkyō.* Tokyo: Hyōronsha, 1970.

Yoshinaga, Toshimi. "Japanese Buddhist Temples in Honolulu," *Social Process in Hawaii* 3 (1937), pp. 36–42.

Young, Charles H., and Helen R. Y. Reid. *The Japanese Canadians.* Toronto: University of Toronto Press, 1938.

Yu, Henry. "On a Stage Built by Others: Creating an Intellectual History of Asian Americans," *Amerasia Journal* 26, no. 1 (2000): pp. 141–61.

Zen bunka kenkyūsho, ed. *Zensō ryūgaku kotohajime.* Kyoto: Zen bunka kenkyūsho, 1990.

Internet Sources

On Gyōmei Kubose:
http://www.brightdawn.org/history.htm.

On Sunya Pratt, conducting services during internment:
Tacoma Buddhist Temple website: www.tacomabt.org

On Ryūsaku Tsunoda:
http://www.columbia.edu/cu/alumni/Magazine/Spring2002/AsianStudies.html

Index

Numbers in boldface refer to photographs.

About the Author

Michihiro Ama received his Ph.D. in East Asian Languages and Literatures from the University of California, Irvine. He is currently an assistant professor of Japanese at the University of Alaska, Anchorage. The focus of his scholarship is Japanese Buddhism and literature, and he has published several articles on Shin Buddhism. He was also guest editor of the featured articles on Natsume Soseki and Buddhism in *The Eastern Buddhist* (n.s.) 38 (2007), nos. 1/2.